The Nitpicker's Guide for NEXT GENERATION TREKKERS VOLUME II

D1471085

The Nitpicker's Guide for
NEXT GENERATION
TREKKERS
VOLUME II

PHIL FARRAND

TITAN BOOKS

**THE NITPICKER'S GUIDE FOR
NEXT GENERATION TREKKERS VOLUME II**
ISBN 1 85286 671 3

Published by
Titan Books Ltd
42-44 Dolben Street
London SE1 0UP

First Titan edition November 1995
10 9 8 7 6 5 4 3 2 1

Developed and produced by Ettlinger Editorial Projects, New York.

Cover illustration © 1995 Bob Larkin.

British Library Cataloguing-in-Publication Data. A catalogue record for
this book is available from the British Library.

Printed and bound in Great Britain by Cox and Wyman Ltd, Reading,
Berkshire.

*Dedicated to Steve Ettlinger,
super-agent by night,
mild-mannered book producer by day,
without whom there would be no Guides*

TABLE OF CONTENTS

THE MOVIE

GUILD SUBMISSIONS

FIRST SEASON

SECOND SEASON

THIRD SEASON

SIXTH SEASON

★ ACKNOWLEDGMENTS

T he book that you hold in your hands is the focal point of a great deal of time and energy from a wide variety of individuals, both intentionally and unintentionally.

Obviously, this book would not exist without the high-quality product generated by the vast juggernaut that comprises the *Star Trek* division at Paramount Pictures. From executive producer Rick Berman to the lowliest PA (production assistant), all have contributed to make *Star Trek: The Next Generation* worth watching. And, since it's worth watching, it's worth nitpicking. I thank you again, ladies and gentlemen, for your work.

As with the *Classic Guide,* Steve Ettlinger served not only as agent, but book producer as well. He and his assistant, Jamie Winnick coordinated William Drennan's copyediting, Jeff Fitschen's typesetting, Margo Zelie's proofreading, Liz McCollum's and John Long's manuscript preparation, and Jane Farnol's indexing. This makes the third one we've put out the door together, Steve.

Eric Wybenga came on board as editor for this installment of the *Nitpicker's Guide.* (My former editor, Jeanne Cavelos found herself intrigued by teaching and decided to find a quiet spot among the forests of New England. She has settled at a small college with a crop of new writers.) Who can say what wonderful tomes will come from this union? Of course, change is always a bit disconcerting. Thankfully, my trepidation quickly subsided after my first phone conversation with Eric. He is a Trekker, a nitpicker, and—best of all— a very capable editor. It's been a joy working with you, Eric. My thanks also to Diane Bartoli, Candace Chaplin, Ingrid Restrick, and the rest of the able individuals at Dell Publishing.

My wife Lynette and daughter Elizabeth still stand beside me. They continue to lend me their strength, and because of that I am privileged.

"World-renowned, internationally acclaimed" acknowledgments need to go to Larry Nemecek—authorized *Star Trek* author of *The Star Trek: The Next Generation Companion*—for his assistance.

And it might interest you to know that Nitpicker Central now has a resident solar physicist. Her name is Mitzi Adams. She works for NASA and has shown extraordinary patience while answering all my pesky questions about the real universe of stars and physics. Thanks for your help, Mitzi. (By the way, if you're interested in having a real scientist speak at your convention you can contact the Public Affairs Speakers' Bureau at the Marshall Space Flight Center in Huntsville, AL.)

Thanks also to Gary of Database Systems/Connecting Point here in Springfield. He helped at just the right time with an important piece of equipment. Thanks, as well, to Bill Ross for loaning me his closed-captioned decoder.

Many, many members of the Nit-picker's Guild expended significant amounts of time and energy toward the creation of this *Guide*. I have done my best to give credit where credit is due—hence, the list of names that follows these acknowledgments. Unfortunately, space did not allow inclusion of all the nits sent my way. To everyone who wrote, whether your nit made it in or not, thank you so much for sharing your discoveries with me. I enjoyed them all.

And finally, my everlasting gratitude to you, Jesus Christ, for being a lamp unto my feet and a light unto my path.

Greetings fellow nitpickers! Originally, Eric and I wanted to acknowledge your submissions by placing your names in a block at the end of each nitpicking section. Unfortunately, this book ran long (*very* long). So, because of space considerations, we pulled those acknowledgments and placed everyone in an alphabetical list. Some members of the Guild had more than one acknowledgment line scattered through the text of this book and in those cases I have placed a number after that person's name to indicate the number of nits they contributed. To the almost 850 individuals on this list, I thank you again for writing. (And, to those members of the Guild who don't find your names here: I'm sorry. Someone either beat you to the nit you submitted or I just plain ran out of space! If it's any consolation, you're not alone. As of this writing there are more than 2,000 other members of the Guild not listed here.)

There is at least one person who should be listed here but isn't. When I compiled the *Miscellaneous Data Tote Board* for this installment, the neurons that identified the episode in which our favorite android plays the guitar quit working. (I hate it when that happens.) I frantically polled all my nitpicking buddies and no one could come up with the answer. In desperation (at approximately 3:50 PM Pacific Time on Sunday, March 19, 1995), while on stage during Creation Entertainment's Grand Slam Convention in Pasadena, CA, I asked if anyone in the crowd knew the answer. *Someone* shouted out "Silicon Avatar"—which turned out to be correct. Unfortunately, I didn't have the presence of mind to ask that person to see me after my talk so I could get their name. If you happen to be reading this, I apologize for my oversight. Drop me a line and let me know who you are! (The address is at the back of this book.)

Dax Abbas of Ames, IA (3)
Jennifer L. Adkins of Louisville, KY (3)
Tracy Adshead of Staffordshire, England (2)
Daniel Aguilar of Barcelona, Spain
Jane Allcock of West Midlands, England
Shirsten Caroline Alm of Pembroke, MA
Vince Amarosa of Flemington, NJ
J.B. Anderton of Marissa, IL
jaQ Andrews of Sellersville, PA (4)
Peter Anspach of Highland Park, IL (2)
Mark Aristos Plus of Wrightwood, CA
Eric Ian Armbruster of Hamilton Square, NJ
James S. Armstrong of Richmond, VA
Richard Arnold of West Hollywood, CA (2)
Shane Arnold of Columbia, KY (16)
Jeff Arrington of Carrollton, TX
Scott Arrington of Carrollton, TX
Chris Askew of Salem, MA
Barbara Atkins of Merriam, KS
Jonathan Baca of San Angelo, TX
Ken Bailey of Surrey, England (2)
Dan Baker of Wentworth, MO
Steve Ballard of Fairfax, VA (3)
Michael Ballway of Evanston, IL (3)
Mark Bannister of London, England (5)
Jason Barnes of Springfield, MO (3)
Rodger L. Barnes of Ralston, NE
Bret Barrett of Woodinville, WA

Joe Barron of Philadelphia, PA
Pierre Bastien of Cap-de-la-Madeleine, Quebec (6)
Tom Batt of Springfield, MO
Adrian Baumgartner of Biberist, Switzerland
Aaron and Debrah Beckley of Westhaven, CT (2)
David E. Bedington of Hickory, NC
Terry Beever of Roswell, GA
Christopher R. Behrens of Colleyville, TX
Mark Belanger of Butte, MT (8)
Steven Bell of Cornwall, Ontario
Heather Beltran of San Jose, CA
Guillaume Bergeron of Gatineau, Quebec
Kim Biedermann of Richboro, PA
Frank T. Bitterhof of Berlin, Germany (11)
Lydia M. Blackman of Conway, AR
Roy Blair of Aurora, CO (2)
Evan Blaisdell of Groton, CT (3)
Simon Blake of Wigan, England (5)
David M. Blakeman of Merced, CA (26)
A.D. Blankenship of Point Pleasant, WV (2)
Sanda Blom of Fredencia, Denmark (2)
Kristen Bloom of Ithaca, NY
Louise Blyton of New South Wales, Australia
Micki Boarts of Mullica Hill, NJ
Brian Bock of Omaha, NE
Melissa Boggs of Xenia, OH
Brad Boothe of Bucyrus, OH
Mary Bordelon of Arnaudville, LA (2)
Bob Borst of Ithaca, NY
Christian Boulanger of Sherbrooke, Quebec
Nick Bousman of Menlo Park, CA
Eric J. Bowersox of Isla Vista, CA
Vicki Bowring of Worcs, England
Toni Boyd of Chicago, IL
Greg J. Bradford of New South Wales, Australia
Phyllis Bradley of Escalow, CA (2)
Thomas Bradley of the U.S. Embassy in Tel Aviv, Israel
Michael Brady of North Myrtle Beach, SC (2)
Stephen Brady of Downey, CA
Robert Brenneman of Muskogee, OK
Jonathan Bridge of Salt Lake City, UT (2)
Allie Brightwell of Hampshire, England (3)
Kim Brocklehurst of Baltimore, MD
Sarah Brockley of Easton, MD
Chris Brodbeck of Wichita, KS
Greg W. Brookshier of Knoxville, TN (3)
Stanley Brookshier, Jr. of Knoxville, TN
Julie Brossard of Montreal, Quebec
Matt Brothers of Canton, OH
Brad Brown of Pryor, OK
Daniel Brown of Northridge, CA
Diana Brown of San Ysidro, CA (5)
Laura Brown of Clinton, MO
Susan J. Brown of Salem, MA (3)
Terry L. Brown, Sr. of Omaha, NE
Chris Browne of Grosse Pointe, MI (2)
P. Bryan of Nepean, Ontario
Donna Bryant of Houston, TX (4)
Carin Budka of Parma, OH
Chris Bullers of West Midlands, England
John Burrows of Middlesex, England

Alex Bush of Ottawa, Ontario
Bartley Busse of Neidpath, Saskatchewan
Donald Byrne of Spokane, WA
Ethan H. Calk of San Antonio, TX
Elizabeth Cameron of Bedford, MA
Hilary Evans Cameron of Toronto, Ontario (4)
Chris Campbell of Mader's Cove, Nova Scotia
Paul Campbell of Laplace, LA
Tom Cantrell of Haslett, MI
P.T.H. Carder of Lancashire, United Kingdom (3)
Mark Carlson of Tulsa, OK (5)
Denise M. Caron of North Grafton, MA
David Carpenter of Atlanta, GA
Gene Carpenter of Westlake, OH
Phyllis "Tiny" Carter of Laguna Hills, CA
Cliff Casselman of Ogdensburg, NY
Belinda Cavazoo of Charlotte, NC
Beth Chalecki of Washington, DC
Daniel L. Chamberlin, Jr of Virginia Beach, VA
Frank J. Chambers, Jr. of Chicago, IL
John Chapelhow of Lancaster, United Kingdom
Scott Charrington of Co. Antrim, North Ireland
Christen Chattin of Media, PA
Benjamin Chee of Singapore (3)
Ken L. Cheshire of Lafayette, LA (2)
Adam Chesin of Philadelphia, PA (10)
Dava Chester of Athens, GA (2)
Nancy Childress of Charlottesville, VA
Jason Childs of Ft. Worth, TX (2)
Wade Childs of Ft. Worth, TX (2)
Gary Chillingworth of Herts, England (6)
Robert Chisnall of North Bay, Ontario (3)
Christopher Chortrand of London, Ontario (4)
J. Michael Clark of Defiance, OH (2)
Matt Classen of Smartville, CA
Beth Claus of Saint John, New Brunswick
David Clayton of Victoria, Australia
Brian Clement of Victoria, British Columbia (3)
Michael Coffey of Chicago, IL
Bob Cole of Eglin AFB
Carrie Michelle Coleman of San Diego, CA
Charles A. Coleman of Columbia, MD
James R. Collier of Georgetown, Ontario (2)
Eric Collins (location unknown)
Mark A. Conger of Ann Arbor, MI
Melissa Contreras of Los Angeles, CA
Geoffrey Cook of Hammond, IL (24)
James Cook of Washington, UT
Judy Cook of Batavia, IL
Loree Cook of Oceanside, CA
Timothy R. Cook of Batavia, IL
Michael W. Cooper of Sturtevant, WI
Paul Cope of Springfield, MO
Mairi Cowan of Toronto, Ontario (4)
Dave Cowles of Gaffney, SC
Cindy Craft of Flemington, NJ
Alex Craig of Broomfield, CO
Steve Criddle of Kent, England (2)
Natalie Crosby of Timberlea, Nova Scotia
Kevin Cunnane of Carle Place, NY (2)
Walter J. Czarniecki of Bethel Park, PA
Alia Czarny of Denver, CO (2)
Golden Czemak of APO, AE (4)
Jeremy Dabbs of Hueytown, AL (4)

Laura Dachenbach of Gahanna, OH (2)
Kirstin E. Dand of Northampton, MA
Stephen Daniels of Roxburghshire, Scotland
Linda Darcy of North Grandby, CT
Linda T. Darcy of North Granby, CT
K.V. Davey of Dyfed, England
Scott Davidson of East Lothian, Scotland
Ronda Davies of Lees Summit, MO
Lisa Davila of San Antonio, TX
Benjamin R. Davis of Petaluma, CA
Jack Davis of Columbus, OH (3)
Matthew E. Davis of Parkersburg, WV (2)
Mike Davis (location unknown)
Stuart Davis of East Sussex, England (11)
Elizabeth L. Davoli of Baton Rouge, LA
W. Degnan of Mid Glam, England
Timothy DeHaas of New York City, NY
Irene Deitel of Farmingdale, NY (2)
Dirk DeJong of Isabella, MO
Bill DeLong of Springfield, MO (2)
Noreen A. Demers of Epsom, NH
Jeffrey DeRego of S. Dartmouth, MA
Danny Da Silva of Toronto, Ontario
Robert DeVoe of St. Ann, MO (3)
Robert Di Panfilo of Edmonton, Alberta (4)
Jennifer Diamonti of Newport News, VA
Sara Dickinson of Willshire, England (2)
Nguyen, Diem-Quynh of Centerville, VA
Duane and Elisabeth Dietz of Seguin, TX
Amber DiGerlando of Wind Gap, PA
Chris Discotto of New Britain, CT
Jimmy Dobson, Jr. of Saratoga Springs, NY (2)
Paul Dockree of Kent, England
Jackson Dodd of Berkeley, CA (2)
Peter Doherty of Cambridge, England
Patricia Jazz Douglas of San Antonio, TX (3)
Vassilios A. Draganis of Mannheim, Germany
Gilles Duchesne of Jonquiere, Quebec (2)
Martin Duke of Cambridge, MA (6)
David Dumble of Santa Cruz, CA (3)
Jonathan Dunbar-Meadows of Morgantown, WI
Joey M. Dunn of Port Arthur, TX
Megan Dybvig of Clayton, MO
Erin Dyment of Calgary, Alberta
Alvin L. East of NATO AWACS
Jo Ann Eates of Pittsburgh, PA
Suzanne M. Eckhardt of Killeen, TX
Jonathan S. Edelman of Raleigh, NC (2)
Dan Ehrlich of Berkeley Heights, NJ
Rodger Elliott, Jr. of Butler, PA
Paul Ellner of Lindsborg, KS
V. Elrod of Eureka, CA
Yoko K. Ema of Chicago, IL (7)
Steve Emirzian of Hartford, CT (5)
Dorka Ellen Engberg of Ellensburg, WA (3)
Kelly Ernst of Columbia, MD
Nicole Erwine of La Mesa, CA (3)
Joshua Ethridge of Fayetteville, AR (11)
Michael J. Evans of Sussex, England (3)
Greg Everett of Oakdale, CT
Carolyn Fansler of Harrisburg, PA
Brendan P. Farley of Pittsburg, PA
Elizabeth A.D. Farrand of Springfield, MO
Lynette Farrand of Springfield, MO (3)
J. Seth Farrow of Independence, MO

Bill J. Fasser of Atwater, CA (2)
Gail Feinberg of Russell, KY
Renee Susan Feldstein of Columbus, OH
Alexandra Felton of Diamond Springs, CA
Todd Felton of Victoria, British Columbia (9)
David J. Ferrier of Washington, DC (16)
Lisa Ferrington of Santa Fe, NM (2)
John Fester of St. Louis, MO
Michael Fiek of Victoria, Australia
Carl Fields of Aiken, SC
James Filsell of London, England
Clare Finkel of Surrey, England
Marcy Fiorica of Ames, IA (2)
The First Light Staff of Westminster, CO
Ryan Fisher of Saugus, MA (6)
Missie Fleck of Cary, NC
Jeri Flick of International Falls, MN
Pat Flynn of Ketchum, ID
John H. Foley of New Market, NH (2)
Janett Folster of Hopkinsville, KY
Fredericka Ford of Indianapolis, IN
David Foster of Charleston, WV (21)
Taylor Francis of Conway, AR
Richard Frank of San Antonio, TX
Rebecca L. Franko of Cleveland, OH
Alex Frazer-Harrison of Calgary, Alberta (2)
Kent Frazier of Naubinway, MI
Jeremy Freeman of Bedford, NH (2)
David L. Freitas of S. Dartmouth, MA
Jamie-Ann French of Plymouth, MA (2)
Sanford French of Milton, Ontario
Derek Frentzen of Darumh, NH
Dan Friedman of Yorktown Heights, NY
Ray Fucillo of Abington, MA
Mike Ganley of Gloucestershire, England
David M. Gansz of West Orange, NJ
Graham Garfield of Evanston, IL (5)
Emma Garland of Gloucestershire, England (4)
William J., Jr. Garmer of Pasadena, MD
John Allen Garrison of Knoxville, TN
Jennifer Gartner of Reisterstown, MD (3)
Laurie Gaut of Staffordshire, England (2)
Suzanne Gert of Edmond, OK
David Gibson of Bakersfield, CA
Ann Giddens of Mansfield, MO
Rachel Giddens of Mansfield, MO
Doug Giffin of Milwaukee, WI
Simon Gilchrist of Stroud, Ontario (2)
Janie Gildow of Tipp City, OH (3)
Frederick W. Gilkey of Takoma Park, MD
Linda Gill-Aranha of Vancouver, British
    Columbia (4)
Ruaraidh Gillies of Merseyside, England (4)
Sean Gilpin of Sudbury, Ontario
Anthony J. Girese of Bayide, NY (2)
Frederic G. Glatter of Highland Park, NJ
Jim Glennon of San Francisco, CA
Dana Gold of Great Neck, NY (2)
William Gold of Philadelphia, PA
Andy Golden of Raineville, WV
Steve Goldinger of Tempe, AZ
Suzanne R. Golia of Fairport, NY (3)
Brian Gonigal of Edison, NJ (2)
Rande Goodwin of Windsor, CT (3)
Jeni Gordon of Arcadia, CA

Adam Gow of Kingston, Ontario
Charles Gragg of Ozark, MO (4)
L. Scott Grant of Pembroke Lakes, FL (8)
Jay P. Graves of Albany, GA (4)
Scott Gray of Judsonia, AR
Nancy Green of Byesville, OH
Sally Green of Herts, England
Sara Green of Lake Elsinore, CA (10)
Rochelle Greenwald of Indianapolis, IN
Eric Greve of Drummondville, Quebec
Heather Grimes of Riva, MD
The Guano Groover of West Yorks, England
Kevin P. Grover of Ft. Knox, KY
Steven Gruninger of Niagara Falls, Ontario
John Gutzmer of Oakland, IL (5)
Jason Allan Haase of Pierce City, MO
Jessica Hall of Middlesex, England (2)
Randy Hall of Columbia, MD (2)
John "KRIS" Halvorson of Reese, MI (4)
Gary Harding of Surrey, England
Jeff Harradine of Brockport, NY
Brian Harrington of Co. Cork, Ireland (3)
Jeff Harris of Atchison, KS (8)
Cecelia Harvey of Cape Coral, FL
Jackie Harvey of Kent, England
Rachel Sarah Harvey of Broken Arrow, OK
Michael Hashemi of Littleton, CO (4)
Kim Haught of Fort Worth, TX
Jacob Hawkins of Flagstaff, AZ
John Hedrick of New Palestine, IN (3)
Bill van Heerden of Toronto, Ontario (14)
Linda Heinz of Rio Rancho, NM
Dan Heisman of Warrington, PA (2)
Marty Hemmings of Pictou, Nova Scotia (2)
Pepijn Hendriks of Etten-Leur, The Netherlands
Steven Hewis of Whitby, Ontario (3)
Brad W. Higgins of Phoenix, AZ (8)
Myles S. Hildebrand of Niverville, Manitoba (10)
Jeremy Hill of Springfield, MO
Adam Hincks of Scaborough, Ontario (4)
Jeff Hinton of Manteca, CA
Kevin Hobbs of Nottingham, England
John Hobson of Bolingbrook, IL
Megan Hoffer of Mineola, NY
Jayson Hoffman of London, Ontario (4)
Martin R. Hoffman of Hilton, NY
Sarahjane Hogben of Herts, England
Tim Holder of Holiday, FL (7)
G. Holland of St. Catharines, Ontario
Michael Hollick of Brampton, Ontario (5)
Diane Holmes of San Antonio, TX
John Holtz of Coraopolis, PA
Darrick B. Hom of Oakland, CA (4)
Hilary Homer of London, Ontario
Kailen Hong of Turtleford, Saskatchewan (4)
Lori Hope of Austin, TX
Natalie F. Houck of Indianapolis, IN (2)
Ed Howard of Sloatsburg, NY (2)
Patrick Howard of Vernon Hills, IL
Ronn Hubbard, Jr. of Murray, KY (4)
Otto "Hackman" Huer of the Internet List (6)
Niall H. Huffman of Costa Mesa, CA
Darrin Hull of Willard, MO (2)
Ben and Jyl Hunt of Fayetteville, NC
Charles E. Hunter of St. George, UT

Jack Huskey of Judsonia, AR (2)
Edward Huspeka of Scabourough, Ontario (2)
Ron Hutcheson of E. Missoula, MT
Stu Hutchings of Kent, England
Matt Ingy of Guernsey, Channel Islands
Wendy Inouye of Pleasanton, CA
Analyse Ivey of Swansea, SC (2)
Heather Jacobs of Cincinnati, OH
Jim Jacobson of Spokane, WA (2)
Jeff Jacques of Nepean, Ontario (3)
Gladys Jane of Little Rock, AR (2)
Joel Janovec of San Antonio, TX (3)
James Jarvis of San Francisco, CA
Eliot Jenkins of Independence, MO
Valerie Jennes of Pittsburgh, PA (2)
Paul Jepson of Red Oak, IA
Dennis Jernigan of Boynton, OK
Lisa J. Jimenez of Riverside, CA
David N. Jimerson of Martin, OH
Ryan Jodrell of Cremona, Alberta
Carleton R. Johnson of Alice Springs,
    Australia (2)
Kyle R. Johnson of Revelstoke, British
    Columbia
Michael Johnson of Long Beach, CA (2)
Mikal C. Johnson of Kirkland, WA
Al Johnston of Newcastle upon Tyne,
    United Kingdom (2)
Angela G. Jones of Pineville, LA (4)
Jeremy Jones of Oakdale, MN
Amy Jordan of Claremont, CA
Justina Ju of Vienna, VA
Donald R. Jury of Hollywood, FL
Lois E. Kane of Sedona, AZ (6)
Paul F. Kane of Holbrook, NY (5)
Ben Karas of Whitefish Bay, WI
Rosetta M. Karlan of San Diego, CA
David Karp of Thornhill, Ontario (3)
Ryan T. Kato of Torrance, CA
Ashok Katwala of Essex, England (4)
Lara Kazkaz of Mount Prospect, IL
David Kealy of Essex, England
Margaret Keates of Leicestershire, England
Colin Keevil of Hanover, OH
Katherine M. Keirns of Northborough, MA (2)
Colleen Kellam of Raytown, MO
Ryan Kelly of Old Brookville, NY
Gary R. Kerr of Alton, IL
Justin Kidd of Pueblo, CO
Joshua M. Kielty of Tempe, AZ (3)
Elizabeth Kieronski of Concord, NH
Richard Kilby of N. Yorkshire, England (5)
Anna Kim of North Hills, CA
Sarah King of Chapel Hill, NC
Sheri Kirschner of Olympia, WA
Theodore L. Kisiel of Erie, PA
Ann Wurst Kissinger of Katy, TX
Dom Klyve of Morris, MN
Tracy Knight of Annapolis, MD
Brian Knudtson of Blair, NE
Meg Kolodick of Oil City, PA
Zoran Kovacich of Richmond, CA
Steve Kreisler of Chicago, IL
Paul Kuehn of Lewisville, TX (2)
Kevin L. of Toronto, Ontario

Andrew Lai of Windsor, Ontario (2)
Johnson Lai of Ajax, Ontario (50)
Sue Lajeunesse of Ottawa, Ontario (4)
Anne Laleman of Dekalb, IL
Paul Lalli of Feeding Hills, MA
Francis Lalumiere of Montreal, Quebec (2)
Christopher Lam of Richmond, British Columbia
Andrew LaMance of East Ridge, TN (11)
Doris Lamb of Lakeworth, FL (2)
Jon Lane of Warsaw, NY
Real Laporte of Monteal, Quebec (10)
Wendy A. Largey of Attleborg, MA
Brian Larsen of Warren, MI
Richie Laskaris of Toronto, Ontario
Lori Lawrence of Wichita, KS
B. Keith Lawson of Brazil, IN (5)
Vincent G. Lawyer of Lancaster, VA
Barbara Lay of Irving, TX (8)
Jim Lazar of Milwaukee, WI
Gregory Lea of Houston, TX (3)
Mark Lee of Livermore, CA (4)
Quiton A. Lee of Indianapolis, IN
Young Lee of Baltimore, MD
Murray J. D. Leeder of Calgary, Alberta (8)
Paul J. LeGere of Rotterdam, NY (3)
Steven Lehr of Shiloh, IL
Michael Lehrman of Newton, KS
Michael Leinoff of Glen Falls, NY
Seth Lejeune of Philadelphia, PA
Chris LePage of Port Moddy, British Columbia
Manon Lessard-Belanger of Val D'or, Quebec
Eric Levine of Great Neck, NY
Kendra Levine of Carmichael, CA
Payton Levine of Hockessin, DE
Richard C. Lewis of Bellevue, WA (2)
Kim Wai Li of Surrey, England
Tobi Liedes-Bell of Worland, WY
Paul R. Lilly of Danbury, CT (7)
Jen Lindsay of Mansfield, MA
Andy Lipsett of Newton, MA (3)
Eve LoCastro of Highland Park, NJ (2)
Jeffrey B. Locklear of Richmond, VA
Katy M. Loebrich of Perrysburg, OH (2)
Brian Lombard of Gaithersburg, MD (14)
Sharon Lowachee of Mississuaga, Ontario
Martin Lucero of Orchard Park, NY
Ronnie Luchejko of Wallington, NJ
Nancy Luedke of Wauwatosa, WI
Meike Luessmann of Hamburg, Germany
Zana Lutfiyya of Winnipeg, Manitoba
Garner MacDonald of Dartmouth, Nova
    Scotia (2)
Mike Mader of Independence, MO
William Magalio of Flemington, NJ
T.J. Maher (location unknown)
Christine Mair of West Sussex, England
Gary Makin of Liverpool, England
Karen P. Malcor of Norco, CA
Carl Malstrom of Washington Courthouse, OH
Jeff Manzolli of Boston, MA
Scott Marchino of Bruceville, IN
Felix Mariposa of Oakland, CA (9)
Mike Marletto of Downey, CA
Andy Marquis (location unknown)
Phillip Martin of Anniston, AL (2)

Wells P. Martin of Stamford, CT (4)
Joey Martinez of Bakersfield, CA
Eric Martinson of Bedford, TX
Marty Martyn of Berkley, MI
Craig Mason of Fort Edward, NY (2)
Thomas B. Massey of Lancashire, England (2)
Jenny Matuszewski of Menomonee Falls, WI
Cameron May of Omaha, NE
David H. May of St. Ann, MO
Scott McClenny of Newport, WA
Keith E. McComb of Queens, NY
Jeff McConnell of Altoona, PA
Bob McCourt of Winnipeg, Manitoba
Danny McEvoy of Brighton, England
Mike McGavock of Salina, OK (2)
Laurie McGinn of Lockport, NY
Bob McKee of Metuchen, NJ
David D. McKeehan of Orange Park, FL (2)
Tim McKenny of Lawrenceville, GA (3)
Jim McMahon of Southampton, MA
Mary McMillan of East Haven, CT
Corinne C. McMillen of Stillwater, OK (2)
Ann McNeil of Owen Sound, Ontario (13)
Glen Melanson of Riverview, New Brunswick
Stephen Mendenhall of Ann Arbor, MI (3)
Heather Menge of Marengo, IL
Theodore Merrill of Circleville, OH
Cindy Miller of Des Plaines, IL
Colin L. Miller of Tucson, AZ
Holly Miller of Ballwin, MD
Joshua E. Miller of Gouverneur, NY (2)
Karen Millett of Hants Co., Nova Scotia
Merak Milligan of Seattle, WA (2)
Mike Milligan of Langley, British Columbia (6)
Kyle Millsap of Wichita, KS
Jeff Millward of Taber, Alberta (2)
David Miracle of Louisville, KY
Gary Moldenhauer of Minnetonka, MN (18)
Morgan Moloney of Bellevue, WA
Denise L. Monroe of Palisades Park, NJ
Michael Mooney of Andrews AFB, MD
Anita Moore of Bowie, MD
David T. Moore (location unknown)
John Moore of Memphis, TN (5)
Latrina Moore of Chicago, IL
Margaret Moran of Dublin, Ireland (5)
Laura Morgan of Denver, CO
Jeff Morin of Arlington, VA
Richars S. Morris of Birmingham, England
John Morrison of Garibaldi Highlands,
    British Columbia (3)
Lynne Ann Morse of Ryswyk,
    The Netherlands
Timothy D. Morton of Dundas, Ontario
David Moss of Colchester, VT
Lynn Moss of Bradenton, FL
Tom Mount of Allentown, PA
Anna Mracek of Creve Coeur, MO
Paul T. Mulik of Joplin, MO (4)
Caleb Mullen of Daleville, AL
Edward W. Munlith (location unknown)
Thomas Munn of Lubbock, TX
John Munro of Edinburgh, Scotland
Oso Murillo-Shaw of Dundas, Ontario
Matthew Murray of Bellingham, WA (3)

C. W. Myers of New Martinsville, WV
Talia Myres of Tulsa, OK
Dr. Seph Naficy of Potomac, MD
Tom Napier of North Wales, PA
Barbara Nazimek of Franklin, WI
Larry Nemecek of Burbank, CA
Donna L. Neuman of Lincoln Park, MI
Bill Newman (location unknown)
Robert Nichol of Newmarket, Ontario
Jonah Nicholas of Okanogan, WA
Paula Nolan of East Essex, England
Susan C. Nolan of Mansfield, OH (3)
C. E. Nugent of Louisville, KY
David Nurenberg of Northampton, MA (2)
Shannon T. Nutt of Tulsa, OK
Andrea M. O'Brien of Bayonne, NJ (4)
Johnny O'Brien of River Hebert, Nova Scotia
Merri O'Connor of Chicago, IL
Austen O'Kurley of Bruderheim, Alberta
Brian O'Melia of Phoenix, AZ (3)
Brad O'Sullivan of Glenwood Springs, CO
Jinetta Oakes of Kingston, Ontario
Dan Oates of Romney, WV
Brian S. Oberhauser of Franklin Park, IL (5)
Nathan Orr of Colorado Springs, CO (4)
Scott Orr of Charlotte, NC
Clay Otto of Morris, MN
Mark S. Painter, Sr. of Mont Clare, PA (4)
Robert Palmer of Temecura, CA
Angela Parker of Zachary, LA
James C. Parsons of Ashland, OR (2)
Gayle Patriquen of St. Louis PK, MN
Lee Everett Patterson of University, MS (9)
Randy Pavelich of Edmonton, Alberta
Wesley R. Payne of Denton, TX (2)
Annette G. Pearson of Marshalltown, IA (2)
Tony R. Pecchia of Johnson, RI (2)
Sarah W. J. Pell of Coconut, FL
Ysabelle Pelletier of Drummondville, Quebec
William Penfield of Liverpool, NY
Matthew Penney of St. John's, Newfoundland
D. Penny of Calgary, Alberta
Mark Penny of San Francisco, CA
Christi Pepin of Midland, MI
Brandon Percle of Kenner, LA
Toby Peregrino of Milwaukee, WI
Robyn Perlin of Randolph, MA (2)
Emily A. Perloff of Flourtown, PA
Rachel Perloff of Flourtown, PA
Leslie Perrico of Largo, FL
Robert Pessongnelli of Ardmore, PA
Aaron Peterkin of Winnipeg, Manitoba (2)
Marian Petre of Oxford, England
Geoffrey H. Petts of Hants, England (17)
Brian Phan of San Jose, CA
Danielle Picard of St. Catharine, Ontario
Kevin Kei-Wai Pih of San Jose, CA
Nathan Pinnegar of Bowling Green, KY
Joseph Pintar of New Hartford, NY (2)
Susan Podkowinski of Syracuse, NY (2)
Hays Poole of Raleigh, NC
Lori Porcelli of Syracuse, NY
David D. Porter of Gauteer, MS (2)
Jane Porter of Northants, England (2)
Nicholas Porter of Murphysboro, IL

Bob Potter of Tasmania, Australia (5)
John Potts of London, England (7)
Chuck Powell of Holland, PA (2)
Patricia Pozywak of Elyria, OH (4)
D. Price of Oakland, CA (2)
Deborah Price of Oakland, CA (2)
Shimon Prohow of Tucson, AZ
Tony Pucci of Rochester, MN
Matthew Pugsley of Spartanburg, SC
Ben Puntch of Wichita, KS
Shel Rabin of Boca Raton, FL
Ruth E. Radecki of Santa Maria, CA (4)
Frank Raffaele of Brooklyn, NY
Gary B. Rainey of Pineville, LA
Phillip Ramati of Athens, GA (7)
James Ramsey of Panama City, FL
James H.G. Redekop of London, Ontario (3)
Greg Reid of Toronto, Ontario (12)
Michael A.D. Reid of Atlanta, GA (2)
Adele Reuben of London, England (2)
Miranda Reynolds of Greer, SC
Bob and Kristine Richardson of Parma, OH
Kara Ricks of San Diego, CA
David Rider of Essex, United Kingdom
Bill Rieck of San Antonio, TX
Isabella Rips of Bonn, Germany (4)
Jamie C. Roberts of Philadelphia, PA (2)
Jhaymi Roberts of Roseville, MI
E. Catherine Robler of Westminster, CO (4)
Will Robley of New Carrollton, MA
Brandon Rochelle of Knoxville, TN
Brian S. Roe of Auburn Hills, MI
Jan Rollins of Pittsfield, ME
Thomas G. Romano of Houston, TX (3)
Kim Roney of Syracuse, NY
Alasdair Rooney of Angus, Scotland (2)
Matthew Rorie of McLean, VA
Sarah Rose of Oreland, PA
Warren Roselius of Anchorage, AK (2)
Pam Rosen of Fremont, CA
Barry Rosenfeld of New York, NY
Randy Rosenfeld of New York, NY
Sara Rosenfeld of San Antonio, TX
Lewis G. Rosenthal of Dix Hills, NY
Eric Rost of Omaha, NE
Carrie Rostollan of Saxon, WI (2)
Rob Roszkowski of Jackson Heights, NY
Fred Rothganger of Boston, MA
Keith Rowe of Wray, CO (2)
Don S. Rudolf II of Youngstown, OH (3)
E. Bryan Rumph of Stafford, VA
Angela M. Russo of Roswell, GA (2)
Hilary Ryan of Regina, Saskatchewan (2)
Joe Ryan of Springfield, MO
Jonathan Ryder of Providence, RI
Curt J. Sallinger of Colorado Springs, CO
Elias S. Saltz of Oxford, OH
Samuel R. Sands of Winston-Salem, NC
Scott Saslow of Boca Raton, FL (2)
Sawpna Sathe of Manchestor, MO
Craig Sawyer of Seattle, WA
Louise Scales of Castlegar, British
   Columbia (5)
Clark Scanlon of Council Bluffs, IA (3)
Fred Schaefer of New Haven, CT

Peter Schaub of Solna, Sweden
Peter Schieren of Edmonton, Alberta
Tait Schleisman of Slayton, MN
Brian Scholl of Starkville, MS (2)
Eva Schultz of Joliet, IL (3)
Ian D. Schulze of Hinsdale, IL
William R. Schwab of Lehighton, PA
Carl Schwenk of El Cajon, CA
Bill Scott of Highlands, TX
Douglas Scott of Arlington, TX (9)
Pat Scott of Tucson, AZ
Stephen M., Jr. Scott of Birdseye, IN
Andreas Seagraves of Lexington, KY
Marah Searle of Williamsville, NY
Jennifer Segal of San Diego, CA (3)
Chris Segall of Scarborough, Ontario
Christine Seghers of Sacramento, CA
Jennifer Seghers of Sacramento, CA
Abby Semple of Toronto, Ontario
Ian Senior of Surrey England (10)
Greg Settles of Hixson, TN
Michael S. Sharp of Tulsa, OK (10)
Nick Shaw (Miss) of Middlesex, England (2)
David Shelton of Birmingham, AL
John E. Sherman of Glendale, CA (6)
Ekim Shim of Duesseldorf, Germany
Michael Shiner of Ajax, Ontario
Scott Shirley of Rochester, NY (2)
Margaret Shockley of Lebanon, OR
Mark A. Shore of Staffordshire, England (3)
Alfred Show of San Mateo, CA
Alex Nathan Shumate of Cedar City, UT (5)
Michelle Shuttlesworth of Hanover, PA (2)
Jol Silversmith of Cambridge, MA (3)
Edwin Sirko of Irvine, CA (4)
Caleb Sjogren of Indianapolis, IN (8)
Jennifer Skirkanich of East Northport, NY
Debbie Sleeter of Albuquerque, NM
Barbara Smith of Haverton, PA (3)
Cindy Smith of Medina, OH
David K. Smith of West Trenton, NJ (24)
Debora L. Smith of Sacramento, CA
Jason Smith of Cadillac, MI
Josiah Smith of Gwynne, Alberta
Kathy Smith of Ellesmere, England (2)
Lance Smith of Brighton, MO
Michael Smith of Willowdale, Ontario (4)
Richard Smith of Surrey, England (7)
Sharla Smith of Minneapolis, MN
William R. Sohm of Frederick, MD
Matthew William Spencer of El Paso, TX
Martin Stahl of Marktheidenfeld, Germany (2)
Roland Stamm of Weisbaden Germany
Steven Stark-Riemer of Delmar, NY
Christopher Steeves of Saint John, New
    Brunswick
Michael Stephenson of Brandon, MS
Robert Stevens of Washington, DC (2)
Paul F. Stevenson of Abilene, TX (3)
Andrew Stewart of Derbyshire, England
Michael Stewart of New Orleans, LA
Mike Stewart of San Antonio, TX (2)
David Stiffel of London England
James R. Stilipec of North Pole, AK
Eric Stillwell of Glendale, CA (2)

Nigel Strafford of Surrey, England (9)
R. Clayton Strang of Lynnwood, WA
Mark Straszewski of Trenton, NJ
Eric R. Straub of Niantic, CT (2)
Matthew Strommer of Great Barrington, MA (3)
Steve Stutton of Rincon, GA
Renee Sullivan of Fennville, MI
Michelle Sutherland of London, Ontario
Stephen Swain of London, Ontario
H. Martin Swan of St. Paul, MN (2)
Andre Swartley of Heeston, KS
Barry Tabrah of West Glamorgan, United
    Kingdom (3)
Sharon Taggart of Rush, NY
David Tarbok of Huntertown, IN (5)
Leonard M. Tare of Atwater, CA (2)
Jason Tasse of Pierrefonds, Quebec (2)
Rich Tatum of Springfield, MO
Aaron Tayler of Silt, CO (3)
Lee Taylor of Omaha, NE
Molly Taylor (address unknown)
David Tayman of Springfield, MO
Jeff Tebbetts (location unknown)
Gerhard Thielman of Ridgecrest, CA (2)
Nick Thoma of Ancaster, Ontario
Bill Thomas of Westminster, CO
Teresa K. Thomas of Riverside, OH
Roland R. Thompson of Los Angeles, CA (2)
Andy Tilley of Leeds, England
Christopher Todaro of Danbury, CT (2)
Fred Tourtellotte of Rutherford, NJ
Shane Tourtellotte of Rutherford, NJ
Joan Trolinger of Madison, AL
Tony Troxell of Shirley, IN
Joshua M. Truax of Fridley, MN (26)
Cynthia C.Y. Tsao of Berkeley, CA
Fender Tucker of Shreveport, LA
John S. Turner of Bethany, OK
Steven T. Turner of Baltimore, MD
Jimmy Tuton of Tinley Park, IL (2)
Maureen Tyers of Hanna, Alberta
Rod Tyrrell of Victoria, Australia (3)
Amit Udeshi of Barrington, IL (2)
Daniel J. Udey of Prince Albert, Saskatchewan
Mary Ulrick of Mississauga, Ontario (2)
Jonathan Upton of Sault Ste. Marie, Ontario (3)
Mitch Utterback of San Diego, CA (2)
Meredith Vacek of Lenexa, KS (2)
Melvin P. Valentin of San Francisco, CA (3)
Rich Valliere of Vienna, VA
Tom VanZandt of Agawam, MA
Tami Vaughn of Forest Grove, OR
Timothy Wade, Jr. of Horsehead, NY
Walter Wakefield III of Portland, OR (5)
Cory Waldron of Altoona, IA
Tracy Walker of Lecoma, MO
Charles Wallace of Antioch, CA (2)
Jennifer Wallace of Victoria, British Columbia
Sean Wallace of Rochester, NY
Kate Walsh of Tucson, AZ
Tom J. Walz of Moorhead, MN
Josh Ward of Batavia, IL
Thelma Ward of Middlesex, England
Linda Ware of North Yorkshire, England
Stu Ware of Davenport, IA

Cheryl Warkentin of Hutchinson, KS
Mark Warrington of N. Canton, OH
Erin Warry of Burlington, Ontario
Edward A. Watson of Downington, PA (15)
John Watson of Everett, WA (3)
Paul Watson of Humberside, England (5)
Susan Way of San Diego, CA (2)
Rhiannon Weaver of Honeybrook, PA
S. Webb of Northborough, MA
Bernd Webler of Wiesbaden, Germany
Dirk Weger of Bad Soden, Germany
Wendy A. Weiger of Brookline, MA (3)
Jason Weintraub of Cambridge, MA
Steven Weintraub of New York, NY
Werner Weiss of Rhein, Germany
Jon Wells of Ames, IA (3)
Kari Wendel of Dunkirk, NY (2)
Gary Wesley of Cambs, England (8)
Andrew Weusthoff of St. Louis, MO
Balthasar V. Weymarn of Munich, Germany
Stephen Whitelam of Perthshire,
    Scotland (2)
Michael Whiteman of Mesa, AZ
Christine and Steven Wicklund of Wheeling, IL
Daniel J. Wigdor of Uxbridge, Ontario (2)

Willem de Lind van Wijngaarden of
    Nepean, Ontario
Jeanne Wildman (location unknown)
Laura Wile of Eau Claire, WI
Alma Jo Williams of Ithaca, NY
D. R. Williams of Amsterdam, Holland (2)
Shantelle Williams of Sauk Village, IL
Brad Wilson of Vaduais Heights, MN
Steven H. Wishod of Washington, DC
Darren Witwicki of Winterburn, Alberta
Dave Wolff of Garden City, NY (7)
Yar Woo of New Haven, CT
Geoffrey H. Wood of Cedar Rapids, IA
Robert J. Wooley of St. Paul, MN (3)
David Yalden II of Flinstone, GA (8)
Robin Yates of Lancaster, PA
Justin Yeoman of Whiteriver, AZ
Leanna Yip of Concord, CA
J. A. Young of Fort Ord, CA
Doyle Steven Youngblood of Waldron, AR
Steven Youngblood of Waldron, AR
Eric Zay of Lansing, MI
Andreas Zech of Berlin, Germany (7)
Lee Zion of the USS Kitty Hawk (4)
Alec Zrike of Middletown, NJ (2)

★
INTRODUCTION

Greetings, fellow nitpickers!
This book wraps up some unfinished business with *Star Trek: The Next Generation*. Many have written to ask why *The Nitpicker's Guide for Next Generation Trekkers* doesn't contain reviews for the seventh and final season of *NextGen*. Well, according to the *Trek* scuttlebutt at the time of that *Guide's* writing, there wasn't going to *be* a seventh season of *NextGen*! Of course, once the *Guide* went into production, word came down that the seventh season was on its way. (Arrgh!) Thankfully, as you can see, it all worked out for the best. Not only does this book—Volume II—cover the seventh season of *NextGen*, it also reviews *Star Trek: Generations* and contains a veritable cornucopia of *all new nits* covering the first six seasons of *Star Trek: The Next Generation*—sent in by the thousands of members of the Nitpicker's Guild! (It even contains some selections from *The Nitpicker's Guide to the Nitpicker's Guide for Next Generation Trekkers*. Wink, wink.)

For those unfamiliar with a *Nitpicker's Guide,* let me offer my usual quick tour. For each episode—or movie—I list the title, star date, and a brief summary—in case you haven't seen that particular installment in the *Star Trek* universe. I also add a few ruminations along the way and offer picks for great moments. There are two trivia ques-

tions just to test your knowledge of the episode or movie. Then—as I say—it's on to the *good stuff!* I take the nits for each review and place them in one of four major categories: Plot Oversights, Changed Premises, Equipment Oddities and Continuity and Production Problems.

Plot Oversights is a catchall. Anything that concerns the plot, or won't fit anywhere else, goes here. Under Changed Premises, you'll discover that sometimes information given in one show directly contradicts information in another. In Equipment Oddities I'll point out any technical problems with the machinery of the *Trek* universe. Lastly, the section Continuity and Production Problems will expose errors in the actual creation of the show.

The "reader mail" reviews covering the episodes in the first six seasons of *NextGen* have an occasional, additional category called Alternate Viewpoints and Corrections. This category contains submissions from members of the Nitpicker's Guild who disagreed with something I said in *The Nitpicker's Guide for Next Generation Trekkers* (hereafter referred to as the *NextGen Guide*). It also contains corrections to items that were just plain wrong in the first *Guide*. (Ah well, my humanity rears its ugly head.)

If you happen to have the episodes of *Star Trek: The Next Generation* on videotape, pull them out and grab the remote as you work your way through this *Guide*. If you find something I missed, disagree with a nit I picked, or even find an error in the *Guide* itself, drop me a line at the address in the back of this book. That entry will make you a member of the Nitpicker's Guild.

As always, the Nitpicker's Prime Directive remains in full force. For those who don't remember, the main rule of nitpicking reads, "All nits picked shall derive from sources the creators consider canonical." In other words, anything that Paramount claims is authoritative can be nitpicked. As I understand it, any of the television episodes in any incarnation of *Star Trek* are canonical. So are the movies and the reference materials available from Pocket Books. On the other hand, the creators do not consider the *Star Trek* novels authoritative. Those stories have never actually happened. Trying to prove a nit by citing a passage from a novel violates the Nitpicker's Prime Directive. And, as you know, nitpickers *never* violate the Nitpicker's Prime Directive.

Happy nitpicking!

SEVENTH SEASON

DESCENT, PART II

Star Date: 47025.4

After declaring his loyalty to Lore, Data leads Picard, La Forge, and Troi to a detention cell. Once there, the trio surmises that Lore has disabled Data's ethical program and now controls their colleague through a constant diet of negative emotions.

Meanwhile, Riker and Worf stumble on to another group of Borg, led by Hugh. He explains what has happened. Once he was returned to his ship, Hugh's newfound self-identity quickly spread through the Borg collective (see "I Borg"). Into this confusion, Lore brought a clarity of purpose as well as a promise that they could become fully artificial. Yet, as Lore experimented with converting the Borg's brains from biological to artificial, all the test subjects had developed brain damage.

Unwilling to risk any more Borg, Data begins experimenting with La Forge. Fortunately, Picard manages to reboot Data's ethical program. Lore senses the change and orders Data to kill Picard to prove his loyalty. When Data refuses, Lore tries to kill his brother. At this point, Hugh, Riker, and Worf attack,

throwing the Borg into confusion. In the scuffle, Data fires on Lore and then deactivates him. Data returns to normal, the Borg become less aggressive, and the crew of the *Enterprise* leaves them to explore their individuality.

Trivia Questions

1. What is the name of the frightened Borg that Crosis brings to Lore?

2. How far did Data walk underwater during a sailing trip with La Forge?

GREAT MOMENTS

The creators did a lovely job showing Lore's deactivation. As Data fiddles, Lore's eye slowly turn to grey.

PLOT OVERSIGHTS

• As the episode begins, the ensign at the tactical station informs Crusher—the acting captain—that she has been on the *Enterprise* for only six weeks. Evidently Picard really *was* serious when he said that he was leaving a skeleton crew on the *Enterprise* during the first part of "Descent." This is unbelievable! The most qualified person to operate the tactical station is an ensign who's been on the ship for only six weeks? Just before this episode began, the *Enterprise* had chased a mortal enemy to its lair, an enemy with a huge ship that had already outgunned the *Enterprise* once. The Borg ship probably would be coming back. This is not a situation where you want an inexperienced person manning the weapons. And then, when the Borg ship does return, Crusher calls for a specific fire pattern and the ensign replies, "Uhhhh…right!" ("Uhhhh …right"? I don't think "uhhhh…right" is the desired response in this situation.) Shouldn't Picard be a little more protective of his ship?

• When Hugh goes through his long discourse on how the Borg met Lore, neither Riker nor Worf react to the mention of Data's brother's name. If I'm not mistaken, at this point in the episode only Picard, La Forge, and Troi know that Lore leads the Borg.

• After Data brings La Forge back from the lab, Troi asks the chief engineer if he's in pain. Wait a minute: Shouldn't Troi's empathic powers tell her if La Forge is in pain?

• When Data talks with Lore outside the Borg building, he squints. *Squints!?* This, from an android that looked full into the blinding flash caused by the beings in the Romulan engine core in the episode "Timescape." Must be caused by those negative emotions he feels.

• At the end of this episode, Data shuts off Lore and then tells Picard that the nonfunctioning android must be disassembled. Isn't Lore sentient? Aren't all sentient beings guaranteed certain rights under Federation law? Isn't this the equivalent of murder?

• Just before the crew rides out into the sunset, Hugh tells Picard that the Borg on the planet can't go back to the collective. From this, I assume that there still is a collective. I thought they all operated as one group mind. If the self-awareness of Hugh devastated one ship, wouldn't their subspace emanations carry that devastation throughout the rest of the collective consciousness? On the other hand, if the Borg are still out there, why do they seem to have lost all interest in the Federation?

CHANGED PREMISES

• In the previous episode, Troi stressed to Data that emotions are neither positive nor negative. In this episode Troi says that "…the only emotions Data seems to feel are negative."

• After the Borg ship damages the *Enterprise*'s warp drive, Crusher decides to take the ship into the nearby star. She asks a lieutenant to run La Forge's experimental work on metaphasic shielding so they can enter the sun's corona. Evidently La Forge based his work on the Ferengi scientist's "breakthrough" discussed during "Suspicions." *One more time,* shielding to allow the *Enterprise* to enter a star's corona is *not a new ability.* The *Enterprise* does not need metaphasic shielding to do this. In "I Borg," Picard said the *Enterprise* would hide in a star's *chromosphere* to obscure the sensors of the ship coming to rescue Hugh. The chromosphere of a star is the lower part of its atmosphere, the part next to the photosphere—the actual surface of the star. The corona of a star is the uppermost part of the star's atmosphere. In other words, Picard—during "I Borg"—hid the *Enterprise* *below* the star's corona, next to its surface without metaphasic shielding!

EQUIPMENT ODDITIES

• When the Borg ship approaches for

the first time, Crusher orders the transporter chief to beam everyone off the planet. With only twenty seconds to go before the Borg ship fires, there are seventy-three crew members still on the planet. At the last moment, Crusher raises the shields and breaks orbit. She leaves forty-seven people behind. Therefore it takes twenty seconds to beam twenty-six people off the planet. Neither "Descent" nor "Descent, Part II" mention any trouble with transporting through the planet's electromagnetic interference. And "11001001" indicates that there are at least twenty transporters on the *Enterprise*. At six people per transporter, that's 120 individuals the *Enterprise* can transport in one shot. So why does it take twenty seconds to transport twenty-six people? (All the transporter chiefs were probably down on the planet looking for Data!)

• After living in fear of the Borg for more than four seasons, now we find out that all you have to do is pull one of their tubes and they will short-circuit. After Data takes La Forge the second time, Picard feigns injury in the detention cell. The Borg guard comes over to look. Picard reaches up and yanks out one of his facial tubes. The Borg grimaces and falls over. Evidently it's that easy to defeat one of these guys. Oddly enough, at the end of the episode, when the Borg fight among themselves, not one of them uses this tactic. They punch, kick, and body-slam, but nobody reaches up and "detubes" another. Have the Borg somehow managed to tain this activity with shame and embarrassment? ("You're not going to believe this! You

know good old 'fourth of twelve'? He's a 'tube-puller'!") Along the same line, nitpicker Fender Tucker offered, "Isn't a cheektube a fatal accident just waiting to happen? I can hear Grandpa Borg now. 'You would have loved Aunt Erk. Unfortunately, she caught her cheektube on a doorknob back before you were born.'"

• This twenty-fourth-century technology is amazing: Picard rips a small piece of equipment off the Borg he kills and—with La Forge's help—somehow manages to reconfigure it and sends out the exact type of pulse that's needed to restart Data's ethical programming. And he powers the contraption by shoving it into a force field! (Does this seem a bit too "McGyverish" to you?)

• Attempting to destroy the Borg ship as the *Enterprise* hides in a star's corona, the crew directs a particle beam at the star. Dialogue indicates that this particle beam will come from the tractor beam. Yet, in the exterior shot of the ship, the particle beam actually comes from the Battle Section forward phaser array—according to the *Tech Manual*.

• Several times, this episode refers to the chip Dr. Noonian Soong created for Data so that Data could feel emotions. During "Brothers," Lore stole this chip from Soong. At the end of "Descent, Part II," Data holds the recovered chip with a pair of tweezers. He says the chip was damaged when he fired on Lore. The chip indeed sustained heavy damage. In "Brothers," the chip was a small metal sphere. In this episode, the chip is a flat disk with a pie-shaped piece cut out of it.

• Disturbed by the danger of emotions, Data attempts to destroy this chip. Of course, La Forge stops him (allowing the chip to grow into the much larger object that causes Data all the trouble in *Star Trek: Generations*). What's odd here is *how* Data intends to destroy the chip. A small container for the chip rests on Data's desk. It sits on top of a control pad, and he looks like he's preparing to phaser it into oblivion! Is a phaser really so accurate that it can do this and not damage the control panel underneath?

CONTINUITY AND PRODUCTION PROBLEMS

• Does Lieutenant Barnaby look vaguely familiar? Sort of like a Takaran scientist named Jo'Brill who visited the *Enterprise* during "Suspicions"?

• La Forge's laboratory restraints don't seem to work very well. The first scene in the lab shows La Forge strapped to an examination table. A seatbelt-like strap runs across his abdomen, pinning his wrists to the table. Data enters, mimicking Picard's voice as a joke. La Forge responds by trying to pull his wrists free. He almost accomplishes this and then remembers that he's supposed to be helpless and so he shoves his hands back under the restraint.

• During the experiment on La Forge, Data uses a wand to implant nanocortical fibers in La Forge's brain. The process is the same every time. First, he touches the wand to La Forge's skull. Then a cutaway shows Data's face. Finally, the camera returns to La Forge, Data withdraws the wand, and a small cluster of fibers remains, giving the impression that they are buried in La Forge's brain. Of course, the cutaway to Data's face gives the makeup artists time to glue the fibers to La Forge's forehead. The wand is then placed over the fibers so that Data can retract it in the next shot and have it appear that he's implanted them. The only problem is that the first time Data does this, he touches the wand to La Forge's forehead near La Forge's left eyebrow, but when the camera returns, the wand is suddenly in the center.

• At one point, Data visits Lore on a sunny veranda outside the Borg building. There must be some weird spatial anaphasic particle field surrounding the veranda, because on Lore's side all the shadows point to the left, and on Data's side all the shadows point to the right! (By the way, I used the "Technobabble Generator" included in this guide to come up with the cause of these unusual visual anomalies.)

TRIVIA ANSWERS
1. Goval.
2. One kilometer, forty-six meters.

★
LIAISONS

Picard travels to the Iyaaran home world as part of a cultural exchange. On the way, the Iyaaran shuttle crash-lands on a planet, apparently injuring the pilot, Voval. Picard goes for help, but an ambient plasma discharge knocks him to the ground. He awakes inside the wreckage of a freighter and is cared for by a human female named Anna, who explains that she is the sole survivor of the freighter's crash.

Anna thwarts Picard's every attempt to effect their rescue, while claiming to love him. She even wrestles him to the ground to extract a kiss. When Picard pushes her away, Anna leaves, disappointed. Voval then appears, stating that he saw the woman head toward the nearby cliffs. Moments later, Picard locates Anna, apparently suicidal, on the edge of a precipice. Picard notices that Anna wears a necklace that had broken loose during their struggle and realizes that Voval must have brought it to her. Confronted with this fact, Anna changes into Voval. He explains that his race's first contact with humans came from logs left by the woman who survived the

freighter crash seven years ago. The logs recorded her rescue by a man and told of their subsequent romance. Without a concept of love in their society, the Iyaarans decided to restage this incident and learn from it.

Trivia Questions

1. What is Troi's favorite dessert among those at the buffet in Ten-Forward?

2. Where is the antimatter storage facility housed on the *Enterprise*?

RUMINATIONS

The show opens with Worf making final adjustments to his dress uniform before the arrival of an Iyarran shuttle containing two Iyaaran ambassadors. As Picard visits the Iyaaran home world, these two ambassadors will stay on board the ship. A few moments later, Riker enters Worf's quarters, trying to hurry him up. Worf replies that the dress uniforms look like dresses. It's a cute moment, but a long view of the uniforms later doesn't support Worf's statements. The bottom of the dress coat comes to the same level as one of our suit coats, and the men wear pants underneath it. The outfit isn't that different from the getup Worf wears to teach Klingon martial arts. On the other hand, the dress uniforms worn by Picard and Riker in "Manhunt" really did look like dresses. Those dress coats extended to the tops of their knees, and the men wore opaque tights underneath. I wonder if the writer of this episode had the "Manhunt" dress uniforms in mind.

And speaking of men in dresses, I suppose I should add another entry in the Updated Romance Tote Board: "Number of men who kiss Picard." Continuing briefly with this theme, I wonder just how far Voval would have gone in his exploration of the human concept of love if Picard had found Anna attractive and decided to take advantage of their isolation....

GREAT LINES

"You share all of those qualities in abundance. Perhaps you should try to build on your similarities."—Data to Worf, after Worf has described the Iyaaran ambassador, Byleth, as "demanding, temperamental, and rude."

PLOT OVERSIGHTS

• At the beginning of the episode, Riker tells Worf that he will escort the Iyaaran ambassadors around the *Enterprise* for three days. Moments later, Ambassador Byleth states that the next *seven* days will be interesting.

• Again, a member of the *Enterprise* crew shows a lack of knowledge about first aid. After the shuttle crash, Picard lifts Voval's head to place his jacket under it and then actually pulls the guy over a few inches. On top of it all, he doesn't even use the available tricorder to diagnose Voval's condition (as Wesley did for Picard in "Final Mission").

CHANGED PREMISES

• Great confusion surrounds the race known as Tarellians. In the *NextGen Guide* in the review for "Starship Mine," I discussed the progression of this race from plague victims to *Enterprise* employees. In this episode Picard identifies the crashed freighter as Tarellian and then proceeds to comment that he knows Anna is not Tarellian because she is missing two arms. So Tarellians now have four arms?!

CONTINUITY AND PRODUCTION PROBLEMS

• Subtlety suffered a death blow in this episode. Just after Troi escorts the ambassador to taste some chocolate at a buffet, she heads for a table. Delighted with this new thing called "dessert," the ambassador grabs an entire tray of goodies. At this point, an off-camera voice comes clearly sailing through the background chatter and says, "SEX!" Sex? What does sex have to do with this scene?

• As the shuttle heads for the planet, one camera angle shows the backs of the chairs. The emblem on them looks very Romulan. (Could this possibly be a plot to get our beloved Captain Picard into an extremely compromising position and then blackmail him for information later?)

TRIVIA ANSWERS

1. A Ktarian chocolate puff.
2. Deck 42.

★
INTERFACE

Star Date: 47215.5

Using an experimental probe that interfaces directly to his neural inputs, La Forge investigates a tragedy concerning the science vessel *Raman,* as it tried to collect gases from the lower atmosphere of an unusual planet. Something went wrong as the ship tried to reascend into space. La Forge soon discovers that the crew is dead. Impossibly, La Forge also meets his mother— captain of the USS *Hera,* a ship recently reported missing. She tells him that "they" are "dying" and must "go down."

Picard thinks La Forge was hallucinating. Since continued exposure to the high sensory inputs of the probe poses a danger, the captain opts for another plan to retrieve the *Raman.* Believing that his mother is still alive, La Forge disobeys Picard's orders and, with Data's assistance, fires up the probe interface. He soon discovers the truth. When the *Raman* had descended into the atmosphere, it trapped several subspace beings within its hull. When the ship started to ascend, the beings began to die. In desperation, they tried to communicate with the crew but

accidentally killed them. Then La Forge appeared. The beings read his thoughts and took on the appearance of his mother, hoping to persuade him to help them. Endangering his life, La Forge returns the creatures to their home near the surface of the planet.

Trivia Questions

1. What is the name of the admiral whom Picard speaks to on DS3?

2. Name the three other *Star Trek: The Next Generation* episodes that featured LeVar Burton acting without his white contacts or VISOR?

PLOT OVERSIGHTS

• On the *Raman,* La Forge spots a fallen crew member. He walks over and asks Data to increase the power to the probe's tractor beams. This increases the danger to La Forge, but the extra power allows him to pull some debris off the crew member. Then La Forge leans down, feels the crew member's neck, and determines that the guy is dead. Note that the guy's neck was exposed prior to clearing away the debris. Wouldn't it make more sense for La Forge first to check if the guy was still alive and then ask for more power?

• Moving down the hall of the *Raman,* La Forge states that he is detecting atmospheric gases— methane and ammonia—and supposes that there has been a hull breach. Then he comes to a magnetic

9

storage bay and supposes that the crew members have fled there for protection. Then he blows open the door of the bay. If the hall is filled with methane and ammonia because of a hull breach, don't you suppose that blowing open the door of the ship's only refuge is a *really* bad idea?

• Starfleet sure gives up on the *Hera* quickly! They search for six days and list it as lost. So…when the *Enterprise* got stuck in that temporal causality loop for seventeen days in "Cause and Effect," was it listed as lost as well?

EQUIPMENT ODDITIES

• At the very beginning of the episode, the image of La Forge straightens his shirt. This image corresponds to the actual probe. Yet the probe doesn't wear a shirt, and the real La Forge wears an interface jumpsuit.

• Everyone keeps commenting how real the input from the probe must be for La Forge because of his neural implants. Couldn't Data hook the probe interface into a holodeck and then map the movements of a person back onto the probe and provide the same level of realism to ordinary folks like us?

• In school, most of us learn about the five senses: seeing, hearing, smelling, tasting, and touching. Neurologists refer to a *sixth* sense that humans possess, the sense of body position. Barring some neurological problem, humans possess the ability to know the position of an arm or leg without looking at it. Losing this sense can be very disorienting. I assume that receiving conflicting input as to the current position of an arm or leg would be very disorienting as well. Just after La Forge reaches out to touch his "mother" the first time, the scene cuts back to La Forge in the lab. Evidently the probe was manufacturing the sensations of La Forge raising his arms and touching his mother because, in the lab, La Forge's real arms are at his side. In other words, the probe is telling La Forge that his arms are at the level of his chest and, at the same time, his body is telling him that his arms are at his side.

• Speaking of probes, wouldn't it have been simpler for the *Raman to* send a probe down to the lower atmosphere to secure the sample gases? Additionally, can't Picard resolve the issue of whether La Forge is hallucinating by sending an *Enterprise* probe to the planet's surface and scanning for the *Hera*? And wouldn't this be a really great time to have some sort of *normal* visual feed from the interface probe?

CONTINUITY AND PRODUCTION PROBLEMS

• The actor who plays La Forge's mother in this episode also played the captain of the USS *Saratoga* in *Star Trek IV: The Voyage Home.* As I said in the *Classic Guide,* she was probably La Forge's grandmother. (Actually, more like La Forge's great-grandmother.)

TRIVIA ANSWERS
1. Holt.
2. "Hide and Q" and "Future Imperfect."

GAMBIT, PART I

Star Date: 47135.2

After uncovering reports that Picard died in a bar fight with a group of mercenaries, Riker sets course for Baratas III, the mercenaries' next known destination. Shortly after an away team beams down, the mercenaries attack and capture Riker in the scuffle. The mercenaries then beam back to their vessel and warp away, easily evading the sensors of the *Enterprise*. Data reviews the available facts and concludes that the mercenaries are stealing ancient Romulan artifacts. He deduces that their next attack should be on Calder II, and he sets course.

Meanwhile, the mercenaries bring Riker to their leader, Arctus Baran. When Baran decides to keep Riker as a prisoner, everyone objects, including Picard, who is posing as an artifacts smuggler named Galen. Later, Picard visits Riker in his quarters and explains. After finding an archaeological site vandalized, Picard went to look for the culprits. He soon found them but asked too many questions, and they fired their specially-equipped weapons at him. These weapons activated transporters

that whisked Picard to Baran's ship. Once there, Picard convinced them he could be valuable and joined the crew to discover their mission.

Shortly after the mercenaries arrive to plunder Calder II, the *Enterprise* shows up as well. As the episode ends, the mercenaries attack, aided by Riker and Picard.

PLOT OVERSIGHTS

• At the very beginning of the episode, an away team rummages around in a seedy bar, looking for information on Picard. The barkeep reiterates Troi's description of the captain, giving him a height of almost two meters. Two meters is more than six feet, six inches tall!

• The Yridian that supplies the away team with information in the bar must have really bad eyesight. After being questioned, he asks, "Who are you people?" Well, let's see. They carry Starfleet regulation phasers, a Starfleet regulation tricorder, and one of them talks about finding "Starfleet fiber traces" where Picard was supposedly vaporized. Maybe they belong to...*Starfleet*?

• When Riker becomes acting captain and forms an away team to go

Trivia Questions

1. Where is the *Enterprise* scheduled to go when Admiral Chekote puts the ship on detached duty?

2. What is Riker's serial number?

down to Baratas III, Data reminds him that his place is on the bridge. Riker ignores this comment and goes down anyway—only to get captured. Of course, this is the same Riker who clucked every time Picard wanted to go on an away team. Then—after Riker gets captured—Data shows up on an away team. At this point in the show, *he's* the acting captain! In other words, neither Riker nor Data followed the "captains shouldn't go on an away team" rule once the rule applied to them.

• At Calder II, a mercenary tells Baran that they lost a man in their last engagement with Starfleet. That must have happened when we weren't looking, because I only recall a Starfleet officer getting injured during the battle on Baratas III.

CHANGED PREMISES

• After promotion to first officer in "Chain of Command, Part 2," Data changes to a red uniform. Yet in this episode he doesn't, though Picard's "death" means that he is—again—first officer.

EQUIPMENT ODDITIES

• On Baratas III, an away team discovers depressions in the ground. The dialogue seems to indicate that the mercenaries created the depressions when they used their weapons to activate their transporter and collect artifacts to take back to their ship. Yet during a big phaser battle on the surface, a mercenary charges out, grabs a pot, and runs for cover. Why would she do this if she could just fire at it and beam it to their ship?

• The *Enterprise* really needs to get its crew back on the phaser range. Nobody seems to be able to hit *any-thing* except the rocks in the big shoot-out. And why do the Starfleet guys just sit there and watch the mercenaries walk up to Riker and kidnap him? Come on, guys! Fire at somebody!

• Of course, one wonders why the Starfleet team doesn't just crank up their phasers and vaporize the rocks that the mercenaries use for cover.

• The *Tech Manual* states, "the value of phaser energy at warp velocities is close to none." Why then does Data tell the officer at tactical to lock phasers on the mercenary ship as it flees from Baratas III at warp 8.7 and the *Enterprise* pursues it at warp 9?

CONTINUITY AND PRODUCTION PROBLEMS

• When Riker asks Admiral Chekote from Starbase 227 to let him investigate Picard's death, the stars in the ready room window drift from left to right. Since the second season, when the *Enterprise* travels at warp the stars always streak away when viewed through the ready room window at an angle. That means the window must face somewhere between south and southwest—if north is toward the front of the ship. In other words, if the stars are drifting from left to right, the *Enterprise* must be going in reverse. (I wonder if it has one of those little horns that sound when construction vehicles go in reverse…)

TRIVIA ANSWERS

1. The Argus Sector.
2. SC 231-427.

GAMBIT, PART II

Star Dates: 47160.1—47169.2

As the show begins, Picard and Riker help a mercenary ship attack the *Enterprise*. Of course, the pair has ensured that the mercenaries' phasers have little effect. Taking the cue, Data shuts down power, making it appear that the mercenaries—headed by Baran—have succeeded. After the mercenaries leave, the crew of the *Enterprise* discovers a coded message from Picard containing Baran's flight plan. A short time later, Picard and Riker uncover Baran's mission. A mercenary named Talera tells them that an isolationist group on Vulcan has hired Baran to reassemble an ancient Vulcan psionic resonator—a weapon that makes it possible to kill with a single thought.

Meanwhile, the *Enterprise* intercepts a Klingon who is attempting to deliver a component of the resonator to Baran. To retrieve it, Baran orders Picard and Riker to take a team to the *Enterprise*. While on board, Picard "kills" Riker and then returns and mutinies against Baran. Picard—the new captain of the mercenary ship—flies to Vulcan. In an underground sanctuary, Talera quickly assembles the psionic resonator and kills all the mercenaries on the away team except Picard. At this point, Riker appears with a security team from the *Enterprise*. Picard quickly deduces the only way to defeat the resonator. Since it works on aggressive emotions, he orders the away team to remain passive, rendering the weapon useless.

PLOT OVERSIGHTS

• As the show progresses, Picard becomes concerned for his safety on the mercenary ship. At one point, Riker enters Picard's room. Picard spins, grabs a weapon, and points it at Riker. The odd thing is that Picard was sitting with his back to the door. Shouldn't Picard sit with his back against the wall and *face* the door? And another thing: Where did he get this weapon in the first place? Baran rules the ship by fear and intimidation. Does this seem like an atmosphere where weapons would be readily available to disgruntled crew members?

• This next nit spans both a plot oversight and an equipment oddity. Depending upon your point of view, it

Trivia Questions

1. Riker beams the mercenaries to the observation lounge using the transporters of what shuttle?

2. What is the name of the navigation computer file that contains the message Picard sent to the *Enterprise*?

can be either. At one point, mercenaries—including Picard and Riker—beam into an *Enterprise* shuttle bay to steal an artifact. Riker fires his weapon several times and then beams the away team up to the observation lounge. After more phaser fire, Picard goes back to the mercenary ship with everyone except Riker. The entire time the mercenary team visits the *Enterprise*, there is no indication that anyone—except those in their immediate vicinity—is aware of their presence. First, how did the mercenary ship get close enough to transport people over without the crew of the *Enterprise* knowing it? True, the mercenaries' ship is sensor-invisible at warp. But since the *Enterprise* is not traveling at warp, the mercenary ship would have to drop out of warp to dispatch the raiding party. Apparently no one on the bridge noticed. Second, why doesn't someone detect the transporter signatures when the mercenaries beam aboard (as Worf did in "Rascals" when the Ferengi transported over)? Third, what happened to the intruder alerts? Fourth, why doesn't anyone pick up on the phaser fire in the shuttle bay and the observation lounge? (Possibly Riker used his ineffective command codes again and Data mocked up the appropriate responses as he did at the beginning of this episode, but no dialogue indicates this.)

• After the raid on the *Enterprise*, Picard tries to take command of the mercenary vessel. No one has tried this heretofore because of the neural implants each crew member wears. Baran's predecessor installed them

in the crew, and with a touch on a control pad, Baran can inflict pain, or even death. Baran—fed up with the backtalk—decides to kill Picard. He hits the appropriate button and promptly falls to the ground, dead. Picard then explains that he switched transponder codes on the neural implants. This implies that Baran had an implant. Granted, Baran's predecessor probably installed an implant on Baran, but why didn't Baran remove it when he became captain?

• After assuming command of the mercenary ship, Picard goes to Baran's quarters to try to discover where they need to take the artifacts in order to secure payment for their deeds. The action cuts to Riker, on the *Enterprise*, who proceeds to tell a governmental official on Vulcan that the mercenary ship might be headed their way. Then the action cuts back to the mercenary ship, and Picard learns that they should go to Vulcan. So…Riker knew the mercenaries were going to Vulcan before Picard? Does this seem out of sequence to anyone else? (Granted, with some shoving and twisting it can make sense, but it just seems a bit too confusing to me.)

• Evidently the crew of the *Enterprise* has finally managed to domesticate Worf. In the final confrontation, Picard orders Worf to rid himself of all violent and aggressive emotions…and Worf complies! (I guess his blood does not boil anymore. Or maybe Troi has been helping him explore his femininity. Of course, I could come up with several more completely uncalled-for statements exploring the latter theme, but…I believe I shall postpone. Even the thought of Worf in a tutu sends chills up my spine.)

CHANGED PREMISES

• Displeased with Worf's constant sass, Data asks him if he wishes to be relived of first-officer duties. Data claims that the role of the first officer is to carry out the captain's orders. Then he says, "I do not recall Commander Riker ever publicly showing irritation with his captain, as you did a moment ago." Yet in "Sarek," Picard and Riker got into a shouting match on the bridge. Granted, they were inflamed by the telepathically transmitted emotions of Sarek, but Riker was most definitely irritated at Picard and publicly showed it—questioning Picard's indecision over Sarek. Data probably forgot about that incident. Of course, an android never forgets....

• In this episode, Vulcan is a moldy mustard color, but in the *Classic* episode "Amok Time," Vulcan is very red.

CONTINUITY AND PRODUCTION PROBLEMS

• The show opens with an exterior graphic of the mercenary ship pounding the starboard nacelle of the *Enterprise*. Immediately after this shot, the action moves inside, and Worf reports that the *port* nacelle has sustained a hit.

• After the above pounding, Data knows he must simulate battle damage and tells Worf to shut down all power on decks 31 through 37. Interestingly, the exterior shot that follows shows lights burning on those decks!

TRIVIA ANSWERS

1. *Justman.*
2. File 137/Omega.

PHANTASMS

Star Date: 47225.7

Just after the installation of a new warp core in the *Enterprise,* Data begins having nightmares. In one, he sees Worf consuming a piece of "cellular peptide" cake, a piece that came from Troi's left shoulder—on the sheet cake decorated like her uniform in the bizarre dream. Data then begins having accompanying daytime hallucinations. He sees a mouth on Troi's right shoulder and stabs the counselor, attempting to excise it from her.

While doctoring Troi, Crusher notices a strange rash around the wound. Subsequent tests reveal a creature feeding on the counselor's cellular peptides. Crusher then discovers the creatures all over the ship, feeding on the crew. The creatures went undetected at first because they exist "interphasically" just outside the sensory range. Since Data attacked the precise spot where the creature was feeding, Picard wonders if Data senses them on a subconscious level. That would account for his dreams and strange behavior. By analyzing the nightmares, Picard, La Forge, and Data discover a way to defeat the creatures. With La Forge's help, Data sends an interphasic pulse from his positronic network throughout the ship and destroys the parasites. Further investigation shows that the creatures boarded the ship inside a plasma conduit—a part of the new warp core.

Trivia Questions

1. Where did Riker and Worf discover Data attacking Troi?

2. Where did the *Enterprise* get its new warp core?

RUMINATIONS

I find it interesting that the creators chose to represent Troi with a flat *sheet cake.* Cake technology has advanced sufficiently in the twentieth century that sculpted cakes are possible in every conceivable size and shape, yet the creators choose a design that mimicked our beloved counselor in almost cubistic fashion. *(I suppose this was appropriate. It was, after all, supposed to be a really weird dream!)*

GREAT LINES

"I will feed him!"—Worf to Data, after the android attempts to give the Klingon a large list of cutesy requirements for his temporary care of Spot. Nominated by Michael S. Sharp of Tulsa, OK. (The whole scene really is wonderful. Spot steals the show.)

PLOT OVERSIGHTS

• Throughout the show, Data assists La Forge with the installation, testing, and repair of the new warp core. Yet when the warp core first encounters difficulties, La Forge tells Picard that it will take a couple of hours to fix. The next scene shows Data watching Spot sleep. Troi comes in. Data decides to have a dream, and he oversleeps for thirty-five minutes. All this consumes at least fifty minutes of the "couple of hours" La Forge claims it will take to fix the core. Why is Data in his quarters in the first place? The *Enterprise* urgently needs to get its warp drive fixed so it can ferry Picard to a very important dinner. Was there nothing he could do to assist La Forge after the problem occurred?

• Disconcerted by the imagery of the nightmare, Data calls up a holographic representation of Dr. Sigmund Freud. We join the scene as he tells Freud about feasting on Troi cake (with mint frosting). First, why isn't Data telling Troi about this dream? Is he *embarrassed* to disclose it? That hardly seems likely, given that embarrassment is an emotion. Second, Data claims that one of the three scruffy workmen—who make continual appearances in the nightmares—pointed to Troi's shoulder before Data cut it. Yet the actual dream sequence doesn't show this action. Evidently it occurred off-camera.

• Data must really be preoccupied with these nightmares. He almost walks out of Troi's office without the doohickey he brought from Main Engineering. This from a guy who never forgets anything!

• Just before Data attacks her in a turbolift, Troi acts like she senses a stalker. Of course, that would mean that she could sense Data—a feat the great Tam Elbrun was not even capable of in "Tin Man." On the other hand, she did sense emotion from Data in "The Schizoid Man" and "Descent, Part II." What's going on here?

• After discovering the creatures, Crusher calls Picard and Riker to sick bay. Using an interphasic scanner, she illuminates the creature on Troi's shoulder. She also finds one of them on Riker's right temple and another on Picard's throat. The doctor states that the "organisms appear to be attached to our epidermal layer with osmotic tendrils." If I recall correctly, the epidermal layer is also called "skin." Yet when Crusher illuminates the creature on her own person, it is attached to her lab coat, not her skin.

CONTINUITY AND PRODUCTION PROBLEMS

• The show begins with Data's nightmare. He walks down a hall, comes to an intersection, hears a noise, and turns left. Moments later, he comes upon three scruffy workmen. The next shot showing Data's face also shows that the intersection from which the android came has disappeared! Now, this *is* a dream, and weird things happen in dreams (like creators running out of hallway sets to use when filming a sequence!).

• During the second major attempt to get the warp core on line, the warp field collapses and the ship loses power. A subsequent exterior shot of the ship shows a blue glow near the region where the Battle Section connects to the Saucer Module. This glow normally comes from the warp engines, but they are clearly off-line. Pray tell: Whence doth this glow cometh? (It's just a *mystery*, I tell you!)

• Following his attack on Troi, Data meets with Picard in the observation lounge. Picard relieves him of duty and confines him to quarters. Data stands, and you can see gold fingerprints on the tabletop. Did a bit of his makeup rub off?

• Experiencing Data's nightmare on the holodeck, La Forge opens the android's chest to retrieve a telephone receiver. When Data's chest opens, there are about two inches of gold shirt showing, to the left of the cavity. But in the wide shot, the gold strip disappears, indicating that the telephone cavity has suddenly jumped sideways!

• Spot changes after living with Worf for a bit. The cat seems to possess both a higher level of energy and a much whiter stomach. (My guess is that Worf accidently killed Spot during bat'leth practice and somehow procured another cat from a crew member. Data doesn't seem to notice but…he's had a hard week.)

TRIVIA ANSWERS
1. On deck 17, section 3 Alpha.
2. Starbase 84.

DARK PAGE

Star Date: 47254.1

Having taught an exclusively telepathic race called the Cairn to communicate verbally in preparation for a meeting with Federation officials, Lwaxana Troi falls into a coma. Maques, a Cairn delegate, indicates that Lwaxana suffers from "bad thought." He says there is a place in her brain caused by some psychic trauma in the past. With Maques's help, Deanna Troi makes telepathic contact with her mother. Frightened by the intrusion, Lwaxana uses the images of Picard, a wolf, and even Deanna's father to try to push Deanna away. Finally, the image of Lwaxana rushes screaming toward Deanna, and she jolts from the connection.

Searching for the cause of her mother's withdrawal, Deanna reads through her mother's journals of the previous five years, talks with Lwaxana's closest friends on Betazed, and even consults with the Betazoid government, but finds nothing. Picard suggests they go back farther. They discover that Lwaxana's journals contain a seven-year gap. The section covers the time from Lwaxana's marriage until just after Deanna's birth. Deanna ventures back into her mother's mind and uncovers the truth. At one time, the counselor had an older sister named Kestra. In a tragic accident just after Deanna was born, Kestra drowned. All these years, Lwaxana has refused to forgive herself for the incident. With her daughter's help, she finally does.

Trivia Questions

1. How does the jewel plant of Tholar III operate?

2. What is the number on the picture pad that Lwaxana and Deanna view in the last scene of the episode?

GREAT LINES
Really?—A suddenly intrigued Picard to Lwaxana after she explains that, if they were members of the Cairn race, their current conversation would already be concluded.

GREAT MOMENTS
This episode gives Majel Barrett and Marina Sirtis a chance to play some deeply emotional scenes. They do it very well.

In addition, nitpicker Ed Watson of Downingtown, PA, found great amusement at the beginning of this episode when Worf finally resigns himself to the fact that Lwaxana will always call him "Mr. Woof."

PLOT OVERSIGHTS
• Supposedly there is no record of

Lwaxana's first daughter anywhere to be found. Don't Betazoids pride themselves on complete honesty (as stated in "Haven")? In the years that followed the accident why didn't any of the family friends tell Deanna Troi that she had a sister ? Why didn't they mention it when—in this episode—Troi inquired as to whether there was any recent tragedy which might have caused her mother's coma? ("A recent tragedy. Let's see. Well…there was the death of her firstborn daughter thirty-some-odd years ago. But that wasn't recent, so we won't mention it to Deanna, as she frantically searches for the cause of her mother's coma.") Additionally, wouldn't the Starfleet service's record of Deanna's father, Ian Andrew Troi, include family information? Wouldn't it have a record of a daughter who died?

• The review of "Reunion" in the NextGen Guide provides an extensive discussion of the correlation between star dates and earth years. According to the information in that episode under "Plot Oversights," 1000 star date units correspond to approximately one Earth year. Unfortunately, "Dark Page" harshly contradicts this hypothesis. Picard says that Lwaxana started her journals on star date 30620.1, just after her marriage. If 1000 units equal one Earth year, then Lwaxana got married only seventeen years ago! This show also indicates that Deanna was born seven years after the marriage. That would make her currently ten years old, having joined the crew of the Enterprise when she was only three! In addition, Picard also says that Lwaxana erased a seven-year stretch of her journals

thirty years ago. Again, if 1000 units equal one Earth year, Lwaxana erased the journals somewhere around star date 17254. Since Lwaxana started them on star date 30620.1, she erased them a full thirteen years before she wrote them. (Somehow, I don't think that's correct!)

• Troi claims that she spoke with Mr. Homn concerning her mother's coma. First, speaking with Mr. Homn would be a real trick. In all his time on the Enterprise, the only thing he's ever said is, "Thank you for the drinks" (in the episode "Haven"). Setting that fact aside, Deanna claims that Mr. Homn offered no help when she asked about any possible psychic trauma. Yet this same Mr. Homn saved a picture of Kestra when Lwaxana was destroying all evidence of the little girl's existence. Did Homn simply not consider the death of an eldest daughter traumatic enough to mention?

• I have no desire to cast aspersions on Lwaxana or deepen the horrific guilt she has borne over the death of her firstborn daughter but…why didn't she sense that her daughter had left the party and wandered toward the pond?

CHANGED PREMISES

• Where did Troi get her accent? Troi started her life on the Enterprise with an unusual and distinctive pattern of speech. At first I assumed that it came from her mother. Then Lwaxana visited the Enterprise in "Haven." In that episode and all subsequent episodes, Lwaxana sounds like an American. Since accents form early in life and usually change only under rigorous training, the next likely place of origin for Troi's accent became her father—a fact that Lwaxana seems to substantiate in "Haven." Yet in this episode, her father speaks like an American as well. Is Troi's accent some vestige of a rebellious phase in Deanna's life when she refused to speak like her parents? Did she do something at a young age to get herself committed to an old-style parochial school where the Betazoid mistresses demanded that all their students speak with the arcane Betazoid accent of ancient nobility? Or did Lwaxana always despise her husband's accent, and in her memories simply altered it to sound like her own?

• At the end of the episode, Lwaxana looks at a picture that Mr. Homn supposedly saved for her when it appeared that she was determined to destroy every memory of her dead child. Did Homn leave Lwaxana's employ and then return? In "Haven" we learn that Homn is Lwaxana's *new* servant—replacing a Mr. Xelo. Yet this episode states that Homn worked for Lwaxana some thirty years before.

EQUIPMENT ODDITIES

• In one scene, Lwaxana and Deanna board a turbolift. Deanna says, "Deck 8." The doors close. The doors open. Deanna gets off, the doors close, and the signage reads, "12 Turbolift." They should read, "08 Turbolift."

• Looking over Lwaxana's diary, Picard states that there is a seven-year gap. Yet when the camera cuts to the display screen, the deleted records still scroll onto the screen for some time. If Picard hadn't seen all the deleted records, how did he know that there was a seven-year gap?

CONTINUITY AND PRODUCTION PROBLEMS

• It appears that Romulan Proconsul Neral has snuck off and is using his limited telepathic abilities to pose as the head delegate Maques from the Cairn. (Is this some new and devious conspiracy from the archenemies of the Federation?)

• After Maques comes to sick bay in the middle of the night to look in on Lwaxana, Picard, Crusher, and Troi meet with the Cairn in the observation lounge. Toward the end of the meeting, Troi discusses a plan with Picard to use Maques as a telepathic bridge between Lwaxana and herself. Whenever we see the scene from Picard's perspective, Troi's fingers are extended with the tips together. Yet from Troi's perspective, her hands are clasped.

• As Troi rifles through her mother's things, Picard pays a visit. Troi puts down a picture of her father and withdraws her hands to the edge of her mother's suitcase before greeting the captain. The camera angle switches and Troi, again, withdraws her hand to the edge of the suitcase.

TRIVIA ANSWERS

1. It secretes a resin that collects in the blossom of the plant. When the bloom fades, the resin has hardened into a rare and beautiful gem.
2. No. 567.

★
ATTACHED

Star Date: 47304.2

The *Enterprise* flies to Kesprit III in response to an unusual request for associate membership in the Federation. A large portion of the planet is controlled by the "Kes," a democratic people. The "Prit"—isolationists with dispositions bordering on xenophobia—control the rest. The Kes alone have filed for membership. As Picard and Crusher beam down to meet with them, the Prit redirect the transporter beam and capture the two Starfleet officers. A Kes operative quickly frees Picard and Crusher and provides them with an escape map, but not before the Prit install neural transceivers in their cerebral cortexes. The Prit had planned to use the devices to interrogate them. As they flee to safety, the captain and his chief medical officer discover that the devices allow them to read each other's thoughts.

That night, in the flickering light of a campfire, Beverly learns that during her marriage to Jack Crusher, Picard was deeply in love with her. After Jack's death, he felt guilty and said nothing. When she joined the crew of the *Enter-*

Trivia Questions

1. What title does the viewscreen on the port side of the observation lounge carry during this episode?

2. What other episode featured the extinguishing of candlelight to signify the end of a possible romance?

prise several years later, Picard discovered that his feelings had subsided. The next day the two officers make it to the border between the Kes and the Prit and back to the ship in short order. That evening, Picard and Crusher discuss the experience and decide to remain friends.

PLOT OVERSIGHTS

• Picard and Crusher beam down to meet with the Kes officials. The last time Picard and Crusher transported down to a planet to meet with officials was during the episode "When the Bough Breaks." In that episode, Picard lied in order to allow Crusher to come along. This is definitely not a normal away team configuration. (But then, if they didn't go along, they couldn't have the heart-to-heart chat around the fire.)

• And speaking of odd configurations, why is Worf beaming Picard and Crusher to the surface?

• Also, why doesn't Worf wait to confirm transport? He hits a few buttons and then starts to wander off. Then the Kes call and say that the pair haven't arrived. In the *Classic* episode "The Mark of Gideon," Kirk grouses when he thinks Spock left his post at the transporter console before confirming transport. This implies some sort of protocol. Are the twenty-fourth-century transporters so reliable that no one bothers to hail the destination and say, "Didja get 'em?"?

• Early in their escape, Picard and Crusher come to a series of caves. Crusher states that there is a lava flow thirty meters below them. Obviously the caves are quite warm, because Picard takes off his coat and discards it. It makes no sense for Picard to do this. Along with providing the Prit evidence of their escape route, a coat can be an extremely useful tool in this type of situation. A coat can provide warmth and serve as a pillow. Ripped into strips, it can become bandages or a tourniquet. Yet strategically-gifted, analytically-blessed Picard just throws it away. Did he think that the Prit had placed a tracking device in the coat?

• While still in the caves, Picard and Crusher discover that the neural transceivers are transmitting their thoughts. At this Picard says, "Loren said that they would align themselves to our psi-wave patterns." Loren is the name of the security minister for the Prit. While it is true that Minister Loren has spoken with Picard, she never gave her name. How does Picard know it?

• After spotting a Prit guard above them on a ridge, Picard and Crusher decide to head for the Kes-Prit border. Picard states that it is only two kilometers away. Two kilometers is just over one mile. Even at a leisurely stroll of three miles per hour, they should reach the border in twenty minutes. Yet darkness falls, and they stop to build a fire.

First, wouldn't it be better to reach the border and sneak across at night? From the reflection on Picard's head (no offense intended, merely observation!), there apparently is a full moon, so they would have light to navigate their path. Second, is it wise to build a fire and allow the light to broadcast one's location when one is in enemy territory and being pursued? Then again, maybe they were cold and therefore really *needed* to build a fire. Sure would be nice to have…*a coat*! (And then, when Picard lies down, he has to rest his head directly on the ground. Too bad he doesn't have…*a coat* to wad up.) Third, when Crusher turns in for the night, she states that they have a lot of ground to cover. They only had two kilometers to cover in the first place, and they *still* have a lot of ground to cover?

• I must have missed something in the fireside chat between Picard and Crusher. I thought Picard said he didn't have *those* feelings for her anymore. Yet, at the end of the episode, he certainly acts like he does. And what about Neela Daren? Out of sight, out of mind?

• Of course, Picard isn't the only one who demonstrates confusing behavior at the conclusion of this episode. Crusher comes to the captain's quarters wearing a skirt that's slit up to her belly button. She teases him about his "interesting" dreams. She cajoles him into revealing that he still cares for her. And then…and *then*…when he responds to these provocations, she bolts! (I guess it is understandable. After all, if she has a relationship with Picard, it will be the end of her career. Just look at Neela Daren!)

EQUIPMENT ODDITIES

• During their escape from the Prit, Crusher carries a standard medical tricorder. Now that the Nitpicker's Guild Prime Directive allows the citing of other sources besides the television show, I should point out that the *Tech Manual* says a tricorder can function like a communicator, so Crusher should just have called the *Enterprise* for transport!

• To contact the Prit government, Data interfaces with one of their com-links and manages audio-only contact. During this process, Data states that the Prit have "no link designed for extraterrestrial communication." Yet moments after Riker speaks with a nervous secretary, the minister of security contacts the *Enterprise* with rock-solid video communications. I guess Data was wrong about that link business.

• Picard and Crusher experience a sense of nausea if they get too far apart. For some reason, the neural implants cause this. That would be a valuable feature if the nausea was also geared to kick in if prisoners walked out of their cells. Then again, maybe it is and the Kes turned that feature off.

• The first time the pair experience this nausea, they are several strides apart before it gets bad. The next time, Crusher takes just a few steps and the pair begins to collapse. Yet after the fabled fireside chat, Crusher gets up, walks around the fire, and lies down on the opposite side, and no one seems the worse for wear.

• Are the sensors on the *Enterprise* out of commission? Riker never mentions an intensive sweep of the surface for Picard and Crusher. Compare this to Data's sensor pass on the planet in "Bloodlines."

CONTINUITY AND PRODUCTION PROBLEMS

• It must be a thing with medical doctors. At the end of "Birthright, Part 1," Bashir walks down a hallway during an extended conversation with Data. After wishing Data pleasant dreams, Bashir strolls off and suddenly he's wearing white shoes. In this episode, on the second day of the escape from the Prit—before the Prit guy fires at them and the captain goes tumbling down the hill—Picard and Crusher emerge from behind a rock and begin making their way down a hill. If you use freeze-frame you'll see that—instead of regulation Starfleet boots—Crusher now wears dark gray athletic shoes with black laces and studs on the soles! (No wonder it's taking so long to get to the border: Crusher is stopping at the shoe stores along the way! Actually…this footwear probably gave Gates McFadden much better traction as she pursued Picard's stunt double tumbling down the hill.)

TRIVIA ANSWERS

1. Topographical Analysis 0771.
2. Data blew out a candle at the end of "In Theory" after Jenna D'Sora called off their relationship.

Star Dates: 47310.2—47314.5

As the show begins, the *Enterprise* enters the Hekaras Corridor to search for the *Flemming,* a Starfleet medical transport missing for several days. The Federation established the corridor as the only safe passage through this sector of space. The rest of the sector contains an unusually high concentration of tetrion particles, making warp drive dangerous. When the *Enterprise* discovers a debris field, a small object contained within suddenly emits a verteron pulse and robs the *Enterprise* of warp power and subspace communications.

A small craft approaches, and two Hekaran scientists beam aboard. Roval and his sister Sarova admit to planting the verteron probe and claim that the constant use of warp drive in the corridor has weakened the fabric of space. They believe this has endangered their planet. They knew that if they disabled enough ships, Starfleet would investigate. Data reviews their research but states only that their theories *might* be correct. At this, Sarova takes flight and overloads the engines of her craft. The ship explodes and in the

Trivia Questions

1. What was the *Flemming* transporting?

2. What will the *Enterprise* use to control the weather on Hekaras II?

process proves her point by creating the rift she predicted. The *Enterprise* still manages to recover the *Flemming* but shortly afterward learns that the Federation Council has reviewed the incident and will restrict all Starfleet vessels to warp five, except in cases of extreme emergency.

PLOT OVERSIGHTS

• Worf's marksmanship comes into question again. At one point, the *Enterprise* finds a disabled Ferengi ship in the corridor. It attacks and Picard tells Worf to target their weapons array only. The subsequent phaser blast from the *Enterprise* looks like it hits in the region of the Ferengi bridge, not the weapons array.

• Concerning La Forge's change of heart after seeing the creation of the subspace rift, Gerhard Thielman commented, "Chief Engineer La Forge should have maintained greater skepticism over extrapolating a highly nonlinear and universally applied conclusion with extensive ramifications based on a particular galactic zone with potentially unique characteristics." (*Yeah!* I *agree...*I think.)

• This Sarova is one interesting scientist. She is convinced that warp drive will create a subspace rift that will endanger her planet. So she goes out and blows up her ship, thereby creating the rift and...*endangering her planet*! As nitpicker David M. Blakeman pointed out, "That's like protesting the possible danger from a nuclear power plant by causing a nuclear meltdown yourself! What's next? Smokey Bear starting forest fires so we can see how bad they are?"

CHANGED PREMISES

• In this episode, Data continually refers to Spot as "she." Yet in "Phantasms," Data called Spot "he." Given the accuracy of our android friend, it's a safe bet that Spot has changed from a male to a female sometime during the recent episodes.

EQUIPMENT ODDITIES

• What initiates red alert? Just before the Ferengi vessel fires on the *Enterprise*, Riker says, "Shields up!" and the red alert klaxons sound. Just before the verteron pulse hits the *Enterprise*, Picard says, "Shields up, full reverse!" No red alert klaxons. Then, when Sarova blows up her ship, Riker yells, "Prepare for impact, shields up, full reverse!" and the red alert klaxons sound. Why didn't they sound when Picard said it?

• The dialogue seems to indicate that the crew will use a warp pulse to drop-kick the *Enterprise* through the rift at warp speed without any additional help from the warp drive. In the process, the crew of the *Enterprise* plans to rescue the crew of the *Flemming* by beaming them aboard. Wait

a minute: The *Enterprise* will be traveling at warp and the *Flemming* will be stationary, right? Since when did transporters get the capability to transport stationary objects while the ship is at warp? Think about it. According to "A Matter of Honor"—and the *Tech Manual*—safe transport range is 40,000 kilometers. Even at warp 1, the ship travels 40,000 kilometers in about 0.13 second—too little time to effect a transport. But the *Enterprise* must be moving *much* faster than warp 1. Picard and crew hope that they can coast through the rift in 2 minutes—the amount of time it will take for the ship to drop out of warp. The rift is 0.1 light-year across. (A bit of simple math shows that the *Enterprise* would have to travel much, much faster than its maximum speed to cover 0.1 light-year in 2 minutes. Yet...just for the sake of argument, let's say that they aren't flying directly through the rift. Let's say that they are just shooting through a corner of it.) At a nice comfortable speed of say...warp 9, the *Enterprise* covers 40,000 kilometers in about .000088 second. That's not even enough time for the first diagnostic transporter routine to kick in!

CONTINUITY AND PRODUCTION PROBLEMS

• Speaking of Hekaran ships, they seem to favor Talarian design. The footage of the Hekaran ship comes from "Suddenly Human."

TRIVIA ANSWERS

1. Biomemetic gel.
2. Thermal stabilizers.

INHERITANCE

Star Date: 47410.2

The *Enterprise* arrives at Atrea IV to assist with a geological emergency. The planet's core is cooling and is in danger of solidifying. Data and La Forge suggest reliquefying the core using plasma infusion, and the scientists from Atrea readily agree. Before the process begins, a geologist named Dr. Juliana Tainer reveals that she is the former wife of Dr. Noonian Soong and was present at Data's creation. Spending time with his "mother," Data makes some unusual observations. Dr. Tainer blinks at the same intervals as Data, and during a string duet she precisely matches every pitch and intonation from the pair's practice session.

Soon, an accident uncovers the truth. Dr. Tainer is an android. A holographic module inside her brain supplies the missing information. Dr. Noonian Soong explains that the real Tainer was injured in their escape from Omicron Theta. Soong built an exact duplicate of her and transferred her mind to the new android's brain before she died. The android awoke two days later, believing she was human and married to Soong. He never told her the truth and asks Data to do the same. The aging routines Soong created will continue to alter her appearance and—after a long life—will cause her to cease to function. The *Enterprise* successfully reliquefies the core, and Data bids his mother good-bye.

Trivia Questions

1. How long did Noonian and Juliana Soong spend on Mervala IV?

2. What is the designation of the transporter trace ID for Dr. Tainer?

PLOT OVERSIGHTS

• In the big dramatic moment of the episode, we learn that Juliana is an android. At least two members of the crew should have known this as soon as she boarded the ship. Surely, Troi could sense the difference in Juliana and—according to "Heart of Glory"—androids put off a glow that La Forge's VISOR can detect.

• While watching the holographic image of Soong fill Data in on the details of the android Juliana, I kept thinking, "He's going to say it. He's going to say it." When he did, I burst out laughing. (Of course, my wife gave me one of those "Now what did you find wrong with this episode?" looks but…I'm used to that.) In this episode, Soong explains that after converting his wife to an android, he made a terrible mistake. He never told her how much he loved her. He recounts that she left him because of this and that the human Juliana would have done the same. In other words, he relates not only that Juliana left, but also his reactions to her leaving. Bear in mind that at the beginning of the holographic playback Soong says, "I programmed this hologram to answer any question..." Also, in reference to Data, he says, "I even created a response program to answer your questions." All fine and well, except the module containing this information was *inside* Juliana's brain. For the module to contain information on her leaving and Soong's reactions to that leaving, it must have been created *after* Juliana left. But that means that he had to hunt her down, turn her off, stick in the chip, and scurry off! (As my wife said—after I explained the reason for my mirth—"What a thoughtful father.")

• Data struggles with the decision to keep the truth from his mother. Of the many reasons pro and con given by Picard, Crusher, and Troi, they overlook the most obvious and pertinent. If Data does not tell his mother that she is an android and then help reprogram her, she will cease to function after a normal human life span. As an android she could live for hundreds of years. In that time she probably could perfect the stable positronic network, thereby giving herself an endless supply of new android bodies.

• On the other hand—continuing on with this decision to tell or not to tell—is there really an option? Soong states that he programmed her to shut down "in the event the truth was discovered." So how could Data tell her the

truth? Wouldn't the scene go something like this? "Mom, I have something to tell you. You are an andro...(shakes her) Mom, wake up! Okay, now listen. You are an and...MOM! (slap, slap, slap) Wake up! You are an androi...Mother?" (Yes, I know Data probably could reprogram her not to shut down. I just thought it was a funny scene.)

• So let's put the Soong chronology together with what we know from this and other episodes. Soong creates Lore. Lore no good. Soong dismantles Lore. Soong creates Data. Data good. Soong deactivates Data. Programs in colonists' memories. Crystal entity attacks Omicron Theta. Juliana injured. Data left behind. Soong and Juliana go to backwater planet. Juliana in coma. Soong—whose last experience with android construction resulted in a gold-toned, yellow-eyed humanoid who could never pass for human—constructs a replica of Juliana so *flawlessly* that it can still fool the sophisticated equipment of the *Enterprise* many years later. And he accomplishes this feat with his wife seriously injured and in a race against the approaching moment of her death. Where did he get the supplies? How did he make such a large leap in sophistication so quickly after building Data?

• At the very end of the episode, Juliana tells Data that the people of Atrea IV have a saying. They believe that a child born to parents who love each other will have nothing but goodness in his heart, and that explains why Data turned out so well. I really hate to bring this up, but didn't these *same* two people create *Lore*?

CHANGED PREMISES

• After Data treats her to a selection on the violin, Juliana comments that his playing is "beautiful." Data replies that others have noted his playing is technically flawless but never beautiful. Data needs to get his memory checked. Picard in "The Ensigns of Command" noted that Data's playing was "quite beautiful."

• During the episode, Data notices that Dr. Tainer blinks according to the same mathematical formula as himself. One question: If Data's blinking is controlled by a mathematical formula, wouldn't Lal's blinking be controlled that way as well (see "The Offspring")? And if Lal's blinking was controlled by a mathematical formula, why did Data have to teach her to blink?

• Discovering that Juliana is an android, Crusher and La Forge give her a thorough examination in sick bay. At one point La Forge comments that Juliana has an aging program "just like Data's." Excuse me? Exactly *what* aging program does Data have? Did he write one for himself in the recent past? In "Data's Day" Data comments that growing old is something he can never do. In "Silicon Avatar" he says there's no limit on his existence. In "Time's Arrow" he says he accepted that he would outlive his friends and make new friends. (I realize that Brent Spiner is aging, and this line attempts to explain why Data looks several years older than he did at the beginning of the series. But La Forge tosses the line out like Data has always had an aging program. He hasn't. The dialogue of other episodes states this explicitly. So why not add a few words to the dialogue and make it sound like a recent addition?)

EQUIPMENT ODDITIES

• After beaming down to the magma pocket on Atrea IV with Juliana, Data walks over, picks up a fallen pattern enhancer, and sets it back upright. Don't these things need to function correctly to ensure safe transport? Are they able to function even though one is lying flat on the ground?

• The accident that reveals Dr. Tainer's android construction occurs deep under the surface of Atrea IV. Data and Dr. Tainer leap from a cliff, after the subterranean path back to their beam-out point crumbles away. The resulting fall tears Dr. Tainer's arm off, and she shuts down to avoid seeing what clearly is an android arm. The dialogue states that they must return to the beam-out point because they must use the pattern enhancers there for successful transport. But there's an open shaft leading all the way to the surface right above the machinery. Why can't the *Enterprise* beam them up the shaft? They did that in "Legacy."

CONTINUITY AND PRODUCTION PROBLEMS

• The transporter must have a "practicality circuit" built into it. When Dr. Tainer beams down with Data to the magma pockets, she begins the trip with two-inch block heels. She ends it in flats!

TRIVIA ANSWERS

1. Four days.
2. Tainer, Dr. Juliana F-67.

PARALLELS

Star Date: 47391.2

As the episode begins, Worf travels back to the *Enterprise* via shuttle from a bat'leth tournament on Forkas III. Returning to the ship, Worf finds himself in a series of strange discontinuities. His birthday cake changes from chocolate to yellow. He looks up in Engineering to find that La Forge and Data have changed places. Even more disconcerting, Worf suddenly finds himself standing at Tactical, but he doesn't recognize the configuration of the panel. He fails to raise the shields during a Cardassian attack, and the *Enterprise* is severely damaged —La Forge fatally injured. In his quarters, Worf makes an even more astonishing discovery: He's now married to Troi. He confides his confusion to her over these events. Together they enlist the crew's help.

Captain Riker and crew soon uncover the reason for the sudden changes. Evidently Worf's shuttle passed through a quantum fissure in the time/space continuum. The craft's warp engines opened a keyhole into every possible universe, and Worf has

been bouncing through them. Then the fissure widens and *Enterprises* from all the other parallel universes begin appearing. Data theorizes that they can close the fissure and return everyone to their universes by sending Worf back through the fissure in his original shuttle. Our Captain Picard gladly dispatches it, Worf travels back through and everything returns to normal.

Trivia Questions

1. In one of the realities, output from the Argus Array is rerouted to what sector?

2. What does Worf initiate to seal the fissure?

RUMINATIONS

First (as noted by many other nitpickers as well, including Daryle C. Taylor of Chesterfield, MO), I think the creators did themselves a tremendous favor with this episode. Now they can explain all the discontinuities among episodes of Star Trek: The Next Generation. They aren't really mistakes— just reality shifts!

Second, I must say that this episode added to my belief in the inherent harmony of the universe. It's a great comfort to know that, no matter what the quantum state of reality, Troi still has that off-the-shoulder blue dress!

Finally, several nitpickers have written to question why Worf doesn't have a surprise birthday party at the end of the episode when everything has sup-

posedly returned to normal, since he has one at the beginning. It's my humble opinion that Worf's trip through the quantum fissure actually kicked him over to a neighboring reality just as the show began. At the end of the episode, Worf returns to our reality—one in which he has no surprise birthday party.

Oh…one last thing. Several nitpickers noticed that Data's eyes suddenly change to blue when Worf discusses the date of his marriage to Troi with the android in Main Engineering. Note that the creators were very careful to ensure that this change only held until Worf's next jump to another reality. That would make it a nice touch, not a nit.

GREAT LINES

"I know Klingons like to be alone on their birthdays. You probably want to meditate or hit yourself with a pain stick or something."—Troi to Worf, explaining why she talked Riker out of giving Worf a surprise party.

PLOT OVERSIGHTS

• Dizzy from surfing the quantum realities, Worf goes to sick bay, where Crusher claims he came in complaining of the effects of a concussion received during the bat'leth tournament. Worf states he doesn't have a concussion and soon is startled to find that instead of winning the tournament, he now holds the ninth-place trophy. I realize the poor guy is a bit scrambled from these events, but wouldn't it be fairly simple for Crusher to run another scan and see if Worf still has a concussion?

• How is it that only Worf jumps around in quantum realities? Why not his clothes as well, or for that matter, his trophy, too?

• Then there's La Forge's death. In one reality, La Forge dies because Worf didn't recognize the configuration of the Tactical console and couldn't raise the shields. In a scene that follows, Worf, Troi, Data, and Dr. Ogawa gather around La Forge's scantily clad body in sick bay to discuss the cause of Worf's memory lapses. When Data turns on La Forge's VISOR, Worf jumps to a reality where he serves as first officer but La Forge is *still* dead. Why? Wouldn't someone else be running the Tactical station? (On the other hand, La Forge's death could be the result of a completely different attack from the now aggressive Bajorans.) And does anyone else find an astonishing lack of grief at good old Geordi's death in this scene? The poor guy's body is stretched out in the middle of the room—even more scantily clad than in the previous reality, I might add—and everyone seems completely absorbed with Worf's dilemma.

• During the conclusion of the episode, *Enterprises* start popping up everywhere. Luckily, not one materializes on top of another.

CHANGED PREMISES

• Troi and Worf…married. Okaaay! What happened to the idea that human females were too *fragile* (even those only half-human, as in Troi's case), and that Worf would need a Klingon woman for "companionship" ("Yesterday's Enterprise")? And what happened to the practice of driving the fingernails of the female into the palm of her hand until blood starts dripping off her wrist ("The Emissary")? Is Troi just a lot tougher than we've been led to believe? Or has Worf finally given up on the idea of finding a new "rock 'em, sock 'em" playmate after his romp with K'Ehleyr? (They even have children in one reality. I bet that took some DNA encouragement, given K'Ehleyr's comments on the trouble her parents—Klingon and human—had with her conception. By the way, nitpicker Geoffrey Cook had an interesting thought concerning these children: With the talents of both parents, they could beat you up and feel your pain while doing it.)

EQUIPMENT ODDITIES

• At one point, Picard, Data, La Forge, and Worf examine imaging logs from the Argus Array. A close-up of the screen shows four pictures. La Forge identifies one of them as Starbase 47, but it looks more like the subspace relay station from "Aquiel."

• Man, this Argus Array is impressive! It sits three light-years from the edge of Cardassian space, yet La Forge identifies one of the pictures it takes as Utopia Planitia…on *Mars*! (No wonder the Cardassians are nervous about this array.)

• One of the quantum realities features an interesting badge design. It originally appeared as part of Riker's future fantasy in "Future Imperfect."

• Does anyone else think that the explosion of the Borg-infested-reality *Enterprise* at the end of the episode causes too little damage to the adjacent ships?

CONTINUITY AND PRODUCTION PROBLEMS

• At Worf's birthday party, Data hands the Klingon a gift-wrapped painting. Worf receives the gift with the bow facing himself. The shot changes, and the bow dances for a brief moment in the lower left-hand corner of the screen, on Data's side of the package. Then the shot changes back to Worf's perspective, and the bow is back on his side of the gift. Either that, or Data put two bows on the package.

• After Worf unwraps the painting, Troi takes it from his hands and turns it 180 degrees. She gives the impression that Worf held it upside down and that he should know better. Oddly enough, when Troi hangs it on the wall, she does so with the same orientation that Worf used when holding it!

• Just after the very cute scene where Troi knows she's married to Worf but the big guy doesn't realize it, Worf stands facing Troi with the hair on the right side of his head lying in front of his shoulder. As soon as Troi makes the comment "Even for your wife," the shot changes and the hair leaps backward to rest behind his shoulder. (An understandable reaction given that he has just learned that he is married to Troi.)

TRIVIA ANSWERS
1. Sector 19658.
2. An inverse warp field.

THE PEGASUS

Star Date: 47457.1

Admiral Pressman joins the *Enterprise* for a secret mission to recover the USS *Pegasus*—a ship captained by Pressman on which Ensign Riker served as helmsman. The ship disappeared twelve years ago under unusual circumstances. Aware of these facts, Picard confronts Riker and asks for the truth. Riker recommends that he take the matter up with Pressman and informs Picard that he is under orders to remain silent.

Arriving at the Devolin system, the crew finds a Romulan vessel also looking for the *Pegasus*. The *Enterprise* soon locates the missing ship buried deep within a crevice in an asteroid. Beaming over, Pressman and Riker find the true object of the search, an experimental cloaking device that also phases matter. Knowing that such a device violated the terms of the Treaty of Algeron, Pressman's crew mutinied twelve years ago when their captain ran field tests with it. While Pressman and Riker argue about how to proceed, the Romulan warbird returns and seals the *Enterprise* inside the asteroid. Beaming back to the ship,

Riker finally tells Picard the truth. The crew hooks up the cloak, flies out of the asteroid, and decloaks in front of the warbird, knowing that the Romulan commander will inform his superiors that the Federation has violated its agreement with the Romulan Empire not to develop cloaking technology. Picard then places Pressman under arrest.

Trivia Questions

1. What is Admiral Blackman's first name?

2. Who won the art contest for Captain Picard Day?

GREAT LINES

"I don't know. I think the resemblance is rather striking. Wouldn't you agree, Number One?"—Riker doing his impersonation of Picard while holding an entry for "Captain Picard Day."

PLOT OVERSIGHTS

• In the initial briefing in the observation lounge, Pressman tells Picard that the Romulans have found a piece of debris from the *Pegasus*. Yet later in the show we learn that the *Pegasus* never exploded—that it is intact and buried inside an asteroid. So where did the Romulans get their piece of debris? Was Pressman just making that part up to procure a starship for the search?

• Just as the *Enterprise* arrives at the Devolin system, a Romulan warbird decloaks. After some pleasant banter between the warbird's commander and Picard, it moves off. Worf reports that the Romulans are "resuming" their tachyon scans of the system. Resuming? How does Worf know what they were doing before the *Enterprise* arrived? The warbird was cloaked!

• At one point Pressman and Riker have a little chat in Ten-Forward. Note two items about this exchange. First, Riker tells Pressman that he has had his beard for four years. I believe Riker first appeared with the beard in "The Child," the first episode of the second season. This episode occurs about halfway through the seventh season. According to the *Star Trek Chronology,* each season is a year, so Riker has had his beard at least five and one-half years. Second, the conversation eventually turns to the "experiment"— the cloaking device still aboard the *Pegasus.* Pressman tells Riker that he cannot discuss the matter with any of his crewmates. Obviously this is a top-secret affair. Why then are they discussing it in Ten-Forward? Why not in Pressman's quarters?

• Are "Starfleet Security" and "Starfleet Intelligence" the same thing? In Ten-Forward, Pressman tells Riker that he has the personal support of the "chief of Starfleet Security." Yet later, Admiral Blackman tells Picard that the "chief of Starfleet Intelligence" herself is watching the mission.

• As the *Enterprise* creeps into the asteroid's crevice, he tells Pressman that if the passage narrows to 500 meters he will abort the mission. According to the *Tech Manual,* the saucer module is 559.74 meters in diameter. That's 59.74 meters wider than the passage that Picard specifies.

• Once sealed inside the asteroid, Picard seems very concerned about finding a quick exit. Is this a bit of claustrophobia on our good captain's part? Won't Starfleet send someone to look for them and eventually discover their predicament? The ship has plenty of resources and is self-sufficient for long periods of time. Why risk the safety of the crew on an experimental device that had already caused the destruction of one Starfleet vessel? (Of course, it they hadn't, the rest of the seventh season would sure be boring. "Captain's log, star date 47823.5: Still waiting for Starfleet to send a rescue ship. Captain's log, star date 47911.4: Still waiting for Starfleet to send a rescue ship....")

• Well, now we know why Federation ships don't have a cloaking device! All this time, I thought the problem was Federation scientists. In truth, the problem was Federation diplomats! They actually signed an agreement that barred the Federation from developing cloaking technology. What in the world were they thinking!?

• So when Picard uses the phasing cloak to get out of the asteroid, is that a violation of the treaty as well?

• Anthony J. Girese actually wrote me a lovely treatise on the issue of Picard's reactions in this episode and subsequent arrest of Admiral Pressman. Unfortunately, space does not permit its inclusion here. Anthony made a great point concerning the act of decloaking in front of the Romulan warbird after the *Enterprise* exits the asteroid. In essence, Picard converted an internal Federation crisis into a foreign policy crisis and handed the Romulans a diplomatic coup. If I were Starfleet or even the Federation Council, *I would not be happy!*

• After his arrest, Pressman claims to have lots of friends at Starfleet Command. Picard replies that he is going to need them. What does this say about Starfleet Command? Is this not an organization filled with goodness? Have we not been shown how glorious and wonderful humans have finally become in the twenty-fourth century? Are we to believe that power-crazed maniacs still roam the halls of this paragon of virtue? In a word…yes. (And it sure makes for a lot more interesting stories!)

• I wonder if Thomas Riker will have to stand trial for his actions on the *Pegasus* twelve years ago, just as William Riker must. After all, at the time they were the same person!

CHANGED PREMISES

• Are there two Treaties of Algeron? Everyone in this episode refers to a sixty-year time period when the Federation could not develop cloaking technology. Then they also talk about the Treaty of Algeron. It sounds like the Treaty of Algeron was signed by the Federation and the Romulan Empire sixty years ago. But according to *The Star Trek Encyclopedia,* the Treaty of Algeron was signed between Earth—not the Federation—and the Romulan Star Empire in about 2160, more than two hundred years before the time frame of *NextGen* and one year before the founding of the Federation. It is possible that Federation and Romu-

lan negotiators developed an additional treaty sixty years ago, but wouldn't it be less confusing to call that treaty something like "Algeron II"? (If you want to trace the Treaty of Algeron simply through references in the television shows instead of using the *Encyclopedia,* it goes like this: In the *Classic* episode "Balance of Terror," Spock states that more than a hundred years ago a treaty created the Romulan Neutral Zone. In the *NextGen* episode "The Defector," Picard states that the Romulan Neutral Zone was established by the Treaty of Algeron. Therefore the Treaty of Algeron established the Romulan Neutral Zone more than a hundred years before the events in "Balance of Terror.")

EQUIPMENT ODDITIES

• When La Forge first locates the *Pegasus,* Riker walks up the starboard ramp on the bridge as the camera follows. Yet as the camera passes by Worf's Tactical station, you can see that it is completely blank! They search for a mysterious starship with a Romulan warbird nearby and Worf has powered down the Tactical station?

• I wonder if the *Enterprise* could have covered more of the search area if Picard had separated the saucer module. And what about separating the saucer and just taking the battle section down into the asteroid instead of the entire ship?

• Evidently ionizing radiation dies off fairly quickly or the *Enterprise* sensors can cut through it. To keep the Romulans from discovering the *Pegasus,* Data blankets the asteroid with a pulse of radiation, effectively knocking out the warbird's ability to detect the ship. The *Enterprise* then wanders off, pretending to continue the search. When it returns the next day, Data states that he has been taking readings on the *Pegasus* for the past several hours.

• Why is Pressman so concerned about recovering the prototype of the phasing cloak? Shouldn't there be detailed schematics lying around somewhere? Or did the Federation steal the device from another race, like Kirk stole the cloaking device from the Romulans in the *Classic* episode "The *Enterprise* Incident"?

• Discussing the final moments of the *Pegasus* with Picard, Riker states that there was an explosion in Engineering. The damaged area must be buried in the rock face. When he and Pressman beam over to Main Engineering near the end of the episode, there are a few dead bodies lying around, but the rest of the area looks "shipshape in Bristol fashion."

• And speaking of Main Engineering on the *Pegasus,* when the cloak failed, part of a plasma conduit rematerialized inside solid rock. Wouldn't this cause problems, *including* a secondary explosion?

• These Romulan warbirds must have some pretty impressive transporters. When the *Enterprise* first locates the *Pegasus,* Riker says he wouldn't want to try to transport through "that much" solid rock. (We learn later that it's at least 3 kilometers thick.) Yet, after sealing the *Enterprise* in, the Romulan commander acts like it would be no problem to beam the crew of the *Enterprise* up to the warbird.

• During the conclusion of the episode, Picard walks into the brig and releases Riker from his cell. Interestingly, the force field drops *before* Picard finishes keying in the combination.

CONTINUITY AND PRODUCTION PROBLEMS

• Early in the episode, Pressman visits Picard in his quarters, and the two talk about Riker. Picard pours drinks for them and begins reminiscing about his choice of Riker as first officer. He leans back on his couch as he remembers seeing a report about an incident on Altair III. The shot changes from a side view to a front view. In the process, Picard's left hand jumps from the cup portion of the wineglass to the base.

• After La Forge takes some position readings from an asteroid, Riker calls Picard and Pressman to the bridge. The trio stand around a science station on the bridge as La Forge does further scans. A graphic shows the asteroid rolling towards the viewscreen as large brackets form around the celestial object. Horizontal bars proceed away from the brackets to the edge of the viewscreen area. Apparently the visual effects crew didn't get the tip of the bar on the right side masked off correctly. If you'll watch closely, you'll see the mask slip down and a sliver of the upper portion of the bar extend beyond the right margin of the display area.

TRIVIA ANSWERS
1. Margaret.
2. Seven-year-old Paul Menegay.

HOMEWARD

Star Date: 47423.9

In response to a distress call from Dr. Nicholai Rozhenko—Worf's human stepbrother—the *Enterprise* flies to the dying world of Boral II. Its atmosphere is dispersing, and all life there will die in thirty hours. Rozhenko is stationed on the planet as a Federation cultural observer in an observation post. Unable to locate his stepbrother when the *Enterprise* arrives, Worf beams down and discovers that his brother has broken the Prime Directive. Unwilling to watch a village of Boralans die of the storms caused by the dispersion, Rozhenko set up a force field over a series of caves, altered himself to look like a Boralan, and led them inside.

When Picard refuses to set up an atmospheric shield to protect the villagers on a long-term basis, Rozhenko instructs the holodeck to create an exact copy of the caves and then beams the Boralans aboard as the planet's atmosphere completely dissipates. With no other option, Picard uses the resources of the *Enterprise* to locate a suitable world while Worf and Rozhenko lead the Boralans on a journey through the holodeck to a place that looks identical to the new planet. Then the *Enterprise* beams the villagers down to their new home. Having mated with a Boralan woman, Rozhenko stays behind to help them begin a new life.

Trivia Questions

1. To what starbase does Riker set course after Boral II dies?

2. What planet do Crusher and Data reject as a resettlement site for the Boralans?

PLOT OVERSIGHTS

• After undergoing surgical alteration to look like a Boralan, Worf beams to the surface in search of his stepbrother. Soon they return to the *Enterprise* to discuss the plight of the villagers. In the observation lounge meeting that follows, both Worf and Rozhenko have returned to their normal appearance. Yet when leaving the villagers in the cave, Rozhenko indicates that he and Worf will soon return. Obviously Rozhenko plans to come back. Only at the conclusion of the meeting does Rozhenko learn that Picard will not allow him to beam back to the surface. So...why did he change back to his human appearance *before* the meeting in the observation lounge began? If he thought he would be heading right back, why not stay in the Boralan getup?

• In the aforementioned observation

lounge meeting, Crusher attempts to argue for saving the Boralans by saying that if the crew of the *Enterprise* lets the villagers die they would be interfering with their culture. What? Did I miss some subtle point of logic here? By what euphemistic stretch can you equate inactivity—passive in tone and nature—with interference— very much active in tone and nature?

• Troi has counseling appointments at the most inopportune times. When Boral II dies, she's off the bridge. Of course, that's very convenient because if she was on the bridge she might sense that Rozhenko's inner feelings didn't match his outward look of grief.

• At one point, Worf meets the young man who keeps the chronicle for the village—a set of scrolls that contain annotated illustrations showing the group's history. The chronicler states that they had seventeen scrolls originally, but he could grab only six when they left the village for the caves. Describing these events to Worf, the chronicler discovers that he has only five of the scrolls and proposes to go back and look for the sixth. Amazingly enough, Worf lets him go. Of course, the young man finds the entrance to the holodeck and wanders out into the hall—creating a subplot. Knowing that the holodeck was malfunctioning, wouldn't it have been better for Worf to look for the scroll? Or, at the very least, accompany the chronicler in his search?

• Rozhenko seems to forget he's on the holodeck for a moment as the Boralans ascend a hillside. He tells Worf it will be dark in a few hours.

Excuse me, sir. You are on the holodeck. You can make it dark any time you jolly well please! (Yes, the Boralans might notice if the night came a bit sooner or later than normal, but they have swallowed everything else about this experience.)

• And as long as we are on the subject of the hillside ascent, Worf and Rozhenko have a somewhat boisterous discussion about the departure of the chronicler. They discuss that Crusher cannot zap his memory, that he might be coming back, etc., etc. They do this all within earshot of the villagers passing by, yet none of the Boralans picks up enough details from this discussion to raise some difficult questions for the pair. Does anyone else find this odd?

• In due time we learn that Rozhenko has conceived a child with a Boralan female. But how's he going to explain the child's ridgeless nose if it happens to favor humans instead of Boralans?

• It shouldn't come as any great surprise. I did discuss Starfleet's policy of isolation therapy for anyone who has sustained a loss in the *NextGen Guide*. Seems like every time someone goes through a traumatic experience, the next shot shows that person in a room alone. The pattern holds with the Boralan chronicler. When Picard finds out the young man's decision, we see the poor guy sitting in the middle of an empty room with a guard posted at the door. Was Troi *too* busy to fit the guy into her schedule? Even more incredible, after the chronicler commits suicide, Picard moans that he would have liked the chance to have known him better. Well, you had several days,

Picard. From what we saw, you talked with him once in sick bay and then let him pine away in his room until you marched in to ask him what he had decided to do.

• I wonder if the villagers have a sufficiently large gene pool to create a genetically healthy society. (Remember "Up the Long Ladder"?)

• I almost fell out of my seat when I caught this next nit in my initial viewing of this episode. The chronicler stresses the importance of the written historical record of the village to Worf. Specifically he says, "The chronicle is the life of our village. Without that past, our future means nothing." So what happens at the conclusion of the episode? Just before Worf leaves he asks his stepbrother if he can have a scroll. This in itself is the height of arrogance, but even more amazing, his stepbrother actually hands him one! Rozhenko has supposedly served as a cultural observer of the Boralans. He must know how much they value their history. They started out with seventeen scrolls. They could salvage only six before the destruction of their village. The chronicler died with one outside the holodeck. They have only *five* left, and Rozhenko gives one to Worf! This is *unbelievable*! I realize that Rozhenko says that the village must start a new chronicle—evidently since they have begun a new village—but are we really to believe that the Boralans care *nothing* for their present scrolls?

EQUIPMENT ODDITIES

• The *Enterprise* received a holodeck upgrade when we weren't looking.

Suddenly, with this episode, there's a holodeck 5 on deck 10! (Of course, if the holodeck that Rozhenko used wasn't on deck 10, it would be exceedingly difficult for the Boralan chronicler to wander out of the faux caves and into the bar to be greeted by Counselor Troi. Wink, wink.) Also, the holodecks *finally* have some privacy control—as demonstrated when Worf attempts to enter Rozhenko's simulation of the Boralan caves.

• The turbolift behaves very oddly in this episode. After discovering what his stepbrother has done, Worf escorts him off the holodeck and onto a turbolift heading for the main bridge. Remember that Rozhenko's holodeck is on deck 10. The pair boards the turbolift and it starts going down! The main bridge happens to be in the other direction. But here's another little tidbit concerning this scene. Not only does the holodeck go down, it also goes down for at least thirty-four decks! Let's see…they start on deck 10 and go down for thirty-four decks. That would put them on deck 44. Not a good place to be, considering that the *Enterprise* has only *forty-two* decks!

• Those doors on the *Enterprise* somehow know exactly when not to close. The Boralan chronicler spots the edge of the holodeck arch. He touches it, and the full arch appears. He walks into the arch. The doors open. He jumps back. The doors *stay* open! If he backed out of the sensor field for the doors, shouldn't they close? And another thing about these doors: What happened to the security lockout that Rozhenko had in place earlier in the episode?

• I really have only two things to say about the Boralans: They have really cool, futuristic—and some might even say anachronistic—looking flashlights and very, *very* nice boots. In fact, if I didn't know better, I'd say those boots were *manufactured* out of some sort of *rubber*. You can get a good look at them when Worf helps the old man up the hillside.

• When sending Rozhenko and Worf back into the holodeck to take the Boralans on their journey, Picard orders them to keep an open communications line so La Forge can monitor their progress. (It *still* would be really nice to have visual communications in a situation like this, but that's another discussion.) Yet, even with the open communications line, Worf feels the need to tap his hidden communicator not once but twice.

CONTINUITY AND PRODUCTION PROBLEMS

• After arriving at Boral II, Worf attempts to contact his brother. After a plasmonic energy burst buffets the ship, Picard turns and asks Worf if he has received any response. Riker walks up behind the captain and stops directly beside Picard. Then the shot changes to a front view of the pair, and Riker is suddenly behind the captain.

• On his first excursion to the planet, Worf wears a standard-looking mustache. Back on the ship, he attends an observation lounge meeting with his normal Fu Manchu handlebars. Did Crusher just glue some mustache tips on him until his facial hair had a chance to grow out again?

• The stars in the observation lounge windows amaze and confound. Apart from one shot featuring a close-up of Worf, the stars stay still. But right in the middle of the meeting—and only while the camera grabs a close-up of Worf—they move!

• During a hillside ascent on the holodeck, Rozhenko starts out leading the way. Then he urges his wife to keep going while he turns back to speak with Worf. Two men carrying a stretcher pass by the camera before it cuts to Worf helping an old man up the hill. Then Rozhenko arrives. The two walk for a bit, then stop to have an argument. All the while, Boralans walk around them. Finally it appears that Worf and Rozhenko have fallen behind. The pair turn and continue their discussion as they catch up to the pack. *One sentence later,* Worf and Rozhenko not only catch up to the pack, they also lead it again! Almost instantly they are in front of the two guys with the stretcher!

TRIVIA ANSWERS
1. Starbase 87.
2. Drego IV.

SUB ROSA

Star Date: 47488.2 (Perhaps. See below.)

During the graveside ceremony for her recently deceased grandmother, Felisa Howard, on Caldos Colony, Crusher spots a young man who seems oddly drawn to the coffin. She walks back to her grandmother's house and soon is joined by Ned Quint, the groundskeeper. Quint is adamant about one item among Howard's possessions. He blows out a candle that Howard women have always kept lit and demands that Crusher rid herself of its holder. Stunned, Crusher orders Quint out of the house.

Later, Crusher finds that her one hundred-year-old grandmother was having an ongoing affair with a man named Ronin. That night, while sleeping in her quarters on the *Enterprise,* Crusher feels someone caressing her shoulder but startles awake to find the room empty. The next visitation comes at her grandmother's home. Amid her weak protests, Ronin—for the moment only a disembodied voice—touches her with pleasure, and in a very short time convinces her to relight the candle. Ronin, an anaphasic energy being, lives in

the plasma flame of the candle. For centuries he has feasted on the Howard women because of their receptivity to his energy matrix, loving them and poisoning them at the same time by his union with them. With the crew's help, Crusher discovers what's happening and stops Ronin from doing the same to her.

Trivia Questions

1. Where was the *Enterprise* scheduled to go after the stopover at Caldos Colony?

2. When and where does Ronin claim he was born?

PLOT OVERSIGHTS

• Where's Wesley? This is the funeral for his maternal grandmother. Couldn't he get the time off from Starfleet Academy?

• The founders of Caldos Colony adopted a Scottish Highlands theme for their new home. After the graveside service for Felisa Howard, the governor tells Picard that the founders actually brought stones from Scotland to integrate into the buildings. The captain then points out that the alien-looking governor doesn't appear to be Scottish. With all the intermarrying that we have seen on *Star Trek* and *Star Trek: The Next Generation,* why couldn't the governor have Scottish ancestors?

• Beverly has her first experience with Ronin on the *Enterprise* in her quarters, with the candle unlit. Also, at this point in the episode, there's no

41

power transfer beam between the ship and the weather control station—though the station has already started to malfunction. The dialogue of the episode seems to indicate that Ronin needs to live in a plasma stream or an organic host tuned to his needs. Normally he lives in the candle. But the candle isn't lit. Okay, so he's in the plasma conduit in the weather station. That makes sense because he's causing problems there. But how does he get to the *Enterprise*? Later in the show, he travels along the power transfer beam. La Forge hasn't turned on the beam yet. (I'm confused.)

• Over and over, this episode references "the Howard women." At the end of the episode, Crusher tells Troi that Ronin somehow discovered that one of her ancestors had a biochemical makeup that was compatible with his energy matrix. Presumably this biochemical makeup passed down to each subsequent generation of women, who then served as Ronin's hosts. All very well, but Ronin identifies his first host as Jessel Howard. He also says that he took up residence in Jessel's daughter when Jessel died. Since we are led to believe that these events took place somewhere around the seventeenth or eighteenth century, it's likely that this daughter married to conceive and bring *her* daughter into the world. When Jessel's daughter married, she would take the surname of her husband. The pattern would continue for generation after generation until at least the late twentieth century. By this time, women with the proper biochemical makeup would have a surname far, far removed from

"Howard." Yet Beverly Crusher's grandmother was also named Howard. Did Ronin suggest that they revert to Jessel's last name for sentimental reasons once society deemed it acceptable for a woman to carry a surname of her choosing through life?

• I've been told by *several* nitpickers that this episode bears an uncanny resemblance to a book by Anne Rice called *The Witching Hour.*

• Finally, I can't really prove that this is a nit, but there's an aspect to the timeline of this episode that bugs me. We know this much. Even as a child, Crusher remembers that Felisa Howard kept the candle lit. We know that Ronin lived in the candle. We know that all the Howard women—excluding Crusher and her mother—had remarkable green eyes. We know that Ronin took up with Felisa when Felisa's mother died. We know that Felisa describes Ronin in her journals as a thirty-four-year-old male. We know that Crusher's eyes turn to a remarkable green as Ronin begins infusing her with anaphasic energy. The question is this: How long ago did Felisa take up with Ronin? From the dialogue, it sounds like the event happened *several decades* ago. Crusher's mother dies young. Crusher goes to live with her grandmother. Her grandmother has green eyes and the candle. Ronin lives in the candle, and Crusher's transformation at the end of the episode leads us to believe that the green eyes are a *direct* result of anaphasic energy infusion. Also, there's no mention that the great-grandmother lived with Felisa and Beverly. Here's the problem: If that's true—if Felisa took up with Ronin *decades* ago—Beverly should have immediately known there was something wrong when she read Felisa's journals. Felisa describes Ronin as a thirty-four-year-old male. But if Felisa met him *decades* ago, when Felisa's mother died, Crusher would conclude that Ronin would have been between four and fourteen years old at the time! (I doubt that even the fabled Howard women's libido would allow for this! Remember that, at this point, Crusher believes Ronin is a flesh-and-blood lover.)

• The last captain's log—the only captain's log—of the episode begins with "Captain's log, supplemental." Supplemental to what? Interestingly enough, the closed captioning has "Captain's log, star date 47488.2…" (hence the star date I've assigned to this episode). Unfortunately, I'm not sure it's correct. Perhaps the script read like the closed captioning and Patrick Stewart simply misspoke. Or perhaps the script read like the episode and the closed captioning personnel recognized the mistake and corrected it in the captioning.

CONTINUITY AND PRODUCTION PROBLEMS

• Not a nit, just an observation: Is that gravestone that seems to read "McFly" a nod to the *Back to the Future* trilogy?

• Crusher and Troi speak just after the graveside ceremony. Between them in the background you can see the aforementioned gravestone. Then the camera cuts to a wide shot, and the women depart. Next the scene shifts to Picard and the governor of the colony chitchatting among the tombs. If you look closely, you can see that they also stand near the "McFly" gravestone in a spot that was empty in the previous shot.

• Crusher and Troi depart from the cemetery together to go to Felisa Howard's home. We then join Picard and the governor in their conversation, also at the cemetery. Then a really strange thing happens. As the governor tells Picard about visiting Scotland as a boy, the camera shows Troi strolling around in the cemetery! Wasn't she on her way with Beverly to the deceased grandmother's home?

• Finding the Howard home filled with flowers, Crusher calls out for the person inside the house to identify himself or herself. Just before a mirror starts bouncing on the wall, Crusher has her hands at her side. Then the shot changes to a reflection of Crusher in the mirror. Suddenly her hands are at her shoulder.

• The sound effects people got a little "boop" happy in this episode. When Picard visits Crusher in the Howard home, Data calls from the bridge, and the main computer prefaces the page with the "boop" normally reserved for conversations on board the ship. I believe Picard's communicator should have chirped, if anything.

TRIVIA ANSWERS

1. Starbase 621.
2. In 1647 in Glasgow, Scotland.

★

LOWER DECKS

Star Date: 47566.7

This episode focuses on the lives of four junior officers, among them Ensign Sito, a Bajoran and part of Alpha Squadron during her days at the Academy (see "First Duty"). As the episode progresses, it becomes obvious that something is afoot. Picard orders an unexpected course change to the Argaya System. The ship hangs on the border of Cardassian space while La Forge increases the range of the transporter to reach deep inside Cardassian territory and beam an individual directly to sick bay.

Later, Picard discloses the details of the mission to Sito in the hope that she will volunteer to assist. A Cardassian member of the military named Joret Dal has brought vital intelligence to the Federation. He must return safely to Cardassian space to continue his role as a Starfleet operative. Dal wants to pose as a Cardassian bounty hunter returning home with a Bajoran prize, Ensign Sito. Once past the border patrols, Dal will use the shuttle's escape pod to send Sito back across the border into Federation space. Sito agrees. Unfortunately, the time comes and

Trivia Questions

1. From what shuttle bay does Sito depart the ship?

2. What is Ensign Sito's first name?

passes for the return of the escape pod, and soon after, Starfleet intercepts a report that the Cardassians killed an escaping Bajoran prisoner.

PLOT OVERSIGHTS

• The episode opens with Riker and Troi doing crew evaluations in Ten-Forward. Doesn't this seem like a bad arrangement for crew morale? Why aren't Riker and Troi doing these evaluations in private?

• And speaking of crew evaluations, Brad W. Higgins of Phoenix, AZ—an Air Force supervisor—tells me that in the twentieth-century U.S. military, a person's immediate superior is responsible for doing a person's evaluation. This seems like a much more sensible and manageable way of accomplishing this task (instead of making two officers review the entire ship).

• At one point, Sito claims that events at Starfleet Academy concerning Alpha Squadron happened three years ago. Yet "The First Duty" occurs on star date 45703.9, and this episode occurs on star date 47566.7. That's only a difference of 1862.8 star date units. If 1000 star date units equal one year, the events of "The First Duty" occurred less than two years ago. Of course, if Sito had said two years, that would also have caused a timeline problem. Sito had three bars on her collar in "The First Duty." Since Locarno had four, I am assuming that he was a senior and Sito was a junior. At the end of that episode, Locarno was expelled and all the other cadets were forced to retake a year. That means Sito spent two more years at the Academy—as a junior once again and then a senior—and she has been on the *Enterprise* for seven months. Hence the creators opted to have her put the events three years in the past, again relying on the obscuring quality of the star dates.

• Riker is a real scoundrel when it comes to playing poker. During the game featured in this episode, La Forge goes around the table dealing the final face-up card and states that both Crusher and Troi have two pairs, he himself has three sixes and Riker is working on a flush. Our dear first officer then turns to La Forge and says, "Looks like it's just you and me." Excuse me? Either of the ladies' hands are sufficient to win with a card to make three of a kind if Riker doesn't have the flush and La Forge doesn't have another six in the hole. Granted it's not the best position to be in, but bluffing is what poker is all about, isn't it?

• During the junior officers' poker game, Ben—the civilian who works in Ten-Forward—bluffs Ensign Lavelle with a king, jack, ten and an eight when

Lavelle has two sixes and two sevens. I don't play poker, but even I know that it doesn't matter what Ben has for a fifth card— he can't beat two pairs.

EQUIPMENT ODDITIES

• Dal comes aboard the *Enterprise* injured and Crusher tells Ogawa that they will need to synthesize at least a liter of Cardassian blood. Somebody has been upgrading the capabilities of sick bay. In "The Enemy," Crusher had to ask Worf for some blood products to try to save the life of a Romulan.

• Again, the doors read the script. Leaving the senior officers' poker game, La Forge strides up to the door, stops, turns and talks, preparing to turn back. The doors finally decide that he is actually leaving the room, so they pop open.

CONTINUITY AND PRODUCTION PROBLEMS

• Why doesn't Sito wear the Bajoran earring? After all, Worf gets to wear the sash.

• During the senior officers' poker game, it looks like the right side of Worf's Fu Manchu mustache doesn't have the portion of hair that extends down to his goatee.

TRIVIA ANSWERS

1. Shuttle Bay 2. (Look at the floor when Worf is standing and looking out through the open exterior doors after the shuttle departs.)
2. Jaxa.

THINE OWN SELF

Star Date: 47611.2

Data takes a shuttle to recover the remains of a probe that crashed on Barkon IV. Although the probe contains radioactive metal fragments, the crash doesn't concern the crew, since it occurred well away from the pre-industrial humanoid population of the planet. Unfortunately, a power surge in the probe's onboard computer overloads Data's positronic matrix and wipes out his memory. Uncertain of where he is or where he came from, Data wanders into a nearby village with the probe fragments. The village blacksmith makes jewelry from the fragments, and soon many villagers come down with radiation poisoning. Data finds the cause and cure but not before the blacksmith rams a metal rod through him—believing that Data is the cause of the illness. The rod short-circuits the android's power systems. The villagers bury Data, believing he is dead.

Meanwhile, Troi takes the bridge officer's test, hoping to achieve a rank of full commander. Passing all the other sections of the test, Troi faces the one most difficult for her, the engineering portion. Failing it three times, Troi finally realizes the true emphasis of the test—not technical knowledge but the worst decision a commander faces. In the simulation she orders La Forge into a lethal repair operation and saves the ship. As the episode ends, the crew recovers and reactivates Data.

PLOT OVERSIGHTS

• The town magistrate can't decide where he should send his daughter when Data appears at the village. First he tells her to go home. Then he tells her to go home a second time. The third time, he tells her to go to school!

• The Barkonians have some odd social habits. As the village doctor looks over Data for the first time in the town magistrate's house, there's a knock at the door. The town magistrate gets up, opens the door, and it's his daughter! Apparently in the Barkonian culture, it's considered polite to gain entrance to your *own* house by knocking.

• The creators make a simple error in physics during this episode. They have Data bend over and pick up an anvil that several grown men cannot budge. Note that the men are blacksmiths and quite "manly-looking." The anvil must weigh *a lot*! Three hundred pounds doesn't seem unreasonable. The problem is this: Irrespective of Data's strength, there must be an equal amount of weight on either side of the android's center of gravity or he will topple over. The process of bending over and picking up a 300-pound anvil would push Data's center of gravity forward. To stay upright, Data must have more than 300 pounds behind his center of gravity. Come to think of it, "behind" might be precisely the right word, because from the look of things, the weight would need to reside there. (Lead-shielded reactor in the old posterior, maybe?) Unfortunately, "Inheritance" indicates that Data weighs only about 220 pounds (100 kilograms). If that's the case, he shouldn't be able to bend over and lift the anvil off the ground. Shove it out of the way maybe, but not lift it.

• When first arriving in town, Data tells the town magistrate that the box he transports carries the label "RADIOACTIVE." Unfortunately, Data doesn't remember what that means. Later in the show, Data sees the village doctor's magnifying glass and says, "With an increased focal length and an achromatic objective lens, this instrument will have a higher effective magnification." All this, and Data doesn't remember what the word *"radioactive"* means?

CHANGED PREMISES

• We need to examine this whole business of the bridge officer's test in greater detail. First, let's try to figure

out who takes this test and why. From the dialogue at the beginning of the show, it appears that Crusher and Troi are required to take the test to become bridge officers. Presumably you must be a bridge officer to command the ship. Since Data, La Forge, and Worf have commanded some portion of the ship at one time or another, we have to assume that the bridge officer's test applies only to an officer who is not part of Command, Engineering, or Security. That leaves areas such as Science and Medical. (I'm guessing that Medical also encompasses counseling.) In addition, it sounds as if Science and Medical personnel move beyond the rank of lieutenant commander to full commander *only* by taking the bridge officer's test. If the same is true for other types of officers, Data would have taken and passed the test long ago.

Three problems immediately arise from the statements above. During "Encounter at Farpoint," Crusher carries the rank of full commander, but she tells Riker that her interests and duties lay outside the command structure. On one hand, we know that she has taken the bridge officer's test within the past year, since she carries the rank of commander. She told Troi in "Thine Own Self" that she became interested in being a commander only eight years ago. Unfortunately, we also learn from "Thine Own Self" that Crusher took the test to stretch herself in new areas. The bridge officer's test deals with one area: *command*.

Next problem. Pulaski, the much-adored chief medical officer during the second season, also carried the rank of full commander (three solid pips). Yet in "Where Silence Has Lease," Pulaski states that she *isn't* a bridge officer. How did she get to be a commander without taking the bridge officer's test?

One more problem before moving on. If Troi wasn't qualified to command the bridge—because she hadn't taken the bridge officer's test yet—why was she allowed to command the *Enterprise* during the crisis in "Disaster"? I spent a considerable amount of space on this under the Reader Mail review of "Disaster," but need to make one small point to bring it home. Suppose there's an explosion in sick bay. Crusher dies with most of the medical personnel. The facilities are closed off from the rest of the ship. Only three people are healthy enough to tend to the injured. They are La Forge, Barclay, and Nurse Ogawa. Who ya gonna call? La Forge, just because he has the highest rank? Obviously not! You're going to pass the duties to the person most qualified. In "Disaster," the most qualified person was O'Brien, not Troi.

EQUIPMENT ODDITIES

• Starfleet container technology takes a giant leap backward in this episode. Data carries a container labeled "RADIOACTIVE." Yet the town magistrate flips a very twentieth-century-looking latch and opens the lid. What

happened to control pads? What happened to access codes that prevent accidental exposure to lethal contents?

• After Troi passes the exam, Riker enters and says, "End simulation." The people disappear, but the setting remains. I believe the holodeck usually reverts to the black room with the yellow grid markings after an "End simulation" command.

CONTINUITY AND PRODUCTION PROBLEMS

• After finally figuring out the engineering portion of the bridge officer's test, Troi strides onto the holodeck and asks the computer to load up the exam. She then tells the computer to run the program. But if you look at the large display on the front wall of Engineering, you'll see a reflection from the blue doughnut lights on the warp core. Before Troi tells the computer to start the exam, the lights are already moving.

• At the very end of the episode, Crusher reactivates Data in sick bay. He still wears the clothing provided by the villagers. Yet Crusher most likely removed them to repair the damage caused by the blacksmith's metal rod. So why redress him in those clothes? Why not something of Starfleet issue?

TRIVIA ANSWERS
1. Starbase 231.
2. Antimatter Storage Pod 33.

★

MASKS

Star Dates: 47615.2—47618.4

The *Enterprise* comes upon a rogue comet that has traveled on its own for 87-million years. As the *Enterprise*'s sensors begin scanning the interior of the comet, strange artifacts start appearing all over the ship. In addition, computer terminals display previously unknown symbols, and Data comes down with the android equivalent of multiple personality syndrome. Burning away the outer layer of the comet, Picard and crew discover an ancient informational archive that is transforming the *Enterprise* into a representation of the culture that created it.

The symbolism on the artifacts indicates two predominant personages: Masaka and Korgano—sun and moon archetypes, respectively. Through Data, several different characters speak of Masaka's coming and the danger she represents. They also tell Picard that only Korgano can speak with her. A short time later, when Data takes on the persona of Masaka, Picard adopts the role of Korgano and encourages Masaka to sleep so that their hunt can begin again with her rising. Masaka falls asleep,

and everything returns to normal.

PLOT OVERSIGHTS

• This *Enterprise* is a trusting place indeed. Near the beginning of the episode, Crusher and Troi enter the counselor's quarters just before heading to a martial arts class. Crusher finds a strange artifact on a table, its origins unknown, yet both ladies seem unperturbed that someone has entered Troi's quarters without permission. And neither asks the computer who has entered the counselor's quarters in the past twelve hours (as Data did with his quarters during "In Theory").

• In Main Engineering, Picard somehow divines the sex of Masaka before any of the alien personalities in Data identify her as feminine. He says he would like to know Masaka, "to speak with *her*" (emphasis mine).

• Growing desperate, Picard has La Forge locate the symbol for Masaka's temple in the informational archive and send it to the archive's transformational program. With hesitation, La Forge says he's not sure what will happen when he inputs the appropriate symbol. Amazingly enough, only

Trivia Questions

1. What is the name of the boy who sculpts a bird from clay at the beginning of the episode?

2. What title appears on the display in the room where children sculpt clay?

moments later, we see that Picard, Troi, and Worf have positioned themselves in a hall, and it just happens to be the ~~hallway~~ that the archive uses to create Masaka's temple. How did they know where to stand?

• You would think that after seven years, security guards would know a thing or two about Data. Obviously not. When Data takes on the persona of Masaka and escapes from his quarters, he walks right through the doors and catches both security officers offguard as they spin to face him. In other words, they didn't put a force field around the room—or at the very least lock the door so he couldn't unlock it—and they have been standing with their backs to the entrance.

• While discussing the relationship of Masaka and Korgano, Troi says that, like the sun and the moon, only one can be in ascendance at any time. Troi needs to brush up on her astronomy.

• When Data comes to Masaka's temple he wears a mask that he constructed earlier in the show. Just before the temple disappears, Data—wearing the mask—sleeps slumped back on the throne. Moments later, the camera shows Data standing. Didn't he tumble backward when the throne dematerialized? Or did he wake up in time to jump to his feet? And what happened to the mask? He's not wearing it, and it's not in his hands. It still exists, because Data shows it to Picard at the conclusion of the episode.

• In the captain's final log, Picard says that the Federation has dispatched some archaeologists to study the archive. *Archaeologists?* Forget the archaeologists! Get some Federation scientists and engineers out there to figure out how that transformation program works. It can take anything and turn it into anything!

EQUIPMENT ODDITIES

• Early in the program, Picard decides to destroy the informational archive before it does any more damage to the ship. He orders La Forge and Worf to configure a photon torpedo manually. The next scene shows the pair working in Main Engineering with a torpedo lying on the floor between the center island and the warp core. In other words, they retrieved a torpedo from a launcher, lugged it down to Main Engineering just to configure it for a manual launch knowing that afterward they would have to lug it back to the launcher. Wouldn't it make more sense to do the alterations in the torpedo bay?

• After a bunch of snakes appear inside the torpedo mentioned above, La Forge and Worf apparently give up on the possibility of using a photon torpedo to destroy the archive.

CONTINUITY AND PRODUCTION PROBLEMS

• When the informational archive creates Masaka's temple, Picard, Troi, and Worf stand in a hallway. Matter streams by them, and soon they stand on the ground floor of a stone-like structure. Stairs lead up to a second level, where Data shortly appears, wearing Masaka's mask. Picard leaves and then comes back, wearing Korgano's mask. He walks up the stairs to speak with Data. The conversation puts Data to sleep, and the temple disappears. Strangely enough—though both Picard and Data resided on the upper portion of the temple as it disintegrates—the pair does not plummet to the floor that should be several feet beneath them. They once again stand in a hallway.

• At one point the senior staff meets on the main bridge to discuss the situation. A large block of stone sits upright near the former position of the Ops station. For a portion of the meeting, Riker stands with his back to the main viewscreen, with his arm resting on the block. But at the end of the meeting, a reverse angle suddenly shows us the entire viewscreen from Picard's perspective. Wouldn't the big block obscure at least a portion of the screen?

• With few other choices, Picard orders La Forge to send the symbol for Korgano to the informational archive's transformation program. A silver mask appears on the workstation near La Forge. The chief engineer picks up the mask and hands it to Picard. Suddenly the mask has wide cloth ties attached to each side.

• Picard goes to Masaka's temple and dons the mask. In the wide shots, the ties that secure the mask rest very low near the base of the captain's neck. Then the camera cuts to a medium-wide shot as Picard ascends the stair with the ties joining halfway up his head.

TRIVIA ANSWERS
1. Eric.
2. Classroom 7.

EYE OF THE BEHOLDER

Stars Dates: 47622.1—47623.2

When Lieutenant Dan Kwan commits suicide by jumping through a force field into the plasma stream feeding the starboard engine nacelle, Troi and Worf investigate. Having experienced an empathic jolt of fear, rage, and panic from no discernible source in the nacelle tube, Troi returns there with Worf for a second attempt. This time she finds herself back at Utopia Planitia where the *Enterprise* was constructed. She sees a man and a woman kissing, and another person whom she later identifies as Lieutenant Walter Pierce. Troi and Worf question Pierce, but he offers no further information.

That evening, Troi and Worf begin an affair. Yet, the next day, Troi notices Worf paying special attention to an Ensign Calloway. Finding the pair embracing, Troi grabs a phaser and kills Worf before hurrying to the nacelle tube to commit suicide. Just as she prepares to jump, Worf grabs Troi, and she snaps out of the psychic vision. Soon the crew pieces together the remaining facts. Eight years ago, Pierce—partially telepathic

Trivia Questions

1. Where is the *Enterprise* scheduled to take medical supplies during this episode?

2. What does Riker order in Ten-Forward for himself and Lieutenant Corell?

via a Betazoid grandmother—discovered that his girlfriend was in love with another man. He killed them both. Grief-stricken, Pierce destroyed the bodies in the plasma stream and then killed himself. Evidently the subspace energy of the plasma stream imprinted an empathic pattern into the cellular residue present in the nacelle. It temporarily overwhelmed both Kwan and Troi.

PLOT OVERSIGHTS

• Kwan's girlfriend, Ensign Calloway, seems very calm for someone who has just lost a loved one.

• In her first visit to the nacelle tube, Troi reacts with surprise when she bumps into Kwan's supervisor. Shouldn't the counselor sense that someone is in the room? At this point she hasn't yet experienced the flood of emotions that would understandably cloud her empathic awareness.

• Again in the seventh season, the creators have treated us to an episode that is very difficult to nitpick. After all, most of this show occurs in Troi's mind! We can attribute any errors to the good counselor's neurons. But for the sake of completeness, let's see what problems we can uncover! (Just so there's no confusion, I have labeled each of these mistakes, "IHITMO" for "It Happened In Troi's Mind Only." On to the nits!) Reporting her first empathic vision to Picard in the ready room, Troi says that a man looked familiar. Afterward, she searches the data base for the guy, limiting her search to personnel who worked on the *Enterprise* at Utopia Planitia and have served on the *Enterprise* during the past seven years. Oddly, Troi doesn't limit the search to males only! She's looking for a red-haired male, and almost half the people who come up on the screen are females.

• IHITMO: This episode treats us to the seduction of Troi by Worf. Doesn't seem very Klingon-like, though. It's oh, so sweet and genteel (reminds me more of *human* mating).

• Why isn't Riker present for the final debriefing at the end of the episode? Because of Kwan's suicide and his friendship with Troi, the first officer certainly has a vested interest in the situation.

EQUIPMENT ODDITIES

• Evidently the *Enterprise* has several different types of force fields. In the brig, a force field keeps the prisoner inside the cell. In the shuttle bays, force fields keep the atmosphere inside the bay but allow the shuttlecraft to pass through into space. In the nacelle tube, Kwan jumps through the force field to commit suicide. Doesn't this seem like a good place to have a restraining-type force field?

• And speaking of Kwan jumping to his death, why didn't Riker tell O'Brien

to beam him out of the nacelle tube? Too much interference from the plasma stream?

• IHITMO: After matching the DNA of some bone fragments to a woman named Finn, Ensign Calloway tries to pull up a picture of her on a sick bay workstation. At first the display shows some guy named Alfonse D. Pacelli before filling the screen with Finn's information. Just how do these Starfleet data bases work? Even in the twentieth century we have relational data bases that link information together. This allows the data base designer to reference a specific record in a completely different data base using a key field. Presumably the medical data base has the DNA information on Starfleet personnel. Once Calloway matches a name to the DNA (or more likely Finn's serial number) in the medical data base, the computer should directly access the appropriate record in the personnel data base and bring up Finn's information. There's no reason to display Pacelli's picture!

• Early in the episode, Worf raises the isolation door between the warp coils and the engine nacelle tube control room. Immediately, the computer begins counting down the time until the automatic plasma venting system engages. It starts at ninety seconds. Then it gives an eighty-second call. Then Troi takes her vacation from reality in which she kills Worf. Just before Troi jumps into the plasma stream, Worf grabs her, and the computer gives the seventy-second call. A joyful, shocked expression appears on Troi's face and she grabs Worf in a tight hug. The computer forgets to give the sixty-second warning call, even though the time for it comes and goes.

CONTINUITY AND PRODUCTION PROBLEMS

• The episode begins with Kwan's suicide attempt which creates a crisis for the ship. Data notes that they are losing containment in the starboard nacelle tube and, a bit later, the plasma venting system engages. But the graphic of the ship that follows shows plasma coming from the *port* nacelle.

• IHITMO: Everyone addresses the red-haired male named Pierce as "Lieutenant" when his rank pips show him to be an ensign.

• IHITMO: When Troi shoots Worf with the phaser, the blast initially hits him just above his communicator. Then, as he falls, the glow from the residual energy starts dropping and ends beneath the communicator. When the scene changes, the wound is again above his communicator.

TRIVIA ANSWERS

1. Barson II.
2. Two Til'amin Froths.

GENESIS

Star Date: 47653.2

As the episode begins, Crusher gives Spot a prenatal exam and treats Barclay for a sickness not normally associated with humans. Barclay has a dormant gene that makes him susceptible. Crusher injects Barclay with a synthetic T-cell to activate the gene to fight the disease. Meanwhile, the crew tests updated weapons systems, including a new targeting program for the photon torpedoes. When a torpedo goes astray, Picard and Data leave in a shuttle to recover it.

Returning three days later, the pair finds the *Enterprise* in chaos. The crew has "de-evolved" into half-human, half-animal creatures. Radical changes have occurred in the animals aboard the ship as well, and the main power systems are off-line. Even though Spot turned into a lizard before giving birth, the kittens seem unaffected. Data postulates that something in the birth process protected them. He takes a sample from Nurse Ogawa—who is also pregnant—and synthesizes a retrovirus to combat the crew's affliction. Soon after releasing it into the

ship's ventilation system, everyone returns to normal. After the crisis passes, Crusher determines that the synthetic T-cell she injected into Barclay somehow reacted with his system to activate the dormant portions of his DNA. Then the T-cell became airborne and caused the same thing to happen in the rest of the crew.

Trivia Questions

1. What is exoskeleton Worf's approximate weight?

2. What does Crusher name the disease that affects the crew?

RUMINATIONS

My, oh, my, oh, my, did I get the mail on this episode! It ranks with "Encounter at Farpoint" and "The Enemy" in volume of pages received. Of course, "Encounter at Farpoint" is two hours long, and I did throw down the gauntlet when I claimed in the NextGen Guide that I couldn't find anything wrong with "The Enemy." In a way, that might make "Genesis" the all-time most nitpicked episode! As with "The Enemy," I shall attempt to be less verbose in the discussion of these nits.

GREAT MOMENTS

The shuttle's approach to the disabled, ambling, twisting Enterprise really is quite lovely.

PLOT OVERSIGHTS

• Beginning to "de-evolve," Troi goes to her quarters to take a bath. A bit later, Worf walks in. Does this seem right? Anybody can just stroll into Troi's quarters when she is *taking a bath*? Or did Worf use his security override codes to enter unannounced?

• This episode reinforces the budding romance between Troi and Worf. Oddly enough, she seems shocked when he bites her on the cheek. He's a *Klingon,* for crying out loud! Isn't that pretty much standard fare?

• For some reason, after Troi comes to sick bay following her first true encounter with Klingon mating rituals (i.e., after Worf bites her on the cheek), Crusher doesn't use one of her medical doodads to seal and heal the wound completely. She leaves Troi with bite marks. I would expect this from primitive twentieth century medicine, but how many times have we seen Crusher run that little laser thing over a wound and remove every trace? (Of course, if Crusher removed every trace of the wound, then Picard and Data couldn't later deduce that Worf was bashing on the sick bay door to get to Troi. Wink, wink.)

• The medical staff has a very odd chain of command. After Worf sprays Crusher with venom, Nurse Ogawa gives a report on the health of the crew at the next staff meeting. Yet moments earlier, Crusher mentioned two doctors—one of them the fabled, Dr. Selar seen in "The Schizoid Man" and mentioned many times afterward. Wouldn't "command" of the medical facilities pass to one of them?

• And while we're on the subject of

chain of command, why does La Forge dispatch seven security teams to look for Worf after the Klingon attacks Crusher? Isn't this a job for the assistant chief of Security?

• Obviously Starfleet doesn't have isolation procedures when boarding a ship whose condition has mysteriously degraded. Picard just walks right off the shuttle without any sort of protective suit.

• Now let's spend a few moments talking about the premise of this episode. To review, Crusher tells Barclay that he has come down with a sickness because "the T-cell in your DNA that would normally fight off the infection is dormant." She then says that she can activate that gene with a "synthetic T-cell." Once on board the *Enterprise,* Data rattles off the following explanation for what has happened to the crew. "A synthetic T-cell has invaded [Riker's] genetic codes. This T-cell has begun to activate his latent interons." When Picard questions Data on the meaning of the word "interons," Data responds, "They are genetic codes which are normally dormant. They are evolutionary holdovers, sequences of DNA which provided key behavioral and physical characteristics millions of years ago but are no longer necessary." Still later, both Picard and Data begin referring to this synthetic T-cell as the "interon virus." At the end of the episode, Crusher tells Barclay that the synthetic T-cell she injected into him "became airborne and started to spread like a virus."

Wendy A. Weiger—an M.D./Ph.D. student in the Department of Neurobiology at Harvard Medical School at the time of this writing—had this response to the episode: "As a biologist, I noted a confusing discrepancy. The entity causing the process of de-evolution is sometimes referred to as a virus, sometimes a T-cell. T-cells are a type of white blood cell in the human immune system and could not be transmitted from one individual to another except by a blood transfusion. Viruses, on the other hand, can be more easily transmitted and can add genetic information or alter the expression of existing information in human cells. In the context of the show, a virus makes much more sense than a T-cell."

Corinne C. McMillen (who was working on a Master's degree in evolutionary genetics at the time of this writing) submitted: "This is ludicrous. Interons are not 'evolutionary holdovers,' as Data called them. They are sequences in genes that are cut out after the cell has transcribed that gene into a protein. Therefore there is no selection pressure on these sections of DNA. This means that it will not harm the animal, or plant for that matter, if they are changed or mutated over time. These sections of DNA have the highest probability of being the most different and changed from the original. They would not stay the same and still hold the codes for reptilian or amphibian protein. If your interons were turned on all of a sudden, you would probably die. You would not turn into something that had previously lived on Earth. In all likelihood, you would turn into some form of monster that had never been seen before." (Oooooh, now *that* would

have been interesting!)

Finally, Michael Shiner, a former biology teacher, added the following comments—after graciously granting the creators *all* of their premises: "It is quite erroneous to call this 'de-evolution.' Individuals do not evolve, therefore they cannot de-evolve. It is populations that evolve. Evolution has not occurred when a single organism is born with a new trait or a modification of an old one—that is 'variation.' Evolution only occurs when that new feature, if it is useful, has spread throughout the population as a whole in many generations' time. A whale that grew legs would not have de-evolved into a terrestrial ancestor; it would simply be a whale with legs. What happened to the crew, being structural change caused by genetic mishap, can best be described as an exotic form of cancer."

Having said all this, let's move on.

• Spot probably should be a saber-toothed tiger, not a lizard. (I am absolutely certain that *this* would have made the episode more interesting!)

• Barclay turns into a spider, and Data claims Picard is on his way to becoming a lemur or pygmy marmoset. According to the evolutionary theory, the ancestors of *Homo sapiens* do not include arachnids, lemurs, or marmosets. (By the way, Michael Shiner tells me that Walker's *Mammals of the World* describes pygmy marmosets as "brave and resist aggression"—a description that does not match Patrick Stewart's excellent portrayal of a small, frightened animal.)

• Is Alexander on vacation with the grandparents?

• After Worf sprays Crusher with acidlike venom, Ogawa says that Crusher will need reconstructive surgery. Yet, at the end of the episode …she's *fine*! In fact, everybody's fine! Everybody's happy! Everybody's well adjusted! (with the exception of Barclay, of course). It doesn't matter that they have all just mutated into monsters and back, it's a new day! *Life* …is grand! (This episode should have been a two-parter.)

• Speaking of everybody getting back to normal, did Crusher do reconstructive surgery on all 1,011 people Data detected aboard the *Enterprise*? Or do the creators expect us to fall for the old "just switch the DNA and everything will be hunkey-dory fine" trick *again*? Did Troi's gills just disintegrate? Did Worf's exoskeleton fall off?

• Speaking of Worf, Data states earlier in the episode that to find a cure for humanoids, they would need to find a pregnant humanoid. Ogawa fulfills this role. Does it seem likely that a human solution also would apply to Klingons?

• Oh, and one other thing about Worf: After this experience, would you want to serve aboard a ship with him? (Of course, the same might be said for Data after the events in "Brothers.")

EQUIPMENT ODDITIES

• At one point, Troi—in command of the bridge—asks the computer to raise the ambient temperature and humidity. Immediately, Worf tells the computer to restore the environment to its normal settings. If I recall, Troi outranks Worf. Shouldn't the computer ask Troi for confirmation before executing Worf's order?

• After Worf spits on Crusher and finds a hiding place on the ship, La Forge tells Riker that the sensors are having difficulty finding the Klingon. Yet, at the end of the episode, as Worf charges Picard in the Jefferies tube, we see that the Klingon still wears his communicator! (In case you're wondering, even with main power off, Data locates Nurse Ogawa on deck 17 by using her communicator. Why can't La Forge do the same to Worf?)

• Returning to the rendezvous point after a three-day search for the photon torpedo, Data reports that he cannot contact the *Enterprise.* Sensors subsequently show it two light-years distant. Moments later, we see the shuttle approaching the ship. Picard and Data ride in a type 6 shuttle. According to the *Tech Manual,* it can hit a maximum of warp 2 for only thirty-six hours. At warp 2 it would take about two and one-half *months* to travel two light-years. No wonder the ship is in such bad shape.

• There is some question about how the shuttle could land on the *Enterprise* in the first place with main power out. How did Data raise the doors of the shuttle bay? How did they pressurize the bay later?

• On the way to the bridge, Picard and Data stop at Troi's quarters. As Data turns to go into her bathroom, his flashlight isn't lit.

• Why is Data's quarters the only one with independent processing and memory storage units?

• Someone must have upgraded the doors on the *Enterprise.* In "Conspiracy," Admiral Quinn tossed La Forge into a cabin entrance, and the doors blew off their hinges easily—so easily that La Forge sustained no injury during the incident. Yet in this episode, exoskeleton Worf bangs on the door for some time and can't budge them.

• After deducing that Worf has the hots for Troi, Data makes up a pheromone solution and places it in a hypospray. Picard then proceeds to run around the *Enterprise* like a maniac, squirting this stuff in hallways as he attempts to stay ahead of Worf's desire to mate. Wouldn't it be easier to release the compound into the air handling system and just confuse the living daylights out of the prehomonid?

• In the *NextGen Guide,* I had some fun with the sporadically appearing control panels in the turbolift. I noted that they often appeared only when needed. This episode conveniently has a control panel in the turbolift so Picard can use it to close the turbolift door and thereby fend off an attack from Worf.

CONTINUITY AND PRODUCTION PROBLEMS

• Cat lovers tell me Spot doesn't look pregnant at the beginning of this episode.

• As Picard and Data's shuttle departs from the *Enterprise,* it casts a huge shadow on the saucer section, making the shuttle look far out of scale in comparison to the ship.

• As Troi eats a meal in Ten-Forward with Worf, her spoon keeps changing positions. Worf begins telling her about his day, saying that the torpedo malfunction was his fault. At this point, the shot changes from behind Troi featuring Worf to behind Worf featuring Troi. In the first angle, Troi holds the spoon tilted so that the bowl area rests vertically. In the second, the spoon flips so that the bowl is horizontal. Moments later, the spoon again starts out on edge. Then the shot changes and Troi brings the now horizontal spoon into camera range and it suddenly has caviar in it!

• The next scene occurs in Main Engineering and begins with a long shot from the second level of the warp core before moving in closer. Riker, La Forge, and Barclay talk about a problem in the torpedo launcher. An alarm sounds; Barclay goes off to investigate, and La Forge joins him. Behind Riker, a nondescript officer walks over to a workstation. The camera angle changes back to the original long shot, and the officer again walks over to the workstation.

• The model of the shuttle contains writing on the fold-down door in back. The life-size version seen in the shuttle bay does not.

• After Picard and Data leave Main Engineering, an exterior shot of the ship shows all the lights on and the engines idling. Yet, when the action cuts back to sick bay, main power is still off-line.

• As Worf attempts to gain entrance to sick bay, an interior shot shows the door denting under the pressure. Yet a subsequent hallway shot shows the door perfectly smooth.

TRIVIA ANSWERS

1. It is 200 kilograms.
2. Barclay's protomorphosis syndrome.

JOURNEY'S END

Star Dates: 47751.2—47755.3

Wesley Crusher joins the crew during a break from the academy in time to travel to Dorvan V—a world recently deeded to the Cardassians as part of a final negotiated peace. Picard has orders to evacuate the Federation colony on that world. The heritage of the colonists complicates matters. They are descendants of North American Indians. For hundreds of years, they searched for a new homeland and have finally found it.

As Picard discusses the situation with them, Wesley becomes friends with an Indian who claims that a vision foretold Wesley's arrival two years ago. Intrigued, Wesley follows the man to a vision room, where Wesley experiences a visitation from his father. Jack Crusher tells Wesley that he has followed a path for many years that was not his own—that it is time to begin his journey. Wesley knows that what his father says is true. He has become increasingly depressed as his academy graduation date approaches. He resigns from the academy and soon discovers that the Indian who had the

Trivia Questions

1. From where does Admiral Nechayev board the *Enterprise* at the beginning of the episode?

2. Wesley believes La Forge needs to read whose new theories on warp propulsion interrelays?

vision of him is actually the Traveler come to teach him to live on a higher plane of existence. At the same time, Picard works out an agreement whereby the colonists can stay on Dorvan V but will no longer retain the protection of the Federation.

PLOT OVERSIGHTS

• This episode refers to Nechayev as a "fleet admiral," while "Chain of Command, Part 1" called her a "vice-admiral." Is that the same thing? Or did she get a promotion? If she got a promotion, why hasn't the rank insignia on her collar changed?

• I must have missed something in the dialogue because I can't figure out why this problem with Dorvan V exists in the first place. Supposedly the Federation and the Cardassians have worked out this deal where there are some Cardassian colonies in Federation space and vice versa. I'm assuming that these colonies are in different star systems. (Surely, the Federation wouldn't settle a planet in a system that already had a Cardassian colony on another planet in that star system, would they?) Typically, star systems have quite a bit of space between them. It's four and one-half *light-years* to our nearest star system. Remember, the universe is big…really big! So why can't the Federation and the Cardassians draw the border so that Cardassian colonies are in Cardassian space and Federation colonies are in Federation space? The padd that Nechayev hands Picard in the observation lounge has a graphic of the new border. It looks very irregular. I can't see what difference a few more dimples would make.

• In the second meeting between Picard and the colonists, the leader of the group tells Picard that they have discovered a "stain of blood" on his ancestry: One of Picard's forefathers crushed a rebellion in North America ten years after the Pueblo Revolt of 1680. In a stunning display of historical erudition, Troi brings our beloved captain up to speed on the incident. Does anyone else find it extremely curious that (1) the colonists would actually *have* records dating back to the 1600s and (2) Troi—*Troi, mind you*—would know about the Pueblo Revolt of 1680?

• Following the second meeting with the colonists, Picard walks out to find Cardassians roaming the village. So no one called down from the *Enterprise* to inform the captain that a Cardassian ship had arrived and was transporting an away team to the surface?

• During the conclusion of the episode, the Cardassian Gul makes it sound like Cardassia will leave the colony alone. The leader of the colony really doesn't believe this, does he?

CHANGED PREMISES

• Crusher says the Traveler is from "Tau Ceti." "Where No One Has Gone Before" and "Remember Me" put his origin at "Tau Alpha C."

• We need to revisit "Where No One Has Gone Before," the episode where Wesley first meets the Traveler. At the end of the episode, the Traveler tells Picard that Wesley will forget him in time, which is as it should be. Then he tells Picard that it would be best if the captain did not repeat what he is about to say to the others, "especially the mother." The Traveler tells Picard that Wesley is like Mozart. But instead of music, Wesley is gifted in time, energy, propulsion, and the "instruments of this vessel" that make those things possible. First, I don't think Wesley ever forgot the Traveler, especially after the Traveler helped save his mother's life in "Remember Me." Second, Crusher actually refers to the conversation between Picard and the Traveler in this episode so obviously that our dear captain blabbed about it to her. And third, the statements by the Traveler about Wesley's gifting in "Where No One Has Gone Before" don't really fit with trotting off to live on other planes of existence, do they? It doesn't sound like he's going to be doing a whole lot with propulsion systems on Dorvan V.

TRIVIA ANSWERS
1. Starbase 310.
2. Dr. Vassbinder.

FIRSTBORN

Star Date: 47779.4

Hoping to inspire in Alexander an interest in Klingon ways, Worf takes him to a Klingon outpost. At nightfall, three assassins attack the pair. Suddenly K'Mtar, trusted adviser to the House of Mogh, comes to Worf's aide. Back on the ship, K'Mtar produces the assassin's knife—bearing the symbol of the House of Duras—and states that Kurn sent him to protect Worf. With Picard away, Riker starts looking for the Duras sisters to question them about the incident. Meanwhile, K'Mtar tries to en-courage Alexander to dedicate himself to becoming a warrior. As usual, Alexander resists.

When located by the crew, the Duras sisters deny any knowledge of an assassination plot but also express shock at the knife. It does carry the mark of the House of Duras, but it also carries the mark of Lursa's son—a son only recently conceived. K'Mtar finally tells Worf the truth. He has traveled back forty years from the future. He is actually Alexander, who, because he never became a warrior, watched helplessly as assassins killed Worf. He has

traveled back to try to convince himself to take a different path. Worf assures him that his life has value even though he isn't a warrior. As the adult Alexander departs, Worf gains a new appreciation for the unique path his son must follow.

CHANGED PREMISES

• At the end of the episode, the adult Alexander claims he was three years old when his mother died. However, according to the star date Alexander reports for his birth in "New Ground," he was 1041 star date units old when it happened.

CONTINUITY AND PRODUCTION PROBLEMS

• It appears that Romulan Proconsul Neral has snuck off and is using his limited telepathic abilities to pose as the head delegate Maques from the Cairn. (Is this some new and devious conspiracy from the arch enemies of the Federation?)

Trivia Questions

1. What is the cost of Quark's "confidence"?

2. Where does the Yridian captain claim to have procured his magnesite ore?

TRIVIA ANSWERS

1. Twelve bars of gold-pressed latinum.
2. From a Corvallen trader.

BLOODLINES

Star Dates: 47829.1—47831.8

As the episode begins, a probe delivers a message from Picard's archenemy Bok (See "The Battle"). He announces that he has finally found the appropriate revenge for the death of his son. He will soon kill Picard's son, Jason Vigo. The announcement comes as a surprise. Picard wasn't aware that he had a son. Still, Bok apparently believes that Jason is Picard's son. In response, the *Enterprise* flies to Jason's home world.

Beaming the young man aboard, Picard finds a person of less than sterling character. Yet, genetic testing by Crusher proves that Jason is Picard's son. Continuing the threats by utilizing a subspace transporter, Bok initially frustrates La Forge and Data's efforts to track or block him. At the same time, Jason comes down with a rare genetic disorder. Later, when Bok finally snatches Jason from the ship, Data can at least supply the location of Bok's ship. In addition, Crusher discovers that Jason really isn't Picard's son. Evidently Bok resequenced Jason's DNA to make it appear so, but the process sparked

Trivia Questions

1. What is the name of Jason's female security guard?

2. Where are Jason's quarters?

the young man's disease. Hurriedly, Data and La Forge cobble up a subspace transporter and beam Picard over to Bok's ship. Once there, Picard puts an end to Bok's plans by telling his associates that there will be no profit in the venture.

PLOT OVERSIGHTS

• Vigo beams on board with his arms and one foot raised, as if he is climbing a rock face. Moments later, he turns around, assumes a similar stance and asks Picard to beam him back to the surface. He must have a lot of faith in his abilities or the skill of the transporter chief. He's climbing a *rock face*!

• In sick bay, Crusher performs a genetic scan and promptly announces that Jason Vigo's DNA is a combination of his father and mother's, Jean-Luc Picard and Miranda Vigo, respectively. One question: Where did Crusher get a sample of Miranda Vigo's DNA? Miranda wasn't in Starfleet.

• Back on the bridge, La Forge tells Picard, "We've managed to shut down the probe's power systems so we can beam it aboard." Note: La Forge says, "...so we can beam it aboard." *Future* tense. They haven't beamed it aboard yet! Come back with me to the beginning of the episode. The probe appears and sends its message. ("Testing, testing, one, two, three. Is this thing on?") Picard tells Worf to put a tractor beam on the probe. Picard goes to his ready room. An exterior shot of the ship shows no tractor beam from the *Enterprise*. The *Enterprise* flies to Jason's home planet—probably at warp. If the probe isn't on board yet, the *Enterprise* towed the probe at warp! This contradicts technical information supplied in "Samaritan Snare." Once the *Enterprise* arrives at the planet, another exterior shot again shows no tractor beam. Following this shot, La Forge speaks of bringing the probe aboard. (This could have been an equipment oddity or even a continuity problem, but I put it here because I think the tense is wrong on La Forge's statement.)

• Riker needs to brush up on his math. Shortly after Bok beams Vigo off the *Enterprise*, Data locates the Ferengi vessel at a distance of 300 billion kilometers. Riker says it will take 20 minutes to get there at warp 9. Even a rough estimate without using a calculator will show that Riker is off by a wide margin. Light travels at about 300,000 kilometers a second. The distance Data describes is 1 million times that. So…it would take 1 million seconds to get there at the speed of light. At warp 9, the *Enterprise* travels at approximately 1,500 times the speed of light. One hundred divided by 15 is about 6.6. Add four zeros to take 100 to 1 million, and 6.6 becomes 660 seconds. It would take about 660 seconds, or 11 minutes, to get there. (By the way, at maximum warp—9.6—it

would take the *Enterprise* just under 9 minutes to reach Bok's ship. Did it really take Data and La Forge only 9 minutes to cobble up the subspace transporter? And if it took longer, why didn't the *Enterprise* just fly over to Bok's ship instead of using this dangerous technology?)

• Consider Bok's plan. Somehow he must locate an individual with a unique set of characteristics. Bok must find a young person whose mother had an affair with Picard. (I suppose he could attempt to look this up in the *Intergalactic Registry of Sexual Liaisons*.) This same mother had to have another affair in close proximity to the one she had with Picard. (A Starfleet groupie, perhaps?) She had to keep the father's name secret from the child. She also would need to be dead or unavailable, since Picard would certainly try to communicate with her. Once Bok located this young person, he would need a sample of Picard's DNA as well as one of the mother's DNA. He would then synthetically combine the two, staying as close as he could to the young person's current appearance, since the young person probably would notice if he or she suddenly changed sexes or started growing a larger nose. (Remember: The old standby in *Star Trek* genetics is "Switch the DNA and your physical appearance immediately changes." See "Unnatural Selection," "Rascals," "Genesis.") Using this new combination of DNA, Bok would then "resequence" the young person's DNA when the young person wasn't looking and skulk back into the night, leaving the young person completely unaware that anything had happened. I'll let you decide on the feasibility of this plan.

EQUIPMENT ODDITIES

• For some strange reason Bok's probes bear a striking resemblance to the escape pod used by Roga Danar in "The Hunted."

• The show opens with a probe attempting to beam a holographic message onto the bridge of the *Enterprise*. Graphics show the probe transmitting, but initially the ship's shields block reception. Then Picard tells Data to let the message through. Surprisingly, the message starts at the beginning. What was all that stuff that bounced off the shields? Bok banging on the microphone while saying, "Testing, testing, one, two, three. Is this on?"

• Arriving at Vigo's home planet, Data gets the sensors on line, scans for human life signs, and quickly locates eight people, including Vigo, who are 2 kilometers beneath the surface. Someone must have upgraded the sensors after "Attached." In that episode, the crew of the *Enterprise* twiddled their thumbs as Picard and Crusher ran for their lives on the surface of Kesprit III—unable or unwilling to locate the pair with sensors.

• I guess someone upgraded the transporter systems as well. In "Legacy," the transporter could only beam through about 400 meters of solid granite. But in this episode, a transporter plucks Vigo from 2 kilometers (2,000 meters) beneath the surface.

(Granted, he is in a series of caves, so it isn't solid rock, but still....)

• Bok must have a mute button on his subspace transporter. He beams into Picard's quarters in complete silence. He beams out the same way. Then he beams into Picard's ready room in complete silence. But when he beams out, the transporter puts out the familiar Ferengi light and sound show. Why didn't it before? Picard had turned off the lights in his quarters. Even if the background music masked the sound, the sparkly stuff should have reflected off Picard's face. (The nonnitpicking explanation is that the creators didn't want us to know Bok was using a transporter, so they didn't show the effect to prolong the suspense.)

• Near the end of the episode, Bok threatens Vigo with a knife while Picard trains a phaser on the pair. Unless I miss my guess, this is a fairly meaningless threat. Either Bok thinks that he's faster than a phaser, or he thinks that most Starfleet officers are lousy shots!

CONTINUITY AND PRODUCTION PROBLEMS

• Bok seems to have changed a bit since his last appearance, in "The Battle." (Actually, the actor who plays Bok in this episode also starred as a Ferengi in another *NextGen* episode, but I can't remember which one.)

TRIVIA ANSWERS

1. Lieutenant Sandra Rhodes.
2. On deck 9, section 4.

EMERGENCE

Star Date: 47869.2

As Data treats Picard to a scene from *The Tempest* on the holodeck, the *Orient Express*—part of a completely different program—almost runs them down. Then the *Enterprise* unexpectedly jumps to warp to avoid a normally undetectable theta flux distortion. An investigation finds "nodes" scattered throughout the ship. Uncertain of their origin, Data speculates that a recent magnascopic storm may have influenced the ship in unusual ways.

The nodes continue to spread and seize control of vital operations of the ship. The crew soon concludes that an emergent intelligence is growing within the ship. After making several attempts to control its development, Picard decides to let it run its course. In Cargo Bay 5, a much larger version of the nodes begins to form—augmented by an infusion of vertion particles from Tambor Beta-6, a nearby white dwarf star. Unfortunately, the vertion supply runs out before the node in Cargo Bay 5 reaches completion. In response, the *Enterprise* begins a trip at top speed to a new natural vertion source, allocating all available energy, including the portion normally reserved for life support. La Forge quickly finds another potential source in the MacPherson nebula and generates them with a modified photon torpedo. The node grows and soon departs. As it does, all the other nodes disappear, returning the ship to normal.

Trivia Questions

1. What communication system is used by the taxicab on the holodeck?

2. What possible artificial vertion source does La Forge reject?

PLOT OVERSIGHTS

• I realize I may not measure up to the brave and valiant behavioral standards exhibited by the typical Starfleet officer, but when Data determines that the holodeck has independently reactivated itself and is running a collage of programs, I don't think I would have waltzed right in. How many other shows have featured a dangerous holodeck malfunction? Data's report on the status of the holodeck has all the earmarks of another disaster in the making, but our heroes seem to have more faith in their own immortality.

• Worf obviously hasn't worked on many jigsaw puzzles. At the start of the second trip into the holodeck, Worf asks a couple if they have finished the puzzle. A subsequent shot shows

Worf's view, and we see several large open sections that haven't been filled in yet. Offhand, I'd say the answer to Worf's question is "no."

• I realize I may not measure up to the brave and valiant behavioral standards exhibited by the typical Starfleet officer, but I think I would have worn a bulletproof vest and hard hat onto the holodeck once Data discovers that the mortality fail-safe no longer functioned. Instead, our heroes just keep going back in wearing their flimsy little costumes.

• La Forge keeps the great "don't give Picard a straight answer" tradition alive in this episode. Picard sends the chief engineer down to Cargo Bay 5 to investigate. La Forge walks in, sees the large node on the floor, and pages Picard. When the captain asks "What's going on?" La Forge responds that he wishes he could tell him. Why not just describe what you see, Chief Engineer La Forge?

EQUIPMENT ODDITIES

• Why does the ship lurch when it jumps to warp at the beginning of the episode? Does the computer not know how to work the clutch on the warp drive?

• Let me get this straight. There's this thing out there called a theta flux distortion. It can build up and cause a starship to explode, but La Forge says the sensors are not designed to detect it. Why not? I think this would be a good thing to detect. ("Starfleet Headquarters resource management report, star date 47869.2: Three more ships exploded for no apparent reason in the past two months. All signs point to theta flux distortions, but the designers at Utopia Planitia assure this office that there is no need for a fleetwide sensor recalibration.")

• Data and La Forge discover the first node in a Jefferies tube access panel. La Forge tries to probe it with some type of engineering doodad, but the node puts up a force field. Interestingly enough, La Forge's probe rests near the node, but the twinkle shimmer erupts several inches to the left.

• Just before entering the holodeck with Riker and Worf, Data states that a holodeck program is already running. Yet when the trio walks through the doors, you can see the arch. Shouldn't the arch be invisible if the program is already running?

• At one point, a panel short-circuits in Main Engineering, throwing La Forge to the floor. As another officer helps him to his feet, La Forge reaches up and slaps his badge but says nothing. (They're playing with our minds.)

• Celebrating the emergence of a new life form, Troi, Data, and Worf enjoy champagne on the holodeck with the other characters. Then the holodeck program aborts, but the trio still hold their drinks. Did they bring them onto the holodeck from outside? Shouldn't the drinks evaporate as everything else does?

CONTINUITY AND PRODUCTION PROBLEMS

• During the scene from *The Tempest,* Picard complains of the lack of light. Data orders the computer to increase by 20 percent the light from the torches littered throughout the set. Picard says that's much better, and *then* the torch flares up! (I suspect that the light in the scene was coming from more than just the torches.)

• The holodeck recreation of Keystone City has some interesting shadows. When the gangster ascends the subway staircase, sunlight shines on his hat. Moments later, when Troi, Data, and Worf ascend the same staircase, a shadow covers the entire area. Also when Troi, Data, and Worf ascend the stairwell, the shadows originate from the position of the camera. The trio walks toward the camera. The scene flips to a reverse angle, and the trio walks away from the camera. Oddly enough, the shadows *still* originate from the position of the camera, even though it's pointed in the opposite direction! Also, as Data works in the center of the street, long building shadows wash across the street. But when a taxicab tries to run Data down and then rounds the corner, the shadow on the vehicle clearly puts the sun overhead.

• Near the end of the episode, the *Enterprise* flies at warp 9 to a new vertion source. As La Forge discusses possible new artificial vertion sources with Picard and Riker, the stars in the ceiling bubble on the bridge remain stationary.

TRIVIA ANSWERS

1. Sunshine Radio System.
2. Dikon-Alpha, a class 9 pulsar.

PREEMPTIVE STRIKE

Star Dates: 47941.7—47943.2

As the episode begins, Ro rejoins the ship, back from advanced tactical training and a recent promotion to lieutenant. Shortly afterward, Admiral Nechayev comes on board to brief Picard on the latest information concerning the Federation colonists who remained behind when the new peace treaty with the Cardassians went into effect. It placed their worlds either in Cardassian space or the newly formed demilitarized zone. In response to Cardassian incursions, many colonists have formed into resistance groups organized under the banner of the "Maquis." At first the Maquis confined their actions to self-defense, but they have started to take a more aggressive role. Nechayev wants Ro to infiltrate the Maquis and gain more intelligence on the organization.

At first, all goes well. A Maquis cell accepts Ro, and the cell's leader even develops a special friendship with her. Using the information Ro gathers, Picard concocts a plan to lure a massive Maquis strike against an Yridian convoy. Ro baits her cell, and the leader of the cell contacts other Maquis cells to join the effort. Then a trio of Cardassians attacks the colony and murders many in cold blood, including the leader of the cell. Ro rethinks her position, warns the Maquis that the Yridian convoy is a trap, and leaves Starfleet to join their cause.

GREAT MOMENTS

This episode has some unfortunately brief but truly great battle scenes between a Cardassian warship and several Maquis vessels.

PLOT OVERSIGHTS

• Why does Ro wear her Bajoran earring on the left ear? (Everyone else wears theirs on the right.)

• Trying to scrounge up a contact with the Maquis, Ro goes to a bar followed by Data and Worf, who claim they are looking for her. A member of the Maquis pipes up and says she was present a few minutes ago but left. Data and Worf then depart. I would imagine that the owner of the establishment is ready to throttle the Maquis member. Moments before the guy speaks up, Worf says, "If we learn she has been here, this establishment will be closed down." Hearing this, the member of the Marquis admits that Ro had been there! (A side note: Just where is this bar? In the DMZ? Does Starfleet really have jurisdiction here?)

• Getting cold feet about baiting a trap for the Maquis, Ro tells Picard that the colonists have decided against attacking the Yridian convoy. Picard rebuffs her by stating that every intelligence report he gets from Starfleet suggests that the Maquis are eager to strike more targets. Just what intelligence reports is he talking about? At the beginning of the episode, Nechayev said that Starfleet didn't have any reliable intelligence about any of the Maquis cells scattered throughout the DMZ.

CHANGED PREMISES

• I'm a bit confused concerning this whole business of the border between Federation and Cardassian space, the demilitarized zone and the colonists. The creators mentioned the new arrangements in "Journey's End." That episode explained that the Federation and Cardassia had finally settled on an exact border. The plan put some Cardassian colonies in Federation space and vice versa. Also, the agreement established a demilitarized zone (DMZ). In "Journey's End," Nechayev ordered Picard to evacuate Dorvan V, a Federation colony now in Cardassian space. This makes sense. It does no good to leave your people in someone else's territory—especially an aggressive someone else. Those people

will constantly create problems and drag you into new conflicts. The Federation council seemed to understand this in "Journey's End." At the conclusion of the episode, the colonists renounced their Federation citizenship to stay on Dorvan V. Picard made it very clear that whatever happened to them, the Federation would not come to their aid. That was the only way the Federation council would let them stay. Now, "Journey's End" specifically dealt with a colony in Cardassian space. But what about a colony in the DMZ? Doesn't it make sense to apply the same standards to those colonies? Doesn't it seem like the Federation council would make them the same deal? ("Either get out of the DMZ or renounce your Federation citizenship.") *Evidently not!* At several points in the dialogue, "Preemptive Strike" refers to the colonists as Federation citizens. If these guys are Federation citizens, then sooner or later the Maquis will drag the Federation into another war with Cardassia. Period.

EQUIPMENT ODDITIES

• When the trio of Cardassians attacks the colony, their weapons knock people down but don't kill them immediately. Why? Don't they have a disintegrate setting, like Federation phasers? And even if they don't, shouldn't one blast from a Cardassian weapon be lethal? (Of course, if it was lethal, the old man wouldn't have to run out to check on the wounded man, and then the old man wouldn't get killed, and *then* Ro wouldn't have the motivation to leave Starfleet.)

CONTINUITY AND PRODUCTION PROBLEMS

• For some reason, Ro gets a nose job during her time at advanced tactical training. In previous episodes, she had two extra-long ridges that extended up over her eyebrows.

• Why in the world do Picard and Ro pace back and forth in the observation lounge when she comes back for her first meeting after infiltrating the Maquis? Why don't they just sit and have a meeting, as the crew of the *Enterprise* has for the past seven years?

• In the bar, Picard tells Ro that the Yridian convoy will contain six ships. But just before the Maquis attack, Data's screen shows twelve ships in the convoy.

• Near the end of the episode, Picard sends Riker to pose as Ro's brother because the captain is worried about her commitment. Just prior to the Maquis attack, Ro pulls a phaser on Riker and alerts the rest of the Maquis ships to the trap. She then beams aboard another ship and allows Riker to fly himself home. The next scene shows Riker in Picard's ready room concluding a verbal debriefing. He still looks like a Bajoran. At first I thought Riker had gone directly to the ready room after returning to the *Enterprise*. It would make sense for him to explain to Picard immediately what had happened with the raid. It also would explain why he still wore the Bajoran nose and clothes. But at the end of the meeting, Riker hands Picard a padd containing his written report. So...Riker didn't go directly to the ready room? He had time to write a report? Then why didn't he change out of his costume and get Beverly to take the belt sander to his nose?

TRIVIA ANSWERS
1. Cargo Bay 7.
2. Alpha-7.

ALL GOOD THINGS

Star Dates: 47988, 41153.7, (future Star Date unknown), 47988

When a distraught Picard tells the crew that he is shifting through time, Crusher examines him in sick bay and discovers that he is telling the truth. Suddenly Picard jumps forward approximately twenty-five years and finds himself tending a vineyard. In this timeline, he has Irumodic syndrome—a degenerative neurological disease. Jumping backward in time, Picard takes command of the *Enterprise*, duplicating the events that occurred seven years ago.

In both the past and present timelines, Starfleet dispatches the *Enterprise* to the Romulan Neutral Zone. Some sort of anomaly has appeared in the Devron system, and the Romulans are massing starships to investigate. In the future timeline, Picard determines that he must go to the Devron system as well and calls in a favor from Captain Beverly Picard—former wife of Picard and now the captain of the USS *Pasteur*. Although the Neutral Zone no longer exists in the future, Picard obtains permission to enter the now Klingon territory from Governor Worf.

Trivia Questions

1. Under what security lockout does Picard record his captain's log in the past time frame?

2. What starbase is nearest to the Devron system?

Along the way, Picard learns part of the reason for his time shifting. Q brings him to the postatomic horrors courtroom featured in "Encounter at Farpoint" and states that the Q Continuum has finally reached a verdict. They have decided to end humanity's existence, but it will be Picard who actually destroys the race.

In all three timelines, the ships converge on the Devron system. With no anomaly showing in the future, Data suggests using an inverse tachyon pulse to detect it and modifies the deflector dish of the *Pasteur* to accomplish this. When Picard shifts to the other time frames, he suggests that Data do the same there as well. Unknown to the captain at the time, these three converging beams actually create a rift between time and antitime—a construct similar to the relationship between matter and antimatter. Unsealed, the rift will grow backward in time until it disrupts the formation of life on the Earth, thereby erasing humanity from the galaxy. With Q's assistance, Picard eventually discovers this relationship.

In the future timeline, the *Pasteur* is attacked by Klingon warships and subsequently rescued by Riker's *Enterprise*, but not before the *Pasteur's* warp core explodes. Even as Riker's *Enterprise* heads back to Federation territory, Picard convinces the crew to return to the Devron system and assist the other two *Enterprises* in closing the rift. At the cost of all three ships, the crews manage to seal the boundary between time and antitime and save humanity.

Back in the postatomic horrors courtroom, Q congratulates Picard on showing promise before returning him to his present-day *Enterprise*.

RUMINATIONS

*G*reat and fabulous, knee-slapping, rising to our feet, clapping kudos to the creators for the battle scene between the future Enterprise *and the two Klingon warships. It was so wonderful to see the ship finally attack from outside the flight plane of the target vessels. (I really liked that phaser/photon "weapon o' mass destruction" cannon, too!)*

I wonder if Picard actually put this experience in a captain's log that was subsequently forwarded to Starfleet Command. I realize that he told the senior staff, but what about his superiors? Remember that Picard is the only one who has any memories of these events. I can just imagine what the high-muck-a-muck admiral back at Headquarters would say when she read this report. "Okay, let me get this straight. Captain Picard expects us to believe that he saved the entire human race, but none of us can recall anything about the incident. I suppose the next thing you're going to tell me is that he wants a medal for it!"

GREAT LINES

"What?!"—Worf to Troi after seeing her frustration with his minimalist description of a particularly lovely holodeck program as "very stimulating."

PLOT OVERSIGHTS

• At the very beginning of the episode, Picard trots down a hallway, barefoot and in his bathrobe, to interrupt a kiss between Worf and Troi and ask the date. Why doesn't Picard ask the computer while still in his quarters?

• In the future timeline, Picard and La Forge meet with Data at Cambridge University. Attempting to add some distinction to his appearance, Data has colored a broad streak of his hair gray. His housekeeper asks Picard and La Forge to convince him to change it back because he looks like a skunk. Nitpicker Allie Brightwell, who lives in England, informs me—given the lack of skunks in England—that it would be more believable for the housekeeper to say that Data looks like a badger. (Of course, maybe by the twenty-fourth century, skunks have overrun the British Isles.)

• Picard continually battles the perception in the future timeline that he's losing his mind. Yet, in the present timeline, Crusher found positive proof of his travels in time by performing two neural scans. Why not have Crusher do the same thing in the future and lay the issue to rest?

• Does anyone else think that the crew of the past timeline shows an *extraordinary* amount of faith in the very oddly behaving captain?

• What happened to the Romulans? In the present timeline, Tomalak agrees that one ship from either side of the Neutral Zone can investigate the temporal anomaly in the Devron system. That's the last we hear or see of the Romulans.

• In the future timeline, Klingon warships attack the *Pasteur*. Specifically, they attack the *Pasteur* before decloaking. The first blast hits the medical ship, and then Worf reports the warships' appearance. If the warships can fire while cloaking, why decloak?

• This episode contains one of the loveliest plot oversights of the entire series. The creators postulated a thing called "antitime" and based the entire plot on this device, only to find it necessary to violate this basic premise to make the show work. (It is a thing of beauty to a nitpicker!) According to the dialogue, Q received a directive from the Continuum to destroy humanity. To accomplish this goal, he sends Picard skipping back and forth through time. Eventually Picard has the *Pasteur* and two versions of the *Enterprise* beam an inverse tachyon beam at the same point in space. This causes a rupture in the subspace barrier between time and antitime. The rupture grows backward in time, getting larger and larger until it disrupts the formation of life on Earth, thereby destroying the human race. Lest you doubt my interpretation of the events, listen to La Forge in Ten-Forward after Data comes to the conclusion that Picard is telling the truth: "...because antitime operates opposite the way normal time does, the effect would travel backward through the space-time continuum." This was a very clever way for the Continuum to destroy humanity.

Yet, when the *Pasteur* originally arrives at the Devron system, they see no rupture. This lack of temporal anomaly motivates Picard to send the inverse tachyon beam in the first place. Then the crew leaves Riker's *Enterprise*, only to return to find the beginnings of the rupture. *Wait a minute:* That's completely backward! If the rupture grows *backward* in time, Picard and the others should see it when they arrive on the *Pasteur*. But they *shouldn't* see it when they return on the futuristic *Enterprise*. Let's say that Picard created the anomaly at time index "T." You should see the anomaly at any time *prior* to "T," since it grows backward. The temporal anomaly should have been present when the *Pasteur* arrived and then winked out when Picard began the inverse tachyon scan. (Actually, it probably should have winked out when the Klingons attacked, thereby terminating the scan.) When Riker's *Enterprise* returns to the Devron system, the time index is something like "T+2 hours." Therefore they shouldn't see anything. (Of course, if they couldn't see it, they couldn't assist with the sealing of the rupture, and the entire ending for the episode falls apart! I suppose we could say that Q arranged to have the anomaly cloaked when the *Pasteur* arrived and then covertly kicked Riker's *Enterprise* back in time as it returned to the Devron system so it would appear when they arrived. I *suppose* we could say that, but it sure sounds like a strained explanation to me!)

CHANGED PREMISES

• There are lots of little discrepancies in the re-creation of the *Enterprise* of seven years hence. The observation lounge didn't have viewscreens in the first season. Also, the observation lounge viewscreen normally stayed off earlier in the series until someone needed to illustrate a point. In the re-creation of the past, the viewscreens stay on. In the first season, Picard's chair on the bridge had flip-up panels. The chairs for conn and Ops are different. What eventually becomes La Forge's workstation facing the warp core started out as a flat, white area without any controls. In addition, the large master display on the wall in Engineering was originally colored in yellow, not blue, as it was at the end of the series. Lieutenant Torres, not O'Brien, manned the conn as the *Enterprise* traveled to Farpoint prior to the meeting with Q (of course, Picard could have made this change).

• Data first appears in the past timeline with the rank pips of a lieutenant, junior grade (one solid, one hollow). Yet Picard calls him "Commander," and the first time we see him in "Encounter at Farpoint" he holds the rank of lieutenant commander.

• In the present time frame, Picard asks Troi what happened after he came aboard seven years ago. Troi responds that there was a reception in Ten-Forward. Yet, in the entire first season, we never saw Ten-Forward. Major remodeling, maybe?

EQUIPMENT ODDITIES

• In sick bay, Crusher determines that Picard has a defect in his brain that would show up only on a level 4 neurological scan. This scan was never performed before? Even after Picard's experience with the Borg?

• Obviously someone will rework the warp scale in the future. The *Tech Manual* adamantly proclaims that starships cannot go faster than warp 10, but both the *Pasteur* and the *Enterprise* go warp 13 in this episode.

• Can't the *Pasteur* eject its warp core? When a core breach occurs, Riker just beams them aboard the *Enterprise* and then lets the medical ship explode.

• After beaming aboard the *Enterprise* in the future timeline, Picard makes an impassioned plea for Riker's *Enterprise* to keep looking for the temporal anomaly. Out of nowhere, Crusher reaches up and hits Picard with a futuristic-looking hypospray that knocks him unconscious. Where did she get that? She just beamed off her ship with a warp core breach in progress. Does she carry a loaded hypo around in her pocket? (I am really, really suppressing the urge to make a few snide comments about this.)

• Of course, no one even mentions separating the saucer section before dispatching any of the *Enterprises* to almost certain destruction inside the temporal anomaly.

CONTINUITY AND PRODUCTION PROBLEMS

• Considering the location of the observation lounge and the way Earth Station McKinley wraps over the top of the *Enterprise*, shouldn't it show up in the lounge windows?

• When Picard speaks over subspace with Riker at Farpoint in the past timeline, the creators reused footage from "The Arsenal of Freedom" for Riker's end of the conversation. That's Captain Paul Rice in the background.

• This is a gem. In the future timeline, the door signage consists not only of the door plate but also wide vertical strips of color that define the leading edges of the doors. In the past timeline, after telling Picard about her prior relationship with Riker, Troi walks out of the ready room and it looks like the emergency turbolift doors on the other side of the bridge have the future timeline door signage!

• The final scene with Picard joining the senior officers' poker game for the first time really resonated with me. (I still tear up a little when Troi says, "You were always welcome." Sniff, sniff.) Of course, us nitpickers wouldn't feel really fulfilled unless we could find a nit in the final moments of the final episode of the series! (Okay, I admit this is grungy, needlessly excessive nitpicking, but hey…life's short, enjoy the ride.) As Picard deals the cards, an overhead crane shot begins to pull back and rotate. The footage then dissolves to a close-up exterior of the ship featuring the windows on the leading edge of the saucer section. The shot continues rotating for a few moments longer before dropping back and away from the *Enterprise* as it flies off into a nebula (read: "sunset"). Because the creators exactly matched the rotation of the camera between the interior shot of Riker's quarters on deck 8 and the close-up exterior shot of the saucer section windows—also located around deck 8—I assume that they intended to give the impression that the camera had floated through the hull of the *Enterprise* and out into space. If they did, the sequence has a nit in it! To join the poker game, Picard takes a seat directly across from the windows in Riker's quarters. When the scene dissolves to the close-up exterior shot, Picard should still be facing the windows. He isn't. He's facing directly away from the windows. To my way of thinking, the creators should have pointed the *Enterprise* in the other direction—going right to left on the screen instead of left to right. (But then, they never asked me and really don't have any need to do so!)

TRIVIA ANSWERS
1. Omega 327.
2. Starbase 23.

SKIN FLICK TOTE BOARD

1. Number of times we see Picard buck naked: one
2. Number of times Riker treats the audience to a view of his hairy chest: two
3. Number of times Data's gender-identity program malfunctions, resulting in a drag striptease performance on a table in Ten-Forward: none
4. Number of times Data cross-dresses: one
5. Number of times Troi treats the audience to a view of her in a nightgown: six
6. Number of times Crusher gets the "panting hots": three
7. Number of times La Forge lies face up on a slab in sick bay with only a tiny square of cloth to cover him: one
8. Number of times Worf lies face down on a slab in sick bay stripped to the waist: one
9. Number of times we see Starfleet officers manacled: six
10. Number of times the directors choose a full body or cleavage camera pan when shooting Troi: too many to count

REFERENCES

1. Gul Madred slices off Picard's clothing in "Chain of Command, Part 2."

2. Riker meets with Mistress Beata in an open-chested tunic in "Angel One" and he comes in from bat'leth practice with Worf with his shirt open in "The Pegasus."

3. (Thankfully.)

4. As the floozy in "A Fistful of Datas." (Okay, okay. I know it wasn't *really* Data.)

5. After the energy ball impregnates her in "The Child." While enjoying Devinoni Ral's company in "The Price." (Some might count two seperate incidents here.) When the Paxans take control of her in "Clues." While preparing for bed in "Violations." After bedding the young stud in "Man of the People." After bedding Worf in "Eye of the Beholder."

6. For Picard in "The Naked Now." For Odan in "The Host." For Ronin in "Sub Rosa."

7. After he dies in "Parallels."

8. During his operation in "Ethics."

9. Crusher in "The High Ground," Picard in "The High Ground," Picard in "Chain of Command, Part 1," Picard in "Chain of Command, Part 2," Sito in "Lower Decks," and Worf in *Star Trek: Generations*.

10. Actually, I wish I had paid a little closer attention to this—not because it's Troi but because it's fascinating to compare how directors shoot Marina Sirtis (and other female actors) and how they shoot the male actors. I must confess I never really noticed this until nitpicker Allie Brightwell of Hampshire, England pointed out the trip across Troi's cleavage in "Data's Day". By then it was too late to go back and watch all the episodes again. Once I started looking, the contrast in directorial approach had other obvious examples. Two immediately come to mind. In "Timescape," Picard, Troi and Data descend a ladder. The shot begins on Picard's head and shoulders and follows him down. When Data comes down the ladder the director uses a similar technique. However, with Troi, the director starts with her feet and lets Troi descend in one continual shot—a trip that gives us first her feet, then her knees, then her hips, then her stomach, then her chest. In "Masks," just after the formation of Masaka's temple, Picard has several lines of dialogue. While the captain talks, the camera pulls back a bit and drops down to ensure that we have a nice view of Troi's posterior. Then—as the captain continues speaking—Troi wanders up the stairs and the camera stays on her! It's true, she does eventually have a line of dialogue but the entire time she's walking up the stairs, Picard is droning on in the background with nary a chance for us to read his facial expressions, because the director has found something more interesting to watch.

THE MOVIE

STAR TREK GENERATIONS

Star Dates: 48632.4—48650.1

During the christening voyage of the *Enterprise*-B, Captain John Harriman and crew rescue a group of El-Aurians—including Dr. Tolian Soran and Guinan—from a transport vessel trapped in an undulating energy ribbon. Unfortunately, James T. Kirk—aboard as part of the festivities along with Montgomery Scott and Pavel Chekov—is lost when a tendril of the ribbon lashes out and blows a hole in the hull of the *Enterprise*-B.

Seventy-eight years later, Soran fires a stellar probe into a star near the Amargosa Observatory. The probe causes a quantum implosion that halts all nuclear fusion within the star. As it collapses, Soran takes flight on a Klingon Bird-of-Prey commanded by Lursa and B'Etor.

After discussing the matter with Guinan and working in the stellar cartography lab with Data, Picard determines that Soran has calculated the periodic return of the energy ribbon and plans to alter its course to intersect the planet Veridian III. In reality, the energy ribbon is a doorway to a place that Guinan calls the Nexus, a

Trivia Questions

1. What is the vintage of the champagne that christens the *Enterprise*?

2. What is the shield modulation frequency for the *Enterprise*?

place of utter joy where time has no meaning. By bringing the energy ribbon to Veridian III, Soran intends to enter the Nexus again—having entered once already, only to be ripped back to our space-time continuum by the transporters of the *Enterprise*-B.

On the surface of Veridian III, Picard attempts to reason with Soran as Lursa and B'Etor's Bird-of-Prey engages the *Enterprise*. The *Enterprise* wins the battle, but not before sustaining enough damage to cause a warp core breach. Just as saucer separation completes, the star drive section explodes, shoving the saucer section into the atmosphere of Veridian III, where it crash-lands on the surface.

Near the same time, Soran launches another probe, this time destroying the Veridian star. The energy ribbon sweeps past Soran's location, tossing him and Picard into the Nexus. Picard finds himself in a well-adorned home as the father of four beautiful children and husband of a lovely wife. At first, the setting enthralls him, but then he realizes it cannot be real. An echo of Guinan appears and explains that he can leave the Nexus at any time and place. Picard chooses to go back to Veridian III to stop Soran and asks Guinan to come with him. She explains that she cannot but knows someone who can, James T. Kirk. He has lived in the Nexus since the energy ribbon tore into the *Enterprise*-B seventy-eight years ago. The two captains stop Soran, but not before Kirk sustains a fatal injury. After burying the legendary captain, Picard boards a shuttle that takes him back to the unsalvageable remains of the *Enterprise*-D.

RUMINATIONS

*T*his movie represented somewhat of a challenge for me. As a nitpicker, I'm used to having a remote control with review, fast forward, pause, and frame advance buttons. However, at the time of this writing, the movie was not available on videotape. So I had to confine myself to nits I could find by simply watching the movie over and over! Of course, I also had a considerable amount of help from my friends in the Nitpicker's Guild. When this book hits the bookstore shelves, Star Trek Generations no doubt will be available on videotape, and some of the questions I raise may be answered if the creators add in footage shot but not shown for the theater release version of the movie.

Concerning the movie itself, I really enjoyed it even after multiple viewings. Given that this is the first time around the block for most of the individuals who worked on this project to make a movie—as opposed to putting out a television series—I think

they did a fabulous job. And I am looking forward to many more movies to come for the crew of the starship Enterprise. (Did I hear someone say that we will need to do updates to the Nitpicker's Guides?)

There are several items that I feel deserve praise before the nitpicking starts. The opening sequence with the bottle rotating through space was a very nice idea. The graphics throughout the movie were spectacular, especially the crash-landing sequence with the saucer section and the shock wave destroying Veridian III. Of course, Brent Spiner shines in this movie, in a role that is a definite departure for him. When I first heard that the movie would feature Data equipped with Dr. Soong's emotion chip I wondered if the android would simply look goofy. Much to my relief, Brent Spiner pulled it off, and did it well. (But then, maybe the creators knew that he would. After all, there is the scene at the conclusion of "Déjà Q" when Q leaves Data with the gift of laughter.)

There were a few items that I thought were nits but really needed a pause button to confirm. I thought I would alert you to them. Take a look for me. (By now you probably own or can rent a copy of the movie.) Nitpicker Brian Lombard of Gaithersburg, MD, believes you can see La Forge's pupils through his VISOR as Data pulls the emotion chip from its shrine. Jennifer McClain of Springfield, MO, thinks she saw a camera lens in an Engineering display as La Forge returns after his capture by Soran. Steve Emirzian of Hartford, CT, wrote to say that he saw

Worf lose his sash during the crash scene, only to have it magically reappear an instant later. And here's a couple from yours, truly: Punched by Kirk, Soran slides down a rock face with rope in hand. The rope stops his descent, slamming him against an outcropping. Then the knot supporting Soran lets loose. To me it looks like the end of the rope flips off the metal crossbar just before the camera cuts to Soran. Then the camera cuts back and the knot catches on the girder—the same knot that just let loose! Or how about this one? When Soran blows up the metal bridge that supports Kirk, there's a little box thing that bounces away from the legendary captain on his side of the bridge. It looks like it gets stuck in an upright support. Is this the control pad that Kirk wants to fetch? If it is, he didn't need to go to the other side of the bridge, because the pad is already on his side!

GREAT LINES

"Sorry."—Riker to Worf after "mistakenly" asking the computer to remove the plank—on which the Klingon stood above freezing holodeck-created ocean waters—instead of retracting it.

PLOT OVERSIGHTS

• Was there a shortage of command level personnel during the selection process for the captaincy of the *Enterprise*-B? Where did Starfleet dredge up this Harriman guy? He seems completely flustered by the crisis with the El-Aurian transport ships. Even if this is his first time to sit in the big chair,

we have seen over and over during the *Star Trek* saga that many opportunities to command afford themselves to a first officer and even a second officer. Is Harriman's ability to command getting delivered on Tuesday as well? (In case you haven't seen the movie, Harriman keeps telling Kirk that all the good stuff—tractor beam, medical staff, photon torpedoes—will be installed on Tuesday.)

• Once again the creators would have us believe that Starfleet leaves Earth—the headquarters for the Federation—devoid of starship resources. The transports that carry the El-Aurians are only three light-years from the solar system and the *Enterprise*-B is the *only ship in range*.

• Later in the movie, we discover that Crusher has a complete bio on Soran, including the fact that the Borg destroyed the home world of the El-Aurians and that he and other El-Aurians escaped in transports that eventually headed for Earth. In other words, decades prior to the encounter between the *Enterprise*-D and the Borg in "Q Who," the Federation had contact with a race of people who had experienced an onslaught from the Borg. These El-Aurians must be really tight-lipped. Evidently none of the forty-seven people the *Enterprise* "rescued" from the energy ribbon bothered to tell anyone about the destruction of their home planet because Picard acts like he has never heard of the Borg when discussing them with Guinan in "Q Who." (Presumably the biographies of the El-Aurians were updated after "Q Who" to include the information that Guinan so graciously deemed us worthy to receive once we were staring down the cutting beam of a Borg ship!)

• After Scotty suggests rigging the main deflector dish for a resonance burst, Kirk takes off for deck 15 of the Engineering hull and soon reroutes the appropriate controls. Harriman must be really, really understaffed. Moments earlier, helmsman Demora Sulu received a call from Main Engineering. Why not order one of the guys down there to reroute the controls? Aren't they a lot closer to the deflector relays than Kirk, who is all the way up on the main bridge? And wouldn't they be much more familiar with the ship and do the work more efficiently? (Of course, this begs the question: How did Kirk know how to reroute the controls in the first place? He's retired, and this is a brand-new ship. I realize Kirk is supposed to be a Renaissance man, but wouldn't he constantly have to pore over all the technical updates from Starfleet to be this familiar with a new ship?)

• I realize that the news of Robert and René's death is tragic, but isn't Picard's reaction just a little over the top? Think of what this guy has been through. Remember what the Borg did to him? Right after that incident, we see him behind his desk, working. Is it really believable that in the middle of a crisis he would bolt from the bridge and tell Riker to take over?

• The crew of the *Enterprise* continues their tradition of depriving their commanding officers of instant access to information. When a nondescript member of the first away mission to the Amargosa Observatory finds a

dead Romulan, instead of saying something worthwhile such as "Commander, there's a dead Romulan up here," he says, "Commander, you'd better take a look at this."

• My appreciation for Guinan's observational skills dropped a few notches during this movie. Just after being rescued by the first away team to the Amargosa Observatory, Soran waits in Ten-Forward for Picard. He and the captain have an entire conversation, yet Guinan—with all her sensitivities—never notices until Soran sees her and hurries out.

• Having discovered that the Romulan attackers of the observatory were looking for trilithium, Riker tells Worf to send Data and La Forge over on the next away mission. So…why didn't they go over on the *first* away mission? (Because it wasn't in the script, and if they did, La Forge would not have had time to install Data's emotion chip.)

• Shortly after Data and La Forge find a secret lab on the observatory, Soran punches Geordi and frightens Data into submission. He then proceeds to destroy the nearest star. Didn't Data and La Forge come over with an away team? What happened to the other guys? Did Soran incapacitate them as well?

• Granted, hindsight is always 20/20, but this really wasn't the best time to be doodling around with Data's neural net, now, was it? The observatory had just been attacked by Romulans, and an investigation *was* in progress.

• Grieving over the death of his brother and nephew, Picard says that there will be no more Picards to carry on the family line. Why? Is he sterile? Did the Borg really do more to Picard than the creators have told us? See review for "Q Who" and "The Best of Both Worlds" in the Guild Submissions (Reader Mail) section of this tome.

• I had a number of conversations with Mitzi Adams, Nitpicker Central's resident solar physicist, on the issue of what a quantum inhibitor would do to a star. Of course, it completely strains credulity that some dinky little probe could turn off a star. Stars are ancient things. And big! (I mean really big!) But, setting aside our disbelief for a moment, let's grant the creators the premise that Soran can somehow actually turn off all fusion and keep it turned off as the star contracts and reheats its core. As I understand it, there are still two major problems with the physics of what happens on the big screen.

First, both stars produce a massive shock wave. Mitzi tells me that the shock wave in the movie is most similar to a phenomenon known as a supernova. A star begins life fusing two hydrogen atoms into a helium atom. Then it starts on the helium and fuses it together into the next element and so on, until the star has a core composed of iron molecules. Once this happens, the star can no longer generate enough energy to sustain an outward pressure on the gases of the star, and gravity begins drawing the gases inward. The gases hit the iron core and rebound forcefully and rapidly outward, producing the supernova. If you could turn off a star that didn't have an iron

core, it would simply start contracting. No shock wave. So how do we know that the stars don't have an iron core? Well, iron cores only form in really big stars, and when they do, the star turns a reddish color.

The second problem relates to the first. Supposedly Soran destroys the stars to change the pull of gravity on the ribbon. However, gravity is directly related to mass. To change the gravitational attraction of an object you must change its mass. For instance, if our sun suddenly became a black hole, the Earth would not instantly lurch out of orbit and jump across the event horizon because the mass of the sun would remain the same and, therefore, so would its gravitational pull. To weaken the gravitational pull of an object you *must remove mass*. Hence the need for the shock wave. I'm sure the creators viewed the expulsion of this mass as sufficient to account for the change in the ribbon's course. Now consider the Veridian star system. Soran launches the probe. Probe hits star. Star produces shock wave. Ribbon changes course. Ribbon intersects planet. Shock wave destroys planet. Problem: the gravitational pull of the Veridian star would not change until the matter expelled from the star made it to the other side of the ribbon. Let's say you are standing on Earth and our sun explodes. (Let's also say that you could survive this unfortunate occurrence. Wink, wink.) As the mass of the sun moves outward in an expanding sphere, you notice no change. The mass continues moving outward. No change. The sphere of the mass eventually pushes beyond the orbit of the Earth. Now there's change in gravity, because the sphere that intersects your position is smaller than the expanding sphere of matter. In terms of the movie, then, the shock wave might alter the pull of gravity from the star, but only after the shock wave had moved past the ribbon. Therefore, the sequence should go like this: Soran launches the probe. Probe hits star. Star produces shock wave. Shock wave destroys planet. Shock wave crosses ribbon's path. Ribbon changes course to intersect the former position of the planet but can't pick up Soran because he was shredded along with the rest of the planet moments before!

• This Soran guy is quite the genius. After all, he creates a probe that does essentially the same thing as the Tox Uthat as featured in "Captain's Holiday." But that device isn't invented by Kal Dano until the twenty-seventh century. Soran is three hundred years ahead of his time!

• One of the major plot problems with the movie comes from Soran's method of reentering the Nexus ("a place of joy, happiness, and manageable hair," as my wife says). Picard tries to dissuade Soran from launching the probe that will destroy the Veridian star because it will mean the death of 230 million on Veridian IV. Soran claims that this is the *only way* to reenter the Nexus. He must change the course of the energy ribbon so it will intersect with Veridian III. Earlier in the show, when Picard asks why Soran couldn't just fly a ship into the energy ribbon, Data replies that all ships encountering the ribbon have

been severely damaged or destroyed. Wait a minute: How did Soran get into the Nexus in the first place? He got there in a ship. How did Guinan get into the Nexus? She got there in a ship. How did Kirk get into the Nexus? He got there in a ship. Are you beginning to see a pattern? So what if the ships were damaged or destroyed? Soran simply wants to get back to the Nexus. (Then again, why doesn't somebody stick this guy in one of those thruster suits we saw in *Star Trek: The Motion Picture* and fly him into the ribbon?)

• After Lursa and B'Etor release La Forge, Crusher immediately takes him to sick bay. We join the scene as she briefs him on his condition. As part of this discussion she mentions that she has removed the "nanoprobe." What nanoprobe? There's no mention of a nanoprobe in the movie! (Note to all nitpickers: Before you write me, remember the Nitpicker's Prime Directive: "All nits picked shall derive from sources the creators consider canonical." Rough drafts of scripts are *not* canonical. They may explain some questions, but only the events we see on the screen actually happen.)

• As the saucer section of the *Enterprise* screams through the atmosphere on its way to a crash landing, Riker yells for everyone to brace for impact. As nitpicker David T. Moore asked me, "How does one brace for impact in chairs that roll around and have no restraints?"

• After realizing that the fantasy of the Nexus isn't real, Picard asks Guinan to come back with him to help him stop Soran. Guinan, actually an echo of Guinan, says she can't because she is already there. Well...not really. The Guinan that would be "already there" was blown into itty-bitty pieces when the shock wave hit Veridian III.

• These captains of starships need to get out more. Both Picard and Kirk appear in their favorite fantasies wearing Starfleet uniforms! (Well, actually...Starfleet uniforms and panty hose—in the horse riding scene, if William Shatner is to be believed.) Is this really what Picard would wear to open Christmas presents with his children? Is this really what Kirk would wear as he prepares breakfast for Antonia?

• Trying to assimilate the information that Picard gives him about the Nexus, Kirk wanders around his home, looking at various objects. At one point he opens the lid of a box and pulls out a little bag with a gold horseshoe inside. Unfortunately, he never tells us the significance of this item. (Note to nitpickers: Again I remind you of the Nitpicker's Prime Directive.)

• At one point, Kirk asks Picard to get some dill spice from a kitchen cabinet. He tells Picard it is on the second shelf to the left. Picard opens the cabinet, reaches to the *right,* and pulls out the dill.

• Picard's choice of when to return to our space-time continuum deserves a bit of scrutiny. He rejoins our time as he struggles to crawl through a small opening beneath Soran's force field. Personally, I think I would return a tad later. Or maybe several hours earlier and arrest Soran in Ten-Forward. Then again, why not come back a few

days earlier and save Robert and René from burning? Better yet, why not dispatch Kirk to the maiden voyage of the *Enterprise*-B and have him sit on his hands while Harriman fidgets around trying to figure out what to do? In no time, the energy ribbon would destroy the two transporter ships. Soran would be in the Nexus. Guinan would be in the Nexus. True, it would rewrite *NextGen* history, because Guinan would never have been on the show, but it is a better solution. The real problem here is *time.* Whenever you construct a story and give a character control over time, it is inevitable that a multitude of plot oversights will arise.

• Along the same line, there comes a time during Picard and Kirk's attempt to stop Soran when it appears likely that they will not succeed. Why not just stop? Let the probe fire. Let the Nexus grab them again. Get together, figure out a better plan, and take a second run at it.

• Of course, one could argue that Picard never really left the Nexus. Given that this Nexus can supply any fantasy desired, how would you know what was real?

• You have to hand it to Picard. Kirk dies, and the next scene shows Picard completing the legendary captain's burial under a pile of rocks on the highest point in Soran's setup. In other words, Picard dragged Kirk's body all the way to the top of the mountain? (Maybe he wanted a resting place with a nice view. Then again, maybe there are some relatives back on Earth who would want Kirk interned there? Or *maybe—*

since this is one of the greatest captains of all time—Starfleet would want to honor him?)

• Picard and Riker seem pretty calm at the end of the movie for having just lost their starship. And not a word of explanation from Riker? The pair rummage around and find Picard's photo album—tossing aside the extremely rare and prized Kurlan Naiskos in the process—before strolling off to the rescue ship. This is a bit like Dad loaning Son the car keys, Son turning the family vehicle into a pile of smoking, twisted metal, and Dad being okay about it all because Son managed to salvage Dad's favorite cassette tape!

• If the next movie features all seven of our favorite Starfleet *NextGen* officers, it will create a nit. Are we to believe that Starfleet would let them all take a sabbatical while the new ship gets built? Wouldn't the senior officer be reassigned to other postings? (Not that I want the crew split up, mind you. I like this team!)

CHANGED PREMISES

• Near the beginning of the movie, just after Kirk comes on board the *Enterprise*-B as a dignitary for its maiden voyage, a reporter asks the former captain how he feels considering this is the first *Enterprise* in thirty years without him in command. The reporter needs to check her facts. According to *Star Trek: The Motion Picture,* William Decker served as captain of the *Enterprise* prior to Kirk's commandeering her for the mission to V'Ger. And in *Star Trek: The Wrath of Khan,* Spock served as captain of the *Enterprise* until Kirk

assumed that position after receiving the call from Dr. Carol Marcus.

• There is no question that Scott believes Kirk is dead just before the movie jumps seventy-eight years into the future. An energy burst from the ribbon has taken out a chunk of the hull. Scott and Harriman stare out the hole into space. Chekov runs up and asks if anyone was in the room. Scott replies, "Aye." In addition, near the end of the movie, Picard tells Kirk that history records that Kirk died during the maiden voyage of the *Enterprise*-B. Why then does Scott react the way he does when the crew of the *Enterprise*-D rescues him from the transporter beam in the *NextGen* episode "Relics"? Look at the sequence of events. Kirk gets sucked into the Nexus. Everyone thinks he is dead. Sometime later, Scott retires and boards the *Jenolen* to travel to the Norpin Colony. The *Jenolen* crashes into a Dyson Sphere. Scott rigs the transporters to sustain him until help comes. Scott enters the transporter. Seventy-five years later, the *Enterprise*-D comes upon the Dyson Sphere. An away team to the *Jenolen* gets Scott out of the transporter. After hearing that they are from the *Enterprise*, Scott says that he should have known that Kirk would get the ship out of mothballs and come rescue him. According to this movie, in Scott's mind, Kirk is dead! (Now, the transporter *did* show less than a .003 percent degradation in Scott's pattern. I suppose we could say that the degradation wiped out Scott's memory of the event aboard the *Enterprise*-B!)

• In this movie, Soran uses an

experimental compound called trilithium to build a probe that can stop all nuclear fusion within a star. Riker reacts with surprise upon hearing the name of the compound. *"Tri*lithium," he says, accentuating the first syllable. No one seems to have heard of this compound before. Oddly enough, terrorists come on board the *Enterprise* to steal trilithium resin—a by-product of the warp drive—in "Starship Mine." Both Picard and the terrorists refer to it simply as "trilithium." (And it is spelled the same way, in case you are wondering.)

• After receiving a personal message on the holodeck, Picard's mood turns foul and he takes to hiding in his ready room and quarters. Eventually Troi seeks him out and finds the captain reminiscing over an album. Gently, the counselor probes Picard until he breaks down and tells her that his brother Robert and nephew René have died in a fire. Yet, the pictures that Picard views are of people completely different from those who appeared in "Family."

• Angry over the Romulan attack on the observatory, Soran punches B'Etor in the mouth as soon as he boards the Klingon Bird-of-Prey. Although *Star Trek VI: The Undiscovered Country* featured Klingons with purplish blood, B'Etor has red blood like the rest of us.

EQUIPMENT ODDITIES

• I wonder why Starfleet abandoned the *Enterprise*-B design for *Excelsior*-class vessels. In *NextGen*—supposedly set some seventy-five to eighty years later—*Excelsior*-class vessels do not have the angular outcroppings on either side of the belly of the star drive section, like the *Enterprise*-B. If the *Enterprise*-B is a later design of the USS *Excelsior*—as seen in *Star Trek III: The Search for Spock*—shouldn't all the *Excelsior*-class vessels seen in *NextGen* resemble the *Enterprise*-B more than the USS *Excelsior*?

• Starfleet designers often pick unusual places to locate vital equipment. In this movie, Kirk works with the main deflector dish relays and later identifies this place as the deflector control room. Just offhand, I would have guessed that this room would be located directly behind the main deflector dish, but it isn't. Instead the designers of the *Enterprise*-B put the room on the side of the actual dish up at the leading edge of the Engineering hull some distance from the main assembly for the deflector array. (We find this out when the energy ribbon blows a hole in the lip of the deflector dish and Kirk is sucked into the Nexus.)

• Did all the lights burn out on the *Enterprise*-D at the same time? I realize that the subdued lighting is supposed to set the mood for the film, but the change from the television show is a bit drastic.

• Near the end of the scene on the holodeck, Picard receives a call from the bridge. The arch appears on a raised portion of the deck in the center of the sailing ship. Doesn't the arch usually surround the holodeck exit? Moments later, when Picard leaves the holodeck, the doors do appear directly behind the arch. Yet members of the crew of the sailing ship stand *behind* the exit. How can they do this?

Even on the holodeck a person must occupy some physical location. When the doors open, we see the corridor of the *Enterprise*. By simple visual alignment, it's obvious that if members of the sailing ship's crew stand behind the exit doors of the holodeck they cannot be within the physical confines of the holodeck. The only explanation is that all the crew members of the sailing ship are holodeck constructs. The holodeck could project their images on the walls and make it appear that the individuals stand behind the doors. On careful inspection, it does appear that all the members of the senior staff are on Picard's side of the doors. However, even if the crew of the sailing ship is a holodeck construct, the placement of the arch and exit doors still makes no sense. When Picard walks off the holodeck, Troi stands next to the railing of the ship. The arch sits on a raised portion in the center of the deck. When the doors open we see that the floor of the hallway is level with the raised portion of the deck. In the past we have seen that the floor of the hallway is level with the floor of the holodeck. Therefore, since Troi stands at the railing of the ship with the raised portion of the deck adjacent to her, the counselor's feet are below the raised portion of the deck. It follows then that Troi's feet must be *below* the floor of the holodeck. And what about Crusher and Worf? When Picard exits, they are apparently still attempting to climb back on board. Obviously they must be below the floor of the holodeck as well.

• Just after Picard leaves the holodeck, the bridge calls down with a distress call from the Amargosa Observatory. Riker calls for red alert, and the bridge crew hurries to their posts. The action cuts to the main bridge, where everyone shows up in costume—lacking the time to change—even Worf, whose clothes are suddenly dry. Obviously, the holodeck water evaporated as soon as the Klingon slogged off the holodeck. So why didn't Wesley's clothes go instantly dry when he walked off the holodeck in "Encounter at Farpoint"?

• When the away team materializes at the Amargosa Observatory, only Crusher holds a tricorder. If the team is searching for survivors, wouldn't it be a good idea for *all* of them to have tricorders?

• After misinterpreting Crusher's comments on the holodeck and shoving her into the water, Data discusses the situation with La Forge before deciding to install Soong's emotion chip. He walks to a wall and opens a cabinet. The emotion chip hangs suspended—obviously by a thin thread as it swings back and forth—in a container. The creators have again transformed the chip. It started out as a small metal sphere in "Brother." Then Data displays the damaged emotion chip at the end of "Descent, Part II." In that episode, it is a small circle with a pie-shaped wedge removed. In this movie, the emotion chip has suddenly grown to an object approximately one inch square with cylinders embossed on its surface.

• On a related topic, when La Forge begins to install the chip, he takes off the top of Data's head and begins fiddling with an access port. In "Brothers," Soong installed the emotion chip in a side panel directly under Lore's right ear.

• During the scene in stellar cartography when Picard discovers Soran's plan, Data needs to reorient the little desk that sits in front of him. Supposedly the desk has some mechanism that causes it to move, but it's pretty obvious that Data is the one providing the locomotion.

• Discussing the effects of the destruction of the Amargosa Observatory's star, Data mentions that the *Bozeman* had to make a course correction. Evidently the ninety-year-old ship is still in service. (I mentioned this as well in "All Good Things.") As nitpicker Paul F. Kane wondered, "Is Morgan Bateson still the captain? Or is he doing a radio show out of Seattle?" (In "Cause and Effect," Kelsey Grammer—star of the television sitcom *Frasier*, featuring a radio talk show psychiatrist—played Bateson.)

• Continuing on with the scene, Data brings up a graphic of the Veridian system. Without any obvious command from Data, the graphic moves around on the wraparound screen, showing different viewpoints. Yes, it "looks cool." But if I were the user of that system, I would want to throttle the programmer. What's the point of having the graphic continue its movement, especially if the user is trying to look at a specific planet or trying to leave the room? Obviously Stewart and Spiner shot the scene against a blue screen, because if they tried to walk across that little plank between the platform and the door with the graph-

ics moving just as we see it on the film, both of them would tumble off due to vertigo. (Well...maybe Data could make it.)

• The probe that Soran launches from the surface of Veridian III appears to use a chemical propellant. Yet *somehow* it reaches the Veridian star in about eleven seconds. This is nothing short of amazing! (Actually, more like impossible.) It takes light eight minutes to get from the sun to Earth. So if Soran fired his probe with its chemical propellant at our sun from Earth and the probe could travel at the speed of light, it would take eight minutes for it to get there. More than that, you couldn't see an immediate change because it would take another eight minutes for the diminished light to make it back to Earth! Now, I realize that Veridian III might be closer to its star than Earth is to its sun, but it can't be only eleven light-seconds away, because it's an M-class planet. (Of course, I don't think anyone would want to sit in the theater for sixteen minutes while Picard and Soran hurled insults at each other and waited for the probe to do its thing.)

• At one point Picard offers himself in exchange for La Forge, currently held by Lursa and B'Etor. The Duras sisters agree, and moments later Picard steps onto the transporter pad. As he dematerializes, La Forge rematerializes and collapses. Then Picard materializes on the surface of Veridian III without his communicator. This makes sense. Lursa and B'Etor probably removed the communicator to hinder the crew of the *Enterprise* in their efforts to find Picard. There's only one problem. Picard materializes in a blue Starfleet transporter pattern. If the *Enterprise* beamed him down to this location, why can't they find him again, and where is his communicator? Shouldn't Picard rematerialize on the surface in a yellow Klingon transporter pattern?

• La Forge returns to the *Enterprise* with a modified VISOR that transmits a visual picture to the *Enterprise*. Yet no one on the *Enterprise* seems to notice. (In all fairness, I suppose we could say that the guy who would normally catch this type of transmission would be Data, but he is feeling so overjoyed that his buddy has returned safely that he may not be up to his usual efficiency.)

• The crew of the *Enterprise* puts in a pitiful showing when trying to locate Picard on the surface of Veridian III. Granted, the atmosphere's ionization supposedly interferes with the sensors, but Soran has a *50-gigawatt* force field in place on the surface. Why in the world can't the *Enterprise* sensors pick that up?

• When La Forge returns to Engineering after his capture by Soran, you can see a new hallway on the starboard side of the room between the center island and the dilithium chamber.

• Does anyone else find it amazing that something as important and potentially lethal to the ship as the shield modulation frequency is openly displayed in Engineering for anyone to see (like the Borg visitors in "Q Who")?

• For some reason, Riker, Data, La Forge, and Worf all seem to forget

that they can remodulate the shield frequency after the first two Klingon photon torpedoes hit the *Enterprise*.

• Worf seems to forget that Riker orders a full spread of photon torpedoes for the cloaking Bird-of-Prey. Instead, he fires only one.

• And Riker and La Forge seem to forget that they could eject the warp core instead of taking a course of action that trashes the entire ship. (Yet, somehow, I doubt the review board investigating this incident will remember any of these things either!)

• Why did the bubble window in the top of the bridge break? It sits on the very top of the saucer section. I didn't see anything hit that area. Besides, isn't it made from transparent aluminum, like the rest of the windows in the hull? In the last exterior shot of the crash scene, we see that the windows of Ten-Forward remain intact. Wouldn't they take much more punishment than the bubble window during the crash?

• Kirk has an interesting clock in his house in the Nexus. It plays the normal tune at the top of the hour and then stops. Since the hands indicate that it is eleven o'clock, one would expect it to chime eleven times.

• Near the end of the movie, Data and Troi search through the rubble of the saucer section, looking for Spot. Troi asks Data why he decided not to remove the emotion chip. Wait a minute: Earlier in the movie, Picard said Crusher could not remove the chip because it had fused with his neural network. Did Troi not get this bit of information?

• Didn't anyone remove the bug from La Forge's VISOR?

CONTINUITY AND PRODUCTION PROBLEMS

• The red-haired navigator aboard the *Enterprise*-B also played a security officer who escorted Wesley around the *Enterprise*-D in "Peak Performance." The African-American transporter chief aboard the *Enterprise*-B played a terrorist in "Captain's Holiday" and now stars as Vulcan Tactical/Security Officer Tuvok in *Star Trek: Voyager.*

• For some reason, the communicators suddenly change in this movie and everyone begins wearing *Star Trek: Deep Space Nine* style uniforms (except the women, thankfully).

• Attempting to get into the spirit of the moment during the holodeck celebration of Worf's promotion, Data shoves Crusher into the sea. Falling overboard, she knocks Worf back into the water, and his pants look bloody right at the knees. Perhaps he skinned them while trying to climb back into the boat.

• During the first away mission to the Amargosa Observatory, Worf finds Soran buried under some rubble. He bends over to begin uncovering the doctor as Riker approaches. The camera angle changes. Worf is suddenly upright and then bends over again.

• After returning from the first away mission, Riker reports to Picard in the ready room and then exits into complete darkness. Now, either the bridge crew is playing a game of "lights out" hide-and-seek, or the creators didn't actually attach the ready room set to the main bridge set. (The scene showing the two sets attached at the end of the movie is probably an entirely different set constructed to show the battle damage.) This happens again when Troi enters Picard's quarters to discuss the death of his relatives.

• La Forge has on the wrong jacket when he returns to Engineering after his capture by Soran. Look at the sleeves. They are way too long!

• The footage of the Bird-of-Prey exploding comes from *Star Trek VI: The Undiscovered Country.*

• In one of the great moments in this film—just after the destruction of the Bird-of-Prey—Data clenches his fist and exclaims, "Yes!" As the camera pans just prior to this moment, watch the middle guy in the three nondescript officers standing by the rail behind Data. He makes a little "yes" gesture and then he realizes that Data is going to do that, so he sheepishly looks over at the android.

• The evacuation sequence just prior to saucer separation raises a few questions. Why is Crusher evacuating sick bay? Isn't it *in* the saucer section? And why are there so many children in the warp drive section?

• In the Nexus, Picard has a lovely, politely sophisticated wife who seems enthralled with her husband. Her character becomes all the more interesting when you realize that she looks just like Ensign Janet Brooks of "The Loss," whose husband had died a short while before the episode. Just why would an ensign on board the *Enterprise* turn up as Picard's wife in the Nexus—with a British accent, no less? (Hmmmm? Next thing you know we're going to find out her husband died under mysterious circumstances.)

• So...the new design of the communicators—the one with the rectangle behind the chevron? Was that a Starfleet-wide design change from the oval behind the chevron, or just a communicator change? I ask because at the end of the movie— when Troi and Data find Spot—one of the blue barrels behind them has the old oval design.

TRIVIA ANSWERS

1. Star date 2265A.D.
2. Frequency 257.4.

TRIATHLON TRIVIA ON DEVICES

MATCH THE DEVICE TO THE
DESCRIPTION TO THE EPISODE

DEVICE	DESCRIPTION	EPISODE
1. aceton assimilators	A. Its destruction made Satie suspicious	a. "The Nth Degree"
2. anbo-jytsu sticks	B. Folded-space transport device	b. "Heart of Glory"
3. Class-8 probe	C. Built by Dr. Paul Stubbs	c. "Descent, Part II"
4. cloaking device	D. The *Pegasus* had one	d. "The Drumhead"
5. Custodian	E. It grew a new backbone for Worf	e. "The Game"
6. Cytherian probe	F. Revealed creatures attached to the crew	f. "Samaritan Snare"
7. dilithium chamber hatch	G. Used by the Mariposan colony	g. "Realm of Fear"
8. Echo Papa 607	H. The threat of it entrapped Picard	h. "The Vengeance Factor"
9. Egg, the	I. Kal Dano's quantum phase inhibitor	i. "The Icarus Factor"
10. emergency transponder	J. It freed the bridge crew from submission	j. "Bloodlines"
11. emotion chip	K. Louvois threatened to rule Data with this	k. "The Last Outpost"
12. genetronic replicator	L. Allows vessels to enter a star's corona	l. "Chain of Command, Part 1"
13. hologram generator	M. Designed to keep warring gangs apart	m. "Devil's Due"
14. interphasic scanner	N. Bok used one to kidnap Picard's "son"	n. "Phantasms"
15. invasive program	O. Used by Yuta to kill her enemies	o. "The Battle"
16. inverter	P. Stopped transporter psychosis	p. "Starship Mine"
17. laser drill	Q. Used to put Picard to sleep	q. "Redemption II"
18. Merculite rockets	R. Bok used it on Picard	r. "Ethics"
19. metagenic weapon	S. Made Barclay temporarily brilliant	s. "Gambit, Part II"
20. metaphasic shielding	T. Riker used one to relieve a captain	t. "I Borg"
21. microvirus	U. Helped save colonists on Bersallis III	u. "Booby Trap"
22. multiphase tractor beam	V. Ardra used a cheap copy for her tricks	v. "Legacy"
23. multiplex-pattern buffers	W. Produces a baryon particle sweep	w. "Sub Rosa"
24. neural calipers	X. One killed Arthur Malencon	x. "When the Bough Breaks"

25.	painstik	Y.	Weapon used by renegade Klingons	y.	"Reunion"
26.	palm beacon	Z.	Uses thoughts to kill	z.	"The Masterpiece Society"
27.	particle fountain	AA.	Drained energy from the *Enterprise*	aa.	"The Arsenal of Freedom"
28.	phasing cloak	BB.	Used to keep the Romulans out	bb.	"The High Ground"
29.	plasma-flame candle	CC.	Designed to destroy the Borg	cc.	"Evolution"
30.	proximity detectors	DD.	Created a Mintakan duck blind	dd.	"The Emissary"
31.	psionic resonator	EE.	Aledean computer interface	ee.	"Suspicions"
32.	Remmler Array	FF.	Stolen by the Ferengi	ff.	"The *Pegasus*"
33.	subspace transporter	GG.	Ronin often lived there	gg.	"Captain's Holiday"
34.	T-9 energy converter	HH.	Data killed Lore and then retrieved it	hh.	"The Measure of a Man"
35.	tachyon detection grid	II.	Used to ensure that K'mpec was dead	ii.	"Home Soil"
36.	thermal deflectors	JJ.	Dr. Farallon's project	jj.	"Up the Long Ladder"
37.	Thought Maker	KK.	Saved the colony on Moab IV	kk.	"Lessons"
38.	toaster	LL.	Father and son reconcile with these	ll.	"Who Watches the Watchers"
39.	Tox Uthat	MM.	Made by the arms merchants of Minos	mm.	"The Quality of Life"
40.	Yoshimitsu computers	NN.	K'Ehleyr rode in one	nn.	"A Matter of Honor"

SCORING
(BASED ON NUMBER OF CORRECT ANSWERS)

0–10	Normal
11–19	Good
20–29	Excellent retention of technical details
30–40	Technobabble guru

DEVICES ANSWER KEY: **1.** AA u **2.** LL i **3.** NN dd **4.** V m **5.** EE x **6.** S a **7.** A d **8.** MM aa **9.** C cc **10.** T nn **11.** HH c **12.** E r **13.** DD ll **14.** F n **15.** CC t **16.** B bb **17.** X ii **18.** Y b **19.** H l **20.** L ee **21.** O h **22.** KK z **23.** P g **24.** Q f **25.** II y **26.** J e **27.** JJ mm **28.** D ff **29.** GG w **30.** M v **31.** Z s **32.** W p **33.** N j **34.** FF k **35.** BB q **36.** U kk **37.** R o **38.** K hh **39.** I gg **40.** G jj

GUILD

SUBMISSIONS

(READER MAIL)

FIRST
SEASON

ENCOUNTER AT FARPOINT

Star Dates: 41153.7—41174.2

Passing Q's first examination of humanity, Picard determines that Farpoint Station—a state-of-the-art spaceport supposedly built by the technologically inferior Bandi people of Deneb IV—is actually an imprisoned shape-shifting creature.

RUMINATIONS

While I usually try to treat premieres gently, many members of the Nit-picker's Guild saw no reason for such a practice. I will leave it up to you to decide which of the following nits should be considered legitimate and which should fall into the "give them a little grace because it's their first time around the block" category.

TRIVIA QUESTIONS

1. Who was the first person among the crew frozen by Q?

2. At what planet did Riker to refuse to allow the captain of the *Hood* to transport to the surface?

ALTERNATE VIEWPOINTS AND CORRECTIONS

• Ed Howard of Sloatsburg, NY, responded to my references in the *NextGen Guide* on page 4 concerning Dr. McCoy with, "Who is that?" He did so to hold me to the original Nit-picker's Guild Prime Directive that "The information in this book comes solely from the *[Star Trek: The Next Generation]* television series." (Gotta watch these nitpickers! They'll get you every time.)

• I had great fun in the *NextGen Guide* in my review of this episode with the main computer telling Riker to turn *right* to enter the holodeck and the commander turning *left* but still managing to enter the holodeck! (See page 5.) Then the letters started coming in suggesting that the computer did indeed give Riker the correct information because the commander had turned to face the computer. Therefore, Riker's right was now in the direction of the holodeck entrance. John DiGianno of East Elmhurst, NY, sent the first such letter. I can understand this viewpoint, having watched this segment of tape several times. However, I offer the following argument for my original position. If you pause the tape after the computer says, "The next hatchway on your *right*," you will find that Riker has not completed his turn. In fact his chest is not even facing the right side of the hallway yet. In addition, he is still traveling forward. The computer cannot know that Riker will spin to face back down the hall. Because of this, there are only two possible interpretations of the computer's instructions. "Right" is either back down the hall, or "right" is determined by Riker's direction of travel. I simply cannot figure out how "right" could mean the direction in which Riker eventually goes.

Now, if Riker had completed the turn and stopped, then "right" would have made *perfect* sense.

• On page 5 of the *NextGen Guide,* I pointed out a continuity and production problem. I said that some ferns "skew" sideways as Riker and Data walk behind them on the holodeck. James R. Stilipec of North Pole, AK, notified me that the pair actually passes behind a mold-encrusted tree trunk! (Pick, pick, pick, pick, pick…snicker, snicker.)

PLOT OVERSIGHTS

• Moments after arriving on the bridge, Picard uses the word "snoop." Presumably Picard is not the only sentient being in the Federation who still understands what the word means. Therefore it is likely that the word still exists in the dictionaries of the twenty-fourth century. Yet Data doesn't know the word. In fact, his interactions with and understanding of humans in this and the next few episodes of the series seem greatly underdeveloped for someone who has been exposed to humans for *twenty-six* years—as we learn later in "Datalore."

• Coming back from the first commercial break, the title and opening credits roll as Picard makes a log entry. As the episode moves to the bridge, Picard stares at Q—who suddenly appeared just prior to the commercial break. It looks like the scene picks up exactly where it left off. If that's what happened, when did Picard have time to make a log entry? And how did he accomplish it without moving his lips?

• Moments after the saucer separation, Q whisks Picard, Troi, Data, and Yar away to stand trial for the crimes of humanity. This begs the question: Why is Data in this group? Troi might qualify, given that she is half human, but Data? He's an android. Does Q actually believe that because Dr. Soong—a human—built Data, the android should stand trial for the *crimes of humanity?* Or does Q simply not care and has included Data because he happened to be on the bridge?

• Of course, the next question must be: Why isn't O'Brien included in the group that Q puts on trial? At the time, O'Brien mans the helm of the battle bridge, and he is definitely human.

• The powers of the shape-shifting alien seem to extend for some distance. When Riker meets with Groppler Zorn for the first time, a bowl of apples magically appears on Zorn's desk. Yet Zorn's office is in the neighboring old Bandi city, not Farpoint Station. Concerning the same incident, from what source does the alien manufacture these apples? The end of the episode reveals that Farpoint Station itself is the alien. Does this mean that any manifestation of the alien is a part of itself? In other words, is Riker eating a part of the alien as he happily chomps away on the apple?

• In reviewing the logs of the incident with Q, Riker apparently never sees Troi. Later, when Picard introduces them on the bridge, he looks shocked to see her. How could he miss her in the logs?

• Troi gives an interesting description of her physiology when Zorn asks Picard why he brought a telepath to their first meeting. The counselor says she is only half Betazoid, that her father was "a Starfleet officer." Why wouldn't Troi say that her father was "human"? Does Troi believe that the only good Starfleet officer is a human officer? Or—worse yet—do Starfleet officers have a reputation for gallivanting around the galaxy and siring children and she is therefore expecting her statement to bring a nod of understanding from Zorn?

• And, while we are on the topic of Riker missing things, he apparently also forgets that he wears a communicator as he searches the ship for Data. Instead of simply tapping his badge and saying, "Riker to Data," the commander asks an ensign for assistance. Then again, maybe Riker has some ulterior motive in playing dumb. The ensign *is* quite cute, and she apparently likes the looks of the commander as well. (She checks him out as he leaves.)

• According to Michael and Denise Okuda in *Star Trek Chronology: The History of the Future,* Data is incorrect when he tells Riker that he graduated with the "class of '78." So…an android—who remembers everything to which he is exposed—got this wrong?

• During the away team's investigation, an alien vessel approaches and begins firing on the old Bandi city. Riker orders Troi, Yar, and La Forge to beam back to the *Enterprise.* When Troi cries out in fear for Riker's safety, the first officer snaps that she has her orders and addresses her as "Lieutenant." However, Troi's rank is clearly lieutenant commander, and the normal abbreviation for this rank is "Commander."

CHANGED PREMISES

• Just after Picard walks out of the shadows in the first few moments of this episode, he takes a tour through Main Engineering. Twice, crew members stop, put their heels together, and nod in a very formal manner. Strangely enough, this salute never reappears in any subsequent episodes.

• The *Classic Trek* episode "Space Seed" indicates that the "eugenics wars" took place on Earth near the end of the twentieth century and were worldwide. Yet, in this episode, Q claims that World War III occurred in the twenty-first century. Why weren't the eugenics wars called World War III, and the latter war, World War IV?

• Back on the subject of Data, the creators definitely did not know that the android could not use contractions in this episode! (This was later established in "The Offspring.") Data refers to Q in the courtroom by saying, "At least we're acquainted with the judge." When speaking with Admiral McCoy, he comments that McCoy "shouldn't" have to put up with the time and trouble of a shuttlecraft and informs the admiral, "I'm an android." Later he admits to Riker—as they wander through the marketplace of Farpoint Station—"I can't see as well as Geordi."

• While shopping with Riker and her son, Crusher accuses the soon-to-be first officer of making work for himself to impress his new captain. She expresses her lack of enthusiasm for his activities by stating that her duties and interests are "outside of the command structure." Things certainly can change in six years. By the time "Descent" rolls around, Crusher finds herself sitting in the big chair during a very dangerous crisis.

• Data displays a considerable amount of emotion while pulling Wesley from the holodeck stream. He grins broadly and seems quite pleased at Wesley's shock over his strength.

• Upon seeing Picard outside the holodeck, a sopping wet Wesley immediately offers to clean up the water dripping from his person. Why would this be necessary? According to Riker in "Up the Long Ladder," the ship cleans itself.

• And finally, after this episode, Troi no longer deeply experiences the emotions she senses. If she had continued her blubbering every time she felt sorrow and her teary-eyed proclamations every time she felt love ("Great joy…and happiness"), it would have been a very long seven seasons indeed!

EQUIPMENT ODDITIES

• After Q disappears to make preparations for the trial of the crew of the *Enterprise*, Picard orders that all further communications will be accomplished "using printouts only." In the entire run of the series, does anyone out there remember seeing a printer on the *Enterprise*-D?

• Attempting to make a strategic withdrawal after the first encounter with Q, Picard orders the *Enterprise* to accelerate to maximum warp. He then separates the saucer from the battle section. Many have written to say that they find it amazing that the saucer section would remain at warp for some time *after* separation—since the saucer section has no warp drive. However, Picard does state that the battle section

will decelerate to allow the saucer to stay out ahead. It is possible that Data kept the warp fields extended around the saucer and then downshifted while simultaneously slamming on the brakes right after separation to keep the battle section from slicing the saucer section in two. After all, Data commented that there was no margin for error in the operation.

• Escorting Riker out of the holodeck, Data demonstrates that they are near a wall of the holodeck by tossing a rock. When it hits the wall and bounces off, a portion of the scenery blurs momentarily. Does this seem right? Shouldn't the holodeck preserve the illusion of the moment? Shouldn't it dematerialize the rock and then project an image of the rock arching beautifully to a landing?

• When the alien vessel approaches, Picard raises the *Enterprise*'s shields. Yet, a short time later, part of the away team beams back and there is no mention of dropping the shields for an instant. Does the transporter chief have the prerogative to drop the shields momentarily to accomplish transport? Or does the transporter somehow sequence its operation with the shield generators to allow beaming to the *Enterprise* when the ship's shields are raised?

• Near the end of the episode, Picard orders Yar to rig the main phasers to feed the Farpoint Station alien with an energy beam. Oddly enough, when the beam appears, it comes from the center of the bottom side of the saucer, not the phaser ring. Coincidentally, this is precisely the location of the original *Enterprise*'s phasers. Also—during this feeding—the port nacelle is white instead of its usual blue.

CONTINUITY AND PRODUCTION PROBLEMS

• Data shows off some interesting mannerisms in this show. When Picard first appears on the bridge, a camera pan reveals the second officer wiggling his fingers just before placing them over the controls of his station. Much later, as the android walks up to the transporter pad—preparing to beam over to the alien vessel—it looks like he's scratching his left armpit! These are probably just imitative remnants from the last captain under whom Data served. (That captain must have been one of those finger-wiggling, pit-scratching types.)

• Troi senses Q's presence seconds before the appearance of his force field. In a close-up, the klaxons sound and both Picard and Troi jerk their heads—Picard toward the viewscreen and Troi toward her monitor. The scene cuts to a wide shot of the bridge, and the pair repeat their head movements.

• Soon after the battle section of the *Enterprise* arrives at Deneb IV, Riker beams aboard. As he exits the transporter room, the shot clearly shows both a red- and a blue-uniformed crew member in the hall near him. When the shot changes to the hall, both crew members disappear.

• Zorn has a fascinating stained-glass window in his office. Just before it blows out during the alien assault on the old Bandi city, a camera angle clearly shows that the darker pieces of glass spell out "Zorn"—in English lettering, no less! (Probably the lettering really isn't in English, the Universal Translator simply changed it so we could read it.)

• Believe it or not, Troi wasn't the only member of the senior staff to wear the "cosmic cheerleader outfit" (as Marina Sirtis calls it). If you'll look closely at the very end of the episode, you'll see Yar wearing a miniskirt as well.

TRIVIA ANSWERS

1. Lieutenant Torres.
2. Altair III.

THE NAKED NOW

Star Dates: 41209.2–41209.3

Picard's crew battles to overcome the intoxicating effects of a strange type of alcoholic water—much the same as Kirk's crew did many years ago in the *Classic* episode "The Naked Time"—and narrowly avert destruction.

TRIVIA QUESTIONS

1. How many people froze to death in Engineering on the *Tsiolkovsky*?

2. Who is the chief engineer of the *Enterprise* during this episode?

ALTERNATE VIEWPOINTS AND CORRECTIONS

• Nitpicker Carol G. Olsen of Richardson, TX, pointed out that La Forge is only a lieutenant, junior grade during the first season, not a lieutenant commander as I refer to him on page 7 of the *NextGen Guide*.

• I find that my interpretation of the events in this episode is in dispute with the official reference manuals from Pocket Books. All refer to the entity that effects the crew in this episode—and in "The Naked Time"—as a "virus" or "disease." I, on the other hand, maintain that the entity is an intoxicating complex water molecule created by the intense gravitational flux of the collapsing star. Several have written me to point out this discrepancy. I offer the following sections of dialogue from "The Naked Now." In sick bay, Picard asks Crusher if there is any chance that the events on the *Tsiolkovsky* could be repeated on the *Enterprise*. Crusher responds, "If you mean a disease, sir, I'd say there's no chance of it." She goes on to explain that they used full decontamination when the away team returned. Then, after Data finds the logs of "The Naked Time," Picard—*reading* from the aforementioned logs—describes the problem-causing agents as "complex strings of water molecules which acquired carbon from the body and acted…acted on the brain like alcohol." Also, following Yar's departure from Troi's quarters, the counselor contacts Picard to tell her that Yar is "infected." Picard rebuts this by saying, "It's not actually an infection." "Yes, sir, it's more like intoxication," Troi agrees. Finally Crusher herself identifies the substance as "a water-carbon complex." Sounds pretty conclusive, doesn't it? And then there's Dr. McCoy's line in "The Naked Time," "It's the water!"

PLOT OVERSIGHTS

• The dedication plaque of the *Tsiolkovsky* raises an interesting point. For the most part, Starfleet appears to use the Roman alphabet for its computer displays. Yet the dedication plaque uses the Cyrillic alphabet for the name of the ship. Do other Starfleet vessels use this policy? Does the dedication plaque of the USS *Yamato* use Japanese katakana characters?

• Picard seems a bit confused about his computer terminology, but it is an easy mistake to make. He orders Data to download the information about the incident in "The Naked Time" to Crusher. To be absolutely correct, he should order Data to *upload* the information.

• Deciding to take over Main Engineering, Wesley plays a recording of Picard's voice and orders the chief engineer and her assistant to leave their posts. Interestingly enough, neither acknowledge the hails. They simply nod and leave. (Of course, if they did acknowledge the hails with something like, "On my way, sir," Picard would respond, "On your way to where? I want you to stay in Main Engineering!" And then it would be a short show.)

• After discovering that Yar is indeed plastered, Picard sends Data to escort her to sick bay. Just how many people will fit in sick bay? There are more than a thousand people on this ship, and it appears that the intoxication is spreading rapidly. Wouldn't it make more sense to lock everyone in their quarters?

• After Wesley commandeers Main Engineering, Riker heads down there to regain control. A force field blocks the doorway to the main control area, but Riker never thinks of using a phaser to cut through the curved window that separates them. (And even if Starfleet constructed the window from some impenetrable material, why not cut through the deck plates from above or below?)

• At the beginning of the episode, the *Enterprise* approaches the *Tsiolkovsky*. The science vessel orbits a dying star. The episode contains no mention that the *Enterprise* ever moved back from this close position. Yet, when the star collapses, the crew suddenly has fifteen minutes to respond.

• After seeing La Forge's rapid recovery in response to her antidote, Crusher injects herself and Picard with the formula. For some reason they take much longer to recover.

• Near the end of the episode, Wesley receives congratulations for saving the *Enterprise*. Doesn't it matter that he destroyed a very expensive science ship to get the *Enterprise* out of a scrape that *he* caused in the first place? Granted, he was drunk, but he doesn't even get a slap on the wrist. (I know. I know. It happened when we weren't looking, right?)

• In one of the last exchanges of the show, Yar forcefully tells Data that their intimate interlude "never happened." She seems quite determined not to discuss it ever again. Evidently she changed her mind or engaged Data's services for a second time because, in "The Measure of a Man," Data states that he gave his word to Yar that he would not tell anyone what happened between them. If they never spoke of the incident again, how could Data give Yar his word that he would not reveal it?

• How does an alcohol-like substance get transmitted by touch? Sticking your hand in a glass of vodka won't make you drunk.

CHANGED PREMISES

• Data continues using contractions in this episode. (I'll get off this kick *soon*.) After the bridge crew hears an explosion from the *Tsiolkovsky,* he tells Picard, "What we've just heard is impossible." Then, while aboard the *Tsiolkovsky,* Data corrects Riker by saying, "Correction, sir: That's blown out." Finally, after Yar beguilingly asks when Picard wanted her to report to sick bay, Data replies, "I'm sure he meant now."

EQUIPMENT ODDITIES

• Presumably someone scanned the *Tsiolkovsky* before beaming over the away team. After all, Picard and the others just heard someone blow an escape hatch, but the away team arrives without benefit of environmental suits. Even if life support still functions on the *Tsiolkovsky,* what about contamination? When Spock and Tormolen beam down to the research station on Psi 2000 in "The Naked Time," they wear isolation suits. Doesn't that make sense? Or do twenty-fourth-century crews have so much faith in their decontamination technology that they don't worry about catching kooties?

• Crusher reviews the scans of the dead crew members on the *Tsiolkovsky* but finds nothing unusual. Why can't La Forge's tricorder detect this big chain of H_2O molecules (as displayed on the screen when Data finds the records from "The Naked Time")? Surely someone has programmed the scanners to look for this type of configuration. It almost led to the destruction of Kirk's *Enterprise*.

• Oddly enough, even after La Forge wanders out of sick bay, the display above his bed continues to register his vital signs!

• During Data's first scan of the records, a parrot briefly appears on the screen wearing a Starfleet uniform. Would this be a tribute to the "Great Bird of the Galaxy" himself, Gene Roddenberry?

• As Data complies with Picard's order to "download" the information, the computer terminal emits a strange clicking sound and the normal "boops" do not sound even though it looks like Data presses several keys.

• Evidently the restraint system in sick bay gets an upgrade between this episode and "Time Squared." In this episode, Crusher secures La Forge with seat belt straps. In "Time Squared," Pulaski uses a force field to hold Picard's duplicate in place.

• While in Main Engineering, Wesley brings up a picture of the *Tsiolkovsky* on the viewer. The picture does not show the tractor beam enveloping the science vessel.

• Everyone seems shocked and amazed that Wesley can create a reverse tractor beam in such a short amount of time. Just when did Starfleet technology lose this capability? In the *Classic Trek* episode, "Who Mourns for Adonais?" Sulu punches a few buttons on the bridge and rigs the tractor beam to repel.

CONTINUITY AND PRODUCTION PROBLEMS

• At the very beginning of the episode, Picard makes a log entry stating that the *Enterprise* is heading for the USS *Tsiolkovsky* at warp 7. Subsequent outside shots of the ship show it traveling at impulse.

• It turns out to be a strange day for La Forge. Not only is he the first to become intoxicated with the strange water, he also is the victim of a pillow thief! When first seen in a sick bay bed, La Forge has two flat pillows under his head. At this point Crusher walks back into her office to consult her desktop terminal. The scene cuts back to La Forge, who sits up and strolls out of sick bay. By this time, the pillow thief has already struck, because both of La Forge's pillows have disappeared.

• For the most part, the special-effects people do a good job in this episode making objects float in response to Wesley's tractor beam. However, at the very beginning of the scene with the chair, you can see three black strings suspending it from the ceiling.

• After Data finds the logs from the events in "The Naked Time," the camera angle changes to show a diagram of the *Constitution*-class *Enterprise*. Unfortunately, the diagram details the refit, movie version of Kirk's *Enterprise*, not the original version of the television series. (You can tell the difference by the shape of the engine nacelles. The original *Enterprise* nacelles were round in the front. The refit, movie nacelles were slanted.)

• Shortly after discovering that Yar has invaded her quarters, Troi reaches out to comfort the inebriated chief of Security. Yar takes her hand as they talk for a few moments. From one camera angle, there's a piece of cloth caught between their hands; from the other, there isn't.

TRIVIA ANSWERS

1. Ten.
2. MacDougal.

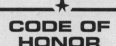

CODE OF HONOR

Star Dates: 41235.25–41235.32

After Lutan—an inhabitant of Ligon II—kidnaps Yar from the *Enterprise,* Picard must allow his Security chief to engage in a fight to the death with Yareena, Lutan's wife, to fulfill Ligonian customs and earn the right for the Federation to acquire a much-needed vaccine.

TRIVIA QUESTIONS

1. What starbase dispatches the message to the *Enterprise* concerning the outbreak on Styris IV?

2. What disease affects the inhabitants of Styris IV?

ALTERNATE VIEWPOINTS AND CORRECTIONS

• Anna Schulrud of Milwaukee, WI, found no contradiction in Picard's con-

versations during this episode. On page 11 of the *NextGen Guide,* I noted that Picard first tells Lutan he is aware of similarities between Ligonian customs and an ancient Earth culture he admires and then later calls these same customs "pompous strutting charades." Anna believes Picard was simply bootlicking (or "being polite," as Sharla Smith of Minneapolis, MN, wrote).

PLOT OVERSIGHTS

• When the Ligonians first beam themselves aboard the *Enterprise,* Yar gives them the coordinates of Cargo Bay 1. Does this seem like an unusual place to welcome persons of high status in Ligonian culture? (Probably the creators wanted to justify building the cargo bay set and so wrote it into this script!)

• After Troi states that she and Data believe Picard should go on the away mission to Ligon II, Riker balks. In the process, he begins to tell Data why he thinks it is a bad idea and ends one of his sentences with "sir." Riker is definitely speaking to Data at the time. Normally, lower-ranking officers are not addressed as "sir."

• In the middle of the crisis on Ligon II, Data finds time to visit La Forge's quarters and tell him a joke. Setting aside the fact that the joke is laced with contractions, Data supposedly has a slip of the tongue after La Forge finds no humor in his recitation. A slip of the tongue? From Data? (By the way, Data also says, "I'm here to brief you…" to Riker after he beams up to the ship just before the fight between Yar and Yareena.)

• The dialogue of this episode states that Lutan wanted Yareena to die so that he could inherit her lands. Yet, at the end of the episode, Yareena states that at her death the mating agreement between her and Lutan ceased. She then chooses Hagon as her "first one." Lutan supposedly loses everything with this turn of events. Wait a minute: If Ligonian customs say that Lutan would inherit all Yareena's wealth at her death, isn't Lutan a rich man now? Why enforce the custom concerning the breakage of the mating agreement but not the custom concerning the inheritance of wealth?

• Having finally secured the desperately needed vaccine for the plague on Styris IV, the *Enterprise* sets off for that planet at a rip-roaring warp 3! What happened to warp 9? If it's as bad on that planet as the dialogue seems to indicate, wouldn't you want to get there as fast as possible?

CONTINUITY AND PRODUCTION PROBLEMS

• At one point, Picard seeks out Lutan. He comes upon a conversation between Lutan and his aide Hagon. As Picard walks up to the pair, Hagon's words do not match the movements of his lips.

• This episode proves that Dr. Crusher fancies antiques. Shortly after the crew beams Yar and Yareena up to the *Enterprise,* Crusher runs forward and begins work on Yareena's lifeless body. When the doctor extends her left arm, a small white-faced watch with a leather band appears on her wrist.

• Near the end of the episode,

Picard escorts Lutan and Hagon through the bridge on the way to the observation lounge. Picard allows Lutan and Hagon to enter the small hallway at the back of the bridge before him but emerges into the observation lounge first. Just how long is that hallway? Is there enough space for Lutan and Hagon to get lost? Is that why Picard raced ahead of them to show them how to get to the observation lounge? Also, note that the hallway is actually a fairly steep ramp as it leads down to the lounge. To my recollection, from here on out, the hallway is flat.

TRIVIA ANSWERS

1. Starbase 14.
2. Anchilles Fever.

THE LAST OUTPOST

Star Dates: 41368.4—41368.5

As the *Enterprise* pursues a Ferengi vessel, both ships fall under the control of an energy-draining field—emanating from an ancient outpost of the Tkon Empire. During a joint away mission with the Ferengi to the planet, Riker passes the test given by the outpost's "portal" and arranges the safe release of both ships.

TRIVIA QUESTIONS

1. Where is the Tkon outpost located?

2. What age follows Bastu, Cimi, and Xora in the ages of the Tkon Empire?

PLOT OVERSIGHTS

• Shortly after the energy-draining field seizes the *Enterprise,* Picard sends La Forge to Main Engineering to get a report, since communications are out. The next time we see La Forge—who is currently the helmsman and a lieutenant, junior grade—he has apparently taken over Engineering! What happened to the chief engineer?

• At Picard's request, Data divulges all known information about the Ferengi. When Riker perks up at Data's comparison of the Ferengi to "Yankee traders," the android snidely comments that they probably won't be wearing red, white, and blue or look anything like Uncle Sam. Moments later, Yar asks, "What have bright primary colors got to do with it?" First, I apologize for the grammar of the preceding quote! As nearly as I can tell that *is* what Yar says. Second, I do not believe that white is a "primary" color. The primary colors are yellow, red, and blue—at least in the twentieth century.

• Discipline seems very loose among the bridge officers during this episode. Data whispers little side comments to La Forge, while Picard attempts to negotiate with the Ferengi. When Rik-

er appears on the planet alone, he walks around yelling for the others and eventually stumbles upon Data, who evidently was too preoccupied to respond. Then, when Data and Riker find La Forge hanging upside down and Riker asks if the helmsman is conscious, La Forge shoots back, "Do I look conscious?"

• I mentioned in the *NextGen Guide* that Riker makes no attempt to use his communicator after materializing alone on the planet's surface. In addition, Data makes no attempt to use his tricorder to locate the other members of the away team. True, they find out later that these devices do not function properly, but why not make the attempt?

CHANGED PREMISES

• Supposedly this episode marks the Federation's "first look" at the Ferengi. Yet subsequent events call this into question. In "Captain's Holiday" we find that Vash has worked with a Ferengi named Sovak for several years. With the advent of *Star Trek: Deep Space Nine* a mere five and a half years later, the Ferengi have so fouled their reputation in the Alpha Quadrant that they look forward to opening new markets in the Gamma Quadrant. They certainly have been busy if the events in "The Last Outpost" truly constitute the Federation's "first look" at them.

• Once again, Data's dialogue contains its share of contractions. Sitting at the Ops position near the beginning of the episode, he says, "This shouldn't be," and referring to the portal's assertion that it is the age of Bastu, Data responds, "I'm afraid not." (Actually, Data says, "I'm 'fraid not." Would that count as two contractions?)

• For some reason, all the Ferengi encountered by the crew of the *Enterprise* seem much less animated than those serving on the away team during this episode. Did the "swoop and duck while twirling your arms" thing go out of fashion in Ferengi circles? (I mean no insult, but it really is very reminiscent of the monkeys in *The Wizard of Oz*.)

EQUIPMENT ODDITIES

• On his way to Main Engineering, La Forge walks up the ramp to the turbolift doors. They open well before La Forge reaches them. How did the turbolift know that La Forge was heading for Engineering and not the workstations in the back of the bridge?

• After Yar closes the frequency following the second conversation with the Ferengi, the DaiMon's image remains on the screen for *several seconds*. (It's probably some sort of latent image.)

CONTINUITY AND PRODUCTION PROBLEMS

• The light source for the exterior shot of the two ships and the planet offers an interesting conundrum. Both ships are clearly illuminated by a light source on the left side of the screen. Why then is the planet lit from the right side of the screen?

• When Picard asks the Ferengi if they are withdrawing their surrender, Yar's arms pop back and forth from folded to extended as the shots change.

TRIVIA ANSWERS

1. In the Delphi Ardu star system.
2. Makto.

WHERE NO ONE HAS GONE BEFORE

Star Dates: 41263.1—41263.4

A warp drive adjustment—supervised by Starfleet propulsion expert Kosinski but actually implemented by a being called the Traveler—takes the *Enterprise* to a dimension where thought becomes reality. Realizing the dangers, the Traveler expends his remaining reserves of energy to return the ship to Federation space before fading to another plane of existence.

TRIVIA QUESTIONS

1. What two ships did Kosinski work on prior to the *Enterprise*?

2. What is the location of the *Enterprise* after the first warp experiment?

PLOT OVERSIGHTS

• If Picard is such an ardent explorer, why doesn't he launch a probe or drop a beacon when he finds his ship out in the far-flung reaches of the universe?

• Speaking of the ballerina, when Picard sees her, he identifies her as an ensign. If you use freeze-frame, though, you will find that the woman has no pips on her uniform. She's a crewman, not an ensign!

• Just prior to the final test that brings the *Enterprise* home, Picard tells the crew to center their thoughts on the Traveler's well-being. Then, just for good measure, he orders *battle stations* complete with flashing lights and klaxons! I don't know about you, but this would not help me concentrate on someone's well-being.

CHANGED PREMISES

• Writers have a natural aversion to limits. Just as soon as someone makes a rule about a given environment, writers usually try to find some way to subvert it. I think it's part of those twisted genes that make us want to create our own realities in the first place. I'm sure by this time in the life of *Star Trek: The Next Generation* the creators had decided on the new warp scale. They probably had also decided that at warp 10, a starship would occupy all the points in the universe simultaneously (and that infinite power would be needed to achieve such a speed). So what do the writers do? They have La Forge say that they are *passing* warp 10 during the first test.

• It's contraction time once again, boys and girls—starring our favorite non-contraction-using android, Data! While the *Enterprise* hurtles through space during the first trial, Picard asks about the ship's velocity. Data answers, "It's off the scale." (Surprisingly enough, two people mailed this nit to me on the same day.) Moments later, he also tells Picard, "Captain, we're here," just before suggesting that they look around Galaxy

M33. (I'll slot the rest of the known contractions into the *Updated Conundrum Tote Board*.)

EQUIPMENT ODDITIES

• Starfleet propulsion expert Kosinski's uniform contains a few oddities. First, he wears no communicator. Isn't this standard issue for all Starfleet personnel? Second, his rank insignia is a rectangle, never seen again in the series and most similar to those worn by Starfleet cadets. Is this some sort of specialist rank?

• The first time the *Enterprise* accelerates to warp 1.5 the *Enterprise* disappears without the normal warp flash.

TRIVIA ANSWERS

1. The *Ajax* and the *Fearless*.
2. Galaxy M33.

LONELY AMONG US

Star Dates: 41249.3—41249.4

Sucked into the sensors as the *Enterprise* performs a close pass on an unusual cloud that travels at warp speed, an energy being hops from crew member to crew member—eventually finding Picard and using the captain's command status to order the ship back to its home.

PLOT OVERSIGHTS

• Picard and crew seem terribly nonchalant about the demise of the Selay delegate at the end of this episode. Think of it: A sentient being has been murdered, and his murderers (or her murderers, as the case may be) want the crew to cook the victim so they can feast! Upon hearing this, Picard shrugs and hands the problem to Riker, who turns with only a slightly startled reaction to look at Data as cutesy music plays in the background. Evidently the Selay don't rate very high on the *Enterprise* crew's list of "Races Whose Individual Rights We Should Ardently Defend and Become Instantly Irate At the Mere Hint of Any Violation of Those Rights." (Interestingly enough, Kamala—the *gorgeous* empathic metamorph from "The Perfect Mate"—seems to rate *very* high on this list. Hmmm…I wonder why.)

TRIVIA QUESTIONS

1. Who is the head of the Selay delegation?

2. Where are the home worlds of the Anticans and the Selay located?

CHANGED PREMISES

• When the energy being possesses Picard, the captain begins behaving irrationally. Riker and Crusher meet with him to discuss the situation, but he bullies both of them into submitting to full physicals. At one point, Crusher almost begs Picard to cooperate. These scenes stand in stark contrast to a similar situation in the *Classic Trek* episode "Obsession." In that episode, Kirk begins behaving in

a seemingly irrational way as well. Spock and McCoy meet with him and in a dignified, respectful, and unapologetic way they note that he has given unusual orders. Then they politely request a fuller explanation. There is no question that the two of them combined have the power to relieve him and are prepared to use it.

EQUIPMENT ODDITIES

• To beam out into the cloud, Picard walks up to a completely dark transporter console and touches it. At this, the console lights up and Picard transports into the cloud, energy only. First, if the panel is completely dark, how would a user know where to push? I can see that these panels might have something like a built-in screen saver. But then the first tap would merely bring the panel back to life. Subsequent taps would enter instructions. In any case, one tap from Picard not only manages to bring the console back to life, but also instructs the transporter to perform an *unusual* transport (i.e., do not reconstruct the captain at the end of the transport cycle). Doesn't it seem likely that this type of operation would require more than one poke at the console?

CONTINUITY AND PRODUCTION PROBLEMS

• After the energy discharge hits Worf, he flies backward and falls to the floor. After the opening title sequence, Crusher hurries into the room. It appears that Worf has moved some distance into the center of the room. Do Klingons move around when they are unconscious? Or did La Forge—continuing to demonstrate the crew's lack of knowledge about basic first aid—drag Worf away from the table? (When Worf first falls, La Forge rushes up and flips him over; in much the same way, Worf rushes up to the dead Singh later in the show and flips him over to check his pulse. Is this an approved practice on the *Enterprise*? Is medicine so advanced in the twenty-fourth century that first aid no longer suggests letting an injured person lie still to minimize the danger of further back injury?)

• As the *Enterprise* returns to the energy cloud, an outside shot shows the ship passing overhead. Evidently the creators spliced the film in backward because the "NCC-1701" is backward on the lower portion of the saucer section. They probably thought no one would notice. (Heh, heh, heh, heh.)

TRIVIA ANSWERS

1. Ssestar.
2. In the Beta Renna system.

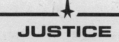

JUSTICE

Star Dates: 41255.6—41255.9

When Wesley unknowingly breaks a law of the Edo—a peaceful race living on Rubicun III—Picard must choose between violating the Prime Directive and allowing the boy to endure the only punishment prescribed by Edo tradition: *death*. (Insert suspenseful music here.)

1. Where does the *Enterprise* deliver a group of colonists prior to the beginning of the episode?

2. What is the name of the Edo woman Picard takes to the *Enterprise*?

PLOT OVERSIGHTS

• Wouldn't contact with the Edo violate the Prime Directive in the first place? The *Classic Trek* episode, "Bread and Circuses" establishes a complete definition of the fabled rule. "No identification of self or mission. No interference with the social development of said planet. No references to space or the fact that there are other worlds or civilizations."

• The Edo display a remarkable calmness at the appearance of the away teams. Clearly they are not technologically advanced, yet they dispassionately accept the materialization of humanoids right before their eyes. Now, I've spent some time watching *Star Trek*, so I would hope that if an alien beamed into my basement, I would smile and say, "Cool." But these people don't even have television! How can they be so unimpressed with this development in their lives? (Just "love-numbed," I guess.) In addition, I suppose I should point out that "First Contact" states that the Federation waits until a race achieves warp drive before making contact. I may be wrong, but I don't think the Edo—with their skimpy outfits and oil-rubbed bodies—qualify.

• Normally to commence transporter operation, Picard says, "Energize."

When ordering the transporter chief to beam the Edo female back to her planet, the captain shouts, "Engage!" He was probably nervous. At the time, the Edo god had started on a collision course for the *Enterprise.*

EQUIPMENT ODDITIES

• If the communicator pins are used to identity people for transport—as demonstrated when Picard removes his communicator and places it on an Edo woman during this episode, preparing her to beam her back to the planet—why doesn't Wesley wear a communicator when he accompanies the away team to the surface?

• The doors on the *Enterprise* can get just a wee bit impatient at times. After Picard tells Crusher that he won't allow the Edo to execute her son, the pair head for the transporter. As Picard walks out of the room, the doors begin to close and then stop to give Crusher a chance to exit as well.

CONTINUITY AND PRODUCTION PROBLEMS

• The "god" vessel in this episode bears a striking resemblance to the Lysian central command in "Conundrum."

• Shortly after Picard beams down to the planet, Crusher calls to inform the captain that Data has awakened from his joining with the Edo "god." The shots of Crusher show Data in the background with an assistant, but they feature sounds normally associated with the main bridge!

TRIVIA ANSWERS

1. The Strnad system.

2. Rivan. (I know. Too easy. There wasn't much to choose from.)

THE BATTLE

Star Date: 41723.9

The normally greed-driven Dai-Mon Bok of the Ferengi suddenly becomes beneficent and returns a salvaged piece of Starfleet equipment—Picard's last command, the USS *Stargazer.* Unknown to the crew of the *Enterprise,* the ship is part of a plan by Bok to seek revenge on Picard for the death of his son in the Battle of Maxia.

TRIVIA QUESTIONS

1. Who is DaiMon Bok's second officer?

2. What is the destination of the *Stargazer* after this episode?

ALTERNATE VIEWPOINTS AND CORRECTIONS

• Several have written to offer reasons why Picard did not set the autodestruct on the *Stargazer* before abandoning her. (I pointed this out on pages 24 and 25 of the *NextGen Guide.*) P. T. H. Carder of Lancashire, England, had an intriguing one, suggesting that there were no command-rank officers left to carry out the order, since autodestruct requires more than just the captain. (This raises an interesting point: How do you set

116

autodestruct if you sustain heavy casualties?)

PLOT OVERSIGHTS

• Under the influence of a thought-making device purchased by Bok to implement his plan, Picard begins experiencing headaches. While waiting for the Ferengi to arrive for a scheduled meeting, the captain goes to sick bay, where Crusher presses a device against his head. Picard immediately proclaims that the pain has gone. To this, Crusher counters that it is still there, merely "cloaked." My dictionary says that pain is a "basic sensation caused by harmful stimuli and marked by discomfort." The cause of the pain might be blocked from creating the sensation, but if the pain is gone, it's gone!

• The Ferengi soon beam aboard, and Picard introduces Riker as the first officer and Data as "second-in-command." Wait a minute: Isn't Data second officer and *third*-in-command?

• The Ferengi ogle Troi for a few moments before turning their attention to Data. They promptly make an offer to buy the android, to which Picard responds that Data is not for sale. When the Ferengi ask why, Riker states that Data is "secondhand merchandise." Don't the words "not for sale" have the connotation that there is a capability to be sold? Isn't Data a sentient being with rights guaranteed under Federation? Let's play a substitution game. Suppose the Ferengi had wanted to buy Troi. Would Picard respond that she's "not for sale," and would Riker give the reason that she is "secondhand mer-

chandise"? And would anyone wish to be within Troi's striking distance when these statements were made?

• Starfleet really isn't going to tow the *Stargazer* back to a starbase, is it? On impulse? At less than the speed of light? Just how close is the nearest starbase? Ten light-years, maybe? Data indicates later that all the main systems of the vessel still function. Why not beam a few crew members over to fly it back to a starbase at warp?

• And speaking of the tow ship, Starfleet seems to approve the assignment of that vessel very quickly, yet moments later we learn that it will take a subspace message an entire day to reach Starfleet and an entire day to return. How did the request for the tow ship get there and back so fast?

• When Riker has his private conversation with Kazago, the Ferengi first officer refers to Bok as "Captain." The commander of a Ferengi vessel is usually called "DaiMon."

• The armchair captains of the Nitpicker's Guild certainly came up with plenty of ways to defeat the Picard Maneuver. The *Enterprise* could disable the *Stargazer*'s weapons systems with some precision phaser fire. Riker also could drop the *Stargazer*'s shields by entering the command codes for the old vessel (à la *Star Trek II: The Wrath of Khan*). Or Riker could simply warp away at high velocity and come back at a more opportune moment.

EQUIPMENT ODDITIES

• Transporters, shields, and tractor beams all behave oddly during the end of this episode. Bok orders the *Stargazer* to raise its shields, gives

Picard a lecture, and then beams off without lowering the shields. Then Riker locks a tractor beam on the *Stargazer* with its shields still up. (Remember that the Borg couldn't lock their tractor beam on the *Enterprise* until they drained her shields in "The Best of Both Worlds.") And finally, the *Enterprise* beams Picard back even though the *Stargazer* apparently *still* has her shields up.

CONTINUITY AND PRODUCTION PROBLEMS

• Shortly after long-range sensors pick up the USS *Stargazer,* La Forge says that he reads it as a *Constellation*-class starship. However, if you watch his lips, he actually says a *Constitution*-class starship. Of course, the original *Enterprise* was a *Constitution*-class starship and doesn't look anything like the *Stargazer.* The creators caught this nit and fixed it by overdubbing La Forge's dialogue.

• The ghostly crew of the *Stargazer* all wear *Next Generation*-style uniforms. Interestingly enough, Jack Crusher served with Picard on the *Stargazer,* and he wears a movie-style uniform in his holographic appearance during "Family."

TRIVIA ANSWERS

1. Rata.
2. Xendi Starbase 9.

HIDE AND Q

Star Dates: 41590.5–41591.4

Having evaluated their recent contact with humanity, the Q Continuum sends Q back to the *Enterprise* to try to entice Riker into joining them. Although Q offers Riker immortality and almost limitless power, the first officer refuses, preferring to live with those he trusts.

TRIVIA QUESTIONS

1. In what form does Q initially appear?

2. Where does the *Enterprise* drop off Troi for a shuttle visit home?

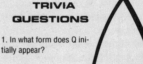

ALTERNATE VIEWPOINTS AND CORRECTIONS

• After Q makes Riker omnipotent, Picard struggles with how to counsel his first officer. In his log entry, the captain states that this situation is beyond his experience, beyond anyone's experience. In the *NextGen Guide* I mentioned that Picard must not be a student of previous vessels named the *Enterprise* because Kirk faced a man turned god in "Where No Man Has Gone Before." P. T. H. Carder of Lancashire, England, wrote to say that Kirk sank the facts regarding Gary Mitchell—the man who received the powers—in his formal report. Possibly all that survived in the Starfleet records was a stern warning on the dangers of transversing the Great Barrier (the cause of the change in Mitchell).

PLOT OVERSIGHTS

• At one point, Worf goes on a reconnaissance mission to spy out the enemy on Q's game planet. La Forge gives Riker updates on the Klingon's progress and states that—even at a great distance—he could see the freckles on Worf's nose if he had any. If La Forge can see that well, why don't they just have him look the situation over from their current position instead of sending Worf?

• La Forge seems "descriptionally challenged" in this episode. Searching for a term to explain the creatures they fought on Q's planet, he describes them to Picard as "animal things." (The moniker was originally assigned by Worf.) Wouldn't the phrase, "hairy, pig-faced humanoids dressing in French soldier uniforms and carrying weapons that look like muskets but actually discharge energy packets" be a bit more useful to Picard?

• The lack of first-aid knowledge continues among the crew of the *Enterprise*. When the away team reaches the injured during their rescue mission, Data digs through a pile of large rocks and uncovers a little girl. Before Crusher can hurry over, the android picks her up!

• Near the end of the episode, Riker tries to give going-away presents to the bridge crew. Oddly enough, after he ages Wesley by ten years—turning him into a larger, more muscular young

man—Wesley retains the voice of a fifteen-year-old. (One other grungy little side note: Since the series ran for seven years, shouldn't Wesley Crusher near the end of the series be closer in appearance to the aged version of Wesley in this episode than the normal teen version? Wink, wink.)

• After Riker ages Wesley, La Forge says, "Hey, Wes...not bad." To what is La Forge referring? It can't be Wesley's new ruggedly handsome good looks, because we find out later that La Forge can't tell what others look like physically: When Riker gives him eyes, he looks at Yar and says she is even more beautiful that he imagined. Or was that just a come-on line?

CHANGED PREMISES

• I mentioned this in my review of "Q Who" in the *NextGen Guide,* but in this episode, Picard and Q make a bet that Picard wins. The prize for winning the bet is supposed to be that Q will keep out of humanity's way *forever.* Of course he doesn't, because then there wouldn't be any more Q episodes.

• Although Worf responds to the snapping, snarling Klingon warrior babette that Riker provides by saying, "She is from a world now alien to me," subsequent episodes suggest differently. He recites with pleasure the mating rituals of Klingons to Wesley in "The Dauphin." He falls into a foul mood when inhibited from participating in a ritual marking a decade since his Age of Ascension during "The Icarus Factor." He mates with K'Ehleyr in Klingon fashion in "The Emissary." He fights for his family's honor in "Sins of the Father." (My guess is that the warrior babette was shorting out his neurons and he would have said anything to try to convince Riker to get rid of her!)

• After first appearing in an admiral's uniform, Q next changes to a French field marshal's outfit—a higher designation in rank. When Riker notes this, Q responds by incredulously asking if Riker thought he would go from an admiral to anything else. Obviously Q believes himself superior to the humans he meets. Why then does he take the rank of captain in subsequent shows like "Q Who"? (Does he idolize Picard?)

EQUIPMENT ODDITIES

• The turbolift doors retain their ability to sense when someone needs to make a dramatic exit. After Riker asks for a meeting with the bridge crew, he stalks into the upper turbolift and then turns around to glare at Picard. The shot changes to show a reaction of the captain and then back to Riker. *Finally* the doors decide the time is right, and they close. Of course, Riker may have been controlling them with his newly acquired powers.

TRIVIA ANSWERS

1. An Aldebaran serpent.
2. Starbase G-6.

HAVEN

Star Dates: 41294.5—41294.6

When a plague ship approaches the beautiful planet of Haven, Picard traps it in a tractor beam to prevent the Tarellians from spreading the disease they carry to the inhabitants below. Surprisingly, the Tarellians have actually come for Wyatt Miller, a young doctor who has experienced a mystic connection with a young Tarellian woman since childhood.

TRIVIA QUESTIONS

1. Who is the first electorine of Haven?

2. What race destroyed the last known Tarellian plague ship?

ALTERNATE VIEWPOINTS AND CORRECTIONS

• On page 18 of the *NextGen Guide,* I quoted Troi as saying, "The years I'd spent on this mission" and used that quotation to question how long the *Enterprise* has been in service. David Foster of Charleston, WV, informed me that Troi really says, "The years I'd spend on this mission." In fact—upon checking the dialogue again—I find that David is right! Sorry, sorry. I think the fact that Troi changes tense in the middle of her dialogue threw me. In explaining why she didn't mention the genetic bonding to Picard she says, "I was certain it would never happen, Captain: the years I'd spend on this mission, the distance it has taken me away from home." Not listening carefully enough, I smeared the tenses of the last two phrases together.

PLOT OVERSIGHTS

• Does it seem like everyone accepts the fact that Wyatt's fantasy woman actually lives a bit too nonchalantly?

CHANGED PREMISES

• The dialogue between Lwaxana and Deanna Troi in the hallway reveals some interesting facts. Lwaxana had a valet before Mr. Homn, and that valet tried to rid Deanna of her accent—an accent she acquired from her father. On the other hand, Deanna speaks with the image of her father in "Dark Page." Guess what? No accent! In addition, "Dark Page" also shows us a picture of the complete Troi family that Mr. Homn supposedly put away for safekeeping after the death of Deanna's older sister. At the time, Lwaxana had decided to destroy every memory that the first daughter existed. The picture shows us that Deanna was only an infant at the time. This brings us to our second problem: The dialogue in "Haven" states that the valet before Mr. Homn tried to rid Deanna of her accent. Yet the picture demonstrates that Mr. Homn was the valet at least part of the time Deanna was a baby. So...the valet *before* Mr. Homn served the Troi family while Troi was a *baby*? Isn't it a bit

obsessive and compulsive to try to rid an *infant* of an accent?

EQUIPMENT ODDITIES

• Here's a fascinating tidbit of technical information you probably don't know about the starship *Enterprise.* The pictures in the guest quarters have a rotate feature! When Troi visits Wyatt in his quarters, watch the painting on the wall. Note the stars in the lower right-hand corner. They almost form an "L." If you keep watching, you see that, by the end of the scene, the picture has turned 180 degrees and the "L" is now upside down in the upper left-hand corner. (I love this stuff!)

• In the staff meeting that follows the identification of the Tarellian vessel, Dr. Crusher claims that the Tarellians had only advanced technologically to the level of late twentieth-century Earth. So where did they get this ship? It has warp drive—albeit nonfunctioning—and transporters.

• At this juncture, the creators must not have known about the biofilters in the transporter. After all, according to Crusher the virus that afflicted the Tarellians is a crude, twentieth-century beastie—surely no match for twenty-fourth-century technology. Picard could have simply run the Tarellians through the transporter and let them lead normal lives. (You would think that once the crew realized they had biofilters they would locate the Tarellian ship and lend a helping hand to these poor, downtrodden, disease-ridden people.)

• Originally Picard traps the Tarellian vessel in a tractor beam so the

Tarellians can't beam down to Haven. Yet, near the end of the episode, Wyatt beams over to the plague ship with apparently no difficulty. Maybe the transporter automatically communicates with the tractor beam and coordinates the transport?

• "Hero Worship" gives the impression that you have to enter an access code to use the equipment on the *Enterprise,* yet Wyatt walks up to the control console, punches a button, and beams right over to the Tarellian vessel. Did the transporter chief already enter the access code?

CONTINUITY AND PRODUCTION PROBLEMS

• Shortly after beaming aboard, Wyatt Miller's mother comments that Lwaxana Troi won't beam aboard until the Millers have left the transporter room. At this point Picard stands a few feet behind Mrs. Miller. In the next shot he suddenly stands beside her. (This is very convenient, because he can now direct her out of the transporter room. Those Starfleet captains know just how to be in the right place at the right time.)

• During the reception for Wyatt and Deanna, the Millers and Lwaxana discuss the type of ceremony the pair will have. Lwaxana objects to Picard performing the wedding because he is not practiced in the ways of Betazoid joining. At this point Data looks directly at Mr. Homn as the valet consumes yet another drink. In the subsequent long shot, suddenly Data is looking at Picard.

• After Riker dismisses himself from the reception, Deanna follows him onto the holodeck. She begins lecturing him on the human problem of separating platonic and physical love. As she does, a broad grin breaks out over Riker's face, as if he teeters on the edge of laughter. Yet the following close-up has the first officer instantly sullen. (Was this an outtake? Marina Sirtis does seem like she is on the verge of blowing her line.)

• When Troi enters the holodeck, the doors make their typical multi-staged opening and then closing sounds. When Riker leaves the holodeck, the sounds repeat. Between these two events, Wyatt enters the holodeck without the normal accompanying sounds. How did he get on the holodeck without walking through the doors?

• Speaking of getting somewhere without using the doors, Troi makes an amazingly fast appearance on the bridge moments later. As the plague ship closes on the planet Haven, Yar suggests using a phaser blast to disable the vessel. Picard nixes that idea, and instantly Troi is seated in her previously unoccupied chair.

TRIVIA ANSWERS

1. Valeda Innis.
2. The Alcyones.

THE BIG GOODBYE

Star Date: 41997.7

After completing a grueling preparation for contact with the protocol-sensitive Jarada, Picard joins Crusher, Data, and fiction expert Whalen for a relaxing holodeck adventure based on Dixon Hill—a fictional detective of the 1940s. Unfortunately, a sensor probe from the Jarada damages the holodeck and endangers their lives.

RUMINATIONS

Geoffrey Cook of Hammond, IN, alerted me to the perfectly appropriate selection the creators used as the melodic basis for a portion of the background music in this episode. As Picard enters the holodeck's version of Dixon Hill's building, a woman sings, "You came to me from out of nowhere."

TRIVIA QUESTIONS

1. What is the name of Picard's holographic police buddy?

2. To what planet does the *Enterprise* travel so that Picard can greet the Jarada?

PLOT OVERSIGHTS

• The star dates for the first season are severely jumbled. For instance, this episode occurs on star date 41997.7. According to all the subsequent seasons of *NextGen*, the episode should be the last one in the first season. Presumably the creators were still figuring out what to do with the star dates.

• When first entering the holodeck, Picard makes a log entry detailing the workings of the holodeck. Given a total suspension of disbelief, one must ask, "Exactly who will review this entry? Are there twenty-fourth-century Starfleet individuals who do not understand what a holodeck does?" (Actually, we *professional* nitpickers call this sort of thing a "cabbageism." The creators must include dialogue—or monologue—to explain the working of the *Enterprise* to us, the cabbages in the audience! Since the holodeck is still new at this point in the series, the creators must remind us what it does, even though it has appeared in three episodes already—"Encounter at Farpoint," "Code of Honor," and "Haven." By the way, Elias S. Saltz holds the distinction of coining the term "cabbageism" in the Nitpicker's Lexicon.)

• Picard's interest in the pulp detective fiction of fifty-odd years ago raises an interesting point. For the captain, this literature would be about 400 years old! Do these detective stories really contain a level of art to sustain them through the fabled "test of time"? Or has the advent of electronic storage done away with this final standard of determining a creative entity's worth? With data compression and cheap memory, will every book published live in perpetuity in some library's data base? (Now, there's a scary thought: Someone stumbling across the *Nitpicker's Guides* 350 years in the future! If you happen to be reading this in the twenty-fourth century: Hi, from the nitpickers of the twentieth century!)

• The Jarada probe that damages the holodeck actually shakes the bridge. In all likelihood, then, it also shakes the holodeck. Oddly enough, Picard doesn't bother to find out why his beloved craft is bouncing up and down.

• Interestingly enough, the protocol-sensitive Jarada evidently think nothing of demanding Picard's presence before the scheduled arrival time.

• Riker, frustrated that the holodeck will not release Picard, and tense over the arrival of the deadline to greet the Jarada, tells Yar to open a channel. He then angrily *demands* to speak with the insectlike race. Two items: First, just after Riker tells Yar to open hailing frequencies, you can see the reflection of the boom mike in a bright white area on a workstation along the back wall of the main bridge just to the left of the first officer. Second, did Riker doze off during the briefing earlier in the episode? Did he misunderstand that the Jarada are completely devoted to protocol and therefore absolutely certain not to acknowledge his attempt at communication?

• The repair crew seems to be missing at the end of the episode when the gangsters leave the holodeck.

EQUIPMENT ODDITIES

• The holodeck behaves rather strangely in this episode even before the Jarada probe damages it. Picard leaves the holodeck while it displays Dixon Hill's office and asks the computer to store the program. Then he returns with Data and fiction expert Whalen, but when the doors open, they are on the street outside. Why don't they return to the office? Was the squirrelly Felix Leech's entrance into Dix's office the end of one chapter, and the street scene the beginning of the next chapter? And that raises another question: If you are experiencing the holodeck version of a novel, do you have to live through the information the book skips? If Picard does not instruct the computer otherwise, would he have to go back to Dixon Hill's apartment and sleep for seven hours before the action would continue?

• I wonder if the holodeck would have allowed Crusher to take Whalen to a twentieth-century hospital in the holodeck after Leech shot him. Granted it wouldn't be as efficient as sick bay, but she probably could have stabilized his vital signs.

• At one point Wesley claims that if he makes a mistake, the program could abort and everyone inside could vanish. Would you want to play in a room that could vaporize you?

• I'm sure the creators did it for effect, but I wouldn't be doing my duty if I didn't point out that the holodeck ends the Dixon Hill simulation a bit oddly. As Picard walks out, the lights dim and the door closes. Shouldn't the room revert to the holodeck grid? (Or hadn't the creators decided on that transition yet?)

CONTINUITY AND PRODUCTION PROBLEMS

• The lipstick Picard acquires from his first kiss by a holodeck woman seems to move around on his face. In the holodeck, the soon-to-be-iced femme fatale plants one on the captain just below his lips, making a fairly light impression. When Picard leaves the holodeck, the lipstick suddenly resides on and above his lips and has become much darker.

• After entering the holodeck for the second time, Picard gets a paper from a vendor. The man hands the paper to Picard folded, but when Picard receives it the paper is instantly unfolded.

• When Crusher enters the holodeck, someone has already removed the panel underneath the interface display. Yet when La Forge checks on Picard and the others, the panel has been returned to its original location. Did the Jarada probe really damage the holodeck? Or is there a crew member on the *Enterprise* who has it in for Picard and is trying to trap the captain in a dangerous situation? (Then again, maybe the perpetrators' real target was Whalen. After all, he's the one who gets shot, and you know how those fiction experts create enemies wherever they go.)

• When the gangsters walk out into the corridor of the *Enterprise,* the shot from inside the holodeck shows a solid wall opposite the holodeck entrance. Yet the shot from the corridor shows a hallway opposite the holodeck entrance.

TRIVIA ANSWERS

1. McNary.
2. Trona IV.

DATALORE

Star Dates: 41242.4—41242.5

On Omicron Theta, an away team finds a complete set of parts for an android. After reassembly, the android introduces himself as Lore, Data's brother. Barely in time, Data and Wesley discover Lore's evil intent to feed the crew to a malevolent creature called the crystalline entity and quickly beam him out into space.

TRIVIA QUESTIONS

1. What chief engineer oversees the reassembly of Lore?

2. Officers from which ship found Data?

ALTERNATE VIEWPOINTS AND CORRECTIONS

• Doris R. Skiba corresponded to inform me that Lore's hair is not over his ears when Data picks up Lore's head, as I purported on page 36. In fact, Lore's ears haven't been attached yet! I have no excuse for this except that the tape I used to review this episode was of less than excellent quality. Once I taped the episode again I saw my mistake immediately.

PLOT OVERSIGHTS

• Are the engineers running diagnostics on the communications systems during this episode? Twice Picard sends someone to fetch Data instead of just paging the android. At the beginning of the episode, the captain dispatches Wesley to bring Data back to the bridge and, after the discovery of Lore, Crusher tells Data that Picard wants him for a briefing.

• As Data practices his sneezing, Wesley asks if Data has a cold. Realizing that Data doesn't understand the question, Wesley then explains that it is a disease that his mom said people "used to get." If people no longer suffer from colds, why would Wesley ask if Data had one? Does he imagine that there is an android equivalent of the common cold that the engineers have yet to conquer?

• Riker makes a log entry as the away team beams down to the planet. In it he gives the star date as 4124.5—one that would jibe with *Classic Trek*! (Apparently Riker dropped a number.)

• Shortly after arriving on the planet, La Forge proclaims that the soil is *almost* completely lifeless. Yet Riker, in his log moments earlier, labeled it completely dead. (Is this one of those "Princess Bride" things? Is the soil only "mostly dead" and Riker doesn't realize it?)

• Great confusion surrounds the sequence of events concerning the consumption of the planet's life by the crystal entity, the disassembly of Lore, the drawing of the children's pictures, the building of Data, and the like. As near as I can reconstruct from the dialogue, Soong built Lore. Lore contacted the crystal entity. The crystal

entity started coming. Soong deactivated Lore. The colony knew it was in trouble and built a big shelter. The crystal entity arrived and began eating the life on the planet. Everyone ran into the shelter. The children drew pictures of it while Soong dumped the colonists' memories into Data. (I'm not exactly sure *when* Soong constructed him.) Soong put him out on the slab and escaped. (We find this out in "Brothers.") The crystal entity ate everyone except Data. Now, this all makes sense until we factor in the events from "Silicon Avatar." In that episode the crystal entity acts like a giant vacuum cleaner, sucking up all the life on the planet in a relatively short amount of time, fewer than thirty hours—and probably fewer than six. Assuming the crystal entity has only one consumption rate, how could Soong and the colonists possibly accomplish all that they did?

• Picard and Riker's attitudes toward Wesley seem a bit odd in this episode. Riker trusts Wesley enough to send him to check on Data and Lore, but then neither the captain nor the first officer seem interested in hearing what the boy has to say.

• Lore's disposition at the end of this episode needs discussion. Wesley transported Lore into space but obviously didn't disperse his pattern because the android shows up later in "Brothers." Evidently the crystal entity didn't cart him off because Lore claims he drifted in space for two years before a Pakled ship found him (as also revealed in "Brothers.") So why did the *Enterprise* just wander off without him? Couldn't their sensors pick him up and beam him into the brig? Lore is obviously intelligent, self-aware, and probably conscious. Doesn't he deserve the right to trial that any sentient being has under the charter of the Federation? Then again, the crew of the *Enterprise* has demonstrated the ability to kill a dangerous person without benefit of a trial (as Riker did to Yuta in "The Vengeance Factor" and Data finally does to Lore in "Descent II"). So maybe it would have been better for Wesley to fling Lore's atoms out into space and save everyone grief in the future.

CHANGED PREMISES

• Subsequent episodes, such as "The Measure of a Man" and "The Offspring" reveal that Starfleet would love to have more than one Data. Yet, for some reason, in the twenty-six years that Data has been associated with Starfleet, no one has bothered to revisit the android's home world. Does this seem right?

• When Data picks up Lore's head, you can see that Lore's ears are missing. In addition, Soong claimed in "Brothers" that Data and Lore were identical except for a bit of programming. On the other hand, Data tells Crusher in "Unification I" that his ears are not detachable.

EQUIPMENT ODDITIES

• With Lore threatening to kill her son if she doesn't leave, Crusher makes a run for the cargo bay door. As it opens, Lore fires on her. After the crisis passes, both Data and Yar—as well as Picard and Riker—must press the panel beside the car-

go bay door before it will open. Why the change?

• During the fight between Data and Lore in the cargo bay, a phaser goes flying through the air. As it lands on the transporter pad, it breaks into two pieces. (I could make some snide comment here about Starfleet hardware but…I'll let you make up your own punch line on this one.)

CONTINUITY AND PRODUCTION PROBLEMS

• At one point, Yar asks Data if he is expecting Lore to come "up here." Moments later, she then states that the turbolift sensors say Lore went to deck 4. Watch Yar's lips. She actually says "deck 1." Since only the bridge and the observation lounge make up deck 1, the creators had to go back and overdub the line. (See, they really do try to get it right!)

• After drinking some spiked champagne supplied by Lore, Data falls backward but lands on his face. (Gotta admire those android reflexes.)

TRIVIA ANSWERS

1. Lieutenant Commander Argyle.
2. The USS *Tripoli. (Too easy!)*

UPDATED DAMAGE TOTE BOARD

1. Number of times Picard is kidnapped: fourteen
2. Number of times Riker is knocked down: eighteen (maybe nineteen)
3. Number of times Data is electrocuted: eight
4. Number of times La Forge's VISOR is knocked off: four
5. Number of times Worf is shot: six
6. Number of times Yar is killed: two (possibly three)
7. Number of times Wesley is pierced through the heart: one (not counting what Salia did to him)
8. Number of times the ship blows up: ten on screen (possibly as many as thirty other times)
9. Number of times the ship gets knocked for a loop: four
10. Number of times life support degrades on the bridge: four (maybe five)

REFERENCES

1. Q does it in "Encounter at Farpoint." Q does it again in "Hide and Q." Q does it again in "Q Who." The Ansata terrorists take him from the bridge in "The High Ground." Aliens take him from his quarters in "Allegiance." The Borg do it in "The Best of Both Worlds, Part 1." Data and Worf take him from the Borg ship in "The Best of Both Worlds, Part 2." Q does it again in "Qpid." Captain Dathon takes him to a planet in "Darmok." The probe mentally kidnaps him in "The Inner Light." Moriarty holds him in the holodeck in "Ship in a Bottle." Mercenaries grab him in "Gambit, Part 1." The Prit do it in "Attached." Q does it once more in "All Good Things."

2. The Ferengi use their phaser whips on him in "The Last Outpost." Armus pulls him down in "Skin of Evil." Admiral Quinn punches him in "Conspiracy." Captain Kargan backfists him in "A Matter of Honor." His father wallops him in "The Icarus Factor." According to hearsay, Dr. Apgar decks him in "A Matter of Perspective." An explosion on the bridge hurls him to the floor in "Yesterday's *Enterprise*." A sucker punch takes him down in "Sarek." The Borg do it in "The Best of Both Worlds, Part 1." The Paxans stun him in "Clues." The Malcorians beat him up in "First Contact." The storm throws him to the ground, Data knocks him backward, and O'Brien stuns him in "Power Play." A disintegrating *Enterprise* shakes him to the floor in "Cause and Effect." An Arkar-

ian hits him in "Starship Mine." The ship throws him off balance in "Timescape." Picard slugs him in "Gambit, Part 1." (Troi does take Thomas Riker down in "Second Chances.")

3. The Ferengi send energy arcs his way in "The Last Outpost." Picard, possessed by an entity, hits him with a lightning bolt in "Lonely Among Us." Gosheven shocks him with a cattle prod in "The Ensigns of Command." The Calamarain's attack on Q jolts Data as well in "Déjà Q." Varria stuns him in "The Most Toys." One half million amps arc through his body in "Disaster." Bashir's machine sends out a plasma tendril twice in "Birthright, Part 1."

4. Armus knocks it off in "Skin of Evil." An out-of-control turbolift flings it aside in "Contagion." The fall into the pit in "The Enemy" jars it loose. Roga Danar evidently sends it flying in "The Hunted."

5. The Ferengi shoot him with a phaser whip in "The Last Outpost." A terrorist takes him down in "The High Ground," Troi uses a phaser on him in "Power Play." The Ferengi hit him in "Rascals." Data puts a slug in him in "A Fistful of Datas." The Cardassians tag him in "Chain of Command, Part 1."

6. Armus sucks the life energy out of her in "Skin of Evil." According to Sela, the Romulans killed her nineteen years before the events in "Redemption II." (Q does freeze her in "Encounter at Farpoint" and then grants her grace.)

7. One of Q's "vicious animal things" does this to Wesley in "Hide and Q." (Actually, it's more like his stomach!)

8. The senior staff watches a replay of the shuttle's log in "Cause and Effect," Picard watches it happen in "Timescape." One of the *Enterprises* blows up in "Parallels." Three *Enterprises* blow up at the end of "All Good Things." The rest of the times occur during "Cause and Effect." (The repeating cycle takes about 12 hours, and the *Enterprise* is in the loop for for 17.4 days.)

9. The Aldean repulser beam does it in "When the Bough Breaks." Q does it twice in "Q Who." Tin Man does it in "Tin Man." (There are other times when the *Enterprise* gets shoved a great distance but not spun in a circle.)

10. An energy-draining field causes it in "The Last Outpost." The nanites pump poisonous gas onto the bridge in "Evolution." Data shuts off life support to the bridge in "Brothers." Metal parasites degrade life support in "Cost of Living." (How about the Zalkonian choking beam in "Transfigurations"?)

ANGEL ONE

Star Date: 41636.9

Beaming down to planet Angel One to recover the crew of the disabled freighter *Odin,* Riker and an away team discover that the men do not wish to leave, even though their lives are in danger because their presence is upsetting the heavily matriarchal culture.

TRIVIA QUESTIONS

1. What gift does Riker present to Mistress Beata?

2. Wesley states that the effects of the virus he contracts on Quazulu VIII are worse than what disease?

ALTERNATE VIEWPOINTS AND CORRECTIONS

• Unfortunately, my "correctness factor" dropped a notch on page 43 of the *NextGen Guide* when I equated the terms "fixed" orbit with "geosynchronous" orbit. In fact they are two different things according to Ed Howard of Sloatsburg, NY, and Ricky G. Gee of Aurora, CA. A fixed orbit simply means that the ship is in a certain type of orbit around the planet, no matter what the orientation in the X, Y, or Z plane. A geosynchronous orbit would position the *Enterprise* constantly above a given position on the planet.

• Diana Brown of San Ysidro, CA, sent me a letter stating that she finds no problem with Yar moving her hands during transport (as discussed on page 43 of the *NextGen Guide*). If Barclay could reach out and grab a crew member during transport in "Realm of Fear," why can't Yar move her arms? (I agree that Barclay did do that. I am still trying to figure out how people move when they are deconstructed into a slush of energy. In fact, in this episode, not only do Yar's arms move, but also the entire away team does a right face! They start out in something akin to a row, facing each other's backs, and then materialize turned ninety degrees—as noted by David J. Ferrier of Washington, DC.)

• David Shelton of Birmingham, AL, wrote to say that he had no difficulty believing the inhabitants of Angel One would possess a disintegrator beam (contrary to my comments on page 43). Since Data's statement that Angel One possessed midtwentieth-century technology was based on information sixty-two years old, David believes that Angel One is at the twenty-first-century level of technology. David also pointed out that disintegrators are less technologically sophisticated than a replicator. Just because you have one doesn't necessarily mean you can easily develop the other.

PLOT OVERSIGHTS

• Data's knowledge and lack thereof concerning the English language are puzzling in this episode. When Data examines a spray bottle of perfume on the surface of the planet, Troi explains that some cultures view the substance as an aphrodisiac. Data then comments that he is not familiar with the term. Mr. "I am skilled in a wide variety of pleasuring techniques" doesn't know the term "aphrodisiac"? Surprisingly enough, a short time later, while in command of the *Enterprise,* Data demonstrates his knowledge of the word "bingo." (True, he doesn't understand how Crusher applies the term, but he does recognize it as a game.) In other words: bingo has outlasted aphrodisiacs?

• A bit of role reversal might shed some light on this next observation. It's not really a nit, just an interesting point. When Riker prepares to meet with Mistress Beata, he dons an open-chested tunic and tight pants. Yar and Troi giggle and titter at the sight like schoolgirls. But let's turn this around for a moment. Suppose Troi had to dress in a low-cut, high-slit outfit...wait a minute, that's not a good example. Suppose...*Crusher* had to dress in a low-cut, high-slit outfit to meet with some high-ranking medical doctor on a distant planet. Would it be professional for Riker and Data to stand around whistling catcalls and shouting, "Whoa, baby! I *definitely* need some emergency care!"?

• This episode purports that the Prime Directive binds only members of Starfleet, and therefore the survivors of the *Odin* are not required to leave Angel One. In fact, Data claims that forcibly removing them would violate the Prime Directive. Wait a minute: If the point of the Prime Directive is to protect peoples and cultures from outside interference, what is to stop an unscrupulous freighter captain from selling replicators to underdeveloped worlds? Granted, Starfleet's specific rules and regulations should be binding only on Starfleet, but shouldn't the Federation have some corresponding laws that are binding on all those who pass through the sectors under Federation control? Isn't this necessary to enforce the *spirit* of the Prime Directive? Indeed, wouldn't leaving the survivors of the *Odin* on Angel One be disruptive to the natural development of the planet and therefore be interfering with it? If so, wouldn't a strict interpretation of the Prime Directive *demand* that Picard remove them? On the other hand, how in the galaxy is the Federation supposed to police every nonaligned planet in sectors under its control? And what about planets outside Federation control on which the *Enterprise* discovers intelligent life? What's to stop the Ferengi from intercepting Picard's transmissions and wandering up after the *Enterprise* leaves with a cargo bay of high-tech goodies? (This Prime Directive stuff is tough!)

• Why does Picard set out for the Neutral Zone at warp 6 when Data supposedly waited until the last minute to leave Angel One? Has Picard received new intelligence that the Romulans have decided to be nice boys and girls and go home?

EQUIPMENT ODDITIES

• Of course, the creators didn't know about the biofilter on the transporter at this point in the series, so they couldn't have Crusher send the afflicted through it and thereby cure the epidemic.

• The meditation crystal Riker gives Beata makes a return performance with Vash in the *Deep Space Nine* episode "Q-Less." Oddly enough, Vash supposedly has returned with little-seen artifacts from the Gamma Quadrant.

• Those amazing communicators with their ability to know exactly when they should keep transmitting are at it again. After visiting with Ramsey, Yar talks with La Forge. She finishes her conversation and it sounds like she taps her badge to end the transmission. Moments later Yar says "Energize," and they beam away!

CONTINUITY AND PRODUCTION PROBLEMS

• Speaking of the snowball that flies out of the holodeck but shouldn't, we do get a chance to see that wondrous quick-drying Starfleet fabric in action. (See page 105 of the *NextGen Guide* under "Continuity and Production Problems" for "Contagion.") During his rebuke of Wesley, a large wet spot still shows near Picard's right shoulder. The camera angle changes, and suddenly the very same spot is completely dry!

• I noted a continuity problem with Mistress Beata in the *NextGen Guide.* She causes another. When she tells Riker that he attracts her like no other man, her hand disappears from his neck.

• Apparently there was a shortage of extras when the creators filmed this episode. In one scene, La Forge—on the bridge—speaks with Crusher in sick bay. When La Forge talks, you can see a white-haired medical assistant helping a crew member. The first time Crusher talks, the same white-haired medical assistant is herself

helped across sick bay. Then the scene cuts back to the bridge and the same woman *still* helps the crew member. Twins, maybe?

• I guess the engineers in the twenty-fourth century couldn't figure out how to improve the basic design of the thermos. Crusher walks into Picard's quarters with one that looks for all the world like something you could purchase off the shelf today.

TRIVIA ANSWERS

1. An Albeni meditation crystal.
2. Hesperan thumping cough.

11001001

Star Date: 41365.9

Bynars—humanoids who possess an unusually high level of interconnectedness with the main computer on their planet—hijack the *Enterprise* to serve as a temporary storage device while intense solar activity buffets their home world.

RUMINATIONS

Time for a big compliment. Admittedly some of the nitpicking I do is pretty picayune—running timings on dialogue, asserting that if a given amount of time is stated for an operation, the operation should take that long. Since I do drop off the edge occasionally (hopefully just occasionally), it's only fair to praise the creators when they take the time to do something, very minor, exactly correct. Before beaming to the bridge, Riker tells Picard that he has set the transporter for a ten-second delay. This will give him time to join Picard on the transporter pad. Riker hits the button, and the console begins beeping. Each beep marks one second and—at the end of ten beeps—the transporter kicks on! Yes, yes, yes, yes, yes. Flawlessly executed!

TRIVIA QUESTIONS

1. Whom does Crusher intend to meet with on Starbase 74?

2. What time of the day does Riker give for the setting of his jazz bar?

ALTERNATE VIEWPOINTS AND CORRECTIONS

• In the *NextGen Guide* under the trivia answers for this episode, I stated that there are at least twenty transporters on the *Enterprise*. Clark Scanlon of Council Bluffs, IA, wrote to say that, in addition, there were also emergency transporters on the shuttles (as seen in "The Best of Both Worlds, Part 2").

PLOT OVERSIGHTS

• Quinteros introduces a pair of Bynars as "01" and "10." Obviously other Bynars must have longer names, because if the entire population uses only two binary digits there would be only four names to go around ("00," "01," "10," and "11"). I suppose they could do something like "11 son of 01 son of 10."

• The sounds that the Bynars make supposedly come from high-speed data transmissions, but they don't sound much faster than data transmitted on a 300-baud modem ("baud" is a measure of how many bits per second the modem can send and receive). Of course, at the time the creators made this episode, 300 baud was probably considered fast. No longer. (At the time of this writing, 14,400 baud is standard, and 28,800-baud modems are coming on fast. When these modems transmit data they sound like static.)

• A bit of Americentrism slips into the dialogue in this episode. After Picard asks Minuet about her ability to speak French, she says that she simply accessed the "*foreign* languages file." In the twentieth century, we call French a foreign language because we—as Americans—classify everything outside our borders as foreign. Wouldn't the expanded understanding of the multitude of inhabited worlds change the definition of "foreign" for Terrans in the twenty-fourth century? Wouldn't it be natural to use the term to refer to anything outside the boundaries of Earth instead of something merely outside the boundaries of the United States of America? (And even if you don't buy any of that, Minuet is speaking with Picard at the time, and French is definitely not a foreign language to him.)

• The crew of the *Enterprise* passes up another perfectly good time for a saucer separation. Presumably these *Galaxy*-class starships cost lots of money. Why not send the battle section off to explode by itself? It should be much easier to evacuate, since all the families live in the saucer. Is there some regulation against separating while in space dock?

• Of course, I find it highly suspicious that all the lights and klaxons are blaring during the evacuation of the ship, yet neither Picard nor Riker hear anything. Probably the Bynars disabled the holodeck's alert indicators. (I would hate to think that a crew member could miss performing his role during a crisis simply because he was playing on the holodeck and didn't hear the red alert signal.)

• The whole business of the Bynars and their need to back up the data in their main computer by storing it in the Enterprise's main computer seems a bit shortsighted. Supposedly this culture completely depends on their main computer, yet they have no mechanism to back up the information? Doesn't seem very practical, does it?

• Finally, if Riker really wants to get Minuet back, why doesn't he just ask the Bynars to recreate her? Did she consume too many computer resources to be practical on a day-to-day basis?

EQUIPMENT ODDITIES

• Those Federation starship designers certainly work hard to put human qualities into the computer. Answering Riker's query on the reason for the power reductions in certain area of the ship, the computer takes at least two *pronounced* breaths.

• Yet another feather in the cap of the Federation starship designers, when Riker orders the band for his jazz club. He asks for a " 'bone," and the computer properly contextualizes the

request by supplying a trombone instead of a dog bone. (But wouldn't it have been fun to see the latter?)

• The computer has a male voice during two different scenes in this episode. Not really a nit, just an observation.

• Oddly enough, the computer fails to answer a direct question from Data as he and La Forge board a turbolift to make their way to the transporter room and leave the Enterprise. Data asks the computer the location of Captain Picard and the computer responds, "All decks empty." Yet later in the program, Picard asks the computer the location of Data, and the computer responds that he is not on board the Enterprise.

• Data and La Forge hurry off the bridge and head to the transporter room because they have only forty-one seconds left. Question: Why don't they just do a site-to-site transport? I understand that it takes twice the resources to implement a direct transport (and therefore you wouldn't want to try to evacuate an entire ship using this method), but everyone who's going ashore has gone ashore, and if you've got only forty-one seconds, you probably want to make your exit posthaste.

• Bynar's tinkering might also be the reason that the holodeck doors don't automatically fade into the scenery as they do in other episodes. Each time Picard and Riker return to question Minuet, the doors stay visible.

• The act of Picard calling Starbase 74 on his communicator near the end of the episode bothered several nitpickers. When I saw the episode for the first time, it bothered me as well. Then I guessed that the computer on the *Enterprise* had patched through the request. Of course, if the computer can do that, why do you need Yar and Worf to "open hailing frequencies"?

CONTINUITY AND PRODUCTION PROBLEMS

• The initial arrival of Commander Quinteros and the Bynars on the *Enterprise* contains a large editing gaff. The scene shows them approaching the *Enterprise* airlock (as evidenced by a hatch flanked with "NCC 1701-D" and "ENTER…"). The action switches to show Quinteros and the Bynars *entering* the airlock from Starbase 74! And while we are on the subject of this airlock and its umbilical connect between the starbase and the *Enterprise,* the establishing external shot of the ship clearly shows windows and lots of people coming and going, neither of which remain when the scene cuts to the interior of the airlock.

• When Data and La Forge first arrive in Main Engineering, the scene clearly shows that everyone is gone. The pair quickly establishes that the magnetic containment field is collapsing, and Data decides to evacuate the *Enterprise.* He begins making his announcement, and the scene cuts to a shot of a woman seated near a workstation. However, the reflection in the glass shows the warp core pulsing, placing her in Main Engineering!

TRIVIA ANSWERS

1. Dr. Terence Epstein.
2. At 2:00 A.M.

TOO SHORT A SEASON

Star Date: 41309.5

F acing the potential of repeating a mistake made forty years ago when he traded arms for hostages and thereby plunged Mordan IV into civil war, Admiral Mark Jameson gives himself a massive dose of a de-aging drug to restore his youth prior to beginning hostage negotiations yet again on the wartorn planet.

TRIVIA QUESTIONS

1. Where does the *Enterprise* pick up Jameson?

2. From what planet did Jameson procure his de-aging treatment?

PLOT OVERSIGHTS

• Yar doesn't seem to make any effort to protect her senior officers' safety at a key point during the away mission. After barely glancing into a newly opened room, she allows both Jameson and Picard to enter before her. Yes, Worf *follows* Jameson into the room, but shouldn't Yar verify the safety of the potentially dangerous area before allowing an admiral and a captain to enter?

EQUIPMENT ODDITIES

• In the previous episode, Picard used his communicator to call Starbase 74. This begs the question: Why does Starfleet need the tactical officer to route calls when the computer can do it with equal ease? This episode raises another question: Just whose job is it to route communications? En route to Mordan IV, the *Enterprise* receives a transmission from Karnas. La Forge reports the incoming message, and Picard orders Data to open the channel. Meanwhile, Yar stands by with her arms folded. Isn't this her job?

CONTINUITY AND PRODUCTION PROBLEMS

• As Yar and Worf begin to cut through the steelplast wall in the tunnels underneath the capital city on Mordan IV, you can see a dark outline already present on the wall. Presumably this is a cord of some sort of flash powder and will ignite to create the sparks that fly when the phasers bite into the surface.

• Also in this scene, Worf begins his cut by moving sideways. The next shot shows his phaser moving downward. Then the very next shot shows him moving sideways again. Also, as they begin the cut, both Yar and Worf hold their phasers much higher than the top of the cut indicates a few moments later.

TRIVIA ANSWERS

1. Persephone V.
2. Cerebus II.

WHEN THE BOUGH BREAKS

Star Dates: 41509.1—41512.4

After the once-believed-mythical planet of Aldea decloaks in front of the *Enterprise,* its leaders ask for the unthinkable. No longer able to procreate—due to the depletion of the ozone layer of their planet by their pervasive technology—the Aldeans offer to purchase children in exchange for their advanced scientific knowledge.

TRIVIA QUESTIONS

1. What mythical landmass does Riker allude to on Xerxes VII?

2. Who is assigned to tutor Katie in the musical arts?

PLOT OVERSIGHTS

• After the Aldeans kidnap the children, Picard tells Troi to get the parents together for a meeting. The subsequent meeting features Picard, Troi, five single parents, and one couple. Since seven children are taken by the Aldeans, we must assume that two of the children were siblings. That does not explain why five of the six families represented are single-parent families. Is this the creators' view of the future?

• Do all the children of the Federation have parents? Has the coming of the twenty-fourth century done away with orphans? In other words, why doesn't Picard bring up the prospect of adoption to satisfy the childless Aldeans? Or do the Aldeans only want to hand-pick their children from the best and the brightest on the *Enterprise*?

• It must be noted that several nit-pickers found it incredible that the Aldeans could possess such advanced technology and not realize what it was doing to their ozone layer.

• Radue has a sudden change of heart once he sees the massive generator that serves as power source for Aldea. Moments before, he grouses around—calling Picard and his people liars. Then the door opens and the little group walks into the huge chamber (which is done very nicely, by the way), and instantly he starts rambling about how their technology has harmed them.

EQUIPMENT ODDITIES

• At least the Federation has transporters with capabilities similar to those of the Aldeans. When the Aldeans beam Riker, Troi, and Crusher back to the ship, the trio begins the trip seated and ends it standing up. Very impressive. (The *Enterprise*'s transporter does exactly the same thing to Lwaxana Troi in "Ménage à Troi.")

• During the negotiations for the children, Picard convinces Radue to allow Dr. Crusher to speak with Wesley. When she does, she places the med-

ical wand from her tricorder in his palm so he can covertly scan Radue's wife. Very conveniently, the wand fails to emit its normal warble while Wesley waves it back and forth.

CONTINUITY AND PRODUCTION PROBLEMS

• Paged by the bridge, Riker leaves his impromptu meeting with Harry and boards a turbolift. In the lower right-hand corner of the turbolift opening you can see a silver tripod leg—probably from a lightstand.

• The creators had to overdub a few words of dialogue for Riker for some reason. Watch his lips when he says that he is surprised Tasha hasn't heard the stories of Aldea.

• When Radue's wife introduces Wesley to the controlling computer—called the Companion—the shot zooms in until it fills the entire screen. Then it cuts to a side shot, and Radue's wife suddenly has both hands on the display area.

TRIVIA ANSWERS

1. Neinman.
2. Melian.

★

HOME SOIL

Star Dates: 41463.9—41464.8

Unwittingly, a terraforming team on Velara III begins killing the crystal life forms indigenous to the planet. In short order, a detachment of the crystals not only declares war on the team but extends the battle to the *Enterprise* as well.

GREAT LINES

"Ugly bags of mostly water."—the crystal life form referring to humans. Alma Jo Williams of Ithaca, NY, nominated this line, saying that she herself has used it several times with gratifying results.

TRIVIA QUESTIONS

1. How does Luisa Kim introduce herself?

2. What does Arthur Malencon do?

PLOT OVERSIGHTS

• The Pleiades Cluster is only 415 light-years from Earth. Yet, during a log entry, Picard claims that the *Enterprise* is conducting a mapping mission in this region. At warp 9, the *Enterprise* could start at Earth and arrive at the Pleiades Cluster in about three months. Why has it taken so long for the Federation to map this cluster?

• You have to hand it to Data. This android is fast! Shortly after asking La Forge to return power to the laser drill in the pumping station on the surface of the planet, Data realizes the drill has focused on him. The scene shows the drill firing and Data *dodging* the beam. This is a laser. It works with light. Light travels at about 186,000 miles per second. (Faster if you figure it in kilometers…just joking.)

• When Data and La Forge first dis-

cover the crystal life form, it sits in a dark drilling tube. Yet later in the show we discover that the crystal needs light to live.

CHANGED PREMISES

• Why does this crystal life form surprise the crew of the *Enterprise*? Discounting the encounters of unusual life forms by previous crews of the *Enterprise,* Picard's crew has already met Q, a "lonely" energy cloud, a transdimensional "god," and a giant crystal entity—all remarkable in their own right.

EQUIPMENT ODDITIES

• Exactly what does the person on the other end of the conversation see and hear when Picard and crew put their communication on hold? At the beginning of the episode, Picard speaks with Mandl. At one point Troi tells Picard that something is wrong. Picard hits a button and the computer says, "Channel closed." Yet the viewscreen continues to show Mandl. Presumably he's staring at some form of blank screen (perhaps with the Federation symbol and a caption that says, "We apologize for putting you on hold, but we need to talk about you and we didn't want you to overhear our conversation"). After a few moments, Mandl impatiently speaks up, and the bridge hears what he is saying. Evidently the channel is only closed going from Picard to Mandl. Doesn't this seem a bit rude?

CONTINUITY AND PRODUCTION PROBLEMS

• Throughout this entire episode, the creators used the same base shot for every scene featuring a wide angle of the viewscreen with Data and La Forge in the foreground at their posts. When originally filmed, the inside area of the viewscreen no doubt contained a "blue screen." After filming, the creators replaced the blue portions of the film with the footage they desired. They used this particular shot several times during Picard's conversation with head terraformer Mandl at the beginning of the episode and at least twice more in conversation with the crystal life form. Watch Data. He keeps punching the same buttons over and over and over....

TRIVIA ANSWERS

1. As the gardener of Edens.
2. He is a hydraulics specialist.

COMING OF AGE

Star Date: 41416.2

As Wesley competes to enter Starfleet Academy, Admiral Quinn boards the *Enterprise* with Lieutenant Commander Dexter Remmick. With little explanation, Quinn orders Picard to submit to an intensive investigation by Remmick—justifying his actions only by a vague reference to a threat facing the Federation.

RUMINATIONS

There is a series of lovely transitions as Remmick questions members of the senior staff. My favorite comes as Remmick interrogates Data. A desktop terminal sits between them. Data turns it to face Remmick. Remmick turns it back. A hand reaches up and shuts it off. Now the reflection in the terminal shows Worf, and the questioning continues.

TRIVIA QUESTIONS

1. What piece of equipment does Wesley play with in the Starfleet entrance exam testing room?

2. To what does the Zaldan Rondon compare Wesley Crusher?

PLOT OVERSIGHTS

• At one point, Jake Kurland steals a shuttle, attempting to run away from home. Evidently the young man is terribly nervous because—shortly after he is described as skilled in shuttle operation—he unbalances the shuttle engines.

• Does it seem realistic that Wesley doesn't make it into the academy? He's already an acting ensign. Both his parents were officers. He has saved the ship several times. I'm sure Picard would give him a good letter of recommendation. Are the entrance requirements really this stringent? In "Legacy," Ishara Yar pretends that she has an interest in joining Starfleet. Both Worf and Data encourage her to do so. Yet this woman has grown up on a colony run by gangs. Doesn't it seem likely that the academy would stress the necessity of a high-quality education? Or is there another reason why Wesley didn't get picked? Could it be that Starfleet hasn't filled its quota of Benzites in the past hundred years? After all, the testing officer tells Mordock—the guy who eventually wins entrance to the academy—that he will be the first Benzite in Starfleet.

CHANGED PREMISES

• A few shows later we will discover that Quinn was not imagining a crisis brewing in Starfleet. In fact, some beetlelike aliens are systematically seizing control of key members of the admiralty. The episode "Conspiracy" reveals this and another interesting fact: The mother creature controlling the beetles lives in Remmick! Presumably it's already in him during this episode. Quinn is already saying that something is amiss. If the aliens want to take over Starfleet, wouldn't this be the most opportune time to plant a few beetles in the bridge crew of the *Enterprise*? After all, Remmick has had a chance to be alone with all of them. For some reason, Remmick fails to take advantage of the situation.

EQUIPMENT ODDITIES

• Near the end of the episode, Remmick reports his findings to Quinn. He comes to Quinn's quarters and sits in a chair directly in front of Quinn's desk. Evidently, the user interface for raising and lowering chairs won't change much in the next 350 years because Remmick's chair has a little lever that sticks out to the side underneath the seat cushion, just like the one on my office chair!

CONTINUITY AND PRODUCTION PROBLEMS

• On the way to a farewell dinner with Admiral Quinn, Picard encounters Jake Kurland in a corridor. During the exchange and the one that follows with Wesley, Picard has no pips on his dress uniform. "Manhunt" shows Picard wearing a similar dress uniform, with the standard four pips in a row near his right shoulder.

TRIVIA ANSWERS

1. A flux coordinating sensor unit.
2. A Bulgallian sludge rat.

HEART OF GLORY

Star Date: 41503.7

The rescue of a trio of Klingons from a severely damaged freighter turns dangerous when the crew discovers that the group is wanted by the Klingon Empire. The warriors soon escape from the brig, and one of them ends up in Main Engineering with a weapon pointed at the warp core.

PLOT OVERSIGHTS

• When the away team first arrives on the freighter, does it seem like a good time to engage in small talk? Another five seconds of "show and tell" with LaForge's VISOR and everyone would have died when the freighter exploded.

• On the way to rescue the Klingons, Data makes the statement that all routes are *equally* dangerous. La Forge responds to this statement by asking which route is least dangerous. Evidently La Forge wasn't paying attention during the previous line of dialogue.

• Under the category of "What Kind of Security Officer Is Worf?" this episode has a pair of Klingons admitting to Worf that they took over a freighter, stranded its crew, and destroyed a Klingon cruiser. What is Worf's response to this turn of events? He takes them on a tour of some of the most strategic portions of the *Enterprise*!

• The armchair captains of the Nitpicker's Guild came up with two plausible methods for handling the crisis at the end of this episode when Korris trains a Klingon phaser on the warp core. In the *NextGen Guide* I suggested separating the saucer section to put the families of crew members out of danger. Others came up with better options. Why not transport the guy out of there and deactivate his weapon, as O'Brien did to Data in "The Most Toys"? Or why not turn off the warp core? La Forge does this in "Galaxy's Child," and it seems to go dead very quickly.

TRIVIA QUESTIONS

1. To what does Picard compare the output of La Forge's VISOR when La Forge gets a closer look at the flaw in the bulkhead of the freighter?

2. What is the name of the Klingon cruiser that the renegades destroy?

CHANGED PREMISES

• During the rescue of the three Klingons, La Forge tests a new gizmo called a visual acuity transmitter. It allows Picard to display the output of La Forge's VISOR on the main viewscreen. At one point Picard comments that the output shows a glow around Data, to which La Forge responds, "Of course, he's an android." Picard then replies that La Forge says that as if they all see Data with a glow. To this La Forge responds, "Don't you?" Now come back to "Hide and Q." At the end of that episode, Riker—temporarily given the power of the Q— gives La Forge new eyes. La Forge takes a good look at everyone on the bridge but finally decides that he would rather be the way he was. There is no indication that Riker took away La Forge's memory of natural sight, yet in "Heart of Glory," La Forge acts as if he has never seen through normal eyes. Of course, the other "glowing android" problem shows up in "Inheritance." In that episode, Data's mother shows up, and she is an android but nobody—including La Forge—knows it. If she is a Soong android, wouldn't she glow as well?

• The Klingon death scream seen in this episode apparently evolved sometime between the time of *Star Trek VI: The Undiscovered Country* and the time frame for "Heart of Glory." When Gorkon dies, no one hollers.

• Korris makes reference to his home world as "Kling." He says he refuses to let the traitors of Kling pick the meat from his bones. Kling? Now, there's a warrior-sounding name! Oddly enough, *Star Trek VI: The Undiscov-*

ered Country named the Klingon home world Qo'noS (or "Kronos" for us non-Klingons).

EQUIPMENT ODDITIES

• Evidently that blue area in the middle of the transporter platform can beam stuff around as well. When Yar finally gets the away team and the Klingons off the ship, the one holding the injured Klingon materializes in the center of the platform.

• The final admission by the Klingon renegades that they actually destroyed a Klingon cruiser raises an interesting point. Earlier in the episode, the renegades claimed they went into battle with only a battery of "ancient Merculite rockets." Are we to believe that a bunch of rockets with *chemical propellants* destroyed a Klingon cruiser filled with the most paranoid warriors in the galaxy? These rockets had to be insufferably slow compared with phasers, photons, or warp drive.

• During the crisis with Korris and the warp core, dialogue indicates that the Klingon points a weapon at the dilithium chamber. In fact, the *Technical Manual* indicates that the dilithium chamber is the wider metal chamber, with the hatch in the front in the center of the warp core. Korris actually points his phaser at a magnetic constriction segment.

• Falling to the floor after sustaining a phaser burst from Worf, Korris smashes through the glass and lands with a thud on the clear panel below, cracking it. Does this seem right? Is it really possible for some poor hapless ensign to die a horrible death because the flooring is made from

obviously fragile *glass*? What happened to transparent aluminum?

1. Spectrography indicating metal fatigue.
2. The *T'Acog.*

THE ARSENAL OF FREEDOM

Star Date: 41798.2

When all intelligent life ceases on the planet Minos, a Starfleet vessel goes to investigate but disappears as well. The crew of the *Enterprise* soon discovers that the inhabitants of the planet—widely known for their manufacturing and marketing of weapons systems—have built the ultimate machine of destruction.

TRIVIA QUESTIONS

1. Where is planet Minos located?

2. How far is it from ground level to the floor of the cavern that holds Picard and Crusher?

PLOT OVERSIGHTS

• Picard demonstrates that his senior officers aren't the only ones with a lack of first-aid knowledge. After falling into a cavern, he immediately tries to move Crusher. She groans in pain and he stops. Good thing she was awake! Otherwise he might have done additional damage by grinding the jagged edges of her broken bones through her muscles.

• When the cloaked starship-killer first appears, Worf reports a disturbance off the port bow, but the outside shot of the ship shows the weapon fired from directly ahead.

• One has to wonder at the competency of the *Enterprise*'s computer targeting systems or at the very least the competency of the guy operating the controls. At one point the cloaked starship-killer fires from behind the *Enterprise* and slightly to starboard as the ship turns to port. That means the direction of turn puts the cloaked starship-killer directly behind the ship. When Worf fires, the phasers and photon torpedoes fire directly *ahead* of the ship into empty space. Worf then slams his fist into the console and yells, "We missed!" Oh, really!?

EQUIPMENT ODDITIES

• For the great majority of this episode, Data's tricorder makes no sound, although Yar's and Crusher's do.

• While the fourth and final probe pursues Riker and Yar, Picard and Data stand in front of the main display for the weapons system. Two squares indicate Riker and Yar's position. The scene cuts to the surface, and the pair takes cover behind some rocks. The scene returns to the cavern, and the two squares stay motionless in the upper right-hand portion of the screen as Picard tries to figure out how to turn off the machine. Then, just before the captain agrees to pur-

chase the device, the display shows that the squares have moved to the center of the screen. However, on the next outside shot, we see that Riker and Yar have not moved from their position behind the rocks.

CONTINUITY AND PRODUCTION PROBLEMS

• There's a very odd overdub just after Picard and Crusher arrive on the planet. Data and Yar explain the function of the force field that holds Riker. When they finish, the scene shows a close-up of Picard and Crusher. A flat, emotionless female voice says, "Clever." It can't be Crusher, because her mouth is closed and her lips don't move, but it sure doesn't sound like Yar.

• After tending to Crusher's injuries, Picard begins exploring the cavern into which they have fallen. He finds a dust-covered panel with a flashing light. He wipes the dirt from its surface, tidies it up a bit, and then wipes the dirt from its surface again!

TRIVIA ANSWERS

1. In the Lorenze Cluster.

2. It is 11.75 meters.

SYMBIOSIS

Star Date: unknown

Rescuing two Ornarans, two Brekkians, and several containers of Felicium from a distressed freighter, the crew of the *Enterprise* soon discovers the unique relationship between the two races. For two hundred years, the Brekkians have supplied the Ornarans with Felicium—supposedly to stave off the effects of a deadly plague. In fact, Felicium is a highly addictive drug, and the Brekkians know it.

TRIVIA QUESTIONS

1. What is the name of the Ornaran freighter?

2. How long has T'Jon served as the freighter's captain?

ALTERNATE VIEWPOINTS AND CORRECTIONS

• Alma Jo Williams of Ithaca, NY, wrote to point out that my answer in the *NextGen Guide* to the second trivia question for this episode is incorrect, though the answer was lifted from the dialogue of the episode. On page 60 I stated that the recommended dosage for Felicium is one-hundredth milliliter. Alma Jo responded, "A milliliter is one-thousandth of a liter (approximately one quart) in metric volume measure. The important word here is 'volume'. Used in the context of my daily lab routine such as 'take one hundredth of a milliliter of 12 Normal hydrochloric acid,' this usage is fine because the acid is also liquid. However, when used with dissolved solids— and I believe Felicium is a solid until it is dissolved in whatever solvent (probably distilled sterile water)—the *concentration* or *amount* of the solid (solute) should have been mentioned."

CHANGED PREMISES

• Picard makes an interesting choice at the beginning of this episode. He takes the *Enterprise* into a system to perform some simple studies on the dynamics of its star's heavy flare activity. He endangers the ship with all its families for a close sensor path. Wouldn't a probe suffice?

CONTINUITY AND PRODUCTION PROBLEMS

• Since this was the last episode taped to feature Tasha Yar as a regular on *Star Trek: The Next Generation,* Denise Crosby took a moment to wave good-bye to her fans as Picard and Crusher walk out of the cargo bay near the end of the show. And when Picard and Crusher arrive on the bridge, Tasha is already at her Tactical station.

TRIVIA ANSWERS

1. *Sanction.*
2. Seven years.

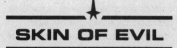

SKIN OF EVIL

Star Dates: 41601.3—41602.1

During an attempt to rescue Troi after her shuttle crash-lands on Vagra II, Yar dies at the hand of the malevolent entity, named Armus, who lives on the planet.

GREAT LINES

"I'm not taking you anywhere."—

Picard to Armus just before beaming back to the *Enterprise*.

TRIVIA QUESTIONS

1. What is the number of the shuttlecraft in which Troi rides?

2. Who is the shuttle's pilot?

ALTERNATE VIEWPOINTS AND CORRECTIONS

• Dale Barkley of Suisun City, CA, was the first to correspond and point out that Yar was never a lieutenant commander, as I stated on page 61 of the *NextGen Guide*.

PLOT OVERSIGHTS

• For some reason, the energy levels that Worf quotes contain *two* decimal points. First he tells Wesley to set the computer for automatic beam-up when the energy level reaches "two-point-six-point-two-zero-five." Then later he says to stand by for transport because the energy level has dropped to "two-point-six-point-three." (Must be that new twenty-fourth-century math.)

CHANGED PREMISES

• At the outset of this nit, I must admit that the first-season star dates have never caused me much concern. Yes, they are all jumbled up and don't make any sense if you apply the standard of the rest of the seasons (in which all the star dates are pleasingly consecutive). I *can* understand how it would bug people. For instance, there

are several episodes that have star dates *later* than the star date for "Skin of Evil" yet still feature Yar—"Angel One," "The Battle," "The Arsenal of Freedom," and "The Big Goodbye."

EQUIPMENT ODDITIES

• The crashed shuttle looks odd for a Starfleet shuttle. It's very round, and the piloting controls are placed about halfway back.

• On his way to sick bay to check on the stricken Tasha Yar, Picard orders the ship to yellow alert. Worf hits the buttons, but the lights over the Klingon's shoulder do not change to reflect the ship's new status.

• Worf indicates that they are going to do a parallel transport for the captain and the counselor. But when it occurs, Troi goes first, then Picard says his great line before the annular confinement surrounds him. (The transporter must have one of those "dramatic line" sensors.)

CONTINUITY AND PRODUCTION PROBLEMS

• As the episode opens, Yar and Worf discuss an upcoming martial arts competition. When they conclude, the scene switches to a close-up of La Forge, with Riker—out of focus—in the background. The first officer is clearly smiling. Then the shot changes to show Picard and Riker, who suddenly wears a solemn expression.

• Shortly after arriving at Vagra II, Worf locates the shuttle. A brief shot of his workstation displays a line graph and what looks like a topographical layout of the area around the shuttle. There's only one problem: The creators use this exact graphic much later in the show to depict the energy fluctuations of Armus. At the time, Picard and Worf even discuss the reasons for the fluctuations. But none of these fluctuations has occurred when the creators first display the graphic because the events are *still in the future.* (Ever feel like you've just entered...*The Twilight Zone?* Doo, doo, doo, doo, doo, doo....)

• I mentioned in the *NextGen Guide* (on page 62) that La Forge's phaser plops to the ground after the rest of the away team runs up to try to help Riker as he sinks into Armus's black goo. I didn't mention that a phaser magically reappears, clean and fresh, on La Forge's belt after Picard beams down. Either La Forge cleaned his off, or Picard brought him down a new one.

• When Armus engulfs Riker and then covers the shuttle, shouldn't there be a bulge to show the first officer's location?

• Just after Picard speaks with Troi in the shuttle, Armus transports him back outside. We see him materialize in a wide shot. We also see Armus standing or kneeling in a sand pit (as if the creators forgot to add in the black slick around him). The shot changes, and suddenly the black slick surrounds him. This happens a second time just before Picard beams away.

• The sound effects guy forgot to dub in a couple of the button-beeping sounds when Wesley works at a science station built into the back of the bridge. When Worf tells the acting ensign to set the computer for automatic beam-up, listen carefully to the first two key presses Wesley makes.

Not only are they missing the characteristic beep, but also you can hear him thumping the Plexiglas.

WE'LL ALWAYS HAVE PARIS

Star Date: 41697.9

The experiments of Dr. Paul Manheim create a door to another dimension, sending ripples of time distortions cascading outward through space. Responding to the crisis, Picard and crew race to find a way to seal the fissure before reality as they know it ceases.

TRIVIA QUESTIONS

1. From what planet did a farming colony also report experiencing a time anomaly?

2. What establishment lies across the square from the Blue Parrot Café on Sarona VII?

ALTERNATE VIEWPOINTS AND CORRECTIONS

• On page 64 of the *NextGen Guide,* I had a little fun with Jenice saying that she waited for Picard all day at the café while at the same time saying that it rained all day *and* the fact that the rendezvous was supposed to occur at an open-air café. John Hobson of Bolingbrook, IL, correctly pointed out that even open-air cafés have tables inside in case of inclement weather.

PLOT OVERSIGHTS

• Here's a brain twister for you. If time replays itself during the fencing match, how does Picard know it? His physical actions repeat themselves. He speaks the same words, so at least a portion of his thought processes are identical to the first time the events occurred. If some of his thoughts are identical, why not all? Indeed, wouldn't his physical state at the beginning of the second pass through the sword salute exactly match his physical state at the beginning of the first pass through the sword salute? And if so, then wouldn't the memory of the sword salute disappear, making the second pass through the sword salute the only one remembered? (Or...maybe not?)

• Ordering a holodeck creation to spend a few moments in contemplative retrospection, Picard tells the computer that he wants a setting twenty-two years ago, on April 9 at 1500 hours, three o'clock. Does this incredibly sophisticated computer really need Picard to remind it that 1500 hours is the same as three o'clock in the afternoon?

• Near the end of the episode, Data grabs a container with a measured portion of antimatter and walks it over to the rip in time. When the next disturbance hits, two more Datas appear, and the trio discusses which of the three of them is in the correct time frame. For some reason, the middle Data decides he is in the correct time frame. If Data walked up to the platform before the disturbance occurred, wouldn't the Data standing at the platform be the one in the correct time frame? (These time things give me a headache sometimes.)

• Just before Jenice Manheim enters the holodeck at the end of the episode, Troi announces herself to the computer. The computer replies by asking the counselor if she wishes to end the current program—the program that Picard is running. So...someone can walk up to a holodeck and just shut off another person's fantasy? Or is Counselor Troi the only one empowered with this ability?

EQUIPMENT ODDITIES

• If the holodeck re-creation of the café in Paris was so accurate, shouldn't it have been raining?

• From a user interface standpoint, an extremely interesting exchange occurs after the final goodbyes between Jenice and Jean-Luc. She strolls back to the location of the holodeck door. When it fails to reappear, she remarks, "So much for my dramatic exit." At this, the door reappears! In other words, anytime a person mentions the word "exit" in any context, the holodeck computer shows you the door? What about other commands, such as "freeze" and "continue"? Do users consciously have to avoid these words or suffer the disrupting consequences?

CONTINUITY AND PRODUCTION PROBLEMS

• Shortly after beaming down to Manheim's lab, Data is attacked by a laser defense system. He dives behind a large rectangular storage container, and it appears that something falls out of his pocket. (Sorry, I can't identify it. It's neither his phaser nor a tricorder.)

TRIVIA ANSWERS

1. Coltar IV.
2. The Zanza Men's Dance Palace.

CONSPIRACY

Star Dates: 41775.5—41780.2

When Captain Walter Keel dies after claiming the existence of a conspiracy to conquer Starfleet, Picard takes the *Enterprise* back to Earth to investigate the charges. In short order, Picard discovers that beetlelike aliens have attached themselves to the brain stems of several admirals in Starfleet and intend to do the same to him.

ALTERNATE VIEWPOINTS AND CORRECTIONS

• On page 67 of the *NextGen Guide,* I mention that a parrot appears in the graphics replaying the Starfleet Command decisions for the past six months. I ask why a parrot would be included in a list of command decisions. A person from Portsmouth, NH,

who wished to remain anonymous alerted me to the fact that the parrot has a human head. (No doubt a homage to the "Great Bird of the Galaxy" himself, Gene Roddenberry.) P. T. H. Carder of Lancashire, England, came up with a funnier explanation. He believes that it is a well-known fact that the Federation is actually controlled through telepathic influence by a race of superparrots, who perch on the shoulder of every commanding officer, issuing orders while screeching "pieces of eight!" Presumably, lapses in concentration by the parrots account for the occasional less-intelligent remarks made and orders given by high-ranking Starfleet officers and other Federation officials. (The explanation is very convenient because when we see one of these bonehead decisions made by Starfleet Command, nitpickers can now yell, "parrot syndrome!")

TRIVIA QUESTIONS

1. What two frigates orbit Dytallix B?

2. Who is the governor of Pacifica?

PLOT OVERSIGHTS

• As the *Enterprise* heads for Dytallix B, Picard tells his bridge crew that no communications should be sent without specific orders from him. Apparently Worf was daydreaming at the time, because once the *Enterprise* nears the abandoned mining planet, the chief of Security says that all attempts at communicating with the ships in orbit have been ignored.

• After realizing Quinn isn't Quinn, Picard hauls Riker back down two halls and into the transporter room. Then the captain makes some outrageous claims that a senior admiral in Starfleet Command is an impostor. Then he orders Riker to keep an eye on Quinn and join him on the planet "in force, if necessary." This is the type of conversation you have in private with your first officer, right? That's why Picard dragged Riker all the way back to the transporter room, right? At the end of the conversation, Picard walks up onto the transporter pad, looks over at the control console, and says, "Energize." That transporter chief sat over there listening to the whole exchange?

• This episode again raises the issue (first broached in "Heart of Glory") of why there are breakables on the *Enterprise*. When Quinn finishes off Riker, the first officer collapses onto a clear coffee table, and it shatters beneath him. (Transparent aluminum, anyone?)

• Shortly after the *Enterprise* arrives at Earth, a senior admiral invites Picard and Riker for dinner. Picard beams down, with orders for Riker to follow. Two admirals meet Picard and escort him to a table with three glasses and a carafe of Andonian tea. One question: How did the admirals know Riker wasn't coming? Shouldn't there be four glasses on the table?

• I noted in the *NextGen Guide* that when Riker calls for Security, La Forge and Worf run down from the bridge. I wondered what happened to the little gold-shirted guys. As an additional question, why aren't La Forge and

Worf carrying phasers? Riker did call for Security. Thankfully, Crusher shows up moments later, and she does remember to bring a phaser! Standard part of a medical kit, maybe? ("If ya can't heal 'em, kill 'em. 'Specially if they gots one of them broken legs.")

• With the arrival of La Forge and Worf, Quinn acts like he wants to beat a hasty retreat. He heads for the door, only to be stopped by La Forge. But what about the beetle thing in the plastic box? Was Quinn just going to leave his comrade behind?

• I may need to rescind part of my skepticism concerning La Forge's assignment to a Security team. After being thrown *through* a set of doors by Quinn, La Forge gets up, shakes his head a few times, and returns to duty. Presumably these doors are fairly strong. After all, Worf—in his reptile state during "Genesis"—pounded on the doors outside sick bay furiously for some time and only dented them. Yet La Forge, shortly after putting on his performance as the human battering ram, goes back to the bridge. Picard better sign that guy up for more Security details!

• Supposedly Quinn performs his superhuman feats because the beetle at the base of his brain is stimulating his adrenaline glands. Does this really makes sense? Wouldn't overadrenalizing an old man like Quinn simply lead to a heart attack? Or is there more to this symbiotic relationship than we've been told?

• Admiral Savar, a Vulcan, doesn't seem to have a very good neck pinch. After Riker yanks out a phaser at the dinner of worms and begins stunning all the infected Starfleet officers in the room, Savar grabs him by the neck. Eventually Picard finds a phaser and shoots Savar, but in the meantime, Riker stares at the ceiling, growling in pain. What happened to the "one touch and they drop like a sack of cement" feature so often demonstrated when Spock used the Vulcan neck pinch in the *Classic* series?

• Supposedly the beetle disappeared from Quinn's body when Picard and Riker killed the mother creature. But— just after the "fryfest"—there were a bunch of little dead beetles lying around, and they didn't disappear. And another thing: Even if the beetles did disappear, what happened to the hole in the back of Quinn's neck? If the creature entered through his mouth and then attached itself to the base of his brain, wouldn't it make a hole to climb through?

• I wonder what happened to the homing signal that Remmick sent.

EQUIPMENT ODDITIES

• Reviewing the Starfleet command logs, Data becomes fascinated with an evolving pattern in the command decisions. He begins talking to himself, and the computer becomes confused. When Data launches into a protracted explanation, the computer *cuts him off*! Evidently it grew impatient with Data's verbose descriptions. So the main computer of the *Enterprise,* in essence, offers commentary on the manner in which it is being used? Who programmed this interface? This would be like having a word processor that would offer its own commentary on the sentences I write. ("You

really should rewrite that last sentence. You made use of the passive voice and, structurally, the sentence could stand improvement.")

• What does the biofilter on the transporter really do? Is it on all the time, or only when the crew suspects that something beaming aboard might be dangerous? And, if it is always on, how in the world did it miss a three-inch beetle attached to the back of Quinn's neck?

• In "Home Soil" I commented on Data's ability to dodge a laser beam after it had emitted from the drill. In this episode Picard dodges a phaser blast after the weapon fires!

• As part of the final chase, an admiral fires a phaser at Picard and Riker. As already mentioned, Picard dives to the side. The blast hits a painting of Saturn, and sparks fly. Yet, when the smoke clears, the painting looks just as it did before the blast!

CONTINUITY AND PRODUCTION PROBLEMS

• The creators can't decide on Remmick's rank in this episode. When he beams Quinn up to the *Enterprise* he appears to wear three solid pips, making him a commander. However, at the end of the episode, while seated in front of the galactic map, a close-up shows him with two solid and one hollow pip, the rank of a lieutenant commander.

• Upon examining Quinn, Crusher clearly states that anyone infected by the beetles will have a prong sticking out of his or her neck. Yet, earlier, just before Quinn gives Riker a pasting— there's no prong protuding from the admiral's neck.

TRIVIA ANSWERS

1. The *Renegade* and the *Thomas Paine*.
2. Delaplane.

THE NEUTRAL ZONE

Star Date: 41986.0

The *Enterprise* sets course for the Romulan Neutral Zone to survey damage done to the Federation outposts along the border. Unexpectedly, a Romulan warbird decloaks, and its commanders claim that the same type of damage has occurred to their outposts. Uneasily, both sides agree to cooperate in their investigation of the incident.

RUMINATIONS

Actually, the summary above deals with the subplot of this episode. The majority of this show concerns a space derelict and three twentieth-century humans in cryogenic suspension. Crusher thaws them out, patches them up, and they set off on a discovery of life in the twenty-fourth century. I have to admit I didn't think much of this episode when it first aired. I had my mind in motion to enjoy an episode similar to the Classic Trek *episode "Balance of Terror," where opposing dominions encounter each other after years of silence. I wanted to see Picard pitted as military strategist against a Romulan counterpart, but the episode kept returning to*

scenes featuring the three thawed humans in less than flattering exchanges.

On my last viewing, I find that this episode has a certain charm. It's actually quite fun to see the crew of the Enterprise *at a loss on how they should interact with these "less than perfect" humans. And a few times the "less perfects" actually seem to come out of the encounters victorious.*

GREAT LINES

"But Data, they were already dead. I mean, what more could've happened to them?"—Picard to Data, questioning his second officer's actions in bringing the frozen humans back to the ship.

TRIVIA QUESTIONS

1. According to this episode, what was the last previous contact between the Federation and the Romulan Empire?

2. What is the first Federation outpost that the *Enterprise* encounters as it travels along the Neutral Zone?

ALTERNATE VIEWPOINTS AND CORRECTIONS

• Kristen Bloom of Ithaca, NY, advised me of an error I made on page 68 of the *NextGen Guide*. I referred to the recently thawed human as coming from the late twenty-first century. In fact, they were from the late twentieth century.

PLOT OVERSIGHTS

• Oddly enough, Data waits until

after he and Worf beam over to pronounce that the space relic has a breathable atmosphere. Does this seem right? Granted, Data can survive without oxygen, but what about poor old Worf?

• So the *Enterprise* is heading for a possible confrontation with the Romulans, right? Wouldn't this be a good time to separate the saucer and leave the families with children behind? Or does Picard know that the "headless chicken" look of the battle section probably won't strike terror in the hearts of his enemies?

• When describing cryonics to Picard, Crusher, in a dismissive tone, calls it a fad. Yet apparently the *"fad"* had something going for it. There are three live humans from the twentieth century in her sick bay!

• Why does Troi have to scrounge up a report on the Romulan from limited information sources when— according to "Unification"—Spock has maintained a dialogue with the Romulan Pardek for eighty years?

CHANGED PREMISES

• In the meeting that follows Picard's return, the dialogue states that the last Federation contact with the Romulans occurred more than fifty years ago. But in "Redemption II," Picard has knowledge of the *Enterprise*-C and the battle at Narendra III, an incident that happened approximately twenty-two years before.

• For the first and last time in the series, this episode shows us a Romulan vessel in which the commander and the subcommander sit side by side.

EQUIPMENT ODDITIES

• When Data and Worf board the space relic containing the frozen humans, there is air to breathe, the lights are on, and the vessel has gravity. Attempting to explain this, the creators have Data make a feeble statement about the ancient solar generator still functioning. Yet the solar panels seen in the outside shot seem badly damaged. On top of that, why do you need an oxygen environment for freeze-dried humans? Why do you need light? And why, oh, why, oh, why would you want to *heat* a capsule when you are trying to keep its contents *cold*? Finally, if this vessel comes from the twentieth century, just how is it generating gravity? Yes, it is spinning, but not nearly fast enough for its size, according to Nitpicker Central's resident solar physicist Mitzi Adams.

• The interior of the cryogenic capsules and the interior walls of the transporter room seem to share the same material. Given that the capsules are more than 350 years old, I guess we should conclude that some things never go out of style (or maybe go so far *out* of style that they come back in).

• Whoever put together the movie version *Enterprise* model in Raymond's quarters did it fast. The engine nacelles are on backward!

TRIVIA ANSWERS

1. The Tomed Incident.
2. Science station (or Outpost) Delta 05.

★ MORE PERSONAL FAVORITES

When I wrote the *NextGen Guide,* I never for a minute thought I had found all the nits in the first six seasons of *Star Trek: The Next Generation.* But I must confess that I thought I had found a good percentage, possibly even a majority of them. Boy, was I wrong! It's been so much fun to read the letters sent to the Nitpicker's Guild and say to myself, "Oh, yeah, that's right!" or go scrambling for my tapes, cue an episode up to the right spot, and see something I had missed in every previous viewing. (Thanks again to everyone for writing.) So here's some more "slapping my head in disbelief that I missed them the first time" nits that have become part of my personal favorites. (These nits are also included in the episode reviews.)

1. "Contagion." On the surface of Iconia, Data opens a gateway to other worlds. A series of pictures fills the interior of the gateway, indicating possible destinations. Toronto's City Hall appears in one of the pictures—that's Toronto, as in Toronto, Ontario…in Canada. (Obviously, aliens have already visited the Earth!)

2. "Who Watches the Watchers." The Mintakans have an unusual planet, indeed. While the Mintakan female Nuria speaks with Picard in the observation lounge, two identical-looking continents rotate by behind her. Then at the end of the episode, a third continent with exactly the same shape—except that it faces in the opposite direction—appears as well.

3. "Yesterday's *Enterprise.*" For the majority of the episode, our heroes function in an alternate timeline—one that features a Federation/Klingon conflict. The uniforms of the Starfleet officers differ from the ones we see normally. Among the changes is a wide black cuff at the end of each sleeve. In the final scene, after everything supposedly reverts to normal, La Forge and Guinan have a drink together in Ten-Forward, yet for some reason, La Forge's uniform still has the wide cuffs.

4. "Qpid." At one point Vash—having been transformed into Maid Marion by Q—writes a letter to "Little John" (Riker). She folds it, but in short order Q bursts in and discovers her plan. If you watch carefully, you'll see that Q unfolds the letter and holds it upside down.

5. "The Inner Light." While supposedly staying by Picard's side as the captain lies prostrate on the floor of the main bridge, Crusher somehow manages to get her hair done. Between scenes, it suddenly develops curls.

6. "Tapestry." During a reenactment of the fight between Picard and a band of Nausicaans, one of the stunt doubles loses his wig.

7. "Birthright, Part 1." At the end of this episode, Dr. Julian Bashir walks with Data down a series of hallways. He wears black shoes. Then in the final few moments of the scene, he wanders off. Now he wears white shoes! (Actually, I use this as an excuse to wear white tennis shoes to conventions no matter how formally I dress. I just tell people the shoes are in honor of Dr. Bashir!)

8. "Timescape." A runabout with Picard, Troi, Data, and La Forge aboard begins encountering time anomalies. One such anomaly causes a bowl of fruit to age rapidly. When the captain reaches toward the fruit, he screams and almost instantly produces a hand with long fingernails (supposedly the result of the time acceleration). However, if you back up the tape and watch Picard as he enters the room and begins operating a computer terminal, you'll see that he already has long fingernails on that hand *well before* he reaches for the bowl.

9. "Force of Nature." After several seasons as a male, Spot suddenly decides to become a female just prior to this episode.

10. "Inheritance." Data's mom, Dr. Juliana Tainer, begins a transporter trip with two-inch heels and ends it wearing flats.

SECOND
SEASON

THE CHILD

Star Date: 42073.1

A s the *Enterprise* flies to Odet IX to pick up plasma plague samples, a small energy being enters the ship. When it finds a sleeping Troi, she becomes pregnant, and the child's rapid growth causes uneasiness among the crew—more so after discovering that the boy emits Eichner radiation, which causes a plague specimen to grow, threatening the lives of everyone on board.

TRIVIA QUESTIONS

1. What is the name of the teacher whose classroom Ian visits?

2. Where does the *Enterprise* head at the end of the episode?

ALTERNATE VIEWPOINTS AND CORRECTIONS

• Greg Reid of Toronto, Ontario wrote to remind me that I left out an important change between the first and the second seasons. La Forge became a full lieutenant and chief engineer.

• Edward A. Watson of Coatesville, PA, correctly pointed out that Worf's uniform is gold, not green as I stated on page 76 of the *NextGen Guide*. (Another nitpicker asked if I was color-blind. Well, as a matter of fact...yes!)

PLOT OVERSIGHTS

• Is Science Station Tango Sierra in the Rachelis system? Early in this episode, Picard makes a log entry stating that the Rachelis system has suffered an outbreak of plasma plague and that the *Enterprise* will ferry a shipment of plasma plague specimens to Science Station Tango Sierra so the personnel there can develop an inoculant. Later in the show, however, Picard makes a log entry stating that the *Enterprise* will take the plasma plague specimens to the Rachelis system.

• Presumably humans and Betazoids share something of the same genetic makeup. Yet, during the discussion over Troi's pregnancy, Pulaski states that the offspring is *exactly* the same as Troi in every way and that the child is a boy. Now, here on good 'ol planet Earth, each human carries two chromosomes to determine sex. Females carry two X chromosomes, and males carry an X and a Y chromosome. Since Troi is a female, she would carry an XX configuration. Yet Troi's child—who is the same as Deanna in every way—is a male! Presumably his configuration is XY. Where did he get the Y chromosome?

• At one point, Picard sends Data to confer with Pulaski on the manifest for the plasma plague specimens. Data walks off a turbolift and turns right. He meets Troi, who asks him to help her to sick bay. Data immediately does an about-face and starts walking with Troi in the other direction, and soon they arrive in Pulaski's office adjacent to sick bay. If both Troi and Data were on their way to sick bay, why were they walking in opposite directions?

• When a plasma specimen begins

to grow, Riker takes Data down to the containment area, and Picard asks Pulaski to join them. Specifically, Picard says that they are having difficulty on "cargo deck 5." Pray tell, where is this? I've heard of Cargo Bay 5 and deck 5, but not cargo deck 5.

CHANGED PREMISES

• For some reason, Guinan lies to Wesley in this episode. She tells him that she didn't know Picard before she came on board the ship. Yet in "Time's Arrow, Part II" we learn that Guinan first met Picard in the late nineteenth century.

• There could be an explanation for this, since Ian is unusual in other respects, but toward the end of the episode he tells Troi that he can feel that people on the ship are very worried. At this point he is supposedly equivalent to an eight-year-old child. However, in "Tin Man" Troi states that most Betazoids don't develop their telepathic abilities until adolescence.

EQUIPMENT ODDITIES

• As part of the opening sequence, the creators treat us to an interior view of Shuttle Bay 3. (Actually it's called "Docking Bay 3" in the episode, but the *Technical Manual* lists no such creature, and the set looks just like a Shuttle Bay 3.) The upright, space door of the shuttle bay set isn't slanted at all. Unfortunately, Shuttle Bay 3 resides on the back side of the yoke, and the external doors on the model of the *Enterprise* show a definite incline. (I suppose the shuttle bay could have two doors. But then we should be able to see some space between them.)

• In previous episodes, such as "The

Arsenal of Freedom," transporter chiefs had to push a button to activate the light bars on the transporter console. In this episode O'Brien simply waves his hand over them.

CONTINUITY AND PRODUCTION PROBLEMS

• Diana Muldaur, who played Dr. Pulaski during the second season of *NextGen,* also appeared in two episodes of *Classic Trek.* In "Return to Tomorrow," she starred as Dr. Ann Mulhall; and in "Is There in Truth No Beauty?" she starred as Dr. Miranda Jones.

• When Troi gets going she can really cry up a storm. After the baby is born, Riker kisses her, and her cheeks are dry. Yet, only seconds later, water drips from her upper lip.

• As Ian dies, Pulaski reaches up with her *left* hand to check the pulse at his neck. The shot changes and she pulls her *right* hand back.

TRIVIA ANSWERS

1. Miss Gladstone.
2. The Morgana Quadrant.

WHERE SILENCE HAS LEASE

Star Dates: 42193.6—42194.7

After an area of blackness swallows the ship, the being who lives within, named Nagilum, subjects the crew to series of laboratory experiments. Faced with the prospect of watching Nagilum kill one-third to one-half of his crew merely to investigate death, Picard opts to set the ship's autodestruct, after which the being releases them.

TRIVIA QUESTIONS

1. Where is the ship heading at the beginning of the episode?

2. Toward what star system does Riker instruct Wesley to set course and engage at impulse when Picard decides to try to leave the area of blackness?

ALTERNATE VIEWPOINTS AND CORRECTIONS

• On page 79 of the *NextGen Guide,* I questioned Pulaski's statement that she isn't a bridge officer. I noted that Crusher was a bridge officer because she attended the bridge staff meeting in "Hide and Q." Charleton R. Johnson and Merak Milligan of Seattle, WA, both shed some light on this issue while raising a few additional questions. Charleton noted that Crusher has consistently demonstrated that she is more that just a medical person. She was handpicked to go on a commando mission in "Chain of Command," and she commanded the *Enterprise* in "Descent." Merak recalled that in the seventh-season episode "Thine Own Self," Crusher discusses with Troi that she took the bridge officer's test to move on to commander rank. Then Merak also noted that Pulaski wears the rank pins of a commander! So, if Crusher had to take the bridge officer's test to make commander, doesn't that mean Pulaski also had to take the test, or is there another way to make commander for medical personnel? (See "Disaster" and "Thine Own Self" for more details.)

• Also on page 79 of the *NextGen Guide,* I wondered why Nagilum would choose to spin Pulaski around as he probes the anatomical differences between male and female when Troi is on the bridge. Amy Vincent of New Orleans, LA, felt I added a sensual aspect to the inspection that isn't present, while Rachel Borenstein suggested that Nagilum should have danced with more than just Pulaski. Troi is not only female, she also is half Betazoid and no doubt has some physical difference. Then again, what about Worf? And, although Nagilum recognized Data's distinctiveness in construction, the Thing from the Void doesn't even *offer* the poor android a dance.

PLOT OVERSIGHTS

• In all, the *Enterprise* fires two probes into the area of blackness. Riker says that the second disappears sooner than the first. Yet Wesley pipes up and says he has charted the boundary of the "hole," and the ship can move closer if Picard chooses. Isn't this just a little presumptuous? If the probes disappeared at different locations, doesn't that imply that the boundary moves? And even if the probes actually disappeared at the same location, isn't this a three-dimensional object with lots of outcroppings? How can you know where a boundary is on an object like that with only two plot points?

• While preparing to beam over to the *Yamato,* Worf tells Riker that he's familiar with the ship and suggests that they beam to the aft station of the *Yamato's* bridge. Doesn't the *Yamato* turn out to be almost an exact copy of the *Enterprise*? (aside from the weird spatial distortions, of course). Wouldn't Riker be familiar with the layout of the *Yamato* as well? Or Picard? Or anybody who lives on the *Enterprise*?

CHANGED PREMISES

• In discussing the area of blackness, Riker asks Data if there are any records on anything similar. Data checks and responds that there isn't. However, Kirk's *Enterprise* encountered an area of darkness in "The Immunity Syndrome."

• This episode cinches O'Brien's demotion sometime between "Power Play" and "Realm of Fear." When I noted that O'Brien suddenly wore a single hollow pip in "Realm of Fear" and wondered why he was demoted, I received all manner of letters proclaiming that O'Brien was never an officer, that those pips he wore were really some type of enlisted man's rank, and that the single hollow pip was actually a *promotion* (something like a chief master sergeant). Yet, in this episode, just before beaming over to the *Yamato,* Riker calls O'Brien *"Lieutenant."* (There's a story floating around Trekdom that O'Brien only received a field promotion to lieutenant from Picard and lost it for some reason before "Power Play." Seems a bit convoluted to me.)

• I want to know where Nagilum has met La Forge prior to this incident.

Nagilum refers to the rest of the bridge crew by their last names, but the being is on a first-name basis with La Forge. (When looking over the crew, Nagilum says, "Data...Picard...Riker...Geordi...Haskell.")

EQUIPMENT ODDITIES

• After Riker tells Wesley to fly the *Enterprise* out of the void on impulse, an outside shot of the ship shows it taking off. Then the scene returns to the bridge. If you look closely at the underside of the right armrest of Picard's chair, you'll see that the bulb has burned out. (It comes back on later, so either a Starfleet maintenance crew ran up in the middle of the crisis to replace the bulb, or the later bridge scenes were actually shot before this scene.)

• Riker and Worf make it back to the *Enterprise,* storm out of the transporter room, and storm onto the bridge. Miraculously, the phasers and tricorders they carried have disappeared. Riker seems very anxious to speak his piece to Picard as he stalks off the turbolift. It doesn't seem as if he would take this moment to drop by ship's stores.

CONTINUITY AND PRODUCTION PROBLEMS

• Evidently the events concerning the area of blackness don't hold much interest for Troi. At the beginning of the episode she sits on the bridge with Picard. Then the ship encounters the area of blackness and Picard allows Wesley to take them in for a closer look. Suddenly Troi is gone! Her chair is empty, and she's not back at any of the stations in the aft portion of the bridge. The show proceeds. Pulaski comes up to the bridge. Riker and Worf beam over to the fake *Yamato*. They beam back, and Troi reappears on the bridge.

TRIVIA ANSWERS

1. The Morgana Quadrant. (Kudos to the creators for this accurate bit of information.) At the conclusion of the last episode, Picard set course for the Morgana Quadrant, and at the beginning of this one they are on their way there.

2. The Cornelian Star System.

ELEMENTARY, DEAR DATA

Star Date: 42286.3

When Dr. Pulaski challenges Data to solve a mystery in true Holmesian fashion, La Forge makes the mistake of asking the computer to fashion an adversary that can defeat the android. The computer honors the chief engineer's request by creating a sentient, superintelligent Professor Moriarty.

TRIVIA QUESTIONS

1. Who is the captain of the USS *Victory*?

2. How much did Holmes pay for his violin?

ALTERNATE VIEWPOINTS AND CORRECTIONS

• In the *NextGen Guide* I mistakenly titled this episode "Elementary, *My* Dear Data." (Edward A. Watson of Coatesville, PA, wrote first on this one.)

• Ann McNeil of Owen Sound, Ontario, believes that this episode proves Data has a sense of humor. At the beginning of the show, a young officer asks where La Forge can be reached when he and Data take off for the holodeck. Data responds by making a joke, giving Sherlock Holmes's address. (Of course, the nitpicker in me wants to know why the officer wants to know where they can be reached in the first place. Doesn't the computer keep track of this stuff?)

• Bradley H. Sinor of Broken Arrow, OK, informed me that while my description of Moriarty as "Doctor" on page 81 of the *NextGen Guide* is technically correct, he is more properly referred to as "Professor."

• As part of my nitpicking of this episode in the *NextGen Guide,* I pondered Moriarty's obvious sentience and mentioned that the main computer created him. Then I wondered if that meant the computer was sentient (and if it was, what ramifications *that* fact would cause). Angelia Parker of Zachary, LA, corresponded to reference "Evolution" and that the nanites achieved consciousness though they did not possess consciousness at the beginning. In her mind, the computer would not need to be conscious to create a conscious being. (I understand Angelia's point. The only thing I would add to the nanite discussion is that Wesley provided the means for them to become conscious, and he, of course, was conscious to begin with.)

PLOT OVERSIGHTS

• At one point Data has the computer construct a story in the Holmesian style to prove to Pulaski that he can deduce the answer to an unknown mystery. He, she, and La Forge then enter the holodeck, and Data quickly comes to the right conclusion. Pulaski denounces the victory as a fraud, stating that Data merely recognized the various elements that the computer picked from different Sherlock Holmes stories. Frustrated, La Forge marches to the holodeck exit and calls for the arch. The scene changes to show us Moriarty watching the trio. Apparently he sees the arch. How can Moriarty see the arch? La Forge hasn't instructed the computer to create an adversary that can defeat Data yet.

• At one point Data tells La Forge that the only way Holmes could defeat Moriarty was at the cost of his own life. Hasn't Data read all of Sir Arthur Conan Doyle's stories? Amber DiGerlando tells me that Holmes survived Reidenbach Falls and went on to star in many more books.

• This episode raises a question about the Federation's attitudes toward what constitutes a sentient being (or maybe just Picard's attitudes). For the sake of discussion, let's say that the crew of the *Enterprise* found a way to bring Moriarty off the holodeck. Is it conceivable that he would not be entitled to the rights granted every sentient being in the Federation? He is intelligent, he is conscious of his existence and self-

aware. What then does Moriarty lack? He lacks a body, a housing from which to operate his sentience. In other words, the Federation is willing to accept sentient beings provided they are "just like us." (Tsk, tsk. "Speciesism" rears its ugly head.) The point is this. If Moriarty is sentient—even if he doesn't have a body—Picard should not shut him off and leave him to languish around in the computer for several years, as we discover in "Ship in a Bottle."

EQUIPMENT ODDITIES

• Shortly after beginning his first holodeck adventure with Data as Sherlock Holmes, La Forge snaps a book shut and commands the computer to freeze the program. For some reason, the fire keeps burning!

TRIVIA ANSWERS

1. Zimbata.
2. Fifty-five shillings.

THE OUTRAGEOUS OKONA

Star Date: 42402.7

R esponding to a distress call from a malfunctioning interplanetary cargo carrier, the crew soon discovers that its captain, a rogue named Okona, is involved in a scandal between the twin worlds of Altec and Straleb.

TRIVIA QUESTIONS

1. What is the name of Okona's cargo carrier?

2. What is Okona's first name?

ALTERNATE VIEWPOINTS AND CORRECTIONS

• Greg Goldstein of Philadephia, PA, had some comments about my selection of a great line for this episode in the *NextGen Guide*. I chose a joke told to Data by Okona. "Life is like loading twice your cargo weight onto your spacecraft. If it's canaries and you can keep half of them flying all the time, you're all right." Greg rightly pointed out that if you have a glass box containing a bird, sitting on a scale, and the bird proceeds to flap its wings, the scale will continue to register the bird's weight even though the bird keeps itself suspended in the center of the box. To stay aloft, the bird must exert pressure downward on the air in the box. In turn, the air pushes on the bottom of the box. So the box will weigh the same no matter what the bird does. Therefore, until Okona's vessel broke free of all strong gravitational forces, it wouldn't matter what the canaries were doing, the vessel would still struggle against the weight. (And I think Okona knew this. As I said, he was making a joke. But I found the glass box and the bird thing interesting.)

PLOT OVERSIGHTS

• Shortly after beaming Okona aboard with a malfunctioning part from his vessel, Riker asks him to give the part to Data, who will see to its repair. Okona replies that he is happy to do the work himself. At this point, he addresses Riker as "Commander," but his lips seem to say "Captain."

• Does it strike anyone else as odd that Data goes to Guinan for advice on humor? True, Whoopi Goldberg is a comic, but Guinan?

• When asked by Data what is funny, the holographic comic mentions a briefcase shaped like a fish. Several moments later, Data identifies this object as an "amphibian" briefcase. Fish are not amphibians. Fish would be agrathan, chondrichthian, or osteichthian (according to nitpicker Carl Malmstrom).

• Have you ever wondered what Joe Piscopo actually says when telling Data the accelerated joke on the holodeck? Brian Lombard slowed the tape down and sent me a letter on the results. "[Piscopo's] story has it that a Jew and an Irishman die and go to heaven. They meet St. Peter at the pearly gate, and tell him that they want to return to Earth. St. Peter agrees, on the condition that if they commit their usual sins, they will be returned to heaven. The minute they get back, the Irishman goes to a bar and is instantly sent back to heaven after having a drink. Here the joke stops, and we see Data in Ten-Forward telling Guinan some jokes." Presumably the joke ends with some sort of generalized assumption about Jewish behavior much like the stereotypical assumption, inherent to the joke, that all Irishmen drink. The joke seems a bit out of place for a show like *Star Trek: The Next Generation,* doesn't it?

CONTINUITY AND PRODUCTION PROBLEMS

• After visiting the holodeck and learning some new jokes, Data tries them out on Guinan. When she doesn't find the first one amusing, Data sits at her table with his cigar. From one angle, his elbows are propped up on the table; from the other, his forearms rest on the table.

• The background of the vessel that carries the delegation from Altec looks suspiciously like the main viewer on the battle bridge.

TRIVIA ANSWERS

1. The *Erstwhile*.
2. Thadiun.

LOUD AS A WHISPER

Star Dates: 42477.2—42479.3

D isaster strikes after the *Enterprise* transports peace negotiator Riva and his "chorus"—a trio of translators who function in telepathic concert with their profoundly deaf leader—to war-torn Solari V. A dissenter in the movement for peace murders Riva's chorus, leaving the negotiator feeling completely isolated until he determines to turn this disadvantage into an advantage.

PLOT OVERSIGHTS

• The away team at the beginning of this episode displays an incredible lack of knowledge about Riva. Obviously no one handles Riva's itinerary, or that person would have related all the necessary information to the crew of the *Enterprise* ahead of time. Such preparations would have reduced or eliminated the possibility of a simple protocol breach like the one Picard causes when he speaks to Riva's interpreters and not to Riva himself. But even if Riva doesn't have an advance man, why didn't Worf prepare for his arrival? Surely that would include a review of Riva's file for any special requirements, and a routine security check. If Riva negotiated several important peace treaties between the Federation and the Klingon Empire, wouldn't his file be quite large and detailed? Yet the away team doesn't know what he looks like or even that he is deaf.

• While learning a gestural language, Data views several signs more than once. Why? Doesn't Data remember everything to which he is exposed?

• After Data learns the gestural language, Picard marches into the observation lounge and calls to Riva even before coming into the man's visual range. Surprisingly, Riva turns to face them.

• When Data interprets for Riva in the observation lounge, he says the word "death" *before* Riva signs it! In addition, when Picard responds to Riva's confession, Data signs the word "one" *before* Picard says it. (Data must be working on a new *clairvoyant* subroutine.)

• And speaking of Data's interpretation, why is he interpreting for Picard in the first place? Doesn't Riva read lips?

Later, when Troi and Data talk with Riva, the android makes no attempt to translate for Troi. (Maybe Riva can read only *Troi's* lips. I probably could come up with an explanation for this but...I believe I shall postpone.)

• At one point, after an examination by Pulaski, La Forge asks, "Are you finished?" Pulaski nods, and La Forge replaces his VISOR. Pulaski *nods*? To the blind guy? And he responds?!

• Presumably the warring factions on Solari V will care for Riva during the negotiations. After all, it doesn't look like the crew of the *Enterprise* left Riva a replicator (unless La Forge snuck one onto the table). Having the Solaris provide for Riva's needs seems a bit tricky. After all, you wouldn't want one side thinking the other side is attempting to sway the negotiations by offering Riva a better cut of meat, now, would you?

TRIVIA QUESTIONS

1. How long have the Solaris been at war?

2. What race developed a written language before using hand gestures?

EQUIPMENT ODDITIES

• When Riva, his chorus, and the away team materialize on Solari V, the transporter shows off an interesting feature. Both Riva and his female interpreter wear robes that flap in the wind as they appear. To do this, the transporter would have to measure the wind velocity and direction, calculate its effect on the partially formed cloth, project the correct location for the next molecule, place it, and start the process over until it completely reconstructs the robe!

• The transporter exhibits yet another interesting capability in this episode. When the away team beams down for the second time, both Riker and Worf start the trip empty-handed and end it with their phasers drawn. Obviously the "Hey, you guys! This is a dangerous planet!" circuit cut in and reconstructed them in a more appropriate manner.

CONTINUITY AND PRODUCTION PROBLEMS

• When Riker, Worf, Riva, and his chorus beam down to Solari V, the creators forgot to put the sparklies on Worf. The other five individuals show the usual transporter "static," but Worf just fades in.

• Those clever creators slipped in the Vulcan hand sign among those that flash across the workstation display as Data learns a gestural language from the computer.

• At the very end of the episode, Picard compliments Troi on her performance with Riva. When she enters his office, a holographic representation of a star system orbits above Picard's desk. It makes a series of fairly obnoxious humming sounds. Yet, when the scene cuts to close-ups of Picard and Troi, the representation is apparently sensitive enough to know that it should quiet down and then stop making noise altogether so the music bed can start.

TRIVIA ANSWERS

1. Fifteen centuries.

2. The Leyrons.

THE SCHIZOID MAN

Star Date: 42437.5

Refusing to accept the death of his intellect, Dr. Ira Graves transfers his consciousness into Data before his physical body ceases to function. Then, a series of accidents, caused by Grave's undisciplined emotions finding release in Data's superior strength, convinces the scientist to vacate the android's body.

TRIVIA QUESTIONS

1. From what disease does Graves suffer?

2. At the very end of the episode, Riker makes a joke by asking Data if he remembers wrestling with what animal?

ALTERNATE VIEWPOINTS AND CORRECTIONS

• Diana Brown of San Ysidro, CA, noted that I mistakenly referred to the episode "Disaster" as "Destruction" on page 90 of the *NextGen Guide*.

PLOT OVERSIGHTS

• As the show begins, Pulaski goes to the bridge to discuss a distress call from the home world of Dr. Ira Graves, one of the most brilliant scientists of the Federation. Bear in mind that the crew does not know the nature of the crisis on Gravesworld, and Starfleet believes that Graves teeters on the verge of a significant breakthrough. Isn't there a possibility then that foul forces are afoot? A chance that the *Enterprise* might be rushing into confrontation? If so, why is *Data* in his quarters stroking his beard while the *chief engineer* tries to find a way to tell him it looks goofy?

• Shortly after heading toward Gravesworld, the *Enterprise* receives a distress call from the *Constantinople*. Riker suggests dropping an away team at Gravesworld using a "long-range," "near-warp" transport. In the transporter room, Troi gets tapped to play the cabbagehead in this episode so that the creators can tell us about this long-range, near-warp transport. I discuss the issue of Troi's lack of technical knowledge in "Disaster," but it deserves a touch here as well. Let us assume for the moment that Troi is a specialist and didn't attend the Academy for officer training. Wouldn't Starfleet still have some type of mini-Academy training for their specialists? Does Starfleet really send people into the field for them to discover later that some beaming operations are dangerous? Wouldn't this be covered in a basic introductory course? ("Transporters 101: Beaming Is Fun! The Transporter Is Your Friend!")

• And while we're on the subject of this long-range, near-warp transport, why is it called "long-range"? The *Enterprise* comes out of warp right next to the planet. Why is it done at "near-warp"? The *Enterprise* comes completely out of warp before the process begins. Evidently the "near-warp" aspect comes as the *Enterprise* rockets away during transport. In other words, Picard opts to endanger the lives of the away team because he doesn't want to hang out for *five more seconds* until the beaming operation completes?

• Shortly after beaming down to the planet, Data meets Dr. Ira Graves, who proceeds to claim that he taught Soong all about cybernetics. Either Soong started his career late in life or Graves was a boy genius or Graves is just plain lying. (Knowing Graves, I vote for the third option.) "Brothers" shows us the contemporary state of Dr. Noonian Soong, and Soong looks much older than Graves does in this episode. Granted, the two episodes occur approximately two years apart, but Soong looks at least a decade older than Graves.

• This episode features a Vulcan doctor named Selar (played by Suzie Plakson, who put in a series of wonderful performances as K'Ehleyr and was last seen languishing around in prime-time half-hour sitcom wasteland). Just what type of bedside manner would a Vulcan doctor have?

EQUIPMENT ODDITIES

• The model of the *Stargazer* in Picard's ready room gets moved a lot. When Picard confronts Data over his insubordination, the model faces right. When La Forge comes to Picard's ready room to discuss Data's condition, the model faces left. Finally, when Troi and Selar visit Picard's ready room, the model again faces right. (Mark Belanger, the person who submitted this nit, came up with a plausible explanation: Picard probably reduces his stress level by

"zooming" the *Stargazer* around his office, making the sounds of the warp drive and weapons systems in the process. Of course, when someone "dweedles" at his door, the captain must hurriedly replace the model, jump behind the desk, and assume a more somber posture. It's understandable that he doesn't always get it facing in the proper direction.)

TRIVIA ANSWERS

1. Darnay's disease.
2. A Klingon targ.

UNNATURAL SELECTION

Star Date: 42494.8

A n experiment in genetic engineering runs awry when the enhanced immune systems of the "children" accidently create an agent that causes accelerated aging in normal humans. Just in time, the crew concocts a plan to use the transporter to sample each affected person's DNA and restore them to normal.

TRIVIA QUESTIONS

1. Where is the *Enterprise* heading at the beginning of this episode?

2. Where is the Darwin Genetic Research Station located?

ALTERNATE VIEWPOINTS AND CORRECTIONS

• On page 93 of the *NextGen Guide,* I stated that—with the success of this transporter DNA switcheroo—everyone can now remain young. I observed that you could simply take a sample of your DNA when you were young and then have the transporter reconstitute you when you grew old *if* (and I did say, "if") switching DNA was enough to make wrinkly skin new and turn white hair back to its original color. Many nitpickers missed the satire in my comments. They advised that DNA doesn't have some sort of age stamp associated with it—that DNA does not change with age, therefore it would do no good to take a sample as a young person. They also stated that Pulaski's situation was unique in that her DNA had been altered to create rapid aging. I happen to agree with these statements. Obviously—in my attempt to be a smart aleck—I failed to communicate my point. Indulge me as I try again. The Dr. Pulaski we all know and love gets infected, and her DNA is altered. This causes rapid aging. So Picard puts her in the transporter and fixes her DNA. So far so good; that should stop the rapid aging, right? It does, and Pulaski *should* step off the transporter pad as an old woman, but a *normally aging* old woman. That's not what happens. Not only does switching her DNA stop her rapid aging, it also restores her youth (well…it makes her younger, at least)! *If* —let me say it again—*if* switching your DNA can fix your wrinkles and color your hair, then obviously the scientists and engineers in the twenty-fourth century know something about DNA that we don't. The simple extrapolation of these events is that DNA and a little transporter magic can "de-age" you. Therefore the transporter is a fountain of youth!

PLOT OVERSIGHTS

• Once Pulaski becomes infected, Picard holds a staff meeting and states that she and Data have become the top priorities—that they can no longer consider the crisis at Darwin Station their most immediate concern. What?! The interior view of Darwin Station shows several scientists at work. These scientists are infected and dying, and Picard tells the crew to focus their energies on rescuing Pulaski and Data? What happened to sacrificing your crew for the good of others? (Perhaps Picard's approach in this instance reflects how he feels about the scientists at the genetic research facility. "The Masterpiece Society" certainly gives the impression that the captain has no great love for genetic engineering.)

• And another thing while we are on the topic of Picard's shortsightedness in this episode: O'Brien comes up with a plan to restore Pulaksi's health by using the transporter trace. However, they can find no transporter trace for Pulaski, so they abandon that plan. What a minute: Isn't it likely that at least one of the scientists on the station below would have a transporter trace available? Wouldn't there be some benefit in attempting O'Brien's procedure on personnel at the research facility?

• Desperate to forestall the inevitable,

Picard tells Pulaski that he's going to beam her aboard in suspended animation until they can find a cure. Pulaski says the risk is too great to the ship. Yet, the Darwin Genetic Research Station previously put one of their "children" in suspended animation for a trip to the *Enterprise*. Why don't *they* start putting people in suspended animation? At least that would give the *Enterprise* a bit more time.

• Picard must have a great amount of faith that the "transporter cleansing" process will work. He makes no attempt to isolate the transporter pad with a force field. And when Pulaski finally arrives, everyone runs up and starts hugging her and shaking her hand.

EQUIPMENT ODDITIES

• During the first look at the crew of the *Lantree,* the bridge on the supply ship seems very dark. Data said earlier that all systems were functioning normally, so the lights should be working. Then again, maybe as the crew aged, the bright lights stung their eyes.

• As the *Enterprise* orbits above the Darwin Genetic Research Station, you can clearly see a flashing yellow light on the back of the tail of the star drive section, directly between the engine nacelles. For some reason this light isn't flashing during the opening credits.

• I can't believe I missed this! On page 93 of the *NextGen Guide,* I mentioned that some of the workstations on Darwin Station still use old-fashioned cathode ray tube monitors. It's actually worse than I dreamed. Beside the monitors, it looks like there is an old-fashioned telephone!

• It's a fairly minor point, but at the very end of the episode, Riker tells Worf to arm "photon torpedoes," plural. Then the *Enterprise* fires only one.

CONTINUITY AND PRODUCTION PROBLEMS

• Just after the *Enterprise* warps to the *Lantree*'s location, Picard stands with his hands folded in front of him. Then the shot changes to a reverse angle, and his right hand rests by his side.

• As Pulaski and Data prepare to depart in a shuttle, a wide shot of the shuttle bay clearly shows that the craft sits to the left of the shuttle bay door. Yet, when the shuttle emerges from the *Enterprise,* it comes out on the right side of the shuttle bay door (watch the shuttle's shadow).

• An outside shot of the ship shows the shuttle flying between the engine nacelles and coming to rest parallel to the ship, facing in the same direction as the ship, behind the *Enterprise* and off the port nacelle. If you were sitting in the pilot's chair on the shuttle, the *Enterprise* would be ahead of you and off to the right. Then the shot changes to the interior of the shuttle, and instead the *Enterprise* appears in the background—to the *left* and in front of Data's position. Did Data rotate the shuttle a bit when we weren't looking?

• The Darwin Genetic Research Station gets a slight rework and is used again for a building on Ohniaka III at the beginning of "Descent."

TRIVIA ANSWERS

1. Star Station India.
2. Gagarin IV.

A MATTER OF HONOR

Star Dates: 42506.5–42507.8

When Kargan—captain of the Klingon vessel *Pagh*—comes to believe that the *Enterprise* is responsible for "infecting" his ship with a hull-consuming parasite and vows revenge, Riker—on board the *Pagh* as part of an officer exchange program—assumes command by using an emergency transponder to fool the crew of the *Enterprise* into beaming Kargan onto Picard's bridge. (How's that for a sentence?)

TRIVIA QUESTIONS

1. After the replacement officers beam aboard, which officer does Riker order them to follow?

2. What three Klingon delicacies does Riker name at his "feast before the transfer"?

PLOT OVERSIGHTS

• The dialogue constantly refers to the ship-eating parasite as "sub-atomic." In other words, the parasite is constructed from uncombined quarks? That *is* unusual.

• Shortly after Riker arrives on the *Pagh*, Kargan tells one of his officers to "speak in their language." The officer, Klag, seems to have no difficulty at all with English (i.e., Federation Standard). Nor do any of the other Klingon warriors. They even crack jokes that Riker can understand. I find this situation appalling. Obviously the Klingon education system is vastly superior to that of the Federation! Every Klingon on this ship is bilingual, and the best we've ever seen our Starfleet personnel do is grunt a few curses in Klingon and Romulan.

• Does anyone else find it odd that Wesley wanders away from his post at one point in this episode just to have a chat with Mendon?

CHANGED PREMISES

• In this episode, Klag, the second officer, claims that a Klingon is his work, not his family. Why then does Klingon custom put so much emphasis on family? In "Sins of the Father," Worf must answer for charges against his father. In "New Ground," Worf lectures Alexander on the importance of honor and how it will reflect badly on the family if Alexander is dishonorable.

EQUIPMENT ODDITIES

• The Klingons discover the parasites, and Kargan quickly proclaims that they cannot fix the situation. What about putting a spacesuit on one of these great warriors and sending him outside with a phaser to cut off that section of the ship? Surely it's better to lose a chunk of the hull than the entire craft.

• When Mendon scans the *Pagh*, the graphics show the infestation on the port side of the ship. But when the *Enterprise* removes the parasites at the conclusion of the episode, the cleanup beam strikes the starboard side.

CONTINUITY AND PRODUCTION PROBLEMS

• For some reason, Mendon's uniform has a collar. Maybe the makeup artist found it easier?

• Picard joins Riker in Ten-Forward as the first officer enjoys a feast before transferring to the *Pagh*. Riker hands a drink to Picard, who takes it with his right hand and draws it to his mouth. The camera angle changes, and suddenly Picard holds the cup with his left hand.

• At this same feast, a waiter approaches and loads up Riker's table with more treats. If you watch carefully, the waiter actually places the same bowl on the table twice. He approaches in the wide shot, grabs a spherical bowl, and places it on the table before unloading most of the tray. Moments later, the scene cuts to a close-up of Picard, and the waiter grabs the spherical bowl from the tray again.

TRIVIA ANSWERS

1. Lieutenant Lewis.
2. Pipius claw, heart of targ, and gagh.

THE MEASURE OF A MAN

Star Date: 42523.7

Summoned by Commander Bruce Maddox for a series of dangerous experiments that Maddox hopes will result in the creation of more Soong-type androids,

Data must undergo a trial to determine his status as a sentient being.

TRIVIA QUESTIONS

1. At what hour does Maddox expect Data to report to his office?

2. From what dictionary does Data quote the definition of android?

ALTERNATE VIEWPOINTS AND CORRECTIONS

• Robert Googooian of Burbank, CA, wrote to inform me that JAG stands for "Judge Advocate General" not "Judge Adjutant General," as I stated on page 97 of the *NextGen Guide*.

• Responding to my disbelief on page 98 of the *NextGen Guide* that the word "toaster" would still be in use in the twenty-fourth century, Keith A. Garrett of Memphis TN, came up with an interesting explanation. Keith wondered if the term "toaster" hadn't become generic, given the existence of the Video Toaster (a low-cost, video editing and graphics generation device). Perhaps the term "toaster" came to identify any piece of high technology that could perform complex tasks with ease.

PLOT OVERSIGHTS

• How are starbases numbered? In this episode, the *Enterprise* docks at the newly created Starbase 173. If they are numbered in order of creation, Starfleet must get really busy in the next few months, because Picard and Wesley take a shuttle to

Starbase 515 in "Samaritan Snare." On the other hand, if starbases are numbered by location, how is the scheme implemented? Starbase 173 resides in the 21st Sector, according to JAG officer Captain Phillipa Louvois.

• Bruce Maddox was either a boy genius or doesn't show his age. Looking approximately thirty-five years old, he claims to have evaluated Data on the android's entrance to Starfleet Academy. In the episode "Redemption II," Data states that he has twenty-six years of service to Starfleet. That episode occurs approximately two and one-half years after "The Measure of a Man." So, at this point, Data has been in Starfleet for about twenty-three and one-half years *plus* four years at the Academy. Did Maddox actually evaluate Data when he was seven or eight?

• To make his point that Data is property, Maddox asks Louvois if a starship computer could refuse a refit. Well...what if it did? Would Starfleet simply pull its plug? Or would Starfleet proceed with caution, attempting to determine if the state of the computer had changed in some way?

• While identifying Data at the trial, the computer states that the android is currently assigned to the USS *Enterprise*. Hasn't Data been transferred to Maddox by this point in the episode?

CHANGED PREMISES

• Data's off button seems to move. In this episode, Riker taps Data on the left side and the android flops over, but in "Datalore" the off button appears to be on Data's right side.

EQUIPMENT ODDITIES

• The doors of Starfleet continue their amazing demonstrations of knowing not only when to open but also when *not* to open. During the scene when Picard tells Data about the hearing, the android stands mere inches from the ready room door and it does not open.

CONTINUITY AND PRODUCTION PROBLEMS

• Near the beginning of the episode and again in the middle, the creators use an outside shot of the *Enterprise* coming head on toward the camera as Starbase 173 sits off to the right. This graphic can be interpreted in two ways, and both interpretations have problems. If the shot shows the *Enterprise* approaching, why is Picard already aboard the starbase at the beginning of the episode? And why is the shot reused in the middle of the episode, when intervening shots have shown the *Enterprise* docked? On the other hand, if the shot is supposed to show the *Enterprise* docked at Starbase, why does it drift into view as Picard and Louvois get reacquainted at the beginning of the episode? (Besides that, if the shot supposedly shows the *Enterprise* docked at Starbase 173, the perspectives are off.)

• The courtroom on Starbase 173 bears a remarkable resemblance to the battle bridge.

• As part of his presentation, Riker asks Data to bend a metal bar. Data folds it into a "U" and hands it back to Riker. Supposedly this metal is really, really tough to bend, and Data's performance indicates his great strength. Oddly enough, by the time Louvois holds it, someone has pulled the ends apart so that the bar makes almost a forty-five-degree angle. Data didn't do it. He's still sitting at the witness stand. Maddox didn't do it. He's sitting behind the prosecutor's table. I guess that leaves Riker. (Clark Kent in disguise, maybe?)

TRIVIA ANSWERS

1. At 0900.
2. *Webster's Twenty-fourth Century,* fifth edition.

THE DAUPHIN

Star Date: 42568.8

Wesley falls in love when the *Enterprise* transports a young lady named Salia and her overprotective guardian named Anya to Daled IV, where Salia will assume the planet's leadership. Picard soon discovers that both of the women are actually shapeshifters with advanced capabilities and realizes that Anya's absolute determination that no harm come to Salia could endanger the ship.

ALTERNATE VIEWPOINTS AND CORRECTIONS

• In my second trivia question for this episode on page 99 of the *NextGen Guide,* I asked how many times Salia had been "exposed" to chocolate and answered twice. Mary

M. Kleinsmith of West Falls, NY, wrote to say it was actually three times: twice by Wesley and once by Guinan. I should have asked how many times Salia "tasted" chocolate.

TRIVIA QUESTIONS

1. How long are beans on Thalos VII aged before they are made into Thalian chocolate mousse?

2. From what illness does the patient in sick bay suffer?

PLOT OVERSIGHTS

• For a trained medical professional, Pulaski seems very loose with her descriptions. While on a tour of sick bay, Anya discovers a patient with a virulent, contagious disease. Salia's protector wants the patient destroyed, saying that he poses a threat. Pulaski refuses, stating the air filtration system reduces the possibility of transmission. When pressed by Anya, Pulaski does admit that the "probability is not zero." A short time later, Picard and a team from Security charge into sick bay, and Pulaski states that there is "no chance" of contagion.

• Is rank a factor in how fast Security responds to requests for assistance? In the incident above, Anya morphs into a beast, Pulaski hollers for Security, and a team shows up with *Picard...three seconds* later. (Was the captain loitering out in the hall or just happened to be passing by?) Near the end of the episode, Salia sneaks off to Wesley's quarters, and Anya follows. Again, she morphs into a beast, as does Salia. Wesley slaps his combadge and yells for Security. More than thirty seconds later, the scene goes to a commercial break, and Security still hasn't arrived!

CHANGED PREMISES

• In "Hide and Q," when Riker created a Klingon warriorette for Worf, he claimed that she came from a world now alien to him. Yet in this episode, when Wesley asks about Klingon mating rituals, Worf seems quite enamored with the practices (and treats us to a wonderful performance. "Men do not roar, women roar…").

• At the conslusion of the episode, Data states that a transmission from Daled IV came from a terrawatt source on the planet's surface. Riker immediately reacts, saying that a terrawatt source is more power than the entire ship could generate. However, in "The Masterpiece Society," La Forge tells Hannah Bates that the warp core kicks plasma up into the terrawatt range.

TRIVIA ANSWERS

1. Four hundred years.
2. Andronesian encephalitis.

CONTAGION

Star Date: 42609.1

With his ship increasingly debilitated by a sophisticated computer virus, Picard takes the *Enterprise* into the Neutral Zone to uncover the virus's source—the home planet of the fabled Iconians, a long-dead race that reportedly possessed incredible technologies. Barely in time, La Forge discovers a way to remove the virus before it destroys the ship.

TRIVIA QUESTIONS

1. How many people died on the *Yamato* when the computer unexpectedly dropped a force field in a cargo bay?

2. Who is the subcommander with whom Riker speaks on the Romulan warbird *Haakona*?

PLOT OVERSIGHTS

• Picard makes two oddly placed log entries in this episode. When the *Yamato* explodes, the show fades to a commercial break. It returns with a log entry by Picard who is still staring at the viewscreen. The impression is that we are picking up right where we left, but we can't be because Picard has no time to make a log entry. Then, while down on Iconia, Picard makes a log entry, but the dialogue indicates that the away team cannot communicate with the *Enterprise*.

EQUIPMENT ODDITIES

• When the *Yamato* explodes, Picard orders Worf to raise the shields. When he does, the red alert klaxons sound, and the panels behind the Klingon change to flashing red to indicate the new status. Did Worf turn on red alert when he raised the shields, or does it come on automatically? And if it comes on automatically, why does Riker always say, "Red alert! Shields up!"?

• After reviewing Captain Donald Varley's logs, Picard walks out of his ready room and up to the science stations at the back of the bridge. As he passes the light panel by the turbolift, you can see that the ship is on yellow alert. Moments later, when Data plays back the *Yamato*'s recording of the Iconian probe, a wide shot with Riker in the foreground shows that the light panel has resumed normal status for some reason.

• Shortly after the *Enterprise* drops into orbit around Iconia, a probe launches from the surface. La Forge realizes the damage the probe will do to the ship and tries to warn Picard. Unfortunately, the communications system is out, and La Forge must hop a turbolift. The wild ride that follows deserves a bit of scrutiny. La Forge hops into the turbolift, and it starts traveling backward at a high rate of speed. Accordingly, La Forge flattens against the doors. Then the turbolift changes direction and flies forward. La Forge, in turn, slams against the back of the turbolift. So far, so good. However, in the next few moments, the motion indicator on the turbolift goes top to bottom once and then shows the turbolift going backward again. Yet La Forge stays plastered against the back wall! Even more interesting, some force tosses La Forge out of the turbolift and onto the bridge at the end of the ride, suggesting that the turbolift had been traveling horizontally and has suddenly stopped. The bridge is part of the raised portion on the top of the saucer. There are no horizontal turbolift shafts up there. How could the

turbolift be going sideways?

• At the conclusion of the episode, the Romulan warbird counts down to autodestruct because of the intrusions of the Iconian computer virus. Yet the Romulan chief engineer simply turns everything off, then back on, and everything is fine. Does this seem like something a good, self-respecting autodestruct system should allow? Should Starfleet keep this little maneuver in mind? (Memo to all Starfleet captains: "If you ever find a Romulan warbird in autodestruct mode, just run down to Engineering, turn everything off, turn everything on, and tow it back to Federation space.")

CONTINUITY AND PRODUCTION PROBLEMS

• This episode reveals a *startling* fact about a certain destination as the Iconians fled their planet hundreds of thousands of years ago. Believe it or not, some of them went to...Toronto, Ontario! The semicircular-shaped buildings shown in the Iconian gateway comprise Toronto City Hall. (Proof! Proof, I tell you, that aliens have visited Earth in the distant past!)

• At one point, Worf, carrying Data, steps through the Iconian gateway and instantly materializes on the *Enterprise.* He starts into the gateway with his left arm between Data's legs, grasping Data's left hand, but he appears on the *Enterprise* with his left hand holding Data's left leg and his right hand hiding Data's left hand.

TRIVIA ANSWERS
1. Eighteen.
2. Taris.

THE PICARD TOTE BOARD

1. Number of parts played by Patrick Stewart: seventeen
2. Number of actors who play Jean-Luc Picard: three
3. Number of times we see Picard sleeping alone: seven
4. Number of times we see Picard in repose with a woman: two
5. Number of times we see Picard in bed with Q: two
6. Number of times we see Picard reading a book: four
7. Number of people who call Picard "god" (or "The Picard"): three
8. Number of times Picard decides the fate of an entire planet: at least six
9. Number of times we see Picard with hair on top of his head: three
10. Number of times Picard fixes his hair during a crisis: none

REFERENCES

1. Picard, Picard-plus-energy-being in "Lonely Among Us," Dixon Hill in "The Big Good-bye" and "Manhunt," holodeck soldier in "The Defector," alien Picard in "Allegiance," holodeck swordsman in "Hollow Pursuits," Sarek-Picard in "Sarek," Lwaxana's lover in "Ménage à Troi," Locutus in "The Best of Both Worlds," "The Best of Both Worlds, Part 2" and "I Borg," Robin Hood in "Qpid," a Romulan in "Unification I" and "Unification II," Kamin in "The Inner Light," leader of an acting troupe in "Time's Arrow, Part II," Mot the barber in "Starship Mine," Galen in "Gambit, Part I" and Gambit, Part II," Lwaxana's dream captain in "Dark Page," and Korgano in "Masks."

2. Patrick Stewart, David Tristen Birkin in "Rascals," and Marcus Nash in "Tapestry."

3. Under the influence of the Thought Maker in "The Battle," while sick in "Angel One," before getting the call from Walker Keel in "Conspiracy," in the teaser for "Allegiance," before Jono stabs him in "Suddenly Human," on the floor in "Chain of Command, Part 2," and on Riker's *Enterprise* in "All Good Things."

4. With Vash in "Captain's Holiday" and Crusher in "Attached."

5. After a fight with Vash in "Qpid," and the morning after Marta Batanides in "Tapestry."

6. In a shuttle during "Samaritan Snare," on Risa during "Captain's Holiday," in his ready room during "Darmok," and in his ready room during "Cause and Effect."

7. By Rivan in "Justice" and by both Liko and Nuria in "Who Watches the Watchers."

8. Earth in "Encounter at Farpoint," Bynaus in "11001001," Ornara in "Symbiosis," Drema IV in "Pen Pals," (possibly) Mariposa in "Up the Long Ladder," (possibly) Zalkon in "Transfigurations," (possibly) the Klingon home world in "Redemption, Part II," Earth again in "All Good Things," and Veridian IV in *Star Trek Generations*.

9. In the flashback to Jack Crusher's death in "Violations," as a boy in "Rascals," and as a young man in "Tapestry."

10. Of course, the same cannot be said for Captain Kate Janeway of the USS *Voyager*. No criticism here, just an observation.

THE ROYALE

Star Date: 42625.4

Orbiting the completely inhospitable planet Theta VIII, the crew finds wreckage from an ancient Earth craft and discover an even stranger anachronism below on the surface—a perfect simulation of the events in the pulp novel *Hotel Royale*. Curiosity turns to worry when an away team discovers that they are trapped in a fantasy taken from the novel's pages.

TRIVIA QUESTIONS

1. With what hand does Data win at blackjack?

2. What was the name of Colonel Steven Richey's vessel?

PLOT OVERSIGHTS

• Orbiting Theta VIII, La Forge gives Riker a rundown of the planet. First, he says the surface temperature is -291 degrees Celsius. Somehow the surface temperature of this planet is almost 18 degrees below Absolute Zero (-273.15 degrees Celsius). As of our current scientific understanding, Absolute Zero is as cold as it gets in normal space.

• Science fiction runs a danger whenever it attempts to make specific predictions about the future. For instance, in this episode, Picard tells Riker of Pierre de Fermat's Last Theorem—discovered after the mathematician's death—and mentions that it has remained unsolved for eight hundred years. Given that the theorem is actually unsolved in the twenty-fourth century, Picard probably meant to say it has remained unsolved for seven hundred years, since Fermat died in 1665 (and this episode occurs in about 2365, according to Data's date in "The Neutral Zone"). Also, Ekin Shim of Düsseldorf, Germany, tells me that a proof for Fermat's Last Theorem has been presented and appears to be valid.

• Does anyone else find it odd that Worf doesn't know how to operate a twentieth-century elevator, but seems fairly comfortable with a twentieth-century telephone?

• At one point, the "little lady" in this episode holds a ten and a three in her hand while the dealer at the blackjack table has a face card showing. A dirty old man intent on parting the young woman from her money tells her to take another card, while Data says that the odds favor "standing pat." While I understand the rules of the game, I don't play much blackjack. On the other hand, Chuck Powell of Holland, PA, says that the little lady has only a 39 percent chance of going over twenty-one with the next card (and losing). In addition, since the dealer is showing a face card, the odds say that she must keep taking cards until she reaches seventeen.

EQUIPMENT ODDITIES

• Does the transporter have some sort of heating unit to ensure that objects brought aboard materialize at room temperature? Shortly after beaming a piece of the space wreckage onto the transporter pad, Riker and O'Brien pick it up with their bare hands. From the dialogue, it appears that this metal has orbited an extremely cold planet for hundreds of years. Shouldn't it be *really* cold as well?

CONTINUITY AND PRODUCTION PROBLEMS

• When Data performs a one-handed cut of a deck of cards, he finishes the cut in the wide shot before the camera angle changes to the close-up and he finishes the cut again.

TRIVIA ANSWERS

1. Five of hearts, two of clubs, nine of hearts, two of hearts, and three of spades.
2. Explorer ship, *Charybdis*.

TIME SQUARED

Star Date: 42679.2

When the crew rescues a drifting shuttle, they discover its pilot is an incoherent Jean-Luc Picard from six hours in the future. Ominously, the shuttle's logs show the destruction of the *Enterprise* by an energy vortex. A short time later, when the energy vortex does appear, Picard flies the ship to safety by taking the opposite actions of his future counterpart.

GREAT LINES

"Delicious."—Worf to Riker, evaluating the culinary delights of the Owon eggs. (I love this line because Worf is still an alien at this point in the series. Everyone else is grimacing at the dish, and Worf is shoveling it in with great pleasure.)

TRIVIA QUESTIONS

1. Pulaski brings ale from what planet to Riker's dinner party?

2. The *Enterprise* is en route to what system during this episode?

ALTERNATE VIEWPOINTS AND CORRECTIONS

• There's a little story going around Trekdom that Picard A (the one in our timeline) didn't kill Picard B (the one from six hours in the future) at the conclusion of this episode—that he merely stunned his counterpart. When Picard A shoots Picard B, sparks erupt from his chest. Then Pulaski comes, takes a tricorder reading, walks over to O'Brien, shakes her head, and walks out. Doesn't that give the impression that Picard B is *dead*?

PLOT OVERSIGHTS

• Does the definition of the word "omelette" change in the next three hundred fifty years? At the dinner party that Riker hosts for Pulaski, the dialogue indicates that Riker will fix

omelettes, but the actual dish he prepares looks just like scrambled eggs.

• This whole bit with Picard B being
out of time with the rest of the crew
seems a bit odd. Didn't Kirk and crew
regularly travel in time? They didn't
seem to have any side effects from it.
And why are the shuttle's energy systems out of phase? It comes from only
six hours in the future. Does the Enterprise flip polarities every six hours?

EQUIPMENT ODDITIES

• Shortly after discovering the powerless shuttle, the Enterprise captures
it with a tractor beam and brings it into
Shuttle Bay 2. The scene shows a
wide shot of the interior of Shuttle Bay
2. Looking through the outside door,
you can see the shuttle and a tractor
beam that comes down from directly
above the little craft. One question:
Whence doth this tractor beam
cometh? Remember that Shuttle Bay
2 is on the back side of the yoke that
connects the saucer section to the
star drive portion of the Enterprise.
This piece slopes away from the
saucer section at a fairly quick angle.
To come directly from above, the tractor beam would have to be mounted
on some sort of boom.

• As the Enterprise approaches the
shuttle, Worf declares the small craft
powerless. Yet when Data attempts
to operate the controls, they make a
little buzzing sound.

• Shortly after Picard B arrives in
sick bay, Pulaski walks over to the big
wall display and touches the wall right
beside it. This action engages a force
field over Picard B to keep him from
wandering off. Yet later in the episode,

when Pulaski disables the force field,
the camera angle clearly shows the
location she tapped to engage the
force field, and the area contains no
control panels!

• Near the end of the episode, just
before Picard orders the Enterprise
to fly into the energy vortex, the little
green strips on the underside of the
armrests of his chair are not lit.

CONTINUITY AND
PRODUCTION PROBLEMS

• For the most part, the double Picard
shots work well in this episode. But
in the scene where the Picards leave
sick bay—and just before the pair
board a turbolift—Picard A seems to
be looking into thin air, while Picard B
strides several feet in front of him.

• After disembarking from the turbolift, the Picards walk down a hall. Picard
A stands near Picard B's left side. Then
the pair turns a corner, and Picard A is
suddenly on Picard B's right side.

TRIVIA ANSWERS

1. Ennan VI.
2. The Endicor system.

★

THE ICARUS
FACTOR

Star Date: 42686.4

After Starfleet offers Riker a command, the first officer must undergo a briefing by his estranged
father, Kyle Riker. At first William

Riker will have nothing to do with his dad, but after they hit each other with sticks for a while, they kiss and make up. (Just joking. They don't really kiss.)

GREAT LINES

"If I were not a consummate professional, and an android, I would find this entire procedure insulting."—Data to La Forge on the shipwide inspection of Engineering functions by the technicians from Starbase Montgomery.

TRIVIA QUESTIONS

1. Where did Pulaski's patient pick up a case of the flu?

2. Besides Klingon and Romulan, what other "exotic" languages does Commander Flaherty speak?

ALTERNATE VIEWPOINTS AND CORRECTIONS

• On page 113 of the *NextGen Guide,* I asked why anyone would be enamored of the fact that the first officer of the USS *Aries*—one Commander Flaherty—speaks forty languages, given the existence of the Universal Translator. Mary M. Kleinsmith of West Falls, NY, wrote to say that with the advent of the Universal Translator, individuals no longer *need* to learn other languages. Therefore it has become a lost art and worthy of admiration. Lee Zion of the USS *Kitty Hawk* cited the Universal Translator scene in *Star Trek VI: The Undiscovered Country* to make his point that the person on the other end of the conversation knows when you are using a Univer-

sal Translator and would be much more impressed if someone actually spoke his or her language.

TRIVIA ANSWERS

1. Nasreldine.

2. Giamon and Stroyerian.

PEN PALS

Star Dates: 42695.3—42741.3

Data makes unauthorized contact with a little girl named Sarjenka, who lives on Drema IV. Disturbed that Sarjenka's planet is being torn apart by volcanic eruptions, Data convinces Picard to intervene and save her world by using harmonic vibrations to shatter the planet's naturally aligned dilithium crystals.

TRIVIA QUESTIONS

1. How many geologically similar systems lie in the Selcundi Drema Sector?

2. What by-product results from the breakdown of dilithium?

ALTERNATE VIEWPOINTS AND CORRECTIONS

• When Data beams down to rescue Sarjenka, he encounters a door that vanishes with a wave of his hand in a house furnished in early Flintstones style. On page 116 of the *NextGen Guide,* I noted this disparity. Ed Howard of Sloatsburg, NY reminded me that the style of a house doesn't always reflect the current state of technology. For instance, people build log cabins today and furnish them very simply.

PLOT OVERSIGHTS

• The episode opens with Picard preparing to ride a horse on the holodeck. Just as Picard starts to mount, Riker calls and asks the captain to come up as soon as possible. The first officer says there is something to see that is "spectacular" and a little "terrifying." In response, Picard secures the horse. Does this seem right? Your "Number One" has just told you that there is something "spectacular" and "terrifying" to see on the bridge and you take the time to tie up a holodeck horse!

• There is a blatant plot trick in this episode that I can't believe I missed while compiling the NextGen Guide. After allowing Data to beam down to Drema IV, Picard orders Riker to handle the transport. The pair goes to the transporter room, and Riker beams Data down to Sarjenka's house. Then Picard calls Riker to the bridge. Why? The next time we see Riker, he is watching Picard pace back and forth on the bridge. This is the reason Picard called Riker away from a delicate transport mission? The captain wanted Riker back on the bridge so the first officer could watch him pace? The real reason Picard called him away was so the guy handling the transporter would have a lower rank than Data. If Data had decided to bring Sarjenka back to the ship and Riker

was running the controls, there would have been a major discussion before anyone beamed up.

• Pulaski must have been "monitoring" the bridge again. It is amazing that the good doctor always seems to know exactly when to do this. Data beams on board with Sarjenka and appears to go straight to the bridge. After the crew saves Drema IV, Picard orders Data to take Sarjenka to sick bay. Then the captain goes to the ready room, calls sick bay, refers to Sarjenka as an "alien," and asks Pulaski to erase her memories. Amazingly enough, Pulaski doesn't say, "What alien?" She simply tells Picard that she will do her best.

CONTINUITY AND PRODUCTION PROBLEMS

• When the senior staff meets on the observation lounge with Riker to discuss his desire to put Wesley in charge of the planetary survey team, the stars behave oddly throughout the scene. In the close-ups of Picard and Riker, the stars move right to left. In the close-ups of Pulaski and La Forge, the stars move left to right. To top it all off, when Wesley enters, all the wide shots show the stars perfectly still!

• After one of his team balks at doing a lengthy test, Wesley goes to Riker for advice. Riker walks over with an oversized root beer mug, setting it down in front of him as he sits. At this point the handle faces to Riker's left. The camera angle changes and the handle suddenly faces to Riker's right. It then switches back when the scene returns to the first camera angle.

• After discovering the vanishing

door in Sarjenka's home, Data takes a few steps forward. The wind begins to blow his hair, the camera angle changes, he takes a few steps, and the wind begins to blow his hair again!

TRIVIA ANSWERS

1. Five.
2. Illium 629.

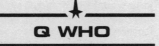

Q WHO

Star Dates: 42761.3—42761.9

After Picard states that the *Enterprise* is ready to meet any challenges that might come its way, Q transports them seven thousand light-years for their first encounter with the Borg. The captain soon realizes that the *Enterprise* is hopelessly outmatched and pleads for Q's further assistance.

GREAT LINES

"Microbrain! Growl for me! Let me know you still care!"—Q to Worf upon seeing the Klingon for the first time after returning to the *Enterprise*. Nominated by Lee Zion of the USS *Kitty Hawk*.

PLOT OVERSIGHTS

• Attempting to convince Picard of his sincerity, Q tells the captain that he is "Willing and able, ready to serve." Several moments later, Picard repeats Q's statement but mixes up the words by saying, "Ready and willing, able to serve."

• One has to wonder how Starfleet Command feels about this incident. Picard doesn't feel like baby-sitting Q, so Q knocks them over to meet the Borg ahead of schedule. Because of this, the Borg head our way, blow up almost forty of our starships, and come within a hairbreadth of destroying the Federation. (I can just hear Admiral Nechayev now: "Now let me get this straight. All he wanted to do was hang around with you boys for a little while and you said, 'No'? Didn't you realize how quickly he would tire of the constant precolonizing mapping missions? A week! One week at the most and Q would have been gone! But *no!* You just had to get him mad, didn't you?")

TRIVIA QUESTIONS

1. Where would Ensign Gomez have done phase work with antimatter if she hadn't been assigned to the *Enterprise*?

2. What three starbases are mentioned in this episode?

CHANGED PREMISES

• When did Guinan change her name and then change it back, and why? Upon hearing Guinan's name, Q seems to indicate that two centuries ago she went by another name. So sometime in the twenty-second century she called herself something else. Yet in "Time's Arrow," Data meets Guinan in the *nineteenth* century and everyone knows her as Guinan.

• Granted, we are dealing with Q here, and everything he says should be suspect. Yet, in this episode when Riker complains that the first time they met Q he put them on trial for the crimes of humanity, Q retorts that they were exonerated. Yet in "True Q," when the subject comes up again, Q says that the jury is still out.

• Based on a warning from Guinan, Picard raises the Enterprise's shields. Afterward, a Borg scout beams into Main Engineering. So the Borg can beam through the Enterprise's shields? And if so, why didn't they use this capability when they wanted to kidnap Picard in "The Best of Both Worlds"?

• In this episode Q tells Picard that the Borg scout is neither male nor female. Also, when Riker beams over to the Borg ship, he concludes that the Borg begin life as humanoids. Assuming the Borg are not like the J'naii of "The Outcast," we must conclude that the Borg start life as either male or female and are "modified" to acquire their asexual designation. This begs the question: Is there something the creators haven't told us about what happened to Picard in "The Best of Both Worlds"? Was there another reason a tear trickled down his cheek?

EQUIPMENT ODDITIES

• For some reason, after Gomez douses him with hot chocolate, Picard opts to walk down a long hall to get to a turbolift when he could step onto the one just to his left. Also, Picard boards the turbolift on deck 36 and requests deck 9, but the motion indicator shows the car going down instead of up. (Q is probably doing that just to see if our good captain is paying attention.)

• When Q abducts Picard in a shuttle, Riker orders the Enterprise into a search pattern. Six hours later, Data says they have investigated the area that a shuttle without warp could cover in the allotted time. However, an outside shot of the shuttle that Q stole shows warp nacelles on the craft. Doesn't this mean that the missing shuttle could travel at warp?

• The shields on the Enterprise seem to have some type of backup system. After realizing that the Borg ship is regenerating, Picard orders the away team back to the Enterprise and blasts away at high warp. The Borg pursue and begin firing a shield-depleting weapon. After the third hit, Worf states, "We have lost shields again." The scene cuts to an outside shot, the Borg ship fires and the weapon detonates across the surface of the Enterprise's shield bubble—the shield bubble that shouldn't exist because the shields are down.

CONTINUITY AND PRODUCTION PROBLEMS

• When Gomez first spills her hot chocolate on Picard, the stain sits on his left hip, fairly confined. The scene goes to a reaction shot from La Forge, and when it returns, the stain is suddenly much larger.

• After the Borg appear, Picard asks Guinan to activate her viewscreen so she can monitor the bridge. Guinan leaves Ten-Forward and walks into an office. She reaches out to press a button on her control panel. The "boop" sounds before she touches anything, and Guinan immediately retracts her finger.

• Evidently Worf decided to relieve the tension caused by the appearance of the Borg scout in Main Engineering with a small ventriloquism demonstration. When the scout begins to interfere with the operation of the ship, Worf turns to a security guard, nods, and says, "Ensign!" Amazingly enough, he does it without moving his lips!

• After dying at the hands of Worf in Engineering, the Borg scout changes position twice in subsequent camera angles.

• When Guinan sits down in the observation lounge with Picard, Riker, and Troi to discuss the first Borg encounter, watch the chair right beside Guinan. A shadow moves across it. (I want to know who else is in the room with them. Why don't the creators tell us who it is? Don't they know we crave this type of information? Don't they realize how much this type of thing *bugs* us? I can't *stand* not knowing! Someone has *got* to tell me!)

• This same conference with the unknown bystander ends when Worf informs Picard that the Borg have locked a tractor beam on the *Enterprise*. Yet the viewscreen showing the Borg ship as Worf begins his announcement doesn't include the tractor beam seen only moments later when the scene switches to an exterior shot.

TRIVIA ANSWERS

1. Rana VI.

2. Starbase 173, Starbase 185 and Starbase 83.

SAMARITAN SNARE

Star Dates: 42779.1—42779.5

As Picard undergoes an operation to replace his faulty cybernetic heart, Riker and the *Enterprise* respond to a distress call from a Pakled vessel. Too late, the first officer discovers that the Pakled plea for help is merely a ruse to kidnap La Forge in an attempt to extort technology from the *Enterprise*.

GREAT LINES

"Uh-huh."—Grebnedlog providing the answer to several of Riker's questions. (Don't you just love this guy's name?) Nominated by Lee Zion of the USS *Kitty Hawk*.

TRIVIA QUESTIONS

1. Where is the *Enterprise* heading at the beginning of the episode?

2. What is the name of the Pakled ship?

ALTERNATE VIEWPOINTS AND CORRECTIONS

• I must have had a brain cramp when I was working on the review of this episode in the *NextGen Guide*. On page 122, under Continuity and Production Problems, I stated that the scene just prior to the launch of the shuttle contains an establishing shot of the shuttle bay and that there is a giant "2" on the floor. Stuart Davis of East Sussex, England, wrote to say that his tape showed a "3" on the floor. I rechecked my tape, and sure enough, it is a "3"!

PLOT OVERSIGHTS

• Of course, the sensible thing would be for Riker to send a team of engineering specialists over to the Pakled ship—instead of just his chief engineer—but then it would be a short episode!

• A small amount of confusion surrounds Wesley's testing in this episode. Supposedly, the tests show that he can continue to earn academy credits with his studies on the *Enterprise.* Wait a minute: When did Wesley get accepted to the academy? He failed his entrance exam in "Coming of Age." What kind of education institution allows you to earn credits before you are even accepted for study?

CHANGED PREMISES

• In this episode, Riker, Troi, Data, and Pulaski judge the Pakleds and determine that they are attempting to develop too quickly. The senior staff seems very smug about making this determination. Yet in the last episode "Q Who," when Q judges that humanity is developing too quickly, Picard spouts off and says that humanity should be the judge of that. Well…if humanity wants to judge the rate of its own development, why shouldn't humanity let the Pakleds judge the rate of their own development? (Hmmm?)

EQUIPMENT ODDITIES

• This episode and "Darmok" provide conflicting information on how the transporters work. In this episode, La Forge dematerializes on the Pakled ship and *then* rematerializes on the bridge of the *Enterprise.* Yet in "Darmok," when La Forge and O'Brien are trying to beam Picard off the planet, one half of the captain is on the transporter pad while the other half is on the planet—indicating that the captain *had begun* to materialize on the pad before completely dematerializing on the planet below.

CONTINUITY AND PRODUCTION PROBLEMS

• Somebody needs to feed those shuttle gremlins before they send anyone else on a trip in Shuttlecraft 01. Watch Picard's sandwich as he tosses Wesley a cloth napkin. Some invisible force gobbles a bite out of the top. Then the camera angle changes and the sandwich becomes whole again. Picard takes a big bite, the scene gives us a look at Wesley, and when it returns to Picard, something has munched the sandwich down to only one bite left! Picard takes it all in stride. He seems completely unperturbed that little invisible imps are devouring his food.

TRIVIA ANSWERS

1. The Epsilon IX Sector.
2. The *Mondor.*

UP THE LONG LADDER

Star Dates: 42823.2—42827.3

Seeking to solve two problems at once, Picard proposes a "marriage" between the Bringloidi—Irish descendants of Earth who had established a "back to nature" settlement on a planet threatened by stellar flares—and a colony of clones in desperate need of fresh DNA on Mariposa.

TRIVIA QUESTIONS

1. When was the SS *Mariposa* loaded with cargo?

2. To what area of the ship does the crew of the *Enterprise* beam the Bringloidi?

ALTERNATE VIEWPOINTS AND CORRECTIONS

• On pages 124 and 125 of the *NextGen Guide,* I noted that the markings on the Mariposan machines looked alien. I asked why they weren't in English, since Mariposans came from Earth. I also pointed out that it had been only around three hundred years since the Mariposans left (actually more like two hundred fifty) and so their script should still be readable. As an example, I noted that Old English documents of the seventeenth century are still readable today. Only a few characters are different than ours. Several nitpickers had corrections to make to these statements, additions to offer and alternate viewpoints to present.

Richard Smith of Surrey, England, advised that Old English was spoken and written from about A.D. 600 to A.D. 1100. By the seventeenth century, the language was an early form of modern English. He also stated that, with the invention of the printing press, the rate of change in the shape of characters greatly decreased. If the Mariposans started out with English labels on their machines, they should still have English labels.

John Hobson of Bolingbrook, IL, wrote to add that in a comparison between seventeenth- and twentieth-century English, only two characters are different: the "long s," which looks similar to an "f," and the "thorn," which looks somewhat like a "y," but is actually a "th." John related that you can actually push back the date of recognizable characters much farther. For example, the inscription on Trajan's Column at Rome—dating from the first half of the second century—has an example of the Roman type family.

Finally, David Shelton of Birmingham, AL, accused me of ethnocentricity since I did not consider that the markings might be katakana characters from the Yoshimitsu computer casings.

PLOT OVERSIGHTS

• How do the Mariposans accelerate the development of the human mind?

In the scene where Riker incinerates both clones, it appears that they are nearly fully grown physically. Do they have completely developed minds as well? Or do the Mariposans have to care for them like any other baby? ("Hello, Ready-Mart? Um, yes, we need some diapers... the largest size you've got." Yeow! Even the thought sends chills up your spine, doesn't it?)

CHANGED PREMISES

• In this episode, Worf orders the food replicator to make real Klingon alcohol. From the expression of the Bringloidi leader who imbibes it, the tonic has quite a kick. Yet in "Relics," Data must go to Guinan's private store to get a bottle of the real stuff. Did some teetotaler reprogram the food dispensers?

EQUIPMENT ODDITIES

• Pulaski is really handy with her little medical wand. She waves it at one Mariposan individual and without a tricorder, and *without even looking* at the wand she determines that she is in the presence of clones. Now, that's a diagnostic doctor for you!

• Suspicious that the Mariposans have illegally extracted cells for cloning, Pulaski scans Riker, La Forge, and herself with a tricorder. Interestingly enough, when she uses the tricorder on herself she doesn't turn it around and point the business end toward her body. Yet somehow the tricorder knows exactly what she wants to do and supplies the appropriate information.

CONTINUITY AND PRODUCTION PROBLEMS

• Watch Riker after the clones stun him. He collapses into the arms of a man, and the guy drags him off camera. Just before he leaves the scene, Riker takes a quick look to the side. (I bet he *thought* he was out of the camera's view.)

• Taking the debilitated Riker and Pulaski to the cloning lab, the Mariposans extract some epithelial cells from their stomachs. The first clone pushes a nasty-looking needle into Pulaski, and it looks like it actually drives down into her. However, the needle that supposedly goes into Riker doesn't have enough tension in its spring. It is obviously retracting into the mechanism.

TRIVIA ANSWERS

1. November 27, 2123.
2. Cargo Hold 7.

✦ MANHUNT

Star Date: 42859.2

Under the guise of traveling as the Betazoid ambassador to a conference on Pacifica, Lwaxana Troi boards the *Enterprise* fully intent on finding a husband. With great discomfort, Picard discovers that Lwaxana has her sights set on him.

GREAT LINES

"Or more?!"—Riker to Counselor Troi after she admits that a Betazoid woman can quadruple her sex drive during the phase…or more. Nominated by David Yalden II of Flintstone, GA.

TRIVIA QUESTIONS

1. The Ooolans of what planet bang rocks together while eating?

2. What is the name of the man who first enters Dixon Hill's office and inquires about Alva?

ALTERNATE VIEWPOINTS AND CORRECTIONS

• At the end of this episode just before beaming down to Pacifica, Lwaxana suddenly springs a surprise on everyone by announcing that the Antidean delegates to the conference are really assassins. On page 127 of the *NextGen Guide,* I asked why Deanna didn't at least get some sense that the Antideans were up to no good—given that Lwaxana labels their minds "primitive." Patricia Pozywak of Elyria, OH, observed that Lwaxana couldn't read their minds until the Antideans awoke from their comas and this was the first time Deanna had encountered them in an animated state. David Yalden II of Flintstone, GA, added that perhaps Deanna hadn't opened her mind to them to probe their intent. (I suppose I merely assumed that the ship's counselor would have some unstated responsibilities. Prior to the transporter scene, the creators showed us the Antideans

awake and feeding in sick bay. Wouldn't it be part of Deanna's portfolio to wander by innocently and give them a scan? (At the very least, she could have given Picard one of her very insightful, awe-inspiring pronouncements, "Captain, they're hiding something!")

PLOT OVERSIGHTS

• Lwaxana Troi sets her first trap for Picard by inviting him to a dinner she describes as an ambassadorial function. Later, as he heads for the dinner, Picard meets Pulaski and inquires if she is coming. She replies that she has already eaten. This gives the impression that Picard expected Pulaski to attend the dinner. Does that mean it is normal for the senior staff to attend "ambassadorial functions"? This would make sense. Yet later, Pulaski reveals Picard's destination to Deanna Troi and the counselor immediately knows her mother is planning something. She eventually arrives at Lwaxana's quarters—presumably to run interference for the captain. The really odd thing about this is that Deanna knew previously that her mother had invited Picard for an "ambassadorial function" dinner. Why is she just now putting two and two together? (Or one and one, as the case may be. I suppose a possible explanation might be that the counselor normally doesn't attend ambassadorial functions and so doesn't find it strange that she wouldn't attend this one until she learns that Lwaxana didn't invite Pulaski either. Unfortunately, that explanation has its own problem because Deanna's *mother* is hosting the dinner. Why *wouldn't* she invite her daughter?)

• It was probably intentional (and a very cute line if it was), but just in case: While in the bar discussing Jimmy Cuzo, Dix's secretary Madeline says that the police would never have captured Cuzo if it wasn't for Hill. Then she adds, "Your testimony got him *arranged*." (Emphasis mine.)

• Why is "Haircut Lapinski" jumpy as he tries to "land on a fraction"? (I can sort out most of the colloquialisms used in the Dixon Hill holodeck program, but this one lost me.)

• Riker doesn't seem to listen very well. Right after he and Data enter Rex's bar, Picard tells them to call him "Dix." A few sentences later, Riker calls him "Captain" again.

• Over and over, Lwaxana demonstrates how distracted the phase has left her in this episode. Not only does she misread Picard more than once, she doesn't recognize that Rex is a holographic construct. I can understand that she might not understand holodecks, but Riker and Picard stand right beside her, and *they* know Rex isn't real. Why can't she read their minds? Her neurons must really be scrambled.

EQUIPMENT ODDITIES

• How quickly we humans forget the state of prior technology. Supposedly, the holodeck creates an accurate representation of San Francisco in 1941, but when Picard turns on the radio, it begins to play almost instantly. A radio available to consumers in 1941 would use tubes, not transistors, and would take a long time to warm up. (On the other hand, the cre-

ators selected a wonderful and appropriate piece of music to spew forth from this anachronistic, instantly-on radio: "Let's Get Away From It All.")

• At one point, Lwaxana determines that her *fiancé,* Will Riker, simply must see how beautiful she looks in a particular dress. She asks the computer to locate the commander. The computer responds, "Riker is in holodeck 3." "Riker"? What happened to "Commander Riker?" Did someone switch the main computer to "informal" mode? Additionally, when the computer shows Lwaxana on the way to holodeck 3, the display does not show the traveling dots that proved so useful when Riker looked for Data during "Encounter at Farpoint."

CONTINUITY AND PRODUCTION PROBLEMS

• Do you recognize the eyes on the second guy who comes into Dixon Hill's office after Picard orders the computer to provide "more ambience, less substance"? It's Gowron! The computer must know all the young up-and-coming Klingons in the Empire and thought it was appropriate to make one of them a thug in Picard's fantasy.

• Marina Sirtis, playing Deanna Troi, covers very nicely when faced with a difficult turbolift exit. Preparing to beam down to Pacifica for a conference, Lwaxana strides out of a turbolift. Engaged in a conversation with her mother at the time, Deanna attempts to exit the turbolift beside Lwaxana. At the last moment she notices that the long train on Lwaxana's dress precludes that possibility. Deciding against stomping on the end of the outfit and yanking Lwaxana backward, Deanna does this darling little dance and eventually hops out into the hall.

TRIVIA ANSWERS

1. Marejaretus VI.
2. Slade Bender.

THE EMISSARY

Star Date: 42901.3

Worf's former girlfriend K'Ehleyr joins the *Enterprise* to assist in a crisis involving the Klingon Empire. A group of warriors, dispatched seventy-five years ago in a sleeper ship, will soon awake, lacking any knowledge of the current peace treaty between the Federation and the Klingon Empire. The *Enterprise* must stop them before they go on a rampage and destroy the defenseless colonies in the region.

RUMINATIONS

I miss K'Ehleyr! She was great, tough, smart, gorgeous—an excellent counterpart for Worf. It's really too bad the creators had to kill her off.

GREAT LINES

"I don't bite. Well ...that's wrong. I do bite."—K'Ehleyr to Worf, trying to get reacquainted.

TRIVIA
QUESTIONS

1. What starbase dispatched K'Ehleyr in the Class 8 probe?

2. Who is the captain of the Klingon vessel *T'Ong*?

PLOT OVERSIGHTS

• This episode never discloses the secret mission of the *T'Ong* and its crew of cryogenically preserved Klingons. (Evidently cryogenics turned out to be more than just a "fad" for the Klingon Empire. See "The Neutral Zone.") The parameters of the mission do raise some questions, however. Seventy-five years is an eternity in weapons development. Did the High Council really believe that the *T'Ong* would be a viable battle horse (battle bird?) seventy-five years after the start of its mission? And were these guys really supposed to thaw out and just start firing at anything that moved and looked like it belonged to the Federation? Did the High Council really believe that seventy-five years in the future their outposts were guaranteed to be distinguishable readily from any other type? There are only a few ways that any of this makes sense. Evidently the *T'Ong* was filled with a bunch of misfits and sent on a "super secret" mission to nowhere! Either that, or the captain of the ship was vying for a place on the High Council and nobody liked him so they dispatched him to the freezer for seventy-five years for the "honor and glory of the Empire."

• After convincing the captain of the *T'Ong* that the Klingon rule the Federation in the present, Worf says, "Welcome to the twenty-fourth century." Why would Worf use a *Terran* measurement of time? Wouldn't the Klingons be more familiar with a time reference based on their emperor's rise to power or the birth of Kahless or some other significant Klingon date?

• Just before beaming over to the *T'Ong*, K'Ehleyr says that the *P'Rang*—a modern Klingon vessel—will arrive in three days. Yet at the beginning of the episode, K'Ehleyr claimed the *P'Rang* was two days behind the *Enterprise*. Now recall that the *Enterprise* dropped out of warp and commenced a search at full impulse for some time. All that time the *P'Rang* was most likely continuing toward the area at warp. Why would the *P'Rang* be *farther* away at the end of the episode than it was at the beginning?

CHANGED PREMISES

• At the conclusion of the episode, Picard congratulates Worf on his first command. Didn't Worf command the saucer section in "Encounter at Farpoint"? Or doesn't that count? And, even if it doesn't count, why does Worf act like he's never sat in the captain's chair before?

EQUIPMENT ODDITIES

• Here's a question: If K'Ehleyr had actually attacked Worf with the holodeck sword after the pair vanquished their enemies during Worf's holodeck exercise program, would the sword have damaged him? Or would the holodeck

have dematerialized it "just in the *nick* of time"? (Sorry, sorry, sorry.)

• During a meeting to discuss options, Data calls Picard from the bridge to report that they are detecting a ship at *extreme sensor range*. Picard tells them to lay in an intercept course and soon marches onto the bridge. The female officer at the conn says she has laid in the course, but Picard tells her to hold position. He wants to see if the *T'Ong* will attack. He asks for a magnification on the viewscreen, and the ship appears. Data says they can't tell if anyone is awake yet (probably because the *T'Ong* is at "extreme sensor range"). Then the *T'Ong* fires, and a blast rocks the *Enterprise*. Hold it! Stop the tape! The *Technical Manual* says that in high resolution mode, the sensors scan out to five light-years. (This is the *minimum* distance they can scan.) We know the *Enterprise* is traveling at impulse (i.e., sublight speed). For the sake of argument, lets say the *T'Ong* is cruising along at warp 9 (which is pretty good for the old Klingon ship). There are only about forty-five seconds from the time Data calls Picard to the time the blast hits the *Enterprise*. Yet at warp 9 it would take the *T'Ong* approximately *twenty-four hours* to travel five light-years and reach the *Enterprise*. Something is off somewhere. The *T'Ong* could not have come within weapons range as fast as it did unless there was a big time skip when we weren't looking, and nothing in the episode indicates this. (Then again, maybe it has some sort of unbelievably fast, long-range phaser. Maybe that's a part of its secret mission!)

CONTINUITY AND PRODUCTION PROBLEMS

• Again with the breakables on the *Enterprise*! In one scene, K'Ehleyr smashes her hand through a clear tabletop and it shatters into many sharp-edged pieces. It is a beautiful scene, but why in the world is the *Enterprise* still using glass?

• K'Ehleyr certainly recovers fast from her mating ritual with Worf. Just before the commercial break, we see blood trickling from her palm. Obviously there *was* a cut. Yet, coming back from the commercial, we glimpse a full view of her left palm and there is no cut, no scab, no scar—nothing to indicate that what we saw before the commercial actually happened.

TRIVIA ANSWERS

1. Starbase 153.
2. K'Temoc.

PEAK PERFORMANCE

Star Date: 42923.4

A battle exercise pitting the *Enterprise* against the eighty-year-old USS *Hathaway*—commanded by Riker—turns serious when Ferengi marauders disable the *Enterprise* and threaten to steal the *Hathaway*.

TRIVIA QUESTIONS

1. La Forge refers to popping the clutch on what vehicle when attempting to describe what will happen if the *Hathaway*'s two-second warp jump fails?

2. Who commands the Ferengi vessel *Kreechta*?

ALTERNATE VIEWPOINTS AND CORRECTIONS

• During the battle exercise, Worf tricks the crew of the *Enterprise* by manufacturing a Romulan warbird for its sensors and main viewscreen. Then, at the end of the episode, he does the same to the Ferengi vessel—this time convincing them that a Federation starship approaches. On pages 132 and 133 of the *NextGen Guide* I wondered how the latter was possible, given that Worf wouldn't know the Security override codes for the Ferengi ship. P. T. H. Carder of Lancashire, England, responded, "Who says Worf doesn't have Security override codes for non-Federation ships? That's why we pay the Intelligence branch!"

PLOT OVERSIGHTS

• With marauders around, why would Starfleet leave a potentially valuable starship unguarded and in orbit around a planet?

• If these Zakdorn are so smart, why haven't we seen any of them in command positions in Starfleet? Huh? Huh?! The only other one we meet runs a Federation *junkyard*! (See "Unification.") Now, there's a job that requires a *master* strategist ("Introducing the new head of the Joint Chiefs of Staff…Fred Sanford!")

• In this episode, Ensign Burke wins the "Fastest Promotion and Demotion in the Galaxy" award. The credits list him as an ensign. He has one pip on his collar. Picard calls him "Ensign" near the end of the episode. Yet, in the middle of the episode, Picard calls him "Lieutenant."

• New vocabulary always intrigues me. While considering the possibilities of using the *Hathaway*'s existing dilithium chamber, Wesley says, "We should be able to do something with these dilithium fragments we scajummed." Scajummed? Is that like…scavenged? (One would expect to find new words cropping up in the twenty-fourth century. Look how the meaning of "hacked" has changed in the past twenty years.)

EQUIPMENT ODDITIES

• Why doesn't Starfleet use holodecks for these simulated battles?

• While explaining the method they will employ to deceive the Ferengi, Data states that the *Enterprise* will fire four photon torpedoes at the *Hathaway*. The *Hathaway* will jump to warp milliseconds before the detonation, making it appear that the ship has been destroyed. However, when the *Enterprise* actually fires, only two photon torpedoes whiz by.

• Just before the strategema rematch between Data and Sirna Kolrami, an outside shot shows the *Enterprise* towing the *Hathaway* (looking suspiciously like footage from "The Battle"). Data holds Kolrami to a stalemate until the great Zakdorn strategist storms

off in a huff. After the episode-ending banter, an exterior shot shows the *Enterprise* accelerating to warp and flashing away. Pray tell: What happened to the *Hathaway*?

TRIVIA ANSWERS

1. Grenthemen water hopper.
2. Bractor.

SHADES OF GRAY

Star Date: 42976.1

When a plant jabs Riker in the leg during a preliminary geological survey on an unexplored planet, Pulaski finds that stimulating the first officer's bad memories slows the growth of the infection, making the microbes pack up their bags and leave.

TRIVIA QUESTIONS

1. What is the name of the unexplored planet?

2. According to Riker, how long did it take a rattlesnake to die after it bit his great-grandfather?

ALTERNATE VIEWPOINTS AND CORRECTIONS

• The prize goes to Paul Ammann of

Santa Rosa, CA, for identifying the "unknown clip of solar activity" listed as part of the second trivia answer on page 135 of the *NextGen Guide*. In fact, the clip comes from the footage of the Genesis Project proposal in *Star Trek II: The Wrath of Khan*.

PLOT OVERSIGHTS

• La Forge demonstrates his incredible bravery (or bravado, depending on your point of view) in this episode when he and Data beam back down to the planet to find a sample of the unknown entity that attacked Riker. Since *something* stuck Riker in the leg, wouldn't it be a sensible precaution to wear some sort of shinguards instead of those flimsy pants?

• Does it seem like Pulaski and La Forge walk awfully close to the deadly vine on the planet without any consequences? I realize that early in the show we aren't supposed to know which vine is the culprit, but it just seems like the vine should attack them as well—but for some reason it doesn't.

• Wendy A. Weiger of Brookline, MA (currently an M.D./Ph.D. student in the Department of Neurobiology at Havard Medical School), sent in the following comments: "Dr. Pulaski uses the term 'endorphin' when she should have used the more general term 'neurotransmitter.' Endorphins are endogenous opioids and represent only a small subset of the neurotransmitters used by the brain to transmit and modify messages between neurons in brain circuitry. The more general term would have made much more sense to me as a neurobiologist in the context of Pulaksi's conversation with Troi."

• Pulaski either loses a few stray neurons in this episode, or we are missing a piece of the episode. Preparing to stimulate Riker's brain by using the machine with all the rods, the good doctor tells an assistant to have a shot of tricordrizine ready in case of seizures. Sometime later she tells Troi that she doesn't want to risk another dose of tricordrizine unless she has to. So when did she administer the first shot? Did Riker go into seizures when we weren't looking, or did Pulaski not give him the first shot and then promptly forget that she didn't give it to him?

• Evidently Troi hasn't been listening. Pulaski is trying to give Riker bad memories so he can experience negative emotions and slow the growth of the microorganisms. Yet, just after Pulaski announces that Riker will die in one-half hour and then attempts yet another refocusing of the machine, a medium-wide shot from the end of Riker's bed shows Troi caressing the first officer's hand! (I don't know about you, but having the ever lovely Counselor Troi caress my hand would definitely *not* evoke negative emotions in me!)

• Supposedly, all the flashbacks in this episode come from Riker's memories. Isn't it odd that Riker doesn't remember anything prior to his time on the *Enterprise*?

EQUIPMENT ODDITIES

• Here's yet another amazing transporter feature. After extracting a nasty-looking thorn from a large vine, Data and La Forge immediately beam back to the ship. A wide shot only moments prior to transport shows them slogging around in a swamp, their boots and lower half of their pant legs drenched with the undoubtedly slimy water. Then, when they materialize on the transporter pad, their boots and pants are suddenly completely *dry*!

TRIVIA ANSWERS

1. Surata IV.
2. Three days.

TRIATHLON TRIVIA ON FOOD AND BEVERAGES

MATCH THE FOOD OR BEVERAGE
TO THE DESCRIPTION TO THE EPISODE

FOOD OR BEVERAGE	DESCRIPTION	EPISODE
1. Aldebaran whiskey	A. Kurn wiped some on his bird meat	a. "Up the Long Ladder"
2. Aldorian ale	B. Lwaxana made some for Timicin	b. "Liaisons"
3. Balso tonic	C. Odell found it packed quite a punch	c. "Cost of Living"
4. banana split	D. Clara Sutter likes eggs this way	d. "Contagion"
5. bregit lung	E. Troi fed some to an ambassador	e. "Ménage à Troi"
6. Calaman sherry	F. Riker made an omelette with them	f. "The Dauphin"
7. caviar	G. A four-handed pianist's bad habit	g. "The Vengeance Factor"
8. chech'tluth	H. When ordered, sausages came instead	h. "Family"
9. Earl Grey tea	I. Lwaxana sent Homn on a hunt for some	i. "The Host"
10. gagh	J. Miles made it for Keiko	j. "Time Squared"
11. heart of targ	K. Data made one after losing at chess	k. "Sins of the Father"
12. Ktarian chocolate puff	L. Keiko made it for Miles	l. "Half a Life"
13. Jestral tea	M. Can be ordered with extra bubbles	m. "A Matter of Honor"
14. Mantickian paté	N. A favorite of Odan's	n. "Relics "
15. Muskan seed punch	O. Sometimes a substitute for tea	o. "Unification II"
16. Owon eggs	P. Part of Riker's last meal	p. "The Wounded"
17. papalla juice	Q. Dish served on the *Pagh*	q. "Suddenly Human"
18. parthas à la Yuta	R. Its beans are aged for 400 years	r. "Conundrum"
19. petrokian sausage	S. Worf asks his mom to make this	s. "Manhunt"
20. pipius claw	T. Picard gave Guinan a bottle	t. "Aquiel"
21. plankton loaf	U. One of Picard's favorite drinks	u. "The Perfect Mate"

22. potato casserole	V. Wesley caught one in the face	v. "Imaginary Friend"
23. purple omelettes	W. Yuta prepared it for Riker	w. "In Theory"
24. *rokeg* blood pie	X. Data orders one for D'Sora	
25. Samarian Sunset	Y. A favorite drink of Uhnari	
26. suck salt	Z. Harodian miners like it	
27. Thalian chocolate mousse	AA. It's what Antedeans eat	
28. uttaberries		
29. vermicula		

SCORING

(BASED ON NUMBER OF CORRECT ANSWERS)

0–5	Normal
6–15	Aware of food
15–29	Have you considered a career as an exofoodologist?

FOOD AND BEVERAGES ANSWER KEY: **1.** T n **2.** Z u **3.** N i **4.** V q **5.** Q m **6.** X w **7.** A k **8.** C a **9.** U d **10.** P m **11.** P m **12.** E b **13.** H c **14.** B l **15.** Y t **16.** F j **17.** M v **18.** W g **19.** O c **20.** P m **21.** L p **22.** J p **23.** D v **24.** S h **25.** K r **26.** G o **27.** R f **28.** I e **29.** AA s

THIRD SEASON

EVOLUTION

Star Date: 43125.8

A s a critical time frame approaches—when the crew of the *Enterprise* must have the main computer to assist in a once-in-a-lifetime experiment monitoring an eruption from the surface of a neutron star—Wesley Crusher's science project goes awry, releasing tiny robots called nanites, which soon start feasting on the computer's memory chips.

TRIVIA QUESTIONS

1. Where does the crew keep Stubbs's "egg"?

2. Who's on first in Stubbs's mental game of baseball?

ALTERNATE VIEWPOINTS AND CORRECTIONS

• Greg Reid of Toronto, Ontario, reminded me that I didn't mention a significant interseasonal change. Between season two and season three, La Forge receives a promotion to lieutenant commander for reasons the creators thought best not to disclose to us.

• Some have found it impossible that Stubbs could know the neutron star would explode every 196 years, given that humans have only had a chance to view, at the most, two eruptions. (By the way, it is 196 years not 197, as stated in the *NextGen Guide.* Thanks to Brian Walton of Lone Jack, MO, for pointing this out.) According to various sources, this episode occurs in A.D. 2366. The last explosion occurred in 2170, and the one before that in 1974. It is possible that these explosions were observed by human scientists, but the one previous to these two would occur in 1778, and two explosions do not a viable pattern make. However, I suspected that there might be another way to establish the pattern without direct observation. I proposed the following scenario to Nitpicker Central's resident solar physicist, Mitzi Adams. Given the state of twenty-fourth century sensors, would it be possible to measure the flow of matter dropping into the neutron star, calculate the accretion rate, and arrive at a detonation time? Mitzi said yes. She also said that the whole idea of a neutron star sucking matter away from a red giant and then expelling it at high velocities is actually a phenomenon that astronomers observe today! (Score one more for the accuracy of the creators!)

PLOT OVERSIGHTS

• At what point does the Federation deign to consider a life form worthy of protection under its laws? Apparently the nanites are intelligent, self-aware, and have the capability to make treaties. Yet at the conclusion of this episode, Dr. Paul Stubbs, murderer of thousands—possibly millions—of nanites, happily processes the information from his probe. True, the other nanites "forgave" him, but if the family of a murder victim forgives the assailant, does the crime go unpunished?

EQUIPMENT ODDITIES

• At the beginning of the episode, the *Enterprise* loses power and begins drifting toward the matter stream between the red giant and the neutron star. As it does, it twists 180 degrees. To halt the progress, Picard calls for reverse impulse engines. Now, if the *Enterprise* is twisting when the engines go into reverse and the ship rotates to face away from the matter stream, wouldn't the engines drive the ship into the stellar material and not from it?

CONTINUITY AND PRODUCTION PROBLEMS

• Near the end of the episode, when Picard decides that he must eradicate the nanites from the ship, he goes to the bridge and tells Worf to prepare to fire up the generators to send a pulse of gamma radiation through the computer core. (One has to wonder what *that* will do to the circuits!) Suddenly Data establishes contact with the nanites. A wide shot from the perspective of Science Station I shows us Data seated in front of the adjacent science station, with Picard and Worf in the background. Note the bubble window in the ceiling of the bridge. It is completely black. The scene goes away for a while and then returns to this same shot. Now there are stars in the bubble window! The difference? Troi is standing behind Data in all her radiant beauty.

TRIVIA ANSWERS

1. Shuttle Bay 2.
2. Lockman.

THE ENSIGNS OF COMMAND

Star Date: 43133.4

Data must convince a group of settlers to leave a world deeded by treaty to the Sheliak Corporate—an ill tempered, condescending, nonhumanoid race—before the Sheliak colonization vessels arrive and clear the planet of its "humanoid infestation." At the same time, Picard struggles to find a way within the bounds of the agreement to forestall the destruction and evacuate the humans.

GREAT LINES

"That's the short definition of 'captain.'" —La Forge to Wesley after the ensign claims Picard wants the impossible.

TRIVIA QUESTIONS

1. What instrument does Miles O'Brien play?

2. Who will play the first violin part for the second concert of the evening?

ALTERNATE VIEWPOINTS AND CORRECTIONS

• Making an attempt at humor, I offered my interpretation of events in this episode as a "guy thing" and a "gal thing" on pages 144 and 145 of the *NextGen Guide.* I noted that the leader of the colony won't listen until Data brings a gun and starts shooting things (a "guy thing") and that a female colonist expects an emotional reaction from Data even though she knows he's an android (a "gal thing"). Doris Lamb of Lake Worth, FL, put a delightful twist on all of this. She wrote, "I think you're all wrong about the 'gal thing'/'guy thing.' Getting an android to do a shoot 'em up (completely out of character), to manipulate 'male thinking'—it's a 'gal thing,' baby, GAL 101. On the other hand, using a woman's talents and leaving the planet without the slightest pang—definite 'guy thing.'" (And, in case you're wondering, "No, I do not mind being called 'baby.'")

EQUIPMENT ODDITIES

• Attempting to make the transporters function in hyperonic radiation, La Forge, O'Brien, and Wesley run a series of tests. As the *Enterprise* orbits the colony, O'Brien beams down and then retrieves a metal canister that returns as a smoking lump of metal. So far, so good. Then the *Enterprise* warps away from the planet to head off the Sheliak. A second scene shows the trio running another test with much the same results. Wait a minute: If the *Enterprise* is at warp, to where are they beaming the cargo? Do they have some way to simulate the effects of hyperonic radiation and simply dematerialize and rematerialize an object through the pattern buffer?

• Evidently anyone can do anyone else's job at any time on the bridge.

Deciding to make a stand against the Sheliak, Picard orders Riker to put the *Enterprise* nose to nose with the colonization vessel. Riker promptly turns his little screen and starts punching in the codes. Isn't this a job for the person at conn? (My guess is that the creators didn't want to pay an actor to show his or her face and say, "Aye, sir" because Wesley is down helping La Forge and O'Brien.)

CONTINUITY AND PRODUCTION PROBLEMS

• I need to talk about uniforms for a moment. For some reason unknown to me, the creators' reuse of uniforms from the first and second seasons has never bothered me. I agree that it is a bit silly for Wesley, as an ensign, to run around in a nice two-piece uniform while the rest of the crew—even those of higher rank—have to wear the old jumpsuits. I can understand why this bothers some nitpickers. For instance, the beginning of this episode features a music conference in Ten-Forward. A few of the officers are wearing the old jumpsuits, in contrast to the newer, sleeker two-piece outfits for male officers. (Wouldn't want to let the women out of their form-fitting, one-piece outfits, now would we?)

TRIVIA ANSWERS

1. Cello (violoncello, to be precise).
2. Ensign Ortiz.

THE SURVIVORS

Star Dates: 43152.4—43153.7

Picard uncovers the truth about the two survivors of a Husnock attack on Delta Rana IV, Kevin and Rishon Uxbridge. In fact, only Kevin Uxbridge still lives. He is a Douwd, a powerful being who reached out in grief and struck down all Husnock everywhere before attempting to recapture the memories of his wife by recreating her image.

TRIVIA QUESTIONS

1. Where did the Uxbridges live before coming to Delta Rana IV?

2. To where does the *Enterprise* set course at the conclusion of this episode?

PLOT OVERSIGHTS

• Riker refers to the habitable area on the planet as "just a few acres." Surely by the twenty-fourth century Starfleet has adopted the metric system! The unit for land area in the metric system is hectare, and it is not equivalent to an acre.

• Kevin Uxbridge makes an odd transportation choice near the end of the episode. When he dematerializes from the bridge, La Forge says he is in the turbolift. Yet when he leaves the ship, he simply disappears. So why did Uxbridge bother with the turbolift when he went from the bridge to Counselor Troi's quarters?

CONTINUITY AND PRODUCTION PROBLEMS

• As the *Enterprise* scans the surface of Delta Rana IV for the first time, Riker stands very close to Picard in the close-ups, with their shoulders overlapping. Then the camera angle changes to a wider shot featuring Wesley at the conn station and Picard in the background but no Riker.

TRIVIA ANSWERS

1. New Martim Vaz.
2. Starbase 133.

WHO WATCHES THE WATCHERS

Star Dates: 43173.5—43174.2

A rescue and repair operation for a group of anthropologists conducting a covert study of an indigenous race on Mintaka III inadvertently convinces an extended family of Mintakans that Picard is an "overseer" or god. With great effort, Picard eventually persuades the Mintakans that the members of the crew of the *Enterprise,* though more advanced, are simply humanoids as well.

TRIVIA QUESTIONS

1. What compound obstructs the *Enterprise*'s sensor sweep of the caves on the planet?

2. How did the Mintakans originally find Dr. Palmer?

ALTERNATE VIEWPOINTS AND CORRECTIONS

• I received quite a few comments on my discussion of "the message" of this episode on pages 149 and 150 of the *NextGen Guide*. In that discussion, I suggested that this episode makes two statements: First, that any belief in the supernatural leads to superstition, ignorance, and fear; Second, that a codified framework will keep religious belief from degenerating into inquisitions, holy wars, and chaos. I dealt with the second statement first, noting that both Christianity and Islam have highly codified beliefs, yet both have engaged in atrocities (as have nonreligious entities such as Germany under Hitler and the Soviet Union under Stalin). Atrocities do not spring from codeless religious systems so much as from certain individuals' desire to exercise control over their existence and the existence of others. Liko, in this episode, drives forward the belief in Picard as overseer, not because of any great love for old traditions, but because he wishes to see his wife resurrected. I received very little disagreement with this portion of my discussion.

Then I stated that if belief in the supernatural leads to superstition, ignorance, and fear, all three categories must apply to the vast majority of the citizens of the United States of America, because in 1986 a Gallup poll found that 96 percent of Americans believed in God or a universal spirit. The letters usually got interesting at this point!

Some tried to accuse me of using statistics to prove the existence of God. However, a careful reading of my original discussion will reveal that it had nothing to do with the argument over the existence of a supernatural being. The topic of discussion was: What are the consequences of simply *holding* a belief in the supernatural? The creators put forth this dialogue: The Mintakans had finally abandoned their belief in the supernatural, and Picard loathed to send them back to the "dark ages of superstition and ignorance and fear." In other words, believing in the supernatural puts you in the categories of being superstitious, ignorant, and fearful. Logically, if the creators' statement is true, and 96 percent of Americans believe in the supernatural, it *must follow* that 96 percent of Americans are fearful, superstitious, and ignorant.

Others responded to my discussion by saying that it didn't belong in the *Nitpicker's Guide.* I realize that religion is a hot topic for many people. But so are race, sexual orientation, child abuse, and a host of other topics that are freely discussed in the communications media of our day. (Several of these topics arise in the *Nitpicker's Guides.*) So why not religion?

Still others tried to say that by the twenty-fourth century we may finally understand that there is no God and therefore Picard's statement is true.

This is a sticky point for nitpickers. For instance, in "The Royale," La Forge states that a planet's temperature is -291 degrees Celsius. That's almost 18 degrees below Absolute Zero! I consider that a nit, but it could be diffused by saying that in the twenty-fourth century, scientists will have discovered temperatures lower than "Absolute" Zero. This is a perfectly legitimate way of tossing almost all nitpicking out the window. On the other hand, if I can use twentieth-century scientific knowledge to nitpick this wonderful twenty-fourth-century setting, why can't I use twentieth-century religious knowledge to do the same? (Especially in a case where the creators brought it up in the first place. Wink, wink.)

PLOT OVERSIGHTS

• The title is a question, right? So where's the question mark?

• After beaming an injured Mintakan up to sick bay and healing his wounds, Crusher leaves him lying on a bed in the ward. This is necessary to the plot so the guy can see Picard and come to believe the captain is the overseer. My question is this: When did privacy curtains go out of style in hospital rooms? At least that would be better than giving this guy the full view of sick bay. And, what about setting up a holodeck simulation just in case the guy wakes up? Shouldn't the crew take some relatively minor precautions?

• It is amazing how quickly the medical team in sick bay can restore a person's appearance. Riker and Troi go down to the planet, surgically altered to look like the Mintakans. Riker grabs

Palmer, beams up to the *Enterprise*, and asks Data if Troi made it back. The episode then cuts to the Mintakans untying an old man. (Riker tied him up when escaping with Palmer.) The Mintakans question Troi. Only seconds into this questioning, Riker strolls onto the bridge in a Starfleet uniform with his face back to normal!

• Data—that lovable android with the positronic brain that remembers everything to which it is exposed—seems to forget Picard's orders in this episode. After locating Nuria, the leader of the Mintakans, the captain tells Data to beam her up as soon as she is alone. Then Picard goes to Transporter Room 1. As he enters, Data says that Nuria is alone. The captain takes the controls and beams her up. Didn't Picard tell Data to beam her up?

• Near the end of the episode, Picard puts himself in harm's way to prove he isn't a god. There's a bit of a problem with this approach. Liko shoots Picard, and Nuria shows him the blood coming from the wound, right? Mintakans are supposedly proto-Vulcan, right? According to *Classic Trek*, Vulcan blood is copper-based and therefore…green! The Mintakans should say, "What is that red guck coming out of the wound?" And another thing while we're on this topic: The guy with the bow evidently had it pointed at the center of Picard's chest. (His daughter shoves his arm to the right, and the arrow hits Picard in the left shoulder.) Why? A Vulcan would not die instantly from that wound because according to the *Classic* episode, "Mudd's Women," Spock's heart is on the left side of his chest.

EQUIPMENT ODDITIES

• Supposedly the generator dies in the anthropologists' outpost. Then it looks like the batteries short out as well. When the away team arrives, La Forge tells everyone not to touch the framework because everything is charged. And charged it is! Electricity flashes and arcs across the metal surfaces. For having no power, there are a lot of sparks dancing around the room. This type of discharge takes a tremendous amount of energy. In addition, Riker, Data, and La Forge all appear to touch the metal framework of the outpost, but none of them is shocked.

• This episode certainly poses an interesting problem for the Universal Translator. Since the Mintakans possess only Bronze Age technological development, we know that *they* don't have a Universal Translator, yet Riker and Troi beam down and converse with them at will. (I freely admit there is no good way around this problem of languages.)

• The transporter—once again— changes someone's position in transit. When rescuing Palmer, Riker squishes the scientist into a cubbyhole. Clearly the man's legs are bent. Yet when the pair materializes on the *Enterprise,* Palmer lies flat on his back.

• The guy in charge of the doors on the *Enterprise* got some chuckles at Picard's expense during this episode. The captain is *trying* to prove to Nuria that he isn't a god, and instead of snapping the doors open like normal as the pair walks out of the transporter room, the guy in the control room parts them with this dramatic "wwwwhh-hoooosssshhh." Of course, Nuria

reacts with awe. (I can almost here the guy giggling in the background.)

• And why, oh, why, oh, why do the Bronze Age Mintakans carry twentieth-century compound bows? Look closely as Liko threatens Picard and you'll see the double string and expertly molded hand grip.

• And, why, oh, why, oh, why does Liko threaten Picard with a blunt tip on his arrow? Aren't these guys hunters? Why would you hunt with a dull tip?

CONTINUITY AND PRODUCTION PROBLEMS

• Undoubtedly Mintaka III contains the strangest geography of any planet visited by the *Enterprise.* As Nuria looks out the observation lounge window you can see a continent rotating toward her that looks like the head of an anteater. The scene cuts away, and when it returns to Nuria, another continent that looks exactly like the first rotates into view! Even more amazing, the conclusion of the episode shows an outside shot of the *Enterprise* and there's yet another continent shaped the same way but facing in the other direction. This is really weird. A planet with three continents shaped the same!

• Great confusion surrounds the model in Picard's ready room. All this time I thought it was a replica of the USS *Stargazer,* NCC-2893—Picard's first command. Yet a close-up of the model—as the captain speaks with Nuria in his ready room—reveals a registry of "NCC-7100." What is this ship, and why is it in the captain's ready room?

TRIVIA ANSWERS

1. Thallium.
2. They followed a hornbuck into a cave.

THE BONDING

Star Date: 43198.7

When Jeremy Aster's mother dies on an away team mission lead by Worf, the Klingon determines to bond with the young boy and make him part of his family. Unfortunately, the energy beings that live on the planet feel a similar responsibility and soon manufacture a duplicate of Marla Aster to entice Jeremy down to the surface.

TRIVIA QUESTIONS

1. Worf's away team was heading from the third tunnel into what room when the explosion occurred?

2. What force field does Picard ask to be dropped the second time the faux Marla Aster tries to take Jeremy to the transporter?

PLOT OVERSIGHTS

• In several places, Jeremy Aster identifies his cat as a male. If the description is correct, then Patches is an unusual cat indeed. Debora L. Smith, D.V.M., tells me that the cat is a calico and—except in very rare genetic anomalies—most calicos are female.

• So what happened to Jeremy after he bonded with Worf? Supposedly they are brothers now, but we never see the kid again! And what about Worf's discommendation? How did that affect Jeremy, if at all?

CONTINUITY AND PRODUCTION PROBLEMS

• While riding in a turbolift with La Forge and Worf, Picard orders the Security chief to Transporter Room 3. He identifies Worf by his rank but pronounces it, "leff-tenant," instead of using the Americanized version, "loo-tenant." It is fairly soft and goes by quickly, but our beloved captain definitely uses the English pronunciation.

TRIVIA ANSWERS

1. The Ceremonial Chamber.
2. Security Force Field 8B.

BOOBY TRAP

Star Date: 43205.6

An ancient Promellian battle cruiser lures the *Enterprise* into a booby trap—an asteroid field filled with energy-draining aceton assimilators placed there by the Promellians' archenemies, the Menthars, over a millennium ago. Working with a holographic construct of engine designer Dr. Leah Brahms, La Forge concocts a plan to allow the *Enterprise* to break free.

TRIVIA QUESTIONS

1. What is the name of the Promellian battle cruiser?

2. Where was the *Enterprise*'s dilithium chamber designed?

PLOT OVERSIGHTS

• Seeking to increase the power output from the warp drive to compensate for the energy drain from the aceton assimilators, La Forge runs a holodeck program of the Utopia Planitia shipbuilding yards on Mars and elicits the help of an engine designer, Leah Brahms. At one point the computer simulation of Brahms gives the dilithium chamber design date as 40052. But the first mission of the *Enterprise,* "Encounter at Farpoint," starts on star date 41153.7. According to various sources, one thousand star date units equal one year. So these dates make it sound like the Starfleet designers and scientists put the final touches on the design of the dilithium chamber—an absolutely vital component of the warp core—barely a year before the *Enterprise* flew its first mission. Does this seem right for a ship as big and complex as a *Galaxy*-class vessel? (In fact, the *Technical Manual* states that the warp core was installed in the *Enterprise* in A.D. 2352, twelve years before Picard and crew meet Q for the first time in A.D. 2364.)

• La Forge jumps to a horribly unsubstantiated conclusion concerning the odds of allowing the computer to take control of flying the *Enterprise* to safety in this episode. We join the scene as the computer fails in a simulation to get the ship out of the asteroid belt. La Forge *changes some parameters,* and the computer succeeds. Then he runs the simulation again *with the same parameters,* and the computer fails. The captain calls, and La Forge pleads for two minutes longer. The chief engineer then starts a completely new simulation, based on shutting off all power and using two thrusters to drift the *Enterprise* out of the asteroid field. Moments later, on the bridge, La Forge tells Picard that either approach has the same chances of success. Both are "even money," to use his words. "Even money" usually means fifty-fifty. So La Forge has determined the odds of the computer controlling the ship on the basis of only two tests? This is an extremely questionable practice. If the results vary from test to test because of the sophistication of the simulation—as they should—La Forge should run thousands, even millions, of tests to determine the odds, not just two! What if the one failure was a fluke and the computer was successful 999 times out of 1,000? Wouldn't you be happy with a 99.9 percent chance of making it out alive?

EQUIPMENT ODDITIES

• Just as Data begins scanning the Promellian vessel, a shot of his console shows a small polygonal graphic with vertical lines. Oddly enough, this graphic appears at the bottom of the Promellian battle cruiser's display when the playback of the captain's final log commences.

• Beaming over to the Promellian

battle cruiser, Picard, Data, and Worf take a look around. Data soon walks up to a console and engages some type of backup battery system to give the bridge some light. One question: Just what is giving this bridge some gravity? (I know it's expensive to simulate, but there are some situations that should require it.)

• When Riker comes into the ready room and Picard tells the first officer that La Forge wishes to turn control over to the computer, watch the doors. They close hard, bounce apart, and then close a second time!

CONTINUITY AND PRODUCTION PROBLEMS

• On the Promellian battle cruiser—as Picard, Data, and Worf take the tour—a plasma conduit sits behind the console at which Worf silences the distress call. Surprisingly enough, it looks just like the ones attached to the *Enterprise*'s dilithium chamber!

• Just after firing a burst of impulse power to get the ship coasting, the crew shuts everything down. Almost all the lights go out on the bridge. (It wouldn't be much of a show if our television screen suddenly went black, now, would it?) Presumably the lights get turned off on the rest of the ship, as well. Yet the external shots of the ship all show several windows lit. (Obviously the visual effects guys just hate it when they have to turn off all the pretty little lights on that model—even if the script calls for it!)

TRIVIA ANSWERS

1. The *Cleponji*.
2. At Outpost Seran-T-1.

THE ENEMY

Star Date: 43349.2

After becoming separated from an away team, La Forge finds himself captured by a Romulan on the surface of Galorndon Core, an inhospitable planet buffeted by severe electromagnetic storms. Realizing the impact of the storms on their bodies, La Forge and the Romulan work together to alert the *Enterprise* to their location.

RUMINATIONS

In the NextGen Guide, *I gave kudos to the creators because I couldn't find anything wrong with this episode. Well …other nitpickers certainly didn't have any trouble finding plenty of nits in it! In fact, I do believe that since the chief nitpicker couldn't come up with anything, all the other nitpickers out there made it their goal to do so. (Wink, wink.) Actually, I feel sorry for this episode in a way. A tremendous amount of energy went in to chainsawing it apart. (I do believe I've created a monster—"Nitpicker Central, the dread of creators everywhere.") While most of my episode files run about one-quarter of an inch, this one is almost an inch thick! Given the preponderance of nits submitted for this show, I will dispense with my somewhat verbose style and list them as tersely as possible—at least for me, that is.*

GREAT LINES

"Galorndon Core, where no good deed goes unpunished."—La Forge to Bochra when the Romulan points his weapon at the chief engineer after receiving La Forge's assistance. Nominated by Alma Jo Williams of Ithaca, NY. (I thought this quotation strangely appropriate, given the next several pages.)

TRIVIA QUESTIONS

1. What is the name of the Romulan scout ship that crashes on Galorndon Core?

2. How does the crew deliver the neutrino pulse to the surface of Galorndon Core?

PLOT OVERSIGHTS

• The away team beams down and finds a destroyed Romulan vessel. Obviously one or more Romulans survived the crash. Then Riker orders the away team to split up. Does this make sense? If there are Romulans running around on the planet, wouldn't you want to stay together?

• Shortly after the Romulan arrives in sick bay, Crusher announces that he suffers from early neural pathway degeneration. Riker asks if it is caused by a head injury, and Crusher responds that there's no obvious cranial trauma. What about that gash in the side of his head, or the fact that Worf palmed him in the face and snapped the poor guy's head back into a rock face?

• Amazingly enough, Wesley is the only one who can figure out that a neutrino beam would cut through the interference. Data just sits there like a human. Then again, when seeing the neutrino beam for the first time, La Forge instantly mutters a "thank you" to Wesley. Maybe the ingenuity quotient on the ship really *is* low, apart from our favorite acting ensign.

• After intercepting the Romulan commander's first transmission, Data identifies its origin as the "Romulan Zone." Now, would that be from the Romulan Neutral Zone, or from within Romulan territory?

• Following the initial conversation with the Romulan commander, Troi says that there is great hostility behind his smile. How does she know this? The guy is six hours away at the Romulan warbird's top speed. That's a long way. If she's doing it with body language, why doesn't she advise Picard of such? If you were captain, wouldn't you want to know if your counselor was actually sensing something or just guessing?

• How come the Romulans get to tool into the Neutral Zone whenever they jolly well please, but they attack us whenever we do it—as in "The Defector"?

• After the probe hits the surface of Galorndon Core, Data describes it as a "neutrino stream," implying a constant flow of information. However, earlier in the show, Wesley called it a "neutrino pulse," indicating a device that transmits intermittently. (Interestingly, the graphics of the probe indicate that Data is more correct, even though Wesley put the thing together.)

• As La Forge wanders around on the planet, a Romulan named Bochra sneaks up behind him and clubs him unconscious. Why risk cranial trauma to your prisoner when a stun from your phaser would do just as well?

• Let's talk about this neutrino beam for a moment. Presumably La Forge cannot see a neutrino until it hits his VISOR. In the same way, a sighted person cannot see unless a photon emits from a light source and strikes the eye or scatters off a surface and then strikes the eye. The problem is this: The probe sends a stream of neutrinos straight up into the atmosphere, directed at the *Enterprise*. I'm told that neutrinos can pass through a humongous amount of solid lead without even slowing down. So it's unlikely that the atmosphere of the planet would even interact with them. Now, if the atmosphere of the planet doesn't deflect the neutrinos, how do they stop their upward momentum, make a right-hand turn, and strike La Forge's VISOR so he can see them? If I understand how these particles work, La Forge would see them only if he looked straight down on the probe!

• Does it make sense that Romulans and Klingons would have similar ribosomes in their blood? Aren't Vulcans and Romulans related? (Or is this Vulcan's dirty little secret, that a sect of emotive Vulcans ran off with Klingon mistresses and produced the Romulan race?)

• How many times is Crusher going to hassle Worf about his potential ribosome contribution? Isn't there some ethical consideration here?

• Why does it take so long for Crusher to tell Picard about the Romulan's

death? One would think that this is an important piece of information. But evidently it occurs, and the good doctor waits to tell Picard until the captain calls to tell her to leave Worf alone. (You have to wonder if Picard isn't really hacked at her. He's just finished groveling in front of Worf—trying to get the Klingon to donate some ribosomes, but he didn't need to, because the Romulan was already dead!)

• When a window in the storm opens, Data says that it will close in nine minutes, forty seconds. Then, one minute and twenty-some-odd seconds later *of continuous dialogue,* Data says the window will close in three minutes. (I believe we lost some time here.)

• Both La Forge and Bochra make the most amazing recovery: Moments before they leave the planet, Bochra can't walk and La Forge can't see. The magnetic fields have been breaking down their synaptic pathways. Yet, once they appear on the *Enterprise,* they perk right up!

• And *finally,* why doesn't Picard send for reinforcements?

EQUIPMENT ODDITIES

• Shortly after beaming down to the planet, Worf announces to Riker and La Forge that the communicators are now "dysfunctional." (I can just imagine the talk show featuring this topic. "Today on Sally Geraldo Raffarivera, 'Dysfunctional Communicators: Their Family Background and Why They Fail to Perform When Sitting on a Klingon's Chest.' You'll hear about their pain. You'll learn the deep inner turmoil they experience as victims in a technology-on-demand universe. And, most of all, you as the audience will be able to ask a bunch of really stupid questions." Sorry, I know I said I wouldn't comment, but this one was too good to pass up.)

• The initial away team consists only of Riker, La Forge, and Worf because the electromagnetic interference on the surface of the planet would wreak havoc with Data's circuits. Why doesn't it affect La Forge's VISOR?

• Here are a few oddities with La Forge's VISOR. He peers into a mud face and sees some rocks. Then he digs them out, washes them off, and *holds them up to the light* so he can see them better. Doesn't the VISOR detect the entire spectrum of electromagnetic energy? With all the energy storms on Galorndon Core, you would think that La Forge would be blind with input. The same type of thing happens moments later when La Forge holds his phaser up to the light to punch in the correct setting.

• La Forge manufactures spikes to climb out of the pit by making a little trench and melting rocks in it. Shouldn't the spikes be flat on one side? They look round as La Forge ascends.

• Why didn't La Forge use his phaser to cut himself hand holds in the rock face?

• When responding to the scout ship's distress call, the Romulan commander says that he will arrive at Galorndon Core in six hours. Then he tells Picard that he will rendezvous with the *Enterprise* at the Federation edge of the Romulan Neutral Zone in about five hours. This dialogue leads us to believe that it would take a Romulan warbird one hour to travel from the Federation edge of the Neutral Zone to Galorndon Core. However, Picard implies that this distance is one-half light-year when he admits his skepticism to the Romulan commander that the Romulan scout ship could be that far off course. So a Romulan warbird can travel one-half light-year in one hour?! That's 4,380 times the speed of light (365 times 24 divided by 2), or more than *twice* the maximum speed of the *Enterprise*! "Tin Man" establishes that Romulan warbirds are slower, not faster, than the *Enterprise*.

• Can La Forge's VISOR see around corners or through walls? He sees the neutrino beam. Then he helps Bochra back *way* into a cave and he can still see the beam!

• The doors once again listen in on conversations and divine when and when not to open. Worf comes into Riker's quarters, sees that the first officer is imbibing, and turns to leave. Although the Klingon's head is inches from the door, it doesn't open.

• The crew of the *Enterprise* beams La Forge and Bochra to the main bridge, but when Picard wants to return Bochra to the Romulan warbird, he makes the poor guy hobble down to the transporter room. Why?

CONTINUITY AND PRODUCTION PROBLEMS

• The palm beacon that Riker carries during the initial away team's trip to the surface appears to have an electrical cord attached to it. Watch carefully after Worf knocks the Romulan unconscious. Riker runs up. The scene cuts to a close-up of the Romulan and then back to Riker and Worf. As Riker drops his hand you can see a white cord running down into his sleeve. (I've been told this is the cord that powers the flashlight.)

• When La Forge falls in the pit, his VISOR clearly lands off to his right. However, a few moments later he picks it up by reaching to his left.

• La Forge lands face down in a mud puddle, yet later his uniform is dirty only to about the level of his communicator.

• As Riker questions the Romulan in sick bay, a medium-wide shot of Riker shows him with his left hand resting beside the Romulan's head. Then his left hand grabs the Romulan's chest, but every time the scene cuts to a close-up of the Romulan, Riker's *right* hand holds the injured male's chest.

• After Wesley figures out that the crew could send down a neutrino beacon, Picard dispatches the ensign to "make it so." Wesley gets up and appears to leave, but there's no door sound to indicate that he boarded a turbolift. Then Data intercepts the message from the Romulan commander, and the show goes to a commercial break. Back from the break, Picard sits down in his chair and sends a message to the Romulan commander. It appears that no time has elapsed during the commercial break, but reverse angles showing the main viewer also show Wesley seated at conn. Later, Wesley returns to the bridge and takes his station as if he's been gone the entire time.

• When Picard attempts to convince Worf to donate his ribosomes to the Romulan, the stars in the ready room travel from right to left. Since the *Enterprise* is orbiting the planet counterclockwise, the stars should travel from left to right.

• At the end of the episode, Picard tells the Romulan commander that he will escort the warbird back to the Neutral Zone. Yet the last scene shows the ships going in different directions. (Actually, I did see this one. I just assumed the commander was taking his ship on the scenic route and Picard would make a loop to catch up to him. Of course, that doesn't explain why Picard didn't execute a 180-degree turn, as he did in "The Best of Both Worlds.")

TRIVIA ANSWERS

1. The *Pi*.
2. Aboard a Class 3 probe.

THE PRICE

Star Date: 43385.6

When "hired gun" negotiator Devinoni Ral sweeps Troi off her feet, she soon learns his secret. Ral is partially empathic, and he uses his abilities to gain the upper hand as he parleys a deal. With Ral currently pitted against the Federation in an attempt to gain the rights to the Barzan wormhole, Troi must decide where her loyalties lay.

RUMINATIONS

A little side tidbit that really isn't a nit. Leslie Diana Russell of Palatka, FL, noted that Troi moved after this episode. A door panel identifies her quarters on deck 9, but in "Violations" Troi travels to deck 8 to return to her quarters.

GREAT LINES

"Fine, fine. Just have your Klingon servant get us some chairs."—DaiMon Goss to Picard, interrupting the captain as he attempts to explain the ground rules of the negotiations for the Barzan wormhole. Nominated by Richard Kilby of North Yorkshire, England.

TRIVIA QUESTIONS

1. To what planet did Ral relocate when he was nineteen?

2. In what sector of the Delta Quadrant does Shuttle 09 appear?

ALTERNATE VIEWPOINTS AND CORRECTIONS

• On page 158 in the *NextGen Guide,* I mentioned my wonder that Data doesn't understand the term "proverbial lemon," given the disclosure that Data understands the term "proverbial" in the episode "The Naked Now." Jeff DeLuzio of London, Ontario, felt that the earlier reference in "The Naked Now"—a "proverbial needle in a haystack"—was self-explanatory, whereas "proverbial lemon" was not. John Potts of London, England, suggested that Data had never heard the term and—even with eight hundred quadrillion bits of memory—probably has gaps in his knowledge of the human language. (A side note here: In "The Measure of a Man," Data

quotes from *Webster's Twenty-fourth Century,* fifth edition dictionary. Has the android committed this mighty tome to memory? If so, does it contain the same second definition for "lemon" as the little Merriam-Webster dictionary that sits on my desk— "something unsatisfactory (as an automobile): dud"?)

PLOT OVERSIGHTS

• As the Federation negotiator confers with Picard in his ready room, Riker states that La Forge has been in "continuous visual contact" with the wormhole. In prior episodes—"Justice" and "Datalore," for example—visual contact for La Forge has meant physically looking at the thing, as opposed to monitoring it on a viewscreen. (These sessions usually result in some highly enlightening report consisting of, "I've never seen anything like it. Light is swirling around. It's half there but not. It's amazing!") Does Riker mean that La Forge has been standing at a window staring at the wormhole ever since the *Enterprise* arrived?

EQUIPMENT ODDITIES

• At one point, Ral visits Riker in Ten-Forward. As Ral approaches, the first officer sips a drink and punches a few buttons on a data padd. After the conversation, Riker gets up and walks off in a huff, leaving the padd behind. (I sure hope it didn't contain any secrets about the ongoing negotiations.)

CONTINUITY AND PRODUCTION PROBLEMS

• During a conversation between Riker and Ral in Ten-Forward, a wide shot establishes that the stars aren't moving. Yet every close-up of Ral shows them traveling.

• At the conclusion of the episode, just after DaiMon Goss fires a missile at the mouth of the wormhole, Picard tells him of the danger to the shuttles scheduled to return at any moment. Goss replies, "Casualties of war, Captain." But his lips mouth another word instead of "Captain." ("Picard," maybe?)

TRIVIA ANSWERS

1. Hurkos III.
2. Sector 3556.

THE VENGEANCE FACTOR

Star Date: 43421.9

Yuta—an Acamarian female and member of the clan Tralesta—boards the *Enterprise* with her sovereign, Marouk, to complete her ancient rite of vengeance. While the sovereign attempts to negotiate a peace treaty with a group of rogue Acamarians known as Gatherers, Yuta uses the opportunity to hunt down members of the Lornak clan and infect them with a genetically engineered microvirus.

GREAT MOMENTS

There is an absolutely gorgeous visual effect in this episode. When Picard speaks with Marouk in Ten-Forward, the camera pans across the room with a wide shot. The ship travels at warp, and the image of the streaking stars in the large windows corresponds exactly to the motion of the camera. Through the rest of the scene, the warp effect stays true to the camera angles. It is really very lovely.

TRIVIA QUESTIONS

1. What is the name of the Gatherer who claims Volnoth's possessions?

2. The rendezvous with what ship was postponed at the end of this episode?

PLOT OVERSIGHTS

• I commented on Yuta's unnecessary death at the conclusion of this episode in the *NextGen Guide,* but I failed to mention that Riker could simply grab her instead of vaporizing her molecules.

EQUIPMENT ODDITIES

• When Crusher asks the computer if any members of Acamarian leader's delegation are from the Tralesta clan, the computer states that clan affiliation is not within the provided records. What? Didn't the computer just give clan affiliation on three other individuals?

• When a group of Gatherers ambushes the away team on Gamma Hromi II, Data states that the vaporization temperature of a given metal is 2,314 degrees. La Forge comments that a level 7 setting on the phaser should do the trick. The away team sets their phasers and they turn portions of the metal into gas. In other words, a phaser set on level 7 can generate temperatures of 2,314 degrees. Now come with me (my little chickadees) to the end of the episode. Riker shoots Yuta. He adjusts the phaser for more power. He shoots her again. He adjusts his phaser for more power. We hear four high-pitched chirps. A close-up shows the power level indicator on the phaser going up one unit for each chirp. The final setting on the phaser has the upper and lower bank of power indicators lit. According to the _Tech Manual,_ that puts the power level at 16! So, on the previous shot, Yuta survived a setting of 12, and setting 7 vaporizes metal at 2,314 degrees!

CONTINUITY AND PRODUCTION PROBLEMS

• After the _Enterprise_ finds Chorgan's ship, the leader of the Gatherers opens fire. As we join the scene, Worf announces from the port side of the Tactical Station that the shields are holding. Picard orders Worf to contact Chorgan's ship. As he does, the shot changes to a front view of Picard, and Worf is suddenly standing on the starboard side of the Tactical station.

• Somebody really needed a drink after Riker fried Yuta at the end of the episode. Before the first officer beams in, Yuta holds a glass of brandy for Chorgan. As she approaches the leader of the Gatherers, Riker materializes and orders Yuta away. In the next few moments, she puts the glass down near the edge of the table halfway between Marouk and Chorgan. Riker kills Yuta, and a wide shot shows Chorgan walk over to Riker to thank the first officer

for saving his life. By now, however, the glass has disappeared.

TRIVIA ANSWERS

1. Temarek.
2. The USS _Goddard_.

THE DEFECTOR

Star Dates: 43462.5–43465.2

Believing that the Romulan Empire is massing for war, Admiral Jarok defects and alerts Picard to a secret base on Nelvana III, a planet in the Neutral Zone that is within striking distance of fifteen Federation sectors. After violating the Neutral Zone to investigate, Picard discovers that the Romulans have fed Jarok false information to test his loyalties, and they lay a trap for the _Enterprise._

TRIVIA QUESTIONS

1. From where does Picard receive his Starfleet command communications during this episode?

2. From what Klingon vessel did the _Enterprise_ receive a communication?

PLOT OVERSIGHTS

• After chasing the scout ship that Jarok pilots into Federation space, a

Romulan warbird turns and cloaks. Then Worf announces that the warbird has reentered the Neutral Zone and is heading toward Romulan territory. Wait a minute: Isn't the warbird cloaked? How does Worf know this?

• Does anyone else find it odd that the *Enterprise* crew doesn't do a quick once-over of the scout ship to preclude the possibility of it self-destructing? Granted, hindsight is always twenty-twenty, but it sure would have been helpful to the Federation if *somebody* had considered that this Romulan guy might blow up his ship.

• At one point Picard asks Data about the spirit of the crew. Wouldn't this question be better asked of Counselor Troi?

EQUIPMENT ODDITIES

• When Picard comments on Data's performance, soldier Patrick Stewart menaces the captain. Data commands the computer to "freeze program," and the soldier stops. Oddly enough, the fire keeps burning and the crickets keep chirping.

• The companels seem to have changed position. In "The Neutral Zone," Riker uses a companel by pressing buttons on the display over the center of the food replicator. Yet, in this episode, Riker gestures to the food replicator while introducing Jarok to his room and then makes an additional gesture to the small rectangle pasted on the wall beside the food replicator and identifies it as the companel.

CONTINUITY AND PRODUCTION PROBLEMS

• This isn't really a nit, but Patrick Stewart puts in a cameo as a soldier

when Data takes the lead in a holodeck recreation of *Henry V.*

• After Jarok arrives, Picard and La Forge look at a local graphic of the Neutral Zone and do a long-range scan of Nelvana III. The creators got a little "movement happy" on this graphic. Motion always appeals to the eye more than a static picture. But in this case, the movement turns out to be silly. The graphic shows static boundaries for the Neutral Zone, with the stars moving slowly in the background. In other words, the Neutral Zone is slowly creeping around the galaxy! Is this some Romulan plot to acquire more territory? Have they figured out how to tap into all the Federation computers and alter the boundaries of their empire? And if a ship waits at what it believes is the edge of the Neutral Zone for too long, will the crew find themselves in violation of the Treaty of Algeron as the boundary passes by them?

TRIVIA ANSWERS

1. Lya III.
2. The *Bortas*.

★

THE HUNTED

Star Date: 43489.2

After apprehending an escaped criminal for the authorities on the planet Angosia III, the crew of the *Enterprise* discovers that Roga Danar isn't a prisoner at all—

merely a mentally and physically enhanced soldier the Angosians are unwilling to retrain.

TRIVIA QUESTIONS

1. In what war did Danar fight?

2. To what rank was he promoted?

PLOT OVERSIGHTS

• This episode points out how few people are actually needed on the bridge. In the opening teaser, as Data attempts to apprehend Danar, several shots show that no one sits at Ops. Granted, this isn't an overwhelming crisis, but is that station *totally* unnecessary to the current operations of the ship? Or is Data performing that function from the captain's chair along with his other duties? Also, at the end of the episode, when Picard boards a turbolift to beam down to the planet, Data, Troi, and Worf join him on the away team. Riker also tags along to tell Worf later that he is personally responsible for the captain's safety. So who is in charge of the bridge? In light of this, does it really matter if anyone "has the conn?"

• Picard supposedly places Danar in a high-security detention cell. Yet Troi waltzes in unannounced, and apparently the only guard around is the lone guy barely seen at the desk in the other room. Obviously the crew of the *Enterprise* doesn't expect anyone to try to bust Danar out of jail.

EQUIPMENT ODDITIES

• After Danar breaks free of the Security guards in the transporter room, Worf wrestles him to the floor as Riker pins his arms. Riker then instructs Worf to adjust his phaser for maximum stun. Worf pulls out his phaser, taps a few buttons, and both rows of bars that indicate phaser strength light up. (See the close-up of Riker's phaser at the conclusion of "The Vengeance Factor.") According to the *Tech Manual,* that's setting 16! At that setting, the phaser could probably blow a hole in the bulkhead!

• Does anyone else find it odd that the walls of the brig are covered with all types of indents and outdents? Why go to all the trouble to manufacture it this way? Why not just a smooth wall? (I suppose even jail cells need interesting decor.)

• There's enough technobabble in the *Tech Manual* about transporter operation that it seems to me at least—and a few other nitpickers—that Danar should not be able to break out of the transporter beam and survive…but maybe there's something in his cells that allows this as well.

• And while we are on the subject of the transporter, I find it amazing that it still manages to function when all the other sensors on the *Enterprise* seem completely blind to Danar. Doesn't the transporter have to lock on to something? Wouldn't its sensors need to see the thing that the transporter dematerializes? Obviously they do, because the crew beams Danar off his escape pod at the beginning of the episode. At first I justified this to myself by saying that the *Enter-*

prise simply couldn't detect Danar's *life signs*. Maybe he looked like a file cabinet to the sensors. But as Danar leads the crew on a merry chase at the end of the episode, *no one* can locate him. Even if he looks like a file cabinet, couldn't Data scan the ship for a file cabinet that moves? (Or does the equipment on the *Enterprise* routinely wander the halls?)

• This is the first and only episode that features large, spacious Jefferies tubes. Later episodes have the small crawlers.

• While escaping from the *Enterprise,* Danar sets a phaser on overload and places it in an access panel on deck 15. When it goes, sparks erupt from the wall, but that's about it. The wall is fine. The corridor is fine. It looks like someone set off a few fire crackers. I don't know. Somehow…I thought a phaser on overload would produce more damage than this. Moments earlier, when Worf finds the phaser on overload in the turbolift, he yells for the bridge crew to seal off the deck. See, now *that's* what an overloading phaser should do. It should take out an entire deck! (Insert manly grunt here.)

CONTINUITY AND PRODUCTION PROBLEMS

• The prime minister gets a word tangled up at the beginning of the episode. On the planet he tells Picard that Lunar V is a maximum-security "sisfility."

TRIVIA ANSWERS

1. The Tarsian War.
2. Subhadar.

THE HIGH GROUND

Star Date: 43510.7

Captured by a terrorist group on Rutia IV, Dr. Crusher must maintain her objectivity as she tends to their injured while the group's charismatic leader pleads their cause. Eventually the group captures Picard as well, but the crew of the *Enterprise* soon locates and rescues them.

TRIVIA QUESTIONS

1. What is the name of the waiter who brings Crusher a bottle of alcohol to serve as an antiseptic?

2. How long ago did the Rutia government deny independence to the Ansata terrorists?

ALTERNATE VIEWPOINTS AND CORRECTIONS

• David Dumble of Santa Cruz, CA, brought up an interesting point concerning the title of this episode. David interprets it in two ways. The more obvious interpretation is the episode's debate over moral "high ground." Is the Federation morally correct in offering medical assistance to the Rutian government, believing itself neutral in the situation and refusing to become involved? The title may also be interpreted in a second way. In the twentieth century, we view space as the "high ground." We feel that whoever controls the atmosphere and beyond will have a strategic edge. In the twenty-fourth century, the *Enterprise* controls the "high ground" and appears to have the strategic edge until the Ansata terrorists lessen that advantage with the dimensional shift.

PLOT OVERSIGHTS

• After a terrorist bomb explodes nearby, Crusher hurries over to treat the wounded. Data reports to Picard that their situation is vulnerable, but the captain allows them to stay on the surface a bit longer because Crusher refuses to leave. Eventually Data and Worf stand on the *other* side of a courtyard and discuss the situation. An Ansata terrorist materializes from nowhere, grabs Crusher, and disappears. Remember that the *only* reason the away team is still on the planet is because Crusher won't leave. Doesn't it seem reasonable that the focus of the other members of the away team should be to assist and protect the doctor? Granted, Worf is doing a tricorder sweep for other bombs, but Data is just wandering around. This raises another issue: Did the Rutia government tell the *Enterprise* that the terrorists had a new toy—a dimensional shift transporter? Later in the show, the chief of Security for the city tells Picard and Riker that the terrorists have been using the device for two months—that with it, a person can materialize right in front of you without any warning. Surely the government would advise Starfleet

visitors—visitors who bring desperately needed medical supplies—of such a grave threat. Yet the initial away team acts like they do not know that the device exists. If they did, why would Commander Data—with his "fancy positronic brain"—leave Crusher exposed when a terrorist might pop in at any moment?

• For all his grousing about Picard leaving the ship and transporting into dangerous situations, Riker does exactly the same thing after the captain gets kidnapped. With Picard in the custody of the Ansata terrorists, Riker commands the *Enterprise.* As soon as Wesley locates the terrorists' hideout, Riker beams down with the hostage rescue team.

EQUIPMENT ODDITIES

• As Crusher doctors the injured in the terrorist bombing at the beginning of the episode, Worf sweeps the area with a tricorder and soon announces that the device can find no other explosive devices in the area. Doesn't this tricorder have some sort of continuous scan mode? If you are going into a dangerous area plagued by terrorist bombings, doesn't it seem like a good idea to set up the tricorder to warn you of any devices in the area?

CONTINUITY AND PRODUCTION PROBLEMS

• Is there some reason that sparks erupt every time someone is shot in this episode?

• Appearing in Main Engineering, an Ansata terrorist fires at La Forge as the chief engineer leaps behind his console. If you use freeze-frame you can see that the weapon leaves a black mark on the wall behind La Forge. Moments later, La Forge stands, and the wall is back to normal. (I guess the ship really does clean itself!)

TRIVIA ANSWERS

1. Katik Shaw.
2. Seventy years.

DÉJÀ Q

Star Date: 43539.1

Stripped of his powers, Q seeks sanctuary from the many enemies he has made over the years as a human on board the *Enterprise*. Then, shortly after the arrival of the Calamarain—intelligent swirls of ionized gas—Q departs the ship in a shuttle, knowing that they will stop at nothing to destroy him. For this selfless act, the Q Continuum restores his powers.

GREAT LINES

"Die."—Worf to Q, after Q asks what he must do to prove to the crew that he is human.

TRIVIA QUESTIONS

1. In what detention cell is Q held?

2. The second Q misplaced what cosmic entity?

PLOT OVERSIGHTS

• Q's first suggestion to help the crew of the *Enterprise* keep a moon from crashing into its planet's surface is to change the gravitational constant of the universe. Q says that doing so will alter the moon's mass. Actually, it would modify the strength of the gravitational attraction, not change the moon's mass, and Q—with his IQ of 2,005—should know that.

• The competency of Worf's Security personnel again comes into question. Just after Data saves Q's life, Crusher and La Forge struggle to repair the android. The doctor asks everyone to leave and, on the way out, Picard tells a guard to stay with Q. Dutifully, the guy pushes Q out into the corridor. Then Q shows up in Picard's ready room. No guard. Q returns to sick bay. No guard. Q goes to the main shuttle bay and steals a shuttlecraft. Guess what? No guard.

EQUIPMENT ODDITIES

• In Ten-Forward, Data tells Q that he occasionally ingests a semiorganic nutrient suspension in a silicon-based liquid medium. He adds that it lubricates his biofunctions. Just what "bio"-functions does Data have?

TRIVIA ANSWERS

1. Detention Cell 3.
2. The entire Deltived Asteroid Belt.

UPDATED ROMANCE TOTE BOARD

1. Number of women who kiss Picard: eight
2. Number of women who have intimate interludes with Riker (interludes that possess a high degree of possibility that there was sexual contact): six (maybe seven)
3. Number of women who fall for Data: three
4. Number of men who make a pass at Troi: ten
5. Number of women who make a pass at Crusher: one
6. Number of women who give La Forge the brush-off: two
7. Number of women snarled at by Worf: four
8. Number of girlfriends for Wesley: three
9. Number of fantasy women in the series: At least seventeen
10. Number of fantasy men: three

REFERENCES

1. Jessica Bradley in "The Big Goodbye," Jenice Manheim in "We'll Always Have Paris," Vash in "Captain's Holiday" and "Qpid," Troi and Marie Picard in "Family," Eline in "The Inner Light," Marta Batanides in "Tapestry," Neela Daren in "Lessons," Anna in "Liaisons," Beverly Crusher in "Attached" and "All Good Things," and Lieutenant Ro in "Preemptive Strike."

2. Mistress Beata in "Angel One," Brenna Odell in "Up the Long Ladder," Lanel in "First Contact," Beverly Crusher in "The Host" (I know—it was really Odan, but it *was* Riker's body), Etana Jol in "The Game," and Ensign Ro in "Conundrum." (Possibly Soren in "The Outcast"?)

3. Yar in "The Naked Now," Ard'rian McKenzie in "The Ensigns of Command," and Jenna D'Sora in "In Theory."

4. Liator in "Justice," Riva in "Loud as a Whisper," Kyle Riker in "The Icarus Factor," Devinoni Ral in "The Price," Barclay in "The Nth Degree," Aaron Conor in "The Masterpiece Society," Thomas Riker in "Second Chances," Dr. Mizan in "Timescape," Jason Vigo in "Bloodlines," and Worf in "Eye of the Beholder."

5. Odan in "The Host." (Please note: The subject is the number of *women* who make a pass at Crusher. Odan, in a female body, does so at the end of "The Host.")

6. Christie Henshaw in "Booby Trap" and Leah Brahms in "Galaxy's Child."

7. The Klingon warriorette in "Hide and Q," K'Ehleyr in "Emissary," B'Etor in "Redemption II," and Kamala in "The Perfect Mate."

8. Salia in "The Dauphin," a blonde in "Evolution," and Robin Lefler in "The Game."

9. Setting aside the pleasure women on Risa ("Captain's Holiday"), Ardra in "Devil's Due," and Kamala in "The Perfect Mate" because they were "real," the fantasy women are: the Klingon warriorette in "Hide and Q," Jessica Bradley in "The Big Goodbye," Minuet in "11001001," the two French lovelies in "We'll Always Have Paris," Madeline of "Manhunt," Rishon Uxbridge in "The Survivors," Leah Brahms in "Booby Trap," the two fanta-babes that Q gives Riker at the end of "Déjà Q," Crusher and Troi in "Hollow Pursuits," Data's dance partner in "Data's Day," the nearly nude dancer in "Cost of Living," Eline in "The Inner Light," Data in "A Fistful of Datas," the Countess Regina Barthalomew in "Ship in a Bottle," Anna in "Liaisons," and the consumable Troi in "Phantasms." (There are others, such as the extras in "The Royale," but the ones listed above had a clear romantic component.)

10. Moriarty in "Elementary, Dear Data," Rex in "Manhunt," and Ronin in "Sub Rosa." (Again, there are others, such as the extras in "The Royale" and Barclay's version of the male members of the senior staff in "Hollow Pursuits," but the ones listed above had a clear romantic component.)

A MATTER OF PERSPECTIVE

Star Dates: 43610.4—43611.6

With Riker accused by authorities on Tanuga IV of murdering Dr. Nel Apgar, Picard convenes a hearing on the holodeck and uses the testimony of various witnesses to construct several simulations of the events leading up to the scientist's death. In the end, Picard convinces the authorities that Apgar died by his own hand.

TRIVIA QUESTIONS

1. What is the name of Apgar's assistant?

2. To what planet does the *Enterprise* set course at the end of the episode?

ALTERNATE VIEWPOINTS AND CORRECTIONS

• Wells P. Martin of Stamford, CT, offered the opinion that Picard should have guessed Dr. Apgar's success very much earlier in the episode. After all, Chief Investigator Krag's hair was done up in Krieger waves.

PLOT OVERSIGHTS

• Picard seems to have a bit of difficulty with Krag's title. For most of the show he refers to Krag correctly as "Chief Investigator," but twice—once in his ready room and once just before putting forth his own interpretation of the events—our good captain refers to Krag as "Chief Inspector."

• In the *NextGen Guide* I wondered why O'Brien didn't testify that he detected no state of discharge with Riker's phaser during transport. However, O'Brien also might be useful in another aspect of the transport. Riker arrives on the *Enterprise* in a relaxed, standing position. Yet in "The Most Toys," Data arrives on the pad in a firing stance, precisely as he left Fajo's ship. If Riker had fired on Apgar's generator, wouldn't he arrive on the *Enterprise* in a similar stance?

EQUIPMENT ODDITIES

• Throughout this episode, whenever anyone tells the computer to "freeze program" on the holodeck, the lights on all the machines keep flashing.

• During this episode, seemingly random energy disruptions chew holes in different parts of the ship. The crew traces these energy disruptions back to the holodeck. Supposedly Apgar's recreated lab on the holodeck has been refocusing the lambda energy emanating from the generator on the surface of the planet and turning it into Krieger waves because the holodeck reproduction is so precise. (Yet, Data states earlier that there the holodeck recreations will have a nominal 8.7% margin of error. I leave it you for to decide it that margin of error is a bit high to produce a copy exact enough to work as well as this one does.) But prior to each incident with the random energy surge, one of the participants in the holodeck hearing commands the computer to "freeze program." Shouldn't this stop the machinery from functioning? And after the second incident, it appears that the hearing is coming back from a recess, so the question must be asked: Did Picard leave the simulation running while everyone stepped out for coffee? Doesn't the crew normally shut down the holodeck in cases like this?

• Let's talk about a table and some chairs. The first time we see the table and chairs used by the persons involved in the hearing, the furniture sits in a holodeck recreation of Apgar's lab. Presumably this table and these chairs are also holodeck recreations. (It would be a lot easier than dragging them in from the outside.) Yet, at the end of the episode when the holodeck program terminates, the table and chairs remain. (Now, there's a scene I would love to see. The explosion terminates the program. The camera slowly pans to the actors. They are sprawled out on the floor in various positions and getting up after the holodeck rudely plopped them on their posteriors.)

TRIVIA ANSWERS

1. Tayna.
2. Emila II.

YESTERDAY'S ENTERPRISE

Star Date: 43625.2

While the *Enterprise*-C assists a Klingon outpost in defending against a surprise attack by Romulans, a fierce volley of photon torpedoes throws it more than two decades into the future, creating an alternate timeline —a timeline in which the Federation fights a losing battle with the Klingons. The *Enterprise*-D finds the *Enterprise*-C, and Guinan convinces Picard to send the ship back. The captain knows that to do so is suicide but also that the sacrifice may lead to peace with the Klingons.

RUMINATIONS

Many nitpickers, including Christopher A. Weuve of Alexandria, VA, nominated this show as the best all-time episode instead of "The Best of Both Worlds."

TRIVIA QUESTIONS

1. Where did the warship *Enterprise* administer a "pasting" to the Klingons?

2. Where does the *Enterprise* go at the conclusion of this episode?

ALTERNATE VIEWPOINTS AND CORRECTIONS

• Brian O'Marra of Little Rock, AR, raised an interesting point. From the warship *Enterprise*'s viewpoint, the crew has fought with the Klingons for the past four years (at least). Yet, on this particular day, Guinan suddenly gives Yar a weird look just because the *Enterprise*-C has come through a temporal rift and suddenly the bartender is convinced that the past twenty-two years should have never occurred. But Yar's dialogue indicates that prior to this day she and Guinan got along fine, so if her perceptions go beyond linear time, as Data theorizes—why is she just now getting weird about knowing Yar? It's a valid point. How is this for a possible solution? Maybe Guinan didn't know the timeline was wrong until the rift opened. Maybe her consciousness extended through the rift, touched a parallel universe, and perceived the original timeline. (Insert theme from *The Twilight Zone* here.)

• Several have written long and complicated discourses over the time-traveling and alternate futures/histories of this episode. Unfortunately, recounting them here would involve too much paper and probably leave everyone confused. Time paradoxes are best discussed interactively, so if you happen to catch me at a convention, we can chat about it. Suffice it to say that—according to your particular view concerning the true state of time and space in the *Star Trek* universe—you may or may not agree that this episode is possible, or you may or may not agree that anyone should know Tasha Yar's identity at the end.

PLOT OVERSIGHTS

• One has to wonder just how much time the warship *Enterprise* would have spent "investigating an unusual radiation anomaly" in the midst of a fierce war with the Klingons if the *Enterprise*-C hadn't wandered through. Was the *Enterprise*-D simply flying through the area and just happened upon it? Or did the *Enterprise*-D actually fly out here to take a look? This does not seem like the kind of activity that would occupy one of the best warships in the fleet during the final throes of a Federation-crushing conflagration.

• Why is Wesley on board this ship? If the alternate timeline is similar to the original timeline, Wesley is only about seventeen or eighteen years old. Presumably he's been through Starfleet academy, because his mother couldn't bring him aboard the *Enterprise* when she joined the ship. The dialogue indicates that there are no children aboard. So Wesley went the traditional route of four years (or maybe slightly less) at Starfleet academy. The war must be going badly for the Federation: They are drafting children.

• Where did the Klingons get the resources to fight this war with the Federation? As of 2293 A.D. (the year of *Star Trek VI: The Undiscovered Country* and seventy-three years prior to this episode), the Klingons had exhausted the resources on their war machine. (Then again, at the time of this episode, there was no *ST VI*! And who knows what can happen in alternate timelines. Wink, wink.)

• While working with the repair crews on the *Enterprise*-C, Yar asks Riker to inform "Lieutenant" La Forge that shields are below minimums. The episode clearly shows La Forge's rank as lieutenant commander, making his shortened rank designation "Commander."

• This is a cheap shot, and certainly no one would expect the creators to build all new sets and a new model of the *Enterprise* just for this one episode, but wouldn't the warship *Enterprise* look very different from the exploration vessel *Enterprise*? And what about Ten-Forward? (All those pretty windows right at the leading edge of the ship…) In all likelihood, the warship *Enterprise* would look more like the USS *Defiant* of *Deep Space Nine*.

• Not only does Guinan show an amazing perceptive ability that goes beyond nonlinear time in this episode, she also displays an aptitude that would be the envy of every waiter alive. At one point Yar and Castillo come into Ten-Forward, and Yar orders two TKLs. Guinan gives Yar a strange look and wanders off, apparently going to fill the order. Picard pages all the senior staff officers. Yar and Castillo leave Ten-Forward. Guinan watches them go as she cleans off a table. Remember that Yar ordered prefab food. Most food service organizations put delivery of the customer's order at a higher priority than cleaning tables—especially in this case, because Guinan simply needed to walk over to the stack of TKLs, pick up two, and toss them toward Yar and Castillo. So why is Guinan cleaning tables when she should be filling Yar's order? Because Guinan can tell when someone is going to order a

meal and then leave without eating or paying for it!

CHANGED PREMISES

• "The Neutral Zone" states that no one has heard from the Romulans in fifty-some-odd years. I am sad to report that Garrett's last wish didn't come true. She told Picard that the *Enterprise*-C would make the battle at Narendra III "one for the history books." Obviously it didn't, because Starfleet doesn't remember that the last contact with the Romulans came not fifty-some-odd years ago but twenty-some-odd years ago. (There is an explanation for this. In fact, we are dealing with three timelines: the original timeline, the alternate timeline, and the restored timeline. It's possible that the events of "The Neutral Zone" occurred slightly differently than we remember them because—at the time of that episode—we were watching the events of the original timeline but now we are watching the restored timeline. Confused enough yet?)

EQUIPMENT ODDITIES

• I hope the transporter straightens out Garrett before she arrives at sick bay with Dr. Crusher. The captain has extensive internal injuries. She does not need to materialize in a seated position and tumble back onto the floor.

• Crusher's tricorder must not be working very well. She walks through the main bridge of the *Enterprise*-C and soon pronounces that all the bridge crew except Garrett are dead. Yet after the doctor beams away, Castillo, quite alive, digs himself out of the wreckage. The wreckage certainly didn't seem sufficient to block the sensors.

• Interestingly enough, the movie insignia pin used by Castillo at the conclusion of this episode acts as a *communicator!* You may recall that in the *Star Trek* movies featuring the original cast, the crew still used some type of hand-held or wrist-mounted communicator. The insignia were merely decorative. This change may explain another anomaly in this episode. There's a definite shortage of movie insignia pins. In fact, only the person who commands the *Enterprise*-C gets to wear one! At first, Garrett has it. Then, after her death, Castillo inherits it. This actually makes sense. Presumably the insignia/communicator pins were just coming into use twenty-two years prior to this episode, and—to ensure that the crew wouldn't become confused and walk around all day slapping their chests at nonfunctioning insignia pins—Starfleet Command decided to remove all the insignia pins except those equipped with communicators. The scarcity of these pins limited their distribution to one per ship. Obviously, the ship's commander would get first dibs.

• As Yar and Castillo walk into sick bay, a close-up clearly shows Castillo's phaser. The design comes from *Star Trek II: The Wrath of Khan!* Since the *Star Trek* movie people seem to have a great affinity for changing hardware almost every movie, the one Castillo carries must be hopelessly outdated. *Star Trek III: The Search for Spock* featured a new phaser, as did *Star Trek V: The Final Frontier.*

• The turbolifts in this episode must be in "car pooling" mode for everyone but the captain. After the senior staff briefing in the captain's ready room, Data exits and turns toward the turbolift, but the doors don't open until Yar joins him beside the door. (Then again, with so many troops on board the warship *Enterprise,* maybe waiting for the turbolift is quite common.)

• At the beginning of the episode, The *Enterprise*-C has no photon torpedoes, but at the end it does. I know the creators have done this type of thing before, but I have never fully understood it. How does one replenish photon torpedoes while hanging in space? Don't you need those flattened tube things and antimatter to make a photon torpedo? I suppose they could just replicate the tubes. Do they get the antimatter out of fuel stores?

• Why didn't anyone think to take away Yar's twenty-fourth-century communicator when she joined the crew of the *Enterprise*-C? Why allow the possibility of the Romulans getting their hands on a communicator from twenty years in the future?

• The warship *Enterprise* takes an amazing amount of punishment at the end of this episode. Shortly after the engagement begins with the three Klingon *K'Vort*-class Birds-of-Prey, Data announces that the shields are buckling. He says, "They will not—" when an explosion cuts him off. From this point until the *Enterprise*-C enters the rift, fifteen to twenty more phaser hits pummel Picard's ship. Contrast this to the Bird-of-Prey that the warship *Enterprise* destroys almost instantly after hitting and then collapsing its shields with one phaser blast.

CONTINUITY AND PRODUCTION PROBLEMS

• In this episode, most of the crew run around with shoulder straps attached to their belts. Most, but not all. None of the senior staff has them. Yet Wesley—who is not invited to the senior staff meeting in Picard's ready room—does not wear one either. Why not?

• During the battle with the Klingons, the Tactical station explodes, killing Riker. He falls to the floor and dies with his head pointing to the right. Then a close-up shows us that his head has instantly turned to the left so that we can get a complete view of the ugly gash in his throat.

• At the very end of the episode, while conversing with Guinan, La Forge still wears the uniform of the alternate timeline. You can clearly see the wide cuffs on his sleeves. (This nit was a very popular one to submit.)

TRIVIA ANSWERS

1. Archer IV.
2. Archer IV.

THE OFFSPRING

Star Date: 43657.0

When Data constructs a daughter named Lal, Picard must defend her against those in Starfleet who wish to take her into their custody and away from Data. Unfortunately, the stress of the situation throws Lal into confusion, causing a complete neural systems failure.

GREAT LINES

"Commander, what are your intentions toward my daughter?"—Data to Riker after he catches Lal smooching the first officer in Ten-Forward. Nominated by Alma Jo Williams of Ithaca, NY.

TRIVIA QUESTIONS

1. At the beginning of this episode, the *Enterprise* is on the way to map what cosmic entity?

2. Where does Admiral Haftel want to take Lal?

PLOT OVERSIGHTS

• When Lal considers the choice of gender and appearance, Troi tells the android that whatever the decision, it will be Lal's for life. Why can't Data just strip the android down and change its sex if it becomes unhappy? For that matter, why can't Data change his sex? Or can he?

• After Lal chooses to be a human female, Data states that he can supply her with more realistic skin and eye color. Obviously Data has grown accustomed to his appearance and even prefers it. Otherwise he would alter his features to be more human-like. ("Unification I" supports this idea as well, since Dr. Crusher can make Data look like a perfect Romulan. Obviously, if he so desired, she could make him look human.)

• Lal has this adorable little strut in her walk, but it raises a question: The unsexed android version of Lal walked quite easily, so why does Lal strut? (It's probably those black leather six-inch stiletto heels she wears. Underneath it all, Lal's a wild woman.)

CHANGED PREMISES

• During this episode, everyone assumes that Lore is dead. Data states that if he dies, Soong's work would be lost. Haftel says that there are only two Soong-type androids in existence—referring to Data and Lal. In the discussions under "Datalore," I mentioned that the episode leaves some ambiguity concerning Lore's disposition at the end. If Wesley simply beamed him into space intact, how can Data and Haftel state their convictions with such assurance? On the other hand, if Wesley scattered Lore's atoms across the cosmos, the attitudes in this episode make sense. But we *know* that Wesley didn't do that, because Lore shows up in "Brothers."

• Attention, all nitpickers! Several times in the course of this and the *NextGen Guide,* I've pointed out that Data uses contractions when he shouldn't. In this episode I have uncovered a plot by the creators to justify Data's contraction usage from this point forward. At the end of the episode, Data states that he downloaded Lal's programs and memories into his own. I suppose that if Lal could use contractions, Data should be able to do so as well. (Of course, this doesn't explain why Riker—in his faux future during "Future Imperfect"—would find it strange that Data can use a contraction. See, the creators had it solved, and then they opened it up again!)

CONTINUITY AND PRODUCTION PROBLEMS

• Taking her cue from the biting lovers, Lal greets Riker as he enters Ten-Forward by hoisting the first officer off his feet and planting a kiss on his lips. The kiss ends with Riker's hands on Lal's side of the bar. Then the shot changes, and Riker's hands are instantly on his side of the bar.

TRIVIA ANSWERS

1. The Selebi Asteroid.
2. The Daystrom Annex on Galor IV.

SINS OF THE FATHER

Star Dates: 43685.2—43689.0

When newly discovered records implicate that the father of Duras—a powerful member of the Klingon High Council—is a traitor, K'mpec allows Worf's father to be accused instead. Worf fights the claim and—though he and Picard soon uncover the truth—he agrees to take discommendation for the sake of the Empire.

ALTERNATE VIEWPOINTS AND CORRECTIONS

• On page 179 of the *NextGen Guide,* I quote Worf as saying the great line "It is a good day to die and the day is not over yet," when in fact he says, "It's a good day to die, Duras, but the day is not yet over."

PLOT OVERSIGHTS

• You really have to hand it to Picard. He really is one of the most considerate Starfleet captains to grace the halls of a vessel named *Enterprise.* Speaking privately with Worf in the ready room, Picard accepts the Klingon's offer to be his *cha'DIch,* the one who will stand by Worf during his challenge. Picard accepts the offer by reciting the appropriate Klingon response and then translates the response into English! Obviously Worf doesn't need Picard to translate, and no one else is in the room, but Picard knows that future generations viewing these log entries may not know Klingon and very graciously provides the English equivalent. (Personally, I have a theory that all the log entries for all ships named *Enterprise* somehow fell into a wormhole that caused them to rematerialize on the desks of the creators at Paramount. Doing the world a tremendous service, the creators decided to edit them together into episodes and show them around the globe.)

TRIVIA QUESTIONS

1. Picard's favorite caviar comes from where on Earth?

2. Where was Kahlest sent for medical attention after the massacre at Khitomer?

CHANGED PREMISES

• At one point, the crew of the *Enterprise* discovers that Worf's nanny, Kahlest, still lives. Seeking evidence to clear Worf, Picard visits her. When asked if Worf's father was a traitor,

Kahlest responds forcefully that Mogh was always loyal to the "emperor." Kahlest must be using the term in a generic sense, because Gowron in "Rightful Heir" says there hasn't been an emperor in three centuries.

EQUIPMENT ODDITIES

• This next issue is applicable to many other episodes, but this is as good a place as any to bring it up. How does the Universal Translator know when *not* to translate? We see many races come and go on the *Enterprise,* even races from worlds that cannot possibly know how to speak "Federation Standard." Rivan of the Edo ("Justice") and Nuria of the Mintakans ("Who Watches the Watchers") come to mind. We must assume that the Universal Translator automatically translates whatever language these individuals speak. However, when Kurn comes on board, he speaks Klingon to Worf on occasion, yet the Universal Translator leaves it alone.

CONTINUITY AND PRODUCTION PROBLEMS

• I distinctly remember a "slap" missing from this episode. When Worf first arrives at the Great Hall on the Klingon Home World to challenge the lies against his father, Duras spews forth some accusations and then backhands Worf. At the time I reviewed this episode for the *NextGen Guide* I remember thinking that sound effect was missing when Duras's hand hits Worf's face. I must have gotten distracted with something else, because the nit never made it into the *NextGen*

Guide. In addition, I have received several letters from nitpickers noting the missing "slap." However, when I reviewed the episode for this book, the sound effect was present. Do the creators ever go back and add in missing sound effects?

• The corridor where assassins attempt to kill Kurn sure looks a lot like an *Enterprise* Jefferies tube as featured in the episode "The Hunted."

TRIVIA ANSWERS

1. The Caspian Sea.
2. Starbase 24.

ALLEGIANCE

Star Date: 43714.1

Aliens kidnap Picard and replace him with a doppelgänger. They intend to explore the concepts of authority and loyalty first on the *Enterprise* by judging the reactions of the crew to this fake captain and second by placing the real captain in a cell with individuals who represent other approaches to dealing with authority.

RUMINATIONS

It is time to compliment the creators once again. At the end of the episode, the faux Picard orders the Enterprise *to a position near a pulsar. A beautiful series of graphics shows the* Enterprise *approaching a star that spins a shaft of light outward every*

one and one-half seconds. Through the rest of the scene, the creators simulated the pulsar's visual effect with off-camera lights, and every one of them pulses at one-and-one-half-second intervals! (Of course, there were a few minor problems when the scene cut to another camera angle, but even I'm not compulsive enough to demand perfection in that area.)

TRIVIA QUESTIONS

1. The *Enterprise* succeeded in eliminating what disease from Cor Caroli V?

2. Where is the nearest pulsar to the *Enterprise's* position?

ALTERNATE VIEWPOINTS AND CORRECTIONS

• I am sad to report that I made a grievous—as well as an auditory—error in my analysis of this episode. On pages 182 and 183 of the *NextGen Guide* I mentioned that Picard taps prime numbers on a control panel near the door of his cell. Supposedly the captain taps the first six prime numbers to show his abductors that he is intelligent. In my review I stated that these numbers would be 1, 2, 3, 5, 7, and 11. Wrong! Error alert! Error alert! Many and varied nitpickers have informed me that 1 is not a prime number, it is "unity." (Sounds like one of those new age words to me! Wink, wink.) Sorry, sorry, sorry. It's been too long since math class. Therefore I should have stated that the first six prime numbers are 2, 3, 5, 7, 11, and 13. That is the grievous mistake. Now for the auditory error. After listening to the sequence again with headphones—and the volume cranked—I find that Picard does not tap four times to represent the last number. (I had great fun pointing out that 4 is not a prime number because it is divisible by 2.) He taps five. Still, the sequence of numbers that Picard taps does little to convince me of any mathematical pattern: 2 3 5 7 3 5 5 7 7 5.

• On page 182 of the *NextGen Guide* I noted that—at the end of the episode—the aliens seem genuinely confused by Picard's agitation over this imprisonment, yet one of the aliens in disguise as a first-year Starfleet academy cadet makes a similar impassioned statement earlier in the episode. Angelia Parker of Zachary, LA, believes that the cadet was merely feigning indignation so the aliens could study Picard's response.

PLOT OVERSIGHTS

• One of Picard's cellmates is a beast man named Esoqq. He has four spindly little teeth that thrust upward from his lower lip. They look like they would impede his ability to put anything in his mouth. They also look quite fragile. One has to wonder how this fierce hunter, warrior, and all-around unpleasant fellow manages to eat anything without first pureeing it in a blender!

• Guinan is conveniently missing in this episode. She and her sensitivities would have proven very valuable when the faux Picard came down to Ten-Forward for a drink and a song.

• And speaking of the drink in Ten-Forward, Picard orders an ale for himself and then ends up shouting, "Ales

for everyone!" Appropriately, "everyone" shouts a cheer of gratitude. Wait a minute: Do people pay for their drinks in Ten-Forward? Why is everyone so happy to get a free drink? Aren't *all* the drinks free?

EQUIPMENT ODDITIES

• So the crew of the *Enterprise* can establish force fields on the bridge, can they (as they do at the end of this episode to trap two of the aliens)? Why then don't they establish some sort of safe zone for the captain? If someone beamed onto the bridge, Worf could hit a button and encapsulate Picard and his chair in a protective covering. Or why don't they set up some macros so Worf could hit a button and capture the people who beam onto the bridge?

TRIVIA ANSWERS

1. The Phyrox plague.
2. In the Lonka Cluster.

CAPTAIN'S HOLIDAY

Star Date: 43745.2

A vacation on the pleasure planet Risa turns to intrigue when a woman named Vash involves Picard in a hunt for the Tox Uthat—a weapon supposedly hidden in the twenty-fourth-century by its time-traveling inventor.

GREAT LINES

"I believe there are two ensigns stationed on deck 39 who know nothing about it."—Riker to Picard after the captain asks if the entire crew is in on the scheme to get him to take a vacation.

TRIVIA QUESTIONS

1. Who wrote *Ethics, Sophistry, and the Alternate Universe*?

2. What is the name of the woman who offers Picard *jamaharon*?

PLOT OVERSIGHTS

• Isn't it inevitable that the Vorgons will eventually acquire the Tox Uthat? They are *time* travelers! By the end of the episode, they know where the Uthat was buried and who dug it up. They can come back a few days earlier, follow her out to the site, and abscond with the weapon. Or better yet, they can go to the site a week before Vash arrives and dig up the weapon themselves. Any way you look at it, the Vorgons will get the Tox Uthat (unless they're stupid or they've used up the last few minutes on their time travel cards). But if the Vorgons will eventually acquire the Tox Uthat, how can Vash find it in the first place? Wouldn't the Vorgons have already taken it?

EQUIPMENT ODDITIES

• Early on, Picard and Riker board a turbolift. The doors close, and you can see they are painted orange. The scene cuts to Picard and then back to Riker, who stands in front of the doors.

Suddenly the doors are gray! What happened here? Just how fast are the maintenance crews on board the flagship of the Federation?

• Sovak's phaser rifle must need a recharge. He fires it at the ceiling of the cave that Vash claims holds the Tox Uthat, but nothing happens. No debris falls. No rocks tumble down. (No chickens squawk as they plummet to the floor.)

CONTINUITY AND PRODUCTION PROBLEMS

• At the very beginning of the episode, Riker makes a log entry stating that the *Enterprise* has left orbit around Gemaris V. An exterior shot of the ship shows it traveling at warp. When the action cuts inside, a wide shot shows the bubble dome in the center of the ceiling on the bridge, and the stars stand perfectly still.

• Upon reaching the cave that supposedly holds the Tox Uthat, Picard assembles a shovel and hands it to Vash. When Picard stretches his arm out, the blade faces Vash. Yet, when she takes the shovel, she grabs it by the handle.

• Having decided to give the Tox Uthat to Picard, Vash picks up a *Horga'hn* and holds the little statue out in front of her. One of her hands rests on the back side of its head. The shot changes to show the front of the *Horga'hn* as its forehead opens, but now Vash's hand has jumped to the top of the statue's head.

TRIVIA ANSWERS

1. Ving Kuda.
2. Joval.

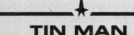

TIN MAN

Star Date: 43779.3

Τhe *Enterprise* ferries an extraordinary telepath named Tam Elbrun to a first encounter with an unusual, recently discovered organic, living spacecraft—designated Tin Man. Despite efforts by the Romulans to stop the *Enterprise,* Elbrun makes contact and soon disappears into the stars with Tin Man, having decided to serve as its companion and crew.

TRIVIA QUESTIONS

1. What probe discovered Tin Man?

2. For what starbase does the *Enterprise* set course at the conclusion of the episode?

ALTERNATE VIEWPOINTS AND CORRECTIONS

• Susan C. Stallings of Oklahoma City, OK, wrote to point out correctly that the answer to the second trivia question on page 187 of the *NextGen Guide* should be forty-seven, not forty.

• Because of the original Nitpicker's Prime Directive—"The information in this book comes solely from the television series"—I was unable in the *NextGen Guide* to give a true accounting of the speed of "impulse,"

because the dialogue in the series never specifies. With the new Nitpicker's Prime Directive—"All nits picked shall derive from sources the creators consider canonical"—I can refer you to the *Technical Manual* and tell you that "full impulse" is one quarter the speed of light. On page 187 I noted that the crew of the *Enterprise* beams Data and Elbrun over to Tin Man while at a distance of 18 minutes by impulse. The figure I gave for this distance should be 81 million kilometers, not 324 million kilometers. This, of course, is still *well* above safe transporter range.

PLOT OVERSIGHTS

• As Data reviews the mission information supplied by Tam Elbrun, Riker notes that Tin Man was discovered at a distance of "23 parsecs" beyond their farthest manned exploration. There are approximately 3.3 light-years in a parsec. In other words, Riker has suddenly decided to switch measuring systems. Why not just say 76 light-years?

• After receiving a warning from Elbrun concerning the first Romulan ship's attack, Tin Man sends out an energy doughnut that destroys the Romulan ship and severely cripples the *Enterprise.* In the aftermath, Riker meets with La Forge in Main Engineering and orders the chief engineer to give top priority to the shields. La Forge finally agrees to this. The episode takes place in sick bay, where we see Picard, Crusher, Troi, and Elbrun. The next scene is in Main Engineering. We see La Forge working on the sensors, and soon he identifies another sensor echo, which everyone immediately assumes is a second Romulan warbird. Two problems: First, the original sensor echo came from the first Romulan warbird because that ship was pushing its limits to beat the *Enterprise* to Tin Man. The dialogue clearly establishes that this "overdriving" is the only reason the warbird shows up on the sensors as an echo. Yet the second warbird does not need to overtax its engines. It is two days behind the first specifically because it did not overtax its engines. So how are the *Enterprise* sensors detecting it? Second: Wasn't La Forge supposed to be working on the shields? After this little discussion about the sensor echo, Riker— now on the bridge—asks La Forge about the shields. The chief engineer gives the lame response that he is "doing the best he can." Well... maybe if he'd quit *fooling around* with the sensors and actually *do some work* on the shields they would get fixed! ("At ease, Phil, at ease." Chuckle, chuckle.)

CHANGED PREMISES

• When the crew first detects a sensor echo following the *Enterprise,* Data claims that there is no known phenomenon capable of traveling at warp. Yet, in "Lonely Among Us," Data identifies the energy cloud as traveling at warp. In addition, the crystalline entity in "Datalore" travels at warp. In neither case does the dialogue of the episode give us any indication that these entities are artificially created devices.

CONTINUITY AND PRODUCTION PROBLEMS

• At the end of this episode, when Tin Man hits the *Enterprise* with a repulser wave and sends it spinning away just before a star goes nova, the ship spins counterclockwise, and the stars on the viewscreen travel horizontally right to left. The same thing happens in "Q Who." The stars should be going from left to right, not right to left! (The ship is spinning to the left. Therefore, a star on the left side of the ship would come into view as the ship turned and disappear from view on the right side of the screen as the ship rotated away from it to the left.)

TRIVIA ANSWERS
1. Vega IX.
2. Starbase 152.

HOLLOW PURSUITS

Star Dates: 43807.4–43808.2

While struggling to overcome his addiction to holodeck fantasies involving members of the senior staff, Lieutenant Reginald Barclay comes back to reality long enough to help La Forge and the Engineering team avert disaster when a contaminant causes the matter and antimatter injectors in the warp core to freeze open.

TRIVIA QUESTIONS

1. Who commands the USS *Zhukov?*

2. Who does La Forge assign to align the matter and antimatter injectors?

ALTERNATE VIEWPOINTS AND CORRECTIONS

• At the conclusion of the episode, Barclay tells the computer to erase all his programs. After the computer dweedles to let him know that it took the requested action, Barclay says, "Except program 9." Many nitpickers wrote to point out the computer should have already deleted program 9. However, the main computer of the *Enterprise* probably has the same feature present on many twentieth-century computers—namely, undelete.

PLOT OVERSIGHTS

• At a mission briefing, Barclay reports on his progress attempting to find a problem with an antigrav unit. Wesley suggests that he look at the flow capacitor. Later, in a counseling session with his fantasy version of Troi, Barclay calls it a "flux" capacitor. The "flux capacitor" was the device that made time travel possible in the *Back to the Future* movies.

• I must say this: La Forge is remarkably calm in high-stress situations. At the end of the program, the ship is on the verge of tearing itself apart. La Forge and company come up with a very plausible solution. But instead of testing it immediately, the chief engi-

neer grabs Barclay and takes a jaunt down to Cargo Bay 5. Now, the ship is going to dissociate in just a few minutes. Why not just try the solution, and if it doesn't work, try something else? The injectors are stuck completely open. How could it get any worse? (Granted, this approach is not always the best, but in this circumstance, I think it's warranted! Of course, if they did just try it, we couldn't have the suspenseful countdown.)

• And speaking of the jaunt to Cargo Bay 5, La Forge and Barclay seem to take their own sweet time strolling down the hall, given that the ship is on the verge of destruction.

EQUIPMENT ODDITIES

• Looking for Barclay, La Forge enters the holodeck and finds fantasy versions of Crusher and Wesley. La Forge acts at first like he thinks they are real. Shouldn't his VISOR spot them as fakes immediately?

• Who has the authority to override whose orders on the holodeck? Looking for Barclay a second time, La Forge accompanies Riker and Troi into one of Barclay's fantasies. Upon seeing Barclay's musketeer versions of Picard, Data, and La Forge, Riker attempts to tell the computer to end the program, but Troi tells the computer to disregard the order. A bit later—after seeing Barclay's recreation of her as the goddess of empathy—Troi attempts to discontinue her fantasy self, but Riker tells the computer to disregard the order. Shouldn't the holodeck computer have some sort of rank-prioritized system for deciding who it is going to obey?

• As the crew investigates the cause of the malfunctions, we discover that the standard scan misses 15,525 substances, at least 2 of which are lethal. This does not inspire confidence on my part!

CONTINUITY AND PRODUCTION PROBLEMS

• Unknowingly contaminated with invidium, an engineer picks up a glass in Ten-Forward. The substance deforms the glass, and La Forge and Data take it to Main Engineering. At one point, La Forge, with Data in Engineering, holds a glass deformed by invidium with his left hand so the camera, sitting behind his left shoulder, can get a good picture of it. Then the shot changes, and La Forge suddenly holds the glass with both hands.

TRIVIA ANSWERS

1. Captain Gleason.
2. Lieutenants Duffy and Costa.

THE MOST TOYS

Star Date: 43872.2

A collector of rare, one-of-a-kind items, Kivas Fajo masterminds a plan to fake Data's death and kidnap the valuable android. Fortunately, the crew of the *Enterprise* uncovers Fajo's plot and comes to Data's rescue.

1. What is the name of Fajo's ship?

2. On what do the Andorians wish to give Fajo a bid?

PLOT OVERSIGHTS

• After Data's death, La Forge and Wesley visit the android's quarters to divide up his stuff. Wesley passes a bench and pauses to look at Data's violin—out of its case and casually lying with its bow on a sitting area. So, Mr. Android "who organizes his closet first by function and then by color from light to dark" simply forgot to put his violin away?

• In the ready room, Picard, Riker, and La Forge discuss the accident that "killed" Data. At one point the captain refers to La Forge as "lieutenant," when in fact La Forge is a lieutenant *commander*.

• Data faces a defining moment at the conclusion of this episode. Fajo claims that if the android does not return to the treasure room, he will execute more members of his crew until Data complies. Data wrestles with this for a moment and decides the killing must stop and so opts to murder Fajo. It's a great moment, especially later, when Data sidesteps Riker's wonderment that the weapon in the android's possession was in a state of discharge. ("Perhaps something occurred during transport," Data tells the first officer innocently. And, yes, he probably is lying here. And, yes, Data's not supposed to lie.) Is killing Fajo really Data's *only* option? Just how big is Fajo's crew? Couldn't Data knock a few heads together and take over the ship? He doesn't seem to have much trouble with the two who try to stop his exit from the ship with Varria.

EQUIPMENT ODDITIES

• Eventually La Forge grows suspicious of Data's death when he reviews the records of the android's shuttle trips to and from Fajo's ship. On the first two trips back to the *Enterprise,* Data announced that he had cleared Fajo's shuttle bay. On the third trip, he did not. La Forge finds this odd, since Data always followed protocol. Interestingly enough, the recording of the preparations for the third shuttle trip does not match the actual events seen at the beginning of the episode. Boarding the shuttle for the third trip, Data says, "Level 1 precautions for incoming material remain in effect." On the recording, Data says, "Level 1 precautions remain in effect." (I want to know who's been editing the transcript and why.)

• The treasure room where Fajo keeps Data contains a safe. When Fajo opens the safe, he operates a locking mechanism with five buttons in a stack. Beginning to enter the combination, he taps the top button and the middle button. Fajo then covers the panel with his right hand as he enters the remaining eight (determined by counting the beeps). Later in the episode, Data attempts to find the combination of the safe by tapping ten buttons as well. Oddly enough, the android begins by tapping the button second from the top instead of the

top button. Doesn't Data remember what button Fajo pressed first? If the android has decided to try all possible combinations without regard to the combination Fajo pressed, he has given himself a much larger task. By starting with the two buttons Fajo pressed, Data would need to test 390,625 combinations (5 raised to the power of 8). On the other hand—if the android has decided to try all possible combinations—the number of combinations he must check grows to 9,765,625.

• And speaking of the combination to this safe, when Fajo opens it, he ends on the bottom button, but when Varria opens it, she ends on the second button from the top.

• Does anyone else think that the "escape pod" in which Data and Varria attempt to escape looks a lot more like a shuttlecraft?

• One of the great tribulations in nitpicking comes when one attempts to choose which piece of conflicting information one will believe. In "The Hunted," Data states that the sensors are calibrated to work on artificial life. Yet, in "Brother," the crew is unable to locate Data and Lore because they do not register on the sensors. Here's the problem: At the end of "The Most Toys," the crew of the *Enterprise* beams Data back home. Note that Data does not wear a communicator. If Data does not wear a communicator, the sensors must be able to sense him if they are going to lock on to him for transport. But…"Brothers" said the sensors couldn't lock on to Data. But…"The Hunted" said they could. So…is this a nit or not? (I personally think the creators do this just to drive us nitpickers insane and get us committed. It's a conspiracy. I just know it is. I think I can hear them coming to get me right now!)

CONTINUITY AND PRODUCTION PROBLEMS

• Attempting to force Data to wear a costume different than his Starfleet uniform, Fajo splashes a vial of liquid on the android. Wherever the liquid touches Data's chest it rapidly dissolves away his uniform. For some reason, however, the splash that falls on Data's right sleeve near his elbow does nothing.

TRIVIA ANSWERS

1. The *Jovis*.
2. A shipment of Tellurian spices.

SAREK

Star Dates: 43917.4—43920.7

As the *Enterprise* transports the renowned Ambassador Sarek to an important meeting with the Legarans, Crusher and Troi uncover a disturbing fact: The Vulcan suffers from Bendii syndrome—a breaking down of emotional control in extreme old age. Knowing that Sarek cannot negotiate in his debilitated condition, Picard suggests a mindmeld. The joining allows the Vulcan to complete his final diplomatic mission.

GREAT MOMENTS

Both Patrick Stewart and Mark Lenard put in excellent performances during this episode. For me, the exchange between Picard and Sarek as the captain attempts to convince the aged Vulcan that he suffers from Bendii syndrome ranks among the best of the series.

TRIVIA QUESTIONS

1. Whom does Worf put on report for insubordination?

2. To test for Bendii syndrome, Crusher must grow a culture from what region of the Vulcan brain?

ALTERNATE VIEWPOINTS AND CORRECTIONS

• Realizing that a mindmeld with Sarek would give the Vulcan the necessary emotional stability so the ambassador could complete his negotiations with the Legarans, Picard calls himself the only logical choice. On pages 193 and 194 of the *NextGen Guide* I noted that there are other logical choices on the *Enterprise*. There is a Vulcan on Sarek's staff and Vulcans serving aboard the *Enterprise*. Several nitpickers had alternate viewpoints. Roland R. Thompson of Los Angeles, CA, believes that while Picard may not be *the* logical choice, he would be more so than a Vulcan. Since Vulcans find strong emotion distasteful, it might be inappropriate for Sarek to complete a mindmeld with another member of his race in his present condition. Geoffrey Cook of

Hammond, IN, wasn't surprised at Sarek's agreement to mind-meld with Picard, given the captain's logical mind and diplomatic skills—adding that Sakkath, the Vulcan who traveled with Sarek, didn't seem too bright! Travis Williamson of Grain Valley, MO, felt that Sarek's wild emotions would overwhelm any Vulcan who mind-melded with the ambassador and possibly kill him. (Kirk asserts that strong emotions will harm Spock in the *Classic* episode "Plato's Stepchildren.")

These are valid viewpoints, but let me offer a few points in response. Until the trip aboard the *Enterprise,* Sakkath held Sarek together emotionally without benefit of a mindmeld. While it is true that strong emotions repulse and even endanger Vulcans, the onslaught Picard experiences is directly attributable to the fact that Picard is human. In discussing the mindmeld with Picard, Sarek says, "Vulcan emotions are extremely intense. No human could control them." For me, this implies that a Vulcan could. If that's true, the mindmeld would pose no danger to another Vulcan. But would it be distasteful for that Vulcan? That answer lies deep in the mores of Vulcan culture.

PLOT OVERSIGHTS

• Paul T. Mulik tells me that the second piece of the all-Mozart concert—featuring a string *quartet* with Data as first violin—is actually from the *Sextet* No. 1, in B♭ by *Johannes Brahms!*

• At one point, Sarek's uncontrolled emotions insight a fisticuffs free-for-all in Ten-Forward. Riker and Worf enter, look around for a few moments, and then scurry up to help La Forge. Once the chief engineer is out of danger, Worf calls for Security. Wouldn't it be a tad more reasonable to call for Security *before* jumping into the fray?

CHANGED PREMISES

• For some reason, Sarek does not offer the Vulcan salute when boarding the *Enterprise*. He did when he boarded the original *Enterprise* in the *Classic* episode "Journey to Babel." Why not here? Has it fallen out of vogue on Vulcan?

CONTINUITY AND PRODUCTION PROBLEMS

• The Legarans will negotiate while they sit in a slime pit heated to 150 degrees Celsius (for those of us still on the Imperial measuring system, that's 302 degrees Fahrenheit). When I was in college, I worked in a cafeteria, loading dishes onto trays and shoving them into a huge dishwashing machine. If I recall correctly, that machine used water heated to 180 degrees Fahrenheit, and steam poured from it constantly. Yet, no heat appears to rise from the pit, and both La Forge and Wesley stand very close.

TRIVIA ANSWERS

1. Ensign DiMato.
2. The metathalamus.

MÉNAGE À TROI

Star Date: 43930.7

DaiMon Tog of the Ferengi falls madly in love with Lwaxana Troi, swearing to have her at all cost. When Lwaxana refuses his affections, Tog kidnaps not only her but the vacationing Riker and Deanna Troi as well. Skillfully, Riker soon escapes from the Ferengi vessel's brig and manages to send a message to the *Enterprise*.

GREAT LINES

"My love is like a fever, longing still for that which longer nurses the disease."— Picard, doing his bad-actor impersonation while trying to convince Tog that he is madly in love with Lwaxana.

TRIVIA QUESTIONS

1. Lwaxana would rather eat what animals than come into the possession of Tog?

2. What is the name of the Ferengi doctor who examines Lwaxana?

PLOT OVERSIGHTS

• Obviously the floor constitutes the Ferengi high place of honor for visiting females. As Lwaxana, Riker, and Deanna awake from their sudden transport and capture, we see Riker and Deanna slowly rising from beds in the detention area, while Lwaxana comes to consciousness on the floor. Given that Tog considers Lwaxana a great prize, does this seem right?

• When did Riker learn to read Ferengi? After busting out of his jail cell, the first officer manipulates the controls of a data terminal with ease, even though the readouts are in Ferengi.

CHANGED PREMISES

• Boy, this Starfleet academy is tough to get into! In "Coming of Age," Mordock took the written exams, and the testing administrator welcomed him to Starfleet academy. In this episode, Wesley has already passed the written exams, and now he has to take some type of oral exams as well! Do these procedures only apply to white, Anglo-Saxon human males?

EQUIPMENT ODDITIES

• Is there some reason why Wesley's communicator is all silver in this episode instead of silver and gold? (I confess that I may not have noticed that it always has been all silver. Perhaps acting ensigns get this type of communicator?)

• The combination to the force field across the front of the Ferengi detention cell seems to change depending on who presses the keys on the control pad. When a Ferengi releases Riker from the cell, he presses the bottom button, then the next-to-bottom button, and finally the top button. He reengages the force field by pressing the buttons in reverse. After knocking out the diminutive guard, Riker released the force field by pressing top, next-to-bottom, and bottom. Wasn't this the command to turn on the force field? And how did Riker know what to press in the first place? It doesn't look like he can see the Ferengi's hand as it works the control panel.

CONTINUITY AND PRODUCTION PROBLEMS

• Interestingly enough, Wesley gets a promotion to ensign at the end of this episode, yet he comes on to the bridge moments later wearing the two-piece outfit associated only with officers on the senior staff.

TRIVIA ANSWERS

1. Orion wing-slugs.
2. Dr. Farek.

TRANS-FIGURATIONS

Star Dates: 43957.2—43960.6

Crusher's efforts to save the life of an unidentified humanoid male that the crew names John Doe places the *Enterprise* in the middle of a civil conflict. Doe's race, the Zalkonians, teeters on the verge of a new energy-only existence, but the Zalkonian authorities have determined to destroy anyone exhibiting signs of the change. The crew's involvement allows Doe enough time to complete his transformation and offer this new level of living to his people.

TRIVIA QUESTIONS

1. During this episode, the *Enterprise* performs a mapping mission on what celestial object?

2. Who commands the Zalkonian ship?

PLOT OVERSIGHTS

• At the beginning of the episode, Riker pages La Forge and asks him to report to a transporter room for an away mission. La Forge simply gets up and leaves Ten-Forward. Wouldn't it be better to acknowledge the order first?

• Again, Data makes observations about the physical surroundings during an away mission at the most interesting times. After the team beams down, he takes out his tricorder and notes that the radiation levels are within acceptable limits. Wouldn't you want to do this *before* you transported to the surface?

• When transporting the Zalkonian captain to the *Enterprise,* does John Doe use some type of freeze ray on the rest of the Zalkonian crew? Their captain beams off the ship just after giving an order to fire all weapons. Not only do they not fire all their weapons, they also act like they don't even notice that he's gone!

• Here's a bit of Terraphobia for you. (Is that a word?) The crew of the *Enterprise* seems very pleased that John Doe has transfigured into a very powerful being, but when humans get powerful in episodes such as "Hide and Q" and the *Classic* show "Where No Man

244

Has Gone Before," everyone gets paranoid. The Zalkonians certainly don't seem to be "pure as the driven snow." Why isn't Picard worried about them receiving great powers?

EQUIPMENT ODDITIES

• At the beginning of the episode, just after the away team beams down, they trudge over quite a little distance to get to John Doe. Wouldn't it be simpler to beam in a little closer?

• During the away mission, Crusher needs to stabilize John Doe before transport, so she hooks him up to La Forge. Then the doctor says, "Three to beam up." Amazingly enough, though the four members of the away team plus John Doe all inhabit a somewhat tight area, the transporter chief knows exactly *whom* to beam up!

• Evidently the crew determines quite rapidly that the piece of machinery they take from John Doe's craft is harmless. (It's the squatty bottle filled with blue gel.) A short time later, Data and La Forge *play* with it in Ten-Forward.

• With the approach of the Zalkonian ship, Data informs Picard that it has come within "weapons range" and then, a few moments later, puts it on the main viewscreen. Isn't this reversed? Can't the *Enterprise*'s sensors normally display a ship on the viewscreen well before it comes into weapons range? And wouldn't it be more helpful to alert Picard when the Zalkonian ship came into communication range (assuming the normal configuration of reaching communication range *before* weapons range)?

THE BEST OF BOTH WORLDS, PART 1

Star Dates: 43989.1—43993.5

D etermined to use a human mouthpiece to aid in their conquest of the Federation, the Borg capture Picard and assimilate him. As the episode ends, Riker orders Worf to fire a high-energy beam through the navigational deflector. He hopes the blast will destroy the Borg vessel, though he knows Picard currently resides on it.

RUMINATIONS

C raig Sawyer of Seattle, WA, noticed that this episode has great and original *music.*

TRIVIA QUESTIONS

1. On what planet did the New Providence colony reside?

2. What ship departed Zeta Alpha II and just over three hours later encountered the Borg?

PLOT OVERSIGHTS

• Picard is strangely absent from

meetings in this episode. Normally we see the captain in the thick of it during a crisis. Yet, in this episode, the senior staff and Shelby develop a plan, and then Riker takes it to the captain. Does Picard have more important business that demands his attention? (Of course, if Picard sat in on the meetings, then Shelby couldn't do an "end run" around Riker and we couldn't have the scene in the turbolift where Shelby tells Riker that he's in her way.)

• And speaking of the famed "You're in my way" conversation in the turbolift, what is with Shelby, anyway? The *Enterprise* is hiding inside a nebula and desperately trying to come up with some way to defend against a foe who threatens the entire Federation, and she is worried about her *career track*? Personally, if I were Shelby I'd be more worried about becoming a Borgette.

• O'Brien must be eavesdropping on the bridge again. The Borg kidnap Picard, knocking out Riker and Worf, too. Riker comes to and asks O'Brien if he can get a fix on the captain. O'Brien knows what Riker is talking about and replies that he cannot. (He probably read the script.)

• (Since the alteration actually occurs here, I should alert you to my comments concerning what the Borg *really* did to Picard. See "Changed Premises" for "Q Who" earlier in this book.)

CHANGED PREMISES

• During a meeting in Main Engineering, Wesley makes the statement that—in the *Enterprise*'s last encounter with the Borg—the ship's best shot "barely scratched the surface." If I

recall correctly, the Borg ship sustained 20 percent damage from that shot—a wee bit more than simply scratching the surface.

• Picard's declaration at the end of this episode, "I am Locutus of Borg," deserves some scrutiny. Later episodes establish that Borg don't normally get assigned names ("Descent") and Borg normally don't refer to themselves as "I" ("I Borg"). In addition, the very name "Locutus" raises some questions. The Borg are soulless, machine-driven humanoids with no individuality. They have no culture, no art, no religion. So just where did they come up with this name? According to Lee Zion of the USS *Kitty Hawk*, "Locutus" means "one who speaks" in Latin. He wondered if Picard—realizing the inevitability of his assimilation—decided to help the Borg pick a really cool name for him as partial compensation for his loss. (See "Changed Premises" in "Q Who" concerning modifications made by the Borg to Picard.)

EQUIPMENT ODDITIES

• The visual effects guys got a little happy with the phaser beam emissions during the first battle with the Borg. Picard tells Worf to fire all weapons, and an exterior shot of the ship shows phasers erupting from the midpoint of the engine pylons. These phaser emissions are never seen again because, according to the *Technical Manual,* there are no phaser arrays at the midpoint of the engine pylons! (There are phaser arrays on the underside of the pylons, but for the phasers to emit as they do in this episode, they would have to shoot up *through* the pylons and then make a right-hand turn.)

• Picard makes an interesting choice of weapons systems when he takes the *Enterprise* out of the nebula. He tells Worf to load "forward torpedo bays." (Is there more than one torpedo bay in the front of the ship?) Considering that the *Enterprise* will make a run for it, one would presume that the Borg will give chase, putting the Borg ship behind the *Enterprise*. Therefore, the more sensible choice would be to load the *aft* torpedo launcher.

• To bring the Borg ship out of warp, Data and Worf begin destroying power distribution nodes. Oddly enough, though the Borg can shield themselves individually from attack, they seem unable to shield these vital areas of their ship. Even more surprising, they fail to adapt to the frequencies of the phasers held by Data and Worf until the pair begin to fire on the Borg themselves. One would think that the destruction of the power distribution nodes would give the Borg enough analysis time to calibrate their shields.

TRIVIA ANSWERS

1. Jouret IV.

2. USS *Lalo*.

★
NITPICKING THE UNIVERSE

most of the nitpicking in the *Guides* occurs on an episode level. Sometimes it's fun to step back a bit and consider the show as a whole to see what nitpicking gems we might uncover.

1. *Windows.* Consider the observation lounge first. It sits behind the main bridge, a blip on the surface of an immense saucer that's more than half a kilometer wide and more than 420 meters long. Yet, never, ever have we seen the top of the saucer section when looking out from inside the observation lounge. (From the side view of the *Enterprise* on page 11 of the *Tech Manual,* it sure looks like you should be able to see the top of the saucer section! Of course, the same can be said for the view out the captain's ready room.) Then there's the windows in Ten-Forward. They slant inward, indicating that the room is on the underside of the saucer section. There's only one problem with that theory: If you count the rows of windows on the top of the saucer section, you discover that deck 11 is the first deck on the underside of the saucer. So should the watering hole really be called Eleven-Forward? But wait! The *Technical Manual* solves this problem by slanting inward the exterior of the last deck on the upper side of the saucer, thereby putting Ten-Forward on the appropriate deck, with inward-slanting windows! Unfortunately, when the creators gave us an "up close and personal" view of the front of the saucer section in the crash scene of *Star Trek Generations,* they didn't slant deck 10 inward, once again demonstrating that Ten-Forward must be on the underside of the saucer (and, in reality, more appropriately called Eleven-Forward!).

2. *Holodeck realities.* How many times must this *entertainment* device malfunction before Picard pulls the plug on the thing? (Yeah, yeah. I know it's *supposed* to be used for other things, such as education and training, but from the looks of it, the crew spends the majority of holotime acting out fantasies.) Crew members go into the holodeck, and more than once it has kidnapped them, put their lives in danger, and even threatened the ship! Obviously someone killed all the lawyers in the twenty-fourth century, because the manufacturer of this item would certainly be sued out of business in short order.

3. *High-powered computers.* Robert Nichol sent me the following observations after watching the workstations on the *Enterprise* fry yet another hapless crew member. "Why do Starfleet computers work on 50,000 volts? Doesn't Starfleet

have the equivalent of an Underwriters Laboratories or Canadian Standards Association to protect poor end users from these overcharged death traps? If General Motors made electronic dashboards that spit at you with every bumper thumper, Ralph Nader would have apoplexy!"

4. *Turbolift quandary.* Why do the turbolifts have only one set of doors? Shouldn't there be an inner set of doors that travel with the turbolift and an outer set of doors that stay on the deck?

5. *Accident prevention.* Why, oh, why, isn't the cargo in the cargo bays strapped down? With all the jostling that goes on aboard the *Enterprise,* you would think that *somebody* would think to add a few mechanical restraints to those tall storage racks containing heavy-looking barrels.

6. *Sound in space.* Okay, okay. I'll say it. Sound doesn't travel in a vacuum. Therefore, we shouldn't be able to hear the *Enterprise* whooshing past us in space. Nor should we hear the fizz of the probes whizzing away from the ship or the phasers firing or photon torpedoes launching or…(The show sure would be boring without all those great sound effects, though, wouldn't it?)

7. *Streaking stars.* Whenever the *Enterprise* flies at warp, we see the lovely streaking stars through every exterior window. (At least we're supposed to!) However, at warp, the *Enterprise* flies faster than the speed of light. The light from the star can move only at the speed of light. If a star sits in front of the *Enterprise,* it makes sense that the crew could see it, since the ship would run into the photons from the star. However, if the star sits beside or behind the *Enterprise,* the photons from those stars could never make it to the *Enterprise* because they can travel only at the speed of light, and the ship is traveling away from them at faster than the speed of light. (However, I do think the view from the observation lounge windows is very nice and would not want to see it replaced with a black backdrop.)

8. *Worf's accent.* Worf was raised by heavily accented Russian foster parents, right? So why doesn't he speak like Pavel Chekov?

9. *Poker, anyone?* The senior staff has the oddest mix of poker buddies. First you've got an android named Data, who can remember every card in the deck. Then you've got an empath named Troi, who can read emotional states and probably tell when you're bluffing. Finally you've got a VISOR-equipped chief engineer named La Forge, who says he can always tell when a human is lying. Would you want to play poker with these people?

10. *The stars of Saturn's rings.* From the third season on, the opening credits of *Star Trek: The Next Generation* have a fairly obvious edit. If you watch as the Saturn-like planet drifts across the screen, you see the star field change directions abruptly at the edge of the rings. The original opening of *Star Trek: The Next Generation* featured a long pullback from an Earth-like planet with a moon to a Jupiter-like planet, then to a Saturn-like planet before the camera panned to find the *Enterprise.* The opening had some problems. As the camera pulled back, the moon orbiting Earth suddenly flew off in the opposite direction of its orbit, and Saturn was lit from the wrong side! For whatever reason, the creators decided to redo the opening footage but only up until the appearance of the *Enterprise.* Unable to match the movement of the stars, they did the next best thing and tried to hide the transition along the edge of the rings. (I suppose it would have cost too much money to reshoot the ship flybys.)

FOURTH SEASON

THE BEST OF BOTH WORLDS, PART 2

Star Date: 44001.4

After viewing the wanton destruction of the Starfleet armada at Wolf 359, Riker devises a plan to kidnap Locutus from the Borg ship. Through a direct neural interface to Locutus, Data gains access to the Borg collective consciousness and implants a command in the regenerative pathway. Just before the destruction of the *Enterprise,* the Borg go to sleep.

TRIVIA QUESTIONS

1. What three ships does Shelby identify at the carnage of Wolf 359?

2. What outpost reported visual contact with the Borg at 1213 hours?

PLOT OVERSIGHTS

• In the first observation lounge meeting, Admiral Hanson addresses Shelby as "Lieutenant." As is the case again and again with Lieutenant Commander La Forge, the proper designation for this rank is "Commander."

• A very minor point but a point to ponder nonetheless, Wesley identi-

fies our solar system as the "Terran system." Since our star is named "Sol," and every other planetary system in *Trek* is named after its star, shouldn't Wesley call it the "solar system"?

• As Data, Troi, and O'Brien ponder why the Borg don't terminate their subspace link with Locutus, Crusher says it would be like asking one of us to cut off an arm or a leg. This seems a reasonable explanation until you remember that the Borg tried to murder Locutus by blowing up the shuttle that had absconded with him.

• At the end of this episode, Riker still wears four pips on his collar when meeting with Picard in the ready room. This seems reasonable. After all, Spock retained his rank of captain even after he continued to serve with Kirk in the *Star Trek* movies. Yet, in the next episode, Riker resumes his rank as commander. Did he take a voluntary reduction? Surely Starfleet wouldn't demote him after he saved the Federation.

• And while we are on the subject of Riker's rank, the battle at Wolf 359 no doubt destroyed a good many command rank personnel. Is it really conceivable that Starfleet would allow an obviously competent commander to remain a first officer under these circumstances? Wouldn't they just order him to take a ship or resign?

• The battle at Wolf 359 destroyed thirty-nine ships according to Admiral Satie in "The Drumhead." At the conclusion of this episode, Shelby claims they will have the fleet restored in "a year." The *Tech Manual* says it took *years* just to build the *Enterprise.*

EQUIPMENT ODDITIES

• This next nit takes a bit of deduction. The *Technical Manual* says there is a restroom that adjoins the main bridge. By the process of elimination, we can determine where this restroom resides. On occasion the creators have shown us a door near the one that leads to the observation lounge. (For instance, Wesley and Mordan have a little chat during "A Matter of Honor" near this door after Mordan realizes his grave error in not telling Picard of the space organism immediately.) This is the only door left unidentified in any episode of *NextGen*. Since the *Tech Manual* claims the existence of a restroom that adjoins the bridge, and this is the only unidentified door, it's fairly safe to assume that this door leads to the restroom. Oddly enough, when Shelby dispatches the crewmen to man the battle bridge, a man and a woman exit this door, after which a man and a woman enter! (Kinda makes ya wonder what they're doin' in there?)

• Apparently the repair technicians on board the *Enterprise* really know their stuff. When Data and Worf leave in the shuttle to make a grab for Picard, we see a lovely close-up of the star drive section—precisely where the Borg cutting tool sliced into Main Engineering during the previous episode. Even though the ship hasn't had a chance to visit a starbase, everything looks perfectly restored.

• Are the Borg shields less powerful than those manufactured by Starfleet? In "The Hunted," when Roga Danar attempts to ram the drive section of his escape craft into the *Enter-* prise, it simply bounces off the shields. In "Relics," La Forge and Scott use the shields of the *Jenolen* to prop open some huge space doors. Yet, in this episode, Data and Worf drive a shuttlecraft right through the Borg shields. Of course, if shuttles can actually fly through the shields, why not just load up a bunch of them with massive charges of antimatter and send them on kamakazi runs?

• As soon as the *Enterprise* reaches our solar system, Riker orders Wesley to drop out of warp and head in on impulse. Wait a minute: Isn't time of the essence here? The Borg are preparing to *pummel* the Earth. In "The Schizoid Man," the *Enterprise* dropped out of warp right next to a planet. Why go crawling up to the encounter with the Borg on impulse?

CONTINUITY AND PRODUCTION PROBLEMS

• As the Borg vessel passes Saturn, traveling from the right side to the center of the screen, the light comes from the right side of both the ship and the planet. Isn't the light coming from our sun? If so, why are the Borg flying parallel to the sun? Are they taking the scenic route to Earth? Shouldn't they be flying *toward* the sun?

TRIVIA ANSWERS

1. The *Kyushu,* the *Tolstoy,* and the *Melbourne.*

2. Jupiter Outpost 92.

FAMILY

Star Date: 44012.3

n eeding to decompress from the violation he experienced at the hands of the Borg, Picard visits his brother in his hometown in France. Meanwhile, Worf's parents visit him on the *Enterprise*—attempting to learn more about his discommendation—and Wesley watches a long-forgotten recording that his father made shortly after his birth.

TRIVIA QUESTIONS

1. From where do Worf's parents transport up to the *Enterprise*?

2. To how many teenagers did Worf give bloody noses when he was seven?

CHANGED PREMISES

• When Worf's father beams on board, he greets O'Brien as a fellow "chief petty officer," a noncommissioned rank. Yet Riker calls O'Brien "Lieutenant" in "Where Silence Has Lease."

EQUIPMENT ODDITIES

• The doors are reading the script again. At the end of the episode, Picard—standing very near the entrance of the transporter room—meets Worf's human parents. Worf's father begins dropping hints that he would like to see the ship, and Worf's mother hustles him inside for transport. Picard turns, listening politely, and the doors close between him and the couple, right in Picard's face. How did they know that Picard didn't want to continue the conversation? Do they have an "obnoxious parent" sensor?

CONTINUITY AND PRODUCTION PROBLEMS

• As Wesley enters the holodeck, the camera gives us a full view of Jack Crusher in his movie-style uniform. He isn't wearing a communicator. Then Wesley starts up the message, and a *NextGen*-style communicator appears on his chest.

• Does anyone else find it odd that Jack Crusher talks to Wesley dressed in a *Classic* movie uniform? Jack supposedly recorded the message only eighteen years ago. Did Starfleet really use the same uniform for that many years?

TRIVIA ANSWERS

1. Earth Station Bobruisk.
2. Five.

BROTHERS

Star Dates: 44085.7—44091.1

D r. Noonian Soong, thought to have died in the attack of the crystalline entity on Omicron Theta, recalls Data by activating a homing device implanted within his brain. Soong has perfected an emotion chip he wishes to give his "son" before he dies. Unfortunately, the homing signal also draws Lore, who steals the chip and seriously injures his father before fleeing.

TRIVIA QUESTIONS

1. Due to the medical emergency aboard the ship, Picard cuts short the crew's liberty on what planet?

2. What panel backs on to Science Station 2 on the main bridge?

ALTERNATE VIEWPOINTS AND CORRECTIONS

• On page 216 of the *NextGen Guide,* I noted that Data operates a panel to the right of the turbolift doors, thereby changing the destination of the turbolift. I stated that—aside from "Power Play" (an episode that shows a panel to the left of the turbolift doors)—this was the only time I could remember seeing a control panel in a turbolift. David J. Ferrier of Washington, DC, wrote to remind me of the control panel that the young girl uses in "Disaster" to secure some optical fiber before she, Picard, and the other two children begin their ascent in the turbolift shaft. I did see this instance when I reviewed that episode. However, the size, location, and shape of the enclosure reminded me a lot of the turbolift's motion indicator. I assumed that the girl had previously removed this cover and the control panels shown normally resided behind it.

PLOT OVERSIGHTS

• Attempting to leave the ship after discovering that O'Brien has disabled the site-to-site transport, Data asks the computer to show him the shortest route to Transporter Room 1. Data doesn't know this already? After all the time he's spent on this ship?

• As Data strolls along to Transporter Room 1, it appears that the Security teams have several good shots at him but fail to take them. In a situation like this, wouldn't it be better to shoot first and ask questions later? (Of course, if they did…it would be a short show.)

• Does it seem like Data should have recognized Soong a lot faster than La Forge, and not the other way around?

• I suppose after you get used to technology it's very difficult to imagine doing things in a primitive twentieth-century way. In this episode, La Forge needs some type of force field power to neutralize the force field around the main bridge. A medical confinement field in sick bay is the only one available. It surrounds a sick child. Picard tells La Forge to confer with Crusher and determine the minimum amount of energy needed to sustain the field. Why not just shut the thing off? The boy is completely enclosed in a glass housing with the exception of a few hand holes. Stuff something in the holes, shut the field off, nullify the field around the main bridge, turn the medical confinement field back on, and pull out the stuff that you shoved in the holes. The boy has a large air space in which to breathe. He won't suffocate.

• Again, the creators give us no indication that anyone went back to

Soong's lab after he died to glean whatever they could from his notes. (I mentioned a similar problem with Dr. Ira Graves's lab in the *NextGen Guide* under "The Schizoid Man.")

• This episode creates some confusion about the timeline of Lore's deactivation and the arrival of the crystalline entity at Omicron Theta. Lore and Soong agree that Soong deactivated Lore because the colonists feared him. Then Soong built Data. Yet in "Datalore" we discover that Lore summoned the crystalline entity, and it rewarded him for the lives it devoured on the planet. These facts won't fit together. If Soong deactivated Lore before building Data, Lore must have contacted the crystalline entity before deactivation. Then a period of time elapsed and the crystalline entity arrived. Just how quickly can Soong throw one of these androids together? And if Lore was deactivated when the crystalline entity arrived, how did the crystalline entity reward Lore? (Put him back together, give him a juice, take him apart, and leave him on the shelf?)

EQUIPMENT ODDITIES

• When life support fails on the main bridge, why doesn't Picard order everyone to the battle bridge? After all, it has a cool captain's chair, really neat displays, a viewscreen, stations for Tactical, Ops, conn. Seems like a logical choice to me.

• Is there some reason that the biofilter on the transporter can't screen out the parasitic infection in the boy? Granted, Data fiddles with the transporters early in the show and makes them almost inoperable, but what about

before the show begins? The boy is already sick in the opening scene.

• Just before beaming off the *Enterprise*, Data seals Riker and O'Brien into the transporter pads with a force field. Yet in the next scene on the *Enterprise*, Riker is back in Main Engineering. Who deactivated the force field? Isn't it under Data's command? Did he put in a "time out" command just to be a nice guy?

TRIVIA ANSWERS

1. Ogus II.
2. J-14 Baker.

SUDDENLY HUMAN

Star Date: 44143.7

When the crew of the *Enterprise* finds a young human male named Jono as part of the injured crew on a Talarian training craft, DNA testing reveals that he is the grandson of an admiral in Starfleet. At first Picard believes that returning the boy to his blood relatives is the proper course, but in time he realizes that Jono is more Talarian than human.

ALTERNATE VIEWPOINTS AND CORRECTIONS

• In my review of this episode, on page 218 of the *NextGen Guide*, I noted that Crusher's skills must be improving, since Picard appears on the bridge shortly after being stabbed by Jono and seems fine, whereas in "Who Watches the Watchers," Picard took an arrow in a similar location and wore a sling even after Crusher's ministrations. Sue Dyke of Shropshire, England, related that even twentieth-century medicine would allow the captain to appear on the bridge a short time later, since the injury dealt solely with skin and the sternum. Sue recounted that she fractured her sternum some years ago and the doctors gave her some painkillers but nothing else—no cast, no sling, nothing.

TRIVIA QUESTIONS

1. Who were Jono's human parents?

2. Where was Captain Endar's son killed?

PLOT OVERSIGHTS

• Obviously, Federation medical technology has removed all fear of radiation contamination. Most of the young Talarian males suffer from radiation injuries. This would imply a radiation *source,* yet the away team beams over without any protective clothing. Even if the radiation source had ceased emitting, wouldn't there be some residual radiation from the surrounding equipment?

EQUIPMENT ODDITIES

• At one point, Jono's human grandmother sends a message saying how overjoyed she is to hear that he is alive.

She also comments that she wonders what he looks like. So the *Enterprise* sent information about Jono to Starfleet and they didn't include a visual?

CONTINUITY AND PRODUCTION PROBLEMS

• Again, during an observation lounge meeting, the stars start out completely still in the wide shots and then move in the close-up! (There must be some sort of production problem with making the stars move in the wide shots. This happens too often to be a simple oversight. I can't believe that the creators are shaking their fists each time and saying, "Rats! We forgot to turn the crank and make the star curtain move…again!")

• I don't quite know how to say this. I admit I'm a bit embarrassed to point it out. But our lovely and sophisticated Dr. Beverly Crusher…well…um…it's just that—during the first observation lounge meeting to discuss Jono—she's…for lack of a better word…*pipless!* Her rank insignia has completely disappeared from her collar. Thankfully, she quickly discovers this egregious oversight and in the following scenes returns fully pipped in all her splendor.

• It's a delightful moment. Wesley gets smacked in the face with a banana split in Ten-Forward. (Not that it's delightful that Wesley gets smacked. Or maybe it is, depending on your viewpoint. It's delightful because it's *messy.*) There is a continuity problem here, though. Jono sits down on Wesley's left. Wesley scoots his bowl over to Jono. Jono takes a spoon and jams it into the bowl. The banana split hits Wesley from his *right* side.

• Just after Jono stabs Picard, the episode moves to sick bay. Picard lies in a bed. A nurse lifts the aluminum foil sheet. Crusher reaches over the sheet awkwardly to use a medical doodad on Picard. The shot changes and suddenly Crusher's hand is under the nurse's arm.

TRIVIA ANSWERS

1. Connor and Moira Rossa.
2. Castal I.

REMEMBER ME

Star Dates: 44161.2—44162.8

A warp core accident traps Crusher in a warp bubble reality shaped by her last thought before entry—a reality in which everyone dear to her begins disappearing. As her universe collapses—due to the shrinkage of the warp bubble—the Traveler ("Where No One Has Gone Before") appears and helps Wesley rescue her.

ALTERNATE VIEWPOINTS AND CORRECTIONS

• In the middle portion of the episode, La Forge and Wesley attempt to create a stable threshold to the warp bubble twice, without success. Each time the threshold appears in Crusher's current location. (It is, after all, her

reality.) Yet, when the Traveler and Wesley make the attempt, Crusher must go to Engineering to find the threshold. On page 220 of the *NextGen Guide,* I suggested that the creators did this simply to add tension to the final moments of the show, that it would make just as much sense to have the threshold appear at Crusher's location again. (As I said, it is, after all, her reality.) Scott Charrington of County Antrim, Northern Ireland, suggested that the stable threshold appeared in Engineering precisely *because* the Traveler helped the third time. On the other hand, Miss Nick Shaw of Middlesex, England, believes that Crusher concluded that the threshold would be in Engineering and therefore it was—since her thoughts controlled her reality.

TRIVIA QUESTIONS

1. Where did Crusher intern with Dr. Dalen Quaice?

2. What Starfleet ship reported normal operations when contacted by the *Enterprise*?

PLOT OVERSIGHTS

• After the Traveler appears to help rescue Crusher from the warp bubble, Picard makes a log entry stating that the *Enterprise* will return to the precise position where the subspace bubble was formed. Subsequent shots show the *Enterprise* reentering the space dock. Is this right? Isn't everything constantly moving in the universe? Planets orbit stars. Stars orbit in galaxies. Galaxies move through the universe. Wouldn't the precise position where the warp bubble originally formed be someplace other than the space dock?

• The computer tells Crusher that her universe is a bubble 705 meters in diameter. Then the bubble begins collapsing and the computer tells her that it can maintain life support for 4 minutes, 17 seconds. A short time later, La Forge says the bubble is collapsing at 15 meters per second and will disappear in about 4 minutes. If the bubble is collapsing at 15 meters per second and it's 705 meters in diameter, it will be gone in 47 seconds, not 4 minutes. To take 4 minutes at 15 meters per second, the bubble would have to be 3,600 meters in diameter at the beginning.

• This episode has given me a new appreciation for an old classic. After all, I thought *The Wizard of Oz* was a fun movie, but I never suspected that it would still be so popular that the chief medical officer of the flagship of the Federation in the *twenty-fourth century* would be so familiar with it that she would describe her situation as, "Click my heels together three times and I'm back in Kansas."

• As the bubble shrinks, the ship rocks due to explosive decompression as the bulkheads evaporate. Amazingly enough, when Crusher makes her run for Engineering, the ship disappears right behind her but the explosive decompression doesn't affect her!

• And speaking of Crusher's jog through the ship, these twenty-fourth century humans are really fit. La Forge

claimed the bubble was contracting at 15 meters per second. That's 54 kilometers an hour! (Or 30 miles per hour for those of us still using the Imperial measuring system. Then again, maybe Crusher competes in the jogging/dancing doctor's competition during the Galactica Olympiad.)

• Poor Wesley. He makes the supreme effort to rescue his mother, collapses in exhaustion afterward, and *nobody* seems to care. He just lies there until his mother finally comes over to help him up.

EQUIPMENT ODDITIES

• Given the number of times aliens pop onto the *Enterprise*—as the Traveler does in this episode—shouldn't Worf have some sort of sensor array that would alert him immediately to an intruder?

• The main computer seems to pick and choose when it's going to answer questions. During a monologue, as Crusher attempts to figure out her situation, she asks, "Could my thought have created this reality?" The computer says nothing. Then she talks for a few moments longer and says, "My thoughts created this reality. Could they get me out of it again? Can it be that simple?" This time the computer answers. Crusher snaps that she wasn't talking to it, and the computer refrains from speaking again until spoken to.

CONTINUITY AND PRODUCTION PROBLEMS

• I'm told that the suitcase that Quaice carries as he beams aboard the *Enterprise* looks just like a Sharp compact video camera case.

• The reflection of a boom mike makes an unscheduled appearance in this episode. After asking the main computer all sorts of questions such as when she came aboard and the purpose of the *Enterprise,* Dr. Crusher walks back onto the bridge and down the ramp toward the captain's chair. Watch the top of the vertical light panel that stands between the turbolift and the Engineering station along the back wall of the bridge.

• When first trapped by the warp bubble, Crusher does not wear her lab coat. She acquires it while inside the warp bubble, and when she jumps through the threshold at the conclusion of the episode, she retains it. In other words, a lab coat created in a warp bubble reality can exist in our reality? Does this apply to other items as well? (Wesley could make quite a business of this if he could figure out how to create these warp bubbles on demand and then establish stable thresholds. I mean, given a large enough warp bubble, maybe you could create an entire *Galaxy*-class starship and fly it back into our reality. Of course, there are other possibilities for this warp bubble stuff if you think about it. A person could conjure up *any* thought, hold it for a moment, have Wesley zap him or her, and then live for a few days in a reality based on that thought.)

TRIVIA ANSWERS

1. Delos IV. (Interestingly enough, Delos is also the star system of the two worlds in "Symbiosis." In fact, one of the two worlds is the fourth planet in the star system, otherwise known as Delos IV! Either there're two Delos systems, or Crusher was feigning ignorance during that

episode. Thanks to Stephen Mendenhall of Ann Arbor, MI, for pointing this out.)
2. The USS *Wellington.*

LEGACY

Star Dates: 44215.2—44225.3

Tracking an escape pod to Turkana IV—Tasha Yar's home planet—an away team finds that one of the colony's two warring factions, the Alliance, has taken the survivors hostage. The other faction, the Coalition, offers Picard help in the form of Ishara Yar, Tasha's sister. Ishara soon betrays the crew's trust by attempting to sabotage an Alliance power plant.

TRIVIA QUESTIONS

1. What card does Data choose during Riker's trick?

2. Who is the engineer of the USS *Archos*?

ALTERNATE VIEWPOINTS AND CORRECTIONS

• I erred in my plot summary of this episode on page 221 of the *NextGen Guide.* I stated that Riker stunned Ishara at the end of the episode when, in fact—As Bill DeLong of Springfield, MO, correctly pointed out—Data stunned Ishara.

PLOT OVERSIGHTS

• In the opening scene of the episode, Riker, Data, Troi, and Worf enjoy a friendly game of poker. At one point, Riker shoves his entire pile of chips into the center of the table and bets Data that he can find any card that the android hides in the deck and furthermore that the android will help him find it. Riker does exactly as he stipulates. Data then describes the method that Riker used to accomplish the feat and *takes the chips.* Hold it: Just because Data figured out how Riker accomplished the task doesn't nullify the bet. Of course, it's a trick! Did anyone really think it wouldn't be a trick? By what logical means does Data deduce that he won the bet?

• Crusher goes along on the initial away team mission, a fact that disturbs Worf greatly, given the anarchy of the colony. Riker's rebuttal to the Security chief is that the hostages may need immediate medical attention. That makes sense. So why doesn't Crusher go along when the actual recovery takes place?

• After Ishara beams back to the colony, an establishing shot shows the *Enterprise* orbiting a planet—presumably Turkana IV. Then the action moves indoors, and Data visits Riker. The android states that it has been "days" since Ishara left. Why is the *Enterprise* still orbiting Turkana IV "days" later? They've rescued the crew of the Archos. Or is this *another* planet? And if so, what planet is it? Did the creators have the *Enterprise* fly off to another planet and *they didn't tell us*?!

EQUIPMENT ODDITIES

• During the actual rescue of the hostages, Riker fires at a Coalition guard, knocking him backward and unconscious. Immediately—without readjusting any settings—Riker joins his phaser to Worf's. The two beams blow the doors off the detention cell. I didn't think a phaser on stun could do that type of damage. (Gasp! Did Riker have his phaser set to kill? Is he guilty *again* of the wanton slaughter of an enemy? See my review of "The Vengeance Factor" in the *NextGen Guide.*)

• Why is Data holding Ishara's proximity detector at the conclusion of the episode? Didn't the crew of the *Enterprise* put it back in Ishara? After all, without it she could infiltrate Alliance headquarters and finish the job she started when Data stunned her.

CONTINUITY AND PRODUCTION PROBLEMS

• After interceding for Ishara with Picard, Data strolls out of the ready room and up the ramp to tell her the good news. In the close-ups it looks like Data wears three solid pips on his collar, the rank of a full commander. (Trying to impress the new girl on the block, eh? On the other hand, it may just be a reflection of some kind.)

• At the very end of the episode, Riker and Data have a heart-to-pump talk. Just after telling Data to sit down, Riker reaches up with his right hand to stroke his beard. The shot changes, and instantly Riker rubs his beard with his left hand.

TRIVIA ANSWERS

1. The jack of hearts.
2. Tan T'su.

REUNION

Star Date: 44246.3

Picard serves as arbiter of succession for the leadership of the Klingon High Council, attempting to discover who poisoned K'mpec among the two seeking the high office, Duras and Gowron. Federation ambassador K'Ehleyr attends the proceedings as well and brings a surprise for Worf, a son named Alexander. Unfortunately, K'Ehleyr grows too curious about Worf's discommendation, and Duras kills her. Enraged, Worf seeks his revenge and kills Duras.

TRIVIA QUESTIONS

1. What ship ferries Duras to the proceedings?

2. For how many generations has Worf's bat'leth been in his family?

ALTERNATE VIEWPOINTS AND CORRECTIONS

• I expressed my wonderment on pages 224 and 225 of the *NextGen Guide* at Alexander's development, given that it's been only a little over a year since his conception during the episode "The Emissary." Patricia Pozywak of Elyria, OH, wrote to remind me that we know little of the gestation period and early development of Klingons. Richard Smith of Surrey, England, suggested that time dilation effects of prolonged travel at relativistic speed might account for the disparity. Several others wrote to suggest that Alexander was conceived during the prior relationship between Worf and K'Ehleyr. This sounds plausible until you remember that Alexander gave his birth date in "New Ground," placing it between the star dates of "The Emissary" and "Reunion." (A birth date that indicates that he was about 1,041 units old at the time of this episode. Those Klingons sure do develop fast! And as long as we are on the subject, the adult Alexander in "Firstborn" claimed to be three years old in this episode.)

PLOT OVERSIGHTS

• When meeting with Picard in this episode, the ailing K'mpec chides the captain by starting the conversation with, "It's about time you arrived!" I felt bad for Picard because it's really not his fault that he's late. Alexander beamed over with K'Ehleyr, and she had to get her son enrolled in preschool first before notifying Picard of K'mpec's invitation. (I'm sure K'Ehleyr couldn't just drop the boy off. There were forms to fill out, payment schedules to arrange, a teacher/student etiquette handbook to go over, a *Special Rules for Klingon Children* pamphlet to examine—"No biting, no backfisting, no palming, no ripping out the heart of your fellow classmate and parading it around the room....")

EQUIPMENT ODDITIES

• Does the main computer use the personal communicators to locate crew members on the *Enterprise*? Seeking vengeance, Worf goes to his quarters grabs his bat'leth, takes off his sash and communicator, and beams over to Duras's ship. Moments later, Riker asks the main computer for Worf's location, and it replies that Worf beamed over from Duras's ship. (I suppose the computer could sense when a communicator is removed and switch to other means of tracking a crew member, but why does the computer locate the spirit-infested Troi, Data, and O'Brien in a turbolift when they remove their communicators in "Power Play"?)

CONTINUITY AND PRODUCTION PROBLEMS

• Right after the first communication with Duras, Picard tells K'Ehleyr to be in Transporter Room 6 in one hour. Standing behind Worf, just to his left, she nods and starts moving to Worf's right. The camera angle changes to show us the area just to Worf's right, but K'Ehleyr has suddenly disappeared. Moments later, the camera returns to K'Ehleyr's original position, but she isn't there either. Did she jump down a Jefferies tube?

• When K'Ehleyr dies, her face starts out turned to the left. Then Worf tells Alexander to look on his mother's dead body and always remember. Now K'Ehleyr's face is turned to her right.

FUTURE IMPERFECT

Star Date: 44286.5

A lonely young alien hidden deep within the caverns of a planet near the Neutral Zone sends out unusual subspace emissions to lure down an away team. Trapping Riker, the boy uses neural scanners and holographic projectors to create simulations drawn from the first officer's mind—one of them set sixteen years in the future.

RUMINATIONS

When I reviewed this episode for the NextGen Guide, I completely missed a very lovely touch added by the creators when they redesigned the communicators. My nitpicking buddy Darrin Hull brought it to my attention. The communicators double as rank insignia. Crusher has three bars behind hers, Nurse Ogawa only has one, and Riker has four.

GREAT LINES

"Shut up! As in 'close your mouth and stop talking!'"—Riker to Picard after he discovers that the future scenario is a fake. Nominated by Matt Cavic of Ballwin, MO.

TRIVIA QUESTIONS

1. On what planet does the young alien live?

2. What is the name of Riker's "great fishing" holodeck program?

PLOT OVERSIGHTS

• As part of the future fantasy set sixteen years hence, Riker awakes in sick bay. A short time later, Crusher implies that he has been in a coma for ten days. If he's been in a coma for ten days, why is he still dressed in his uniform? Does Crusher know that Riker absolutely hates those silly open-backed hospital gowns?

• At one point Troi accompanies Riker to his quarters. As the pair walk through the door, a young boy toots on a trombone. In this future fantasy, the boy is Jean-Luc, Riker's son. The boy looks up and says, "Hi, Dad," and then proceeds with his playing. Now, maybe Crusher got to the little guy ahead of time and told him to act nonchalant, but if your father—your only surviving parent—had just come out of a coma lasting ten days, wouldn't your reaction be a little stronger than "Hi, Dad"?

• After the first fantasy disappears—replaced by a secret Romulan base scenario in which the Romulans have subjected Riker to a holographically generated future—Romulan commander Tomalak asks Riker what gave them away. Riker replies that it was their selection of his wife, since Minuet was herself only a holo-graphically generated character (see "11001001"). Tomalak finds this absurd, since Minuet lives as real as any woman in Riker's mind. This begs a question: Who decided that Minuet would be dead in the first scenario? There are only two possibilities, Riker or the young alien, since those two are the only real individuals involved. Let's consider Riker. Would he want to be part of a holodeck fantasy that featured a living, breathing, flesh-and-blood Minuet? (Yes, yes, yes, yes, yes.) Does it seem reasonable that *Riker* would choose for her to be dead? (No, no, no, no, no.) What about the young alien? Would he want his "mom" in the scenario to be dead? Well... maybe. But he sure *sounds* like he misses his real mom at the conclusion of the episode. With Minuet alive, couldn't he enjoy the company of a larger family unit? (Of course, if Minuet was alive in the future scenario, it would be a short show, since Riker would instantly know that it was fake!)

• When Riker first experiences a computer delay early in the future scenario, Crusher blames it on a "processing attenuator." But later, when questioning La Forge, Riker calls it a "faulty processing accelerator."

• I wonder whatever happened to the young alien. He beams back to the ship with Riker, but that's the last we hear of him.

TRIVIA ANSWERS

1. Alpha Onias III.
2. Curtis Creek.

FINAL MISSION

Star Dates: 44307.3—44307.6

K nowing that Wesley will soon leave for Starfleet Academy, Picard takes him along for a set of negotiations with a group of miners. Unfortunately, the shuttle that the miners send for Picard malfunctions and crashes on an inhospitable moon. When Picard becomes injured, Wesley must use the limited available resources to save the captain's life along with his own.

TRIVIA QUESTIONS

1. Who is the chairman of Gamelan V?

2. What is the name of Captain Dirgo's shuttle?

PLOT OVERSIGHTS

• La Forge tells Picard that he has run safety and operational inspections on the shuttle that comes to pick up the captain. Yet, after the shuttle crashes, its captain—a man named Dirgo—reveals that there aren't any emergency rations. Shouldn't this fact show up in La Forge's *safety* inspection?

• After reaching a cave on the surface of the moon, Picard seems to indicate that he believes it has natural origins. However, the wide shots clearly show a nicely defined, humanoid-size staircase leading downward. Is there a natural process that can create such a structure?

• After discovering the cave, the trio soon finds a fountain that gurgles upward with beautiful-looking water. Unfortunately, an annular force field springs up around the fountain whenever someone approaches. In addition, a sentinel composed of some form of energy stands guard. Dirgo dies while using brute force trying to get to the water, but Wesley eventually finds a way to deactivate both the sentinel and the force field, thereby bringing life-sustaining water to his injured captain. Unfortunately, no one seems interested in the origins of this setting. Who constructed the staircase in the cave? Where did the fountain come from? Who installed the force field and released the sentinel? (My guess would be a race of cruel practical jokemasters who roam the galaxy looking for prime locations with high potentials. "Hey, there's a really hot and dry moon! What say we go down there and build a cool, refreshing fountain and then seal it off with a force field just in case someone crash-lands on the surface? Har, har, har, har!")

• In this episode, Riker exposes the crew to almost lethal levels of radiation as he tows a garbage barge filled with unstable waste products through the asteroid belt of a planetary system and then slingshots it into the sun. I myself mentioned a few other options in the *NextGen Guide*. The armchair captains of the Nitpicker's Guild came up with additional ones. All constitute significantly less risk to the crew. Riker could have slung the barge out of the star system, gone and rescued Picard, and then returned to dispose of it. There's plenty of space between star systems, and the *Enterprise* shouldn't have any difficulty finding the barge again. Then again, the *less* environmentally concerned members of the Nitpicker's Guild wondered why Riker didn't just let the thing break up in the asteroid belt. Nobody needs to fiddle around in there anyway, right? So what if it has a little radiation coming from it?

EQUIPMENT ODDITIES

• At the end of the episode, Crusher and an away team rescue the injured Picard and Wesley. Crew members carry Picard, on a stretcher, out of the cave. Obviously the magnetic fields on the moon must be so severe that the transporters won't function. I can think of no other reason why our good doctor would want to subject a patient with internal injuries to the jostling of a stretcher when the transporter could beam him directly to sick bay.

CONTINUITY AND PRODUCTION PROBLEMS

• After Picard is injured, Wesley and Dirgo argue about how to proceed. During the discussion, Dirgo comes down from a ledge above the fountain, and the dialogue continues with one camera angle showing us Dirgo's back and Wesley's face while the other gives us the reverse of this. Twice Dirgo gestures with his right hand, the camera cuts to a new angle, and he completes the motion with his left hand.

TRIVIA ANSWERS

1. Songi.
2. *Nenebek.*

THE LOSS

Star Date: 44356.9

When a colony of two-dimensional beings unintentionally traps the *Enterprise,* their collective consciousness overpowers Troi, effectively blinding her empathic sense. As Troi struggles with her loss, the ship faces a greater peril: The creatures are dragging the ship toward a cosmic string—an entity with the gravitational forces of a black hole.

TRIVIA QUESTIONS

1. Who mans the conn station during this episode?

2. Where did La Forge see a visual motion pattern similar to the one created by the two-dimensional entities?

PLOT OVERSIGHTS

• Obviously no one has communicated the severity of the crisis facing the *Enterprise* to Troi. After Picard discovers that photon torpedoes have no effect on the two-dimensional beings and the progress toward the cosmic string continues, the episode transitions to Troi clearing out her office. The *Enterprise* sits only hours away from a complete shredding by a cosmic string, and Troi is worried about cleaning out her office? She must have a great deal of faith in the bridge crew.

• To avoid any possible misinterpretation as I reveal this next nit (*perish* the thought), I will quote directly from the episode. While discussing the situation with Data near the end of the episode, Troi says, "You're convinced the string's gravitation is pulling them in." Data replies, "Because the cluster is two-dimensional, I do not have enough direct evidence to support that assumption. However, it is the most reasonable hypothesis." Now, all during the episode, multiple characters—including Data—tell us that the *Enterprise* travels at a constant course and speed toward the cosmic string. Yet, a body under gravitational attraction does not travel at a constant speed. It continually accelerates. Data would know this. If the string travels at a constant speed toward the string, it cannot be solely under the influence of the string's gravitational pull.

CHANGED PREMISES

• After losing her powers, Troi experiences all the stages of grief. In the process, she makes statements such as "How do you people live like this?" and "I don't know what to do. All I see is surfaces. Nothing seems real." These statements give us the impression that Troi has never been without her em-

pathic powers. Yet "Tin Man" clearly establishes that normal Betazoid children are not born with their empathic powers. This transition occurs at adolescence, allowing plenty of times for our beloved counselor to form memories of interacting with humanoids prior to having her empathic sense.

EQUIPMENT ODDITIES

• During the first attempt to break free, Picard orders one-quarter impulse. A shot featuring La Forge in Main Engineering shows a reflection of the blue doughnut lights trotting along. Then Picard takes the ship to one-half impulse. The following shot of La Forge shows the lights moving faster. Finally Picard orders full impulse, and the following shot shows the lights going even faster. I'm confused. I thought the speed of the lights correlated to the current *warp* speed.

• This show demonstrates that a "Klingon Dozen" is…ten! At one point La Forge suggests firing a "half a dozen" photon torpedoes to detonate in front of the two-dimensional creatures. Picard agrees, and Worf punches a series of buttons. The *Enterprise* fires, and *five* photon torpedoes launch and then detonate.

CONTINUITY AND PRODUCTION PROBLEMS

• At the very end of the episode, Riker, Crusher, Troi, and Guinan enjoy a few moments in Ten-Forward. Eventually only Riker and Troi remain at the table. In the shot featuring Troi, her arms rest on the table, with her hands clasped in front of her. In the shot featuring Riker, Troi's arms are folded. As the shots mix back and forth, Troi experiences "flying arm syndrome."

TRIVIA ANSWERS

1. Ensign Allenby.
2. While diving in the coral reefs on Bracas V.

DATA'S DAY

Star Date: 44390.1

A s part of his attempt to keep Bruce Maddox supplied with research information, Data makes a record of an entire day for later transmission to the cyberneticist. During this day, Miles O'Brien and Keiko Ishikawa wed, and the crew discovers that Vulcan ambassador T'Pel is actually a Romulan spy.

TRIVIA QUESTIONS

1. What is the name of the ship that brings T'Pel to the *Enterprise*?

2. Where did Crusher win first place in a tap and jazz competition?

PLOT OVERSIGHTS

• At the very beginning of this episode, Riker relieves Data and begins "day watch." At the end of the episode, Data relieves Worf and begins "night watch." In both cases, the light levels for night watch are much lower than for day watch. Pre- sumably the creators want to give us the impression that evening has settled on the *Enterprise*—in much the same way that airlines dim the lights in their airplanes when flying at night. However, does the analogy really hold? It's *always* dark in space. There is no day or night. Yes, it might be beneficial to dim the lights in the corridors for twelve hours at a time to give the crew a feeling of the normal circadian rhythm of Earth, but how does this benefit the bridge? Does it provide a reminder to the third-shift bridge crew that they are stuck working while everyone else gets to go to bed? Does it help them see their panels better? Does it keep them awake?

• And while we are on the subject of day shift and night shift, isn't it convenient that in the past sixty or so episodes, the vast majority of the challenges faced by the *Enterprise* have occurred during the day shift?

• In the twenty-fourth century, females must outgrow any need for privacy. As Crusher finishes giving Lieutenant Juarez a prenatal exam, Data waltzes right into sick bay. The poor woman is sprawled on a table in the middle of the room, but evidently no one bothered to lock the doors or even put up a "Do Not Disturb" sign.

• After almost refusing Data's request to teach him how to dance, Crusher acquiesces on the basis that Data mention it to no one. She does not want to be known as the "dancing doctor" again. To reinforce her suggestion, she zips her lips—an amazing feat given that zippers do not exists in the twenty-third century (and presumably the twenty-fourth), according to none other than the Great Bird of the Galaxy himself, Gene Roddenberry. Perhaps the motion has remained as one of those interesting anachronistic artifacts.

• Feeling a need to learn to dance, Data meets Crusher on the holodeck. Not understanding that Data desires to dance at Miles and Keiko's wedding, Crusher begins teaching Data how to tap-dance. By watching the doctor's feet, Data learns almost instantaneously, flawlessly replicating each of her movements. Well... almost flawlessly. At one point Crusher executes a movement in which she jumps and lands with her feet crossed. She does this twice in the same segment. Data copies the rhythm of her taps but does not cross his feet, taking instead an easier movement (at least from the perspective of my untrained eye).

• Analyse Ivey tells me that Crusher attempts to teach Data a waltz when she asks the computer for a song that would be more appropriate to a foxtrot. Then, after the good doctor departs, Data quickly abandons the waltz and selects a style of dance more appropriate to the song.

• This good old Data guy really learns fast. Either that, or he deserves a lot more credit for being sly. After awkwardly dancing with Crusher for a few moments, Data asks the holodeck to generate a dance partner, and suddenly the android is as smooth as glass in his movements. It makes me wonder if Data could really dance all along and simply wanted to spend a little time with his hands on the doctor.

EQUIPMENT ODDITIES

• Again we are faced with the age-old question "Who does what on the *Enterprise*?" As O'Brien attempts to beam T'Pel over to the Romulan vessel, the Romulans beam her off the transporter pad—leaving behind a small pile of organic goo in an attempt to convince Picard that T'Pel has died in a transporter accident. As this occurs, both Worf and Data, stationed on the bridge, intervene in the transport process. Is this or is this not O'Brien's job? Do the senior officers not trust him?

• Directly after T'Pel's transporter "accident," Picard speaks with Romulan admiral Mendak. Bear in mind that the *Enterprise* is in the Neutral Zone, head to head with a Romulan warbird, and a Vulcan ambassador has just died under mysterious causes. Yet the indicator panel between the upper turbolift and the Engineering station shows the *Enterprise* at normal status. Wouldn't this be a good time to be on some kind of alert status? If not red alert, how about yellow?

CONTINUITY AND PRODUCTION PROBLEMS

• Paged by sick bay, Crusher cuts short her dance lesson with Data. She grabs a towel from the bar in the holodeck created studio, wipes her brow, and makes a hasty exit. The shot changes, and suddenly the towel reappears on the bar.

TRIVIA ANSWERS

1. The USS *Zhukov*.
2. At St. Louis Academy.

THE WOUNDED

Star Date: 44429.6

O'Brien's former captain acts on his suspicions that the Cardassians are massing weaponry despite a recent peace agreement and illegally destroys a Cardassian research station. While believing that Captain Maxwell's suspicions may be correct, Picard must stop the rogue captain before he plunges the Federation back into war.

TRIVIA QUESTIONS

1. On what ship did O'Brien serve with Maxwell?

2. Where did Worf catch the Cardassian accessing a computer terminal?

ALTERNATE VIEWPOINTS AND CORRECTIONS

• On page 235 of the *NextGen Guide,* I addressed a Cardassian as "Captain Gul Macet." In fact, this is redundant, since "Gul" is the Cardassian designation for "Captain."

• Richard Smith of Surrey, England, wrote to point out that the USS *Phoenix* is a *Nebula*-class starship, not a *"Nebular"*-class starship, as I indicated in the answer for the first trivia question on page 236 of the *NextGen Guide.* In my defense, I might raise the point that Gul Macet identifies the ship as *"Nebular"*-class, and since all the information in the *NextGen Guide* came directly from the television show…(Wink, wink.)

• In my review of this episode, on page 236 I wrote that Data states that the *Phoenix* has moved outside the weapons range of a Cardassian vessel, while the graphic shows the *Phoenix inside* the weapons range circles for the Cardassian vessel. Andrew LaMance of East Ridge, TN, reminded me that the graphic of the weapons range is probably a two-dimensional representation of a sphere. If the *Phoenix* is below the Cardassian vessel it would be possible for the display to look like it indicated the *Phoenix* was *inside* the weapons range when viewed from "above," when in fact the *Phoenix* was still *outside* the weapons range. On the other hand, Andrew agreed that the indicator probably wasn't very useful given this scenario but left open the possibility that we simply do not understand how to read the graphic. John Potts of London, England, thought that perhaps the *Phoenix* jumped into the Cardassian vessel's weapons range at the last moment before firing its photon torpedoes.

PLOT OVERSIGHTS

• After the *Phoenix* destroys a Cardassian vessel and freighter, Picard sets course for the rogue Starfleet vessel at warp 9. Later in the show, Data calls Picard into his ready room and reports that they have "located" the

Phoenix. Haven't they already located the *Phoenix?* Hasn't the *Enterprise* chased the *Phoenix* for some time now?

• With Maxwell threatening to destroy another Cardassian freighter, O'Brien asks for a chance to beam over and talk with him. Picard replies that Maxwell probably won't lower his shields, at which point O'Brien spews out a bunch of sensitive technical information about the *Phoenix* that will allow him to beam through its shields. Amazingly enough, Gul Macet sits on the bridge, listening to the information. Does this seem like a good idea?

EQUIPMENT ODDITIES

• In this episode, Picard on the *Enterprise,* some distance away, watches helplessly as Maxwell on the *Phoenix* hunts down a Cardassian freighter. In desperation, Picard supplies a Cardassian with the prefix codes for the *Phoenix* so the Cardassians can "dismantle" its shields. From the movie *Star Trek II: The Wrath of Khan* I got the impression that prefix codes can be used to seize remote control of a vessel. But if that's true, why doesn't Picard just disable the *Phoenix's* phasers and photons?

CONTINUITY AND PRODUCTION PROBLEMS

• Interestingly enough, the commissioning plaque for the *Phoenix* is in Ben Maxwell's ready room instead of the bridge. New interior decorator, maybe? And, yes, the *Tsiolkovsky* had its dedication plaque in a hallway during "The Naked Now." That ship probably had the same interior decorator as the *Phoenix.*

TRIVIA ANSWERS

1. The *Rutledge.*
2. On deck 35.

DEVIL'S DUE

Star Date: 44474.5

A beautiful con artist poses as Ardra—Ventax II's version of the devil—to reap the benefits of a one-thousand-year contract that's nearing its conclusion. Supposedly the inhabitants of the planet sold their souls to Ardra in exchange for a millennium of peace. Picard challenges the contract in Ventaxian court, with the agreement that if he loses, he will belong to Ardra as well.

TRIVIA QUESTIONS

1. Who heads the Federation science station on Ventax II?

2. How many aliases has Ardra used in this sector alone?

CHANGED PREMISES

• In the *Classic* episode "Day of the Dove," Kang claims that Klingons have no devil. Yet, in this episode, Ardra changes herself into Fek'lhr—a being she groups with other races' versions of the devil. Evidently Ardra is confused, or Kang was being melodramatic.

EQUIPMENT ODDITIES

• Sometimes I feel bad for the creators. The episode starts with Data giving a private rendition of "A Christmas Carol" for Picard. When Picard calls for freeze program, the fire halts in midflame! Excellent! Just as it should! Unfortunately, the candles around the fireplace *keep flickering!*

• And—as long as we are on the subject of this particular "freeze"—for some reason the ghost of Marley disappears shortly afterward, as do the fire and the snowflakes falling outside. Shouldn't the ghost hang around until someone says "End program"?

• At one point, Ardra magically replaces a male crew member who sits at Ops. There's no flash, no glow, and no alarms on Worf's panel, but the show later establishes that she is using standard transporter technology. How did she do this? (On the other hand, where did the poor guy go, and was he conscious at the time?)

• Approaching the *Enterprise* in a shuttle piloted by Data after Ardra flicked him down to the planet, Picard sees his *Galaxy*-class starship disappear. Later dialogue explains that Ardra extended her "cheap copy" of a Romulan cloaking device around it and then set up a subspace field to jam all outside communications. It seems to work pretty well for a "cheap copy." La Forge had to run a special test just to find Ardra's ship. (And if the test wasn't special, why didn't Worf find her ship already?) However, the real question is: When Riker and Worf discovered that she had enveloped them, why didn't they just move the ship? Or did Ardra seize them with

some sort of tractor beam as well? (Pretty powerful and sophisticated equipment for a con artist.)

CONTINUITY AND PRODUCTION PROBLEMS

• Those clever creators tried to show us the same scene twice and get away with it. Just before Picard beams down to the planet, we see an establishing wide shot with buildings in the background and people running toward the camera. A few moments later, the creators use the same footage again but start about two-thirds of the way through.

• Attempting to seduce Picard, Ardra dresses provocatively and blows into his quarters. Picard decides to act the better part of valor and tries to retreat, only to find the door locked. Ardra then drapes herself in the doorway to her quarters. The table between Picard and Ardra contains a Klingon knife. Its handle faces the left side of the screen. Then, just after Picard tells Ardra that he finds her obvious and vulgar, the handle suddenly switches to face the opposite way.

TRIVIA ANSWERS

1. Dr. Clarke.
2. Twenty-three.

MISCELLANEOUS
DATA TOTE BOARD

1. Number of parts played by Brent Spiner: twenty-nine
2. Number of access panels seen on Data: six
3. Number of times Data performs a feat of strength: at least eighteen
4. Number of musical instruments played by Data: three
5. Number of times Data mimicks another person's voice: four
6. Number of times Starfleet tries to violate Data's rights: two
7. Number of times Data works behind the bar in Ten-Forward: two
8. Number of times Data endangers the ship or crew: eight
9. Number of times Data takes the sole and crucial action at the end of the episode to save the ship and crew: four
10. Number of rank promotions received (i.e., Data gets more pips) or even offered to Data while on board the *Enterprise:* none

REFERENCES

1. Data; Dix's sidekick in "The Big Goodbye"; Lore in "Datalore," "Brothers," "Descent," and "Descent, Part II"; Sherlock Holmes in "Lonely Among Us" (sort of), "Elementary, Dear Data," and "Ship in a Bottle"; a comic in "The Outrageous Okana"; Ira Grave in "The Schizoid Man"; nanites in "Evolution"; Henry V in "The Defector"; holodeck swordsman in "Hollow Pursuits"; mannequin in "The Most Toys"; Dr. Noonian Soong in "Brothers," Birthright, Part I," and "Inheritance"; Ebeneezer Scrooge in "Devil's Due"; Friar Tuck in "Qpid"; a Romulan in "Unification I" and "Unification II"; a convict posing as Commander Steven Mullen of the *Essex* in "Power Play"; a Frenchman in "Time's Arrow"; Eli Hollander, Frank Hollander, a Mexican, a nondescript bad guy, and Annie Meyers in "A Fistful of Datas"; Hutch in "Starship Mine"; a shrink in "Frame of Mind"; Jaden in "Thine Own Self"; Eehat, young boy, old man, and Masaka in "Masks"; and Prospero in "Emergence."

2. Left forearm in "The Ensigns of Command"; right side of head in "The Best of Both Worlds, Part 2," "Disaster," "Birthright, Part 1" and "A Fistful of Datas"; left side of head in "Déjà Q" and "Masks"; back of head in "Time's Arrow" and "Time's Arrow, Part II"; complete skullcap and right forearm in *Star Trek: Generations.*

3. Pulls Wesley out of the stream with one hand in "Encounter at Farpoint," opens a door and tosses aside big rocks in "Hide and Q," destroys gun in "The Big Goodbye," opens a door in "Heart of Glory," tosses Yar and jumps down into a deep cavern in "The Arsenal of Freedom," bends bar in "The Measure of a Man," holds Q in "Déjà Q," tosses guy in "The Most Toys," tussles with Picard in "The Best of Both Worlds, Part 2," shoves open a door in "Night Terrors," lifts beams in "Hero Worship," picks up Borg with one hand (several times) in "Descent," jumps down from a high ledge in "Inheritance," and lifts an anvil in "Thine Own Self."

4. The violin in "Elementary, Dear Data," "The Ensigns of Command," and "Sarek," the oboe in "In Theory," and the guitar in "Silicon Avatar."

5. Mimicks Q and Picard in "Encounter at Farpoint," impersonates Picard again in "Brothers," and impersonates Picard again in "Descent, Part II."

6. Commander Bruce Maddox wants to disassemble him in "The Measure of a Man," and Admiral Haftel wants to take his child in "The Offspring." (Possibly even Picard by refusing to initially offer him a command at the begining of "Redemption II"?)

7. Makes Troi a Samarian Sunset in "Conundrum" and offers Scotty Aldebaran whiskey in "Relics."

8. Takes over the *Enterprise* in "Brothers," threatens Worf in "Power Play," provides the matrix for the villains in "A Fistful of Datas," refuses to transport the exocomps in "The Quality of Life," acts ugly in "Descent" and "Descent, Part II," and stabs Troi in "Phantasms" and as Masaka in "Masks."

9. Activates the Bussard collectors in "Night Terrors," decompresses the main shuttle bay in "Cause and Effect," vacates the metal parasites from the ship in "Cost of Living," and develops a cure in "Genesis." (Possibly also when flashing the crew at the end of "The Game." Although Wesley was a part of that "save" as well.)

10. (I suspect a bit of latent androidophobia.)

CLUES

Star Date: 44502.7

When the *Enterprise* discovers their home planet, a powerful race of isolationists called Paxans allows Picard and crew to leave unharmed with one provision: The Paxans will erase all memory of the incident from the humanoid minds on the ship, and Picard will order Data to hide their existence. Unfortunately, little clues begin cropping up that contradict Data's fabricated version of the missing time.

TRIVIA QUESTIONS

1. How many small and extremely unstable wormholes have been mapped near T-tauri star systems in the past one hundred years?

2. What other vessel encounters a wormhole with Data on board?

PLOT OVERSIGHTS

• Shortly after Crusher walks into the ready room with her crop of Diomedian scarlet moss, Picard comments that he didn't realize she was interested in "ethnobotany." I believe he meant to say "exobotany." (Ethnobotany would be something like studying the custom of different races of plants.)

• Just before the Paxans take up housekeeping in her body for the second time, Troi sits up in bed, dressed in one of her frilly nighties. Moments later she shows up at Data's quarters in uniform. Remember that these are xenophobes, a race so intent on keeping others out of their space that they are willing to slaughter everyone on board in exchange for their privacy. A starship has just returned to their space—a ship that they had dispatched and hoped to never see again. In the midst of all this, the Paxans take the time to dress Troi.

• When the crew awakes during Data's recollections at the end of the episode, the android tells Picard that an energy field is attempting to penetrate the shields. Picard immediately reacts as if he understands it is an attack and should take evasive maneuvers. Wait a minute: The last thing Picard knew, the *Enterprise* had just encountered a wormhole. Should he be saying, "What energy field? What's going on? What happened to the wormhole?"?

• Some of the armchair captains of the Nitpicker's Guild found it completely unpalatable that the fearless Picard should so quickly turn tail, run, and even allow the Paxans to muck around in the crew's memories.

• So, at the conclusion of this episode, Picard orders Data never to reveal his knowledge of the Paxans. Wouldn't it be easier just to tell him to delete the appropriate files?

• Picard orders Data never to reveal the existence of the Paxans...eh? Then how come *The Star Trek Encyclopedia* has an entry for them, hmmmmmm? Who *snitched*?

EQUIPMENT ODDITIES

• After supposedly awakening from the stunning effects of a wormhole, Picard orders Data to dispatch a probe to survey an M-class planet in the vicinity of the wormhole. When the probe begins transmitting back its information, Data sits at Ops and narrates the visuals. At first the right side of his communicator tilts downward. Then suddenly it corrects itself.

• Apparently Worf can override the door controls on some quarters but not on others. In this episode the chief of Security must page Security and request that they override the lock on Counselor Troi's door. Yet, in "Allegiance," Worf spoke directly to the computer and ordered it to override the lock on Picard's door.

CONTINUITY AND PRODUCTION PROBLEMS

• At the very beginning of this episode, Guinan comes to the holodeck to enjoy a Dixon Hill fantasy with Picard. Watch her cigarette carefully. It lengthens and shortens throughout the scene. For instance, when Guinan first arrives and introduces herself as "Gloria from Cleveland," the shot shows a somewhat short cigarette with a stack of ash. After Dix's secretary attempts to tell her that he is incommunicado, Guinan's cigarette suddenly grows! (It's a common problem with cigarettes on film.)

• Just before an observation lounge meeting of the senior staff, an establishing shot shows the *Enterprise* rapidly traversing the stars on impulse. Yet during the staff meeting the stars don't move at all.

• After the Paxans evacuate from her a second time, Troi collapses. Both Riker and Data rush to her sides. Riker places his left hand on her leg and grasps her left hand with his *right* hand. Then the shot changes and suddenly he's helping her to her feet by clasping her left hand with his *left* hand.

TRIVIA ANSWERS

1. Thirty-nine.
2. The USS *Trieste*.

FIRST CONTACT

Star Date: unknown

When Riker is captured on Malcor III—a planet on the verge of achieving warp capability and therefore a candidate for "first contact"—Picard meets with the Malcorian president and negotiates the first officer's release. Unfortunately, the president also asks Picard to have the Federation leave them alone.

TRIVIA QUESTIONS

1. How far is it from Earth to Malcor III?

2. What is the name of the Malcorian twit doctor who gives Riker a stimulant near the end of the episode?

ALTERNATE VIEWPOINTS AND CORRECTIONS

• For me, picking up little tidbits of information is all part of the fun of authoring the *Nitpicker's Guides*. Several months after the release of the *NextGen Guide,* I received a letter from Karen P. Malcor of Norco, CA. (Does the name sound familiar?) She politely informed me that I had incorrectly named the planet in this episode "Malcoria III" in my review of this episode in the *NextGen Guide*. She pointed out that the planet's name is actually Malcor III and was named after her. (See, Karen, now you've got another book to add to your list of sci-fi tomes that contain your name!)

PLOT OVERSIGHTS

• Trying to convince Durken to refuse the Federation's offer of relations, Minister of Internal Security Krola shoots himself with a phaser, hoping to frame Riker. Crusher soon appears and asks Picard for permission to beam the pair back to the *Enterprise*. Specifically, the good doctor refers to Riker and a "Marconian male." Obviously Krola isn't native to Malcor III and comes instead from a neighboring world founded by a pioneer of radio here on Earth.

EQUIPMENT ODDITIES

• The *Classic* episode "Patterns of Force" showed McCoy implanting subcutaneous transponders in the forearms of Kirk and Spock. These devices allowed the crew of the original *Enterprise* to locate the pair without benefit of a communicator. Seems like a sensible piece of equipment, doesn't it? Too bad Starfleet forgot how to manufacture them.

CONTINUITY AND PRODUCTION PROBLEMS

• Carolyn Seymour, the actress who plays head scientist Mirasta Yale in this episode, also plays the part of Romulan commanders in "Contagion" and "Face of the Enemy."

• Eventually Durken asks Picard and the Federation to leave his planet alone. He feels his people are not ready for knowledge of other races—that they fear the encroachment of aliens too much. If that's true, the Malcorian Ministry of Internal Security had better keep an eye on the blonde who attends all the high-level meetings with Durken. She's wearing the same outfit as Dr. Apgar's Tanugan assistant Tayna in "A Matter of Perspective." Obviously there's some hostile alien fashion infiltration going on here, and it's reached the highest levels of government.

• At the conclusion of the episode, after being asked by Durken to leave, Picard wonders how the government will keep the arrival of the *Enterprise* a secret when so many have seen Riker. Durken replies that the populace will soon go back to their entertainment shows and forget all about the incident. There will be stories, but they will pass. Mirasta reluctantly agrees. At this point the reflection in Picard's ready room window shows her bow her head. But when the scene cuts to a close-up of her, she instantly looks at Picard.

TRIVIA ANSWERS

1. It is 2,000 light-years.
2. Nilrem.

GALAXY'S CHILD

Star Date: 44614.6

La Forge's anticipation turns to dismay when the real Dr. Leah Brahms ("Booby Trap") visits the *Enterprise*. In addition to being married, the woman is very defensive about the modifications La Forge has made to "her" systems. In the end, the two become friends after working together to solve a crisis in which a large space baby suckles energy from the *Enterprise*.

TRIVIA QUESTIONS

1. Where does the *Enterprise* pick up Dr. Leah Brahms?

2. To what animal does La Forge compare Brahms's unfriendliness?

ALTERNATE VIEWPOINTS AND CORRECTIONS

• Several nitpickers had some interesting viewpoints on the way Brahms and La Forge interact with La Forge's holodeck program. Unfortunately, I'm not sure they are nits. (They would have been *good* ones!) Real Laporte of Montreal, Quebec, wrote to say that Brahms stands and watches her doppelgänger on the holodeck instead of interacting with it. (However, both Brahms and La Forge refer to a replay of the holodeck program, so maybe it is as it should be.) Also, Johnson Lai of Ajax, Ontario, noted that when La Forge stormed out of the holodeck he never said "Computer, exit" and therefore should have wandered into the halls of Utopia Planitia. (The only problem here is that La Forge does say "Freeze program" just after he enters. Does that mean the exit reverts to the real world?)

PLOT OVERSIGHTS

• Near the beginning of the episode, Data reports an odd energy reading. Riker, sitting in the first officer's chair, comes forward to discuss it with the android. Since the *Enterprise* is ahead of schedule, Riker allows Data to veer off course and investigate. Shouldn't Picard be advised of this change before Riker makes it?

• Ooooh, here's a technical one for you. Preparing for a romantic evening with Brahms, La Forge asks the computer for "subdued lighting." The computer drops the lights to zero, and La Forge voices a chuckling objection. Then the computer asks the chief engineer to specify the exact candlepower he desires. According to Elias S. Saltz, there is a difference between the intensity of a point source of light (candlepower) and the overall illumination level. The quantity of light that reaches a surface is denoted as "foot-candles." Since La Forge desired to set the overall illumination level of the room, the computer should more properly ask for foot-candles, not candlepower. In addition, both foot-candles and candlepower are from the Imperial measuring system. The computer is calibrated to the metric measuring system, so *really*...it should have asked for "lux," the metric equivalent of foot-candles. Interestingly enough, lux must be combined with another measurement to determine the exact measured brightness or "luminance" of a room. That measurement deals with the amount of light that reflects from the surfaces in the room. The metric term "nit" refers to the quantity of light reflected from or transmitted through an object. (Nit? Nit!? Did someone say "nit"?) So...you combine "lux" and "nit" to get "luminance."

• In a meeting on the observation lounge, Brahms says that the space baby almost completely covers the door of Shuttle Bay 2. Later in the episode, we see La Forge preparing to evacuate the atmosphere from the shuttle bay, and a giant "2" rests on the floor. Presumably that means it's Shuttle Bay 2. Yet all the exterior shots of the space baby show it on the starboard side of the ship, and according to "Unnatural Selection," "Samaritan Snare," *and* the *Technical Manual,* that's Shuttle Bay 3.

• Since "Booby Trap" establishes that in cases of critical energy supplies the computer considers the holodecks optional, does anyone find it odd that a designer of a starship, namely Dr. Leah Brahms, would suddenly decide to run a holodeck program while attempting to supplement the energy supplies of the *Enterprise*? (I know, La Forge did this in "Booby

Trap" and "great minds think alike," but La Forge did it because he needed Brahms's input.)

• Of course, when Brahms runs the holodeck program she finds the engineer/holobabe version of herself and becomes incensed. One wonders if La Forge shouldn't be a bit incensed himself. She *did* violate his privacy.

• At the conclusion of this episode, the crew is frantic to find a way to wean the space baby from the *Enterprise.* Surprisingly, no one thinks of the solution La Forge used when the aceton assimilators were draining power from the ship in "Booby Trap," the first episode featuring Leah Brahms. Why not just shut everything down? If the milk runs dry, won't the baby quit nursing?

EQUIPMENT ODDITIES

• After attempting to blow the space baby off the *Enterprise,* it begins gobbling up more energy. The dialogue on the bridge indicates that the space baby is consuming so much that the crew must take the engines off-line, use auxiliary generators to power life support, and pour everything else into the "milk" for the suckling. In other words, the warp core is maxed out providing energy for the infant. If that's so, why are the blue doughnut lights just puttering along the next time we see Main Engineering?

TRIVIA ANSWERS

1. Starbase 313.
2. A Circassian plague cat.

NIGHT TERRORS

Star Dates: 44631.2—44642.1

When the *Enterprise* becomes trapped in a Tyken's rift, Dr. Crusher finds that no one can enter REM sleep except Troi, who experiences only nightmares. Soon she and Troi deduce that an alien vessel lies trapped on the other side of the rift and its crew's telepathic calls for help are preventing the *Enterprise*'s crew from dreaming. Working in concert, the two ships generate a powerful explosion that allows both to break free.

TRIVIA QUESTIONS

1. What is the name of the Betazoid found alive on the USS *Brattain*?

2. Who takes over for Ensign Rager at conn?

PLOT OVERSIGHTS

• Ya know, Picard is dangerously close to earning a syndrome. We all know what Kirk suffered from: the Kirk-knows-this-is-the-most-dangerous-planet-in-the-universe-so-he-takes-the-entire-senior-staff-with-him-when-he-beams-down syndrome. For Picard it's turning into the Picard-knows-the-

unexplained-phenomenon-can-endanger-the-ship-so-he-decides-to-hang-around-until-he's-sure-the-ship-is-in-danger syndrome. It shows up here. It shows up in "The Naked Now." It shows up in "In Theory." It shows up in "Hero Worship."

• According to the *Tech Manual,* subspace communications travel about sixty times the maximum warp of any existing or planned starship. In this episode Picard claims they have sent a subspace message about their predicament but because of their distance will have to wait "at least another two weeks" for a response. For the sake of simplicity, let's say that they would have to wait only two weeks for a response. That means a week to get there and a week to get back. In other words, it would take the *Enterprise* at least sixty weeks (more than a year!) at maximum warp to make it back to the nearest starbase or other source of help. Yet, in the previous episode, "Galaxy's Child," the *Enterprise* picked up Dr. Leah Brahms at Starbase 313 and traveled to a Federation outpost in the Guernica system. There're only 16.6 star date units between these two episodes. How did the *Enterprise* get out so far so fast?

• La Forge claims they can't use a photon torpedo to blast free of the rift, but eventually the crew supplies hydrogen for some type of chemical or nuclear explosion. Isn't a matter/anti-matter explosion more powerful than either of these?

• I wonder if separating the saucer section would provide enough oomph for it to coast free of the rift.

• Sure does take Security a long

time to get to Worf's quarters after Troi calls them, doesn't it? It's almost as if *they read the script*!

• Doesn't Guinan dream? She seems fine for the whole episode while everyone else except Troi suffers from lack of REM sleep.

• Obviously there were no Vulcans aboard the *Enterprise* who could mind-meld with the catatonic Betazoid and find out what was going on.

• Given that hydrogen is the most common element in the universe, doesn't it seem a bit odd that the aliens wouldn't have any of it?

CONTINUITY AND PRODUCTION PROBLEMS

• When I originally reviewed this episode I spelled the name of the vessel that Picard and company find trapped in the rift, "Brittain." Then, prior to publication, I checked my spellings against Larry Nemecek's *The Star Trek: The Next Generation Companion.* It spelled the ship's name *"Brattain."* So—understanding that Larry is an expert in the field—I changed the spelling to his version. When Dell released the *NextGen Guide,* I started getting letters stating that the hull of the craft definitely says *"Brittain."* Now, with the publication of Michael Okuda, Denise Okuda, and Debbie Mirek's *The Star Trek Encyclopedia* we learn that, in fact, Larry was right. It is spelled *"Brattain."* The model builders spelled it wrong on the hull! (Glad we got that out of the way! Of course, one wonders what has higher authority in this matter. Is the actual episode more authoritative than the reference books?)

TRIVIA ANSWERS

1. Andrus Hagen.
2. Ensign Lin.

IDENTITY CRISIS

Star Dates: 44664.5—44668.1

Lieutenant Commander Leitjen joins the *Enterprise* in a search for three missing Starfleet officers. Oddly enough, she, La Forge, and the three officers investigated the disappearance of a colony on Tarchannen III five years ago. The investigation soon uncovers that each was infected with a parasite that alters its host's DNA in order to reproduce.

TRIVIA QUESTIONS

1. Who stole the shuttle from the USS *Aries*?

2. What is the name of the transporter technician whom La Forge knocked out of the way before beaming down to Tarchannen III?

PLOT OVERSIGHTS

• At the end of the program, when the away team pursues the altered La Forge, Leitjen tells them to douse their flashlights because it will scare the aliens away. Yet La Forge finds an alien shadow during his analysis of the records from the previous search, and all the members of that away team carried flashlights. Why didn't their lights scare the aliens away? Were the lizard guys just in a mating frenzy and didn't care? (The aliens reproduce by implanting a strand of their DNA into a new host by using a parasite. The episode never really says how the parasite is transmitted. It is possible that the aliens must touch the host.)

• Amazingly enough, once the parasite has its way with La Forge, he can see without his VISOR! Not bad for a man *born* blind. On the other hand, even if the parasite has accomplished this, wouldn't his retina need to absorb *some* light to provide him with visual information? If so, how can La Forge be invisible? Shouldn't there be two little black dots where his pupils are?

• The episode never mentions it, but I'm sure Crusher gave the away team members full physicals when they returned from Tarchannen III and removed any parasites she found. Otherwise the *Enterprise* will be back here in about five years!

• Speaking of those parasites, they supposedly use a humanoid host to procreate. That's funny, I didn't hear any mention of a humanoid population on the surface of Tarchannen III. (I guess they don't procreate very often. Or can these parasites use any animal host?)

EQUIPMENT ODDITIES

• Those sentient doors are reading the scripts again. When entering the holodeck, La Forge takes eight and one-half strides and yet the doors stay open so that we can watch him. Now,

a man's stride will run from two to three feet, so La Forge has strolled at least seventeen feet into the holodeck and the doors still haven't shut. Then the shot changes and we hear the doors closing.

• And speaking of entering the holodeck, why are there night sounds chirping away in the background? Everything else is frozen.

• The creators really need to decide how the computer locates a person. This makes the second time—the first being when Worf rips off his communicator and storms out to kill Duras at the end of "Reunion"—that a Starfleet officer removes his communicator and the computer says they are no longer on the ship. Compare this to "Power Play" when Data, Troi, and O'Brien take off their communicators and leave them in a turbolift. In that episode the computer thinks they are still in the turbolift.

• Worf and a Security team go to La Forge's last known location, holodeck 3. The doors open and Worf says he will search the perimeter. What a minute: Why don't they just *shut the thing off*?

• So the parasite has changed La Forge's DNA and made him invisible to the sensors on the ship, right? Then how does the transporter beam him down to the surface? Did La Forge punch in some type of modification to the transporter to allow it to lock on to him?

• One would think—given the multiple instances of away teams beaming into potential infectious or dangerous situations ("The Naked Now," "The Royale," "Shades of Gray," "Tin Man," "The Best of Both Worlds," "Legacy")—that Starfleet would develop some sort of nonsentient automaton to send ahead with sensors and visual communications. (Granted, it wouldn't make for much of a show, so maybe it's better that the creators send the senior staff out as bait for the baddies!)

TRIVIA ANSWERS

1. Mendez.
2. Hendrick.

THE NTH DEGREE

Star Dates: 44704.2–44705.3

When a Cytherian probe flashes Barclay, his IQ jumps dramatically. Under a compulsion he doesn't understand, Barclay hooks himself into the computer and commandeers the ship. Then he distorts nearby space to take the *Enterprise* to the center of the galaxy to meet with the probe's creators.

ALTERNATE VIEWPOINTS AND CORRECTIONS

• On page 256 of the *NextGen Guide* I stated that this episode featured the first and only time that a shuttle is used to gather information. Usually the large and sophisticated sensor arrays of the *Enterprise* are sufficient for the task. (Of course, the decision to use a shuttle allows Barclay to get flashed.) Frank T. Bitterhof and Andreas Zech of Berlin, Germany, took exception to

my statement. They cited additional examples of shuttles used to collect information, in "The Price" and "In Theory." I should have been more specific in my initial elucidation. I should have said that this is the first and only time a shuttle is used to gather information when the *Enterprise* is nearby and—at the time the information is gathered—no clear threat to the ship exists.

TRIVIA QUESTIONS

1. Where does Picard intend to take the probe the crew finds near the Argus Array?

2. Who mans the conn during this episode?

PLOT OVERSIGHTS

• Troi must be having an off day. After Barclay hooks himself into the computer by creating a neural interface on the holodeck, the counselor visits him and attempts to use her psychological and feminine charms to woo him out of the room. When Barclay refuses, Troi gets huffy and says that Picard will make every attempt to stop him. Predictably, Barclay becomes angry. Now, this woman is supposed to be trained as a counselor. What good will it do to get the guy upset and less amenable to reason?

• Given the events of "Force of Nature" and the new knowledge that "warp is bad for space," would there be some benefit to resurrecting Mr. Barclay's method of travel and studying it further?

• I wonder what happened to all the information that the *Enterprise* brought back from its visit with the Cytherians? I realize that Picard claims it will take forever for the researchers to examine. But isn't there *anything* that Data could start applying to day-to-day operations on the ship?

EQUIPMENT ODDITIES

• La Forge seems to forget for a moment that Barclay has become the computer. The chief engineer crawls through a Jefferies tube trying to reestablish helm control when Barclay pages him. In response, La Forge reaches up and taps his badge when he usually just speaks directly with the computer.

• Working by a junction panel in the Jefferies tube, La Forge pulls out a flashlight and peers inside. A flashlight? On the away teams during "The Enemy," "Future Imperfect," and "Identity Crisis," La Forge didn't carry a flashlight, while the rest of the away team did. This makes sense. After all, La Forge can see all types of energy. Why *would* he need a flashlight?

CONTINUITY AND PRODUCTION PROBLEMS

• When Troi visits Barclay on the holodeck, the doors don't quite completely seal behind her. For some reason, the tongue on the door on the right side of the screen doesn't groove properly, and you can see a vertical shaft of light.

TRIVIA ANSWERS

1. Science Station 402 in the Kohlan system.
2. Ensign Anaya.

QPID

Star Date: 44741.9

Q decides to repay Picard's recent kindness in "Déjà Q" by showing the captain that the emotion he feels for Vash is dangerous. To do so, Q creates a fantasy in which he casts Picard as Robin Hood, Vash as Maid Marion, and the rest of the senior staff as Robin Hood's merry men. Of course, Vash is imprisoned and will be executed if Picard cannot effect a rescue.

RUMINATIONS

I admit it. I missed a "Great Moment" by not alerting readers of the NextGen Guide *to the sequence where Worf smashes La Forge's mandolin. It really is very cute—and very reminiscent of the scene from* Animal House *where John Belushi smashes a guitar. Thanks to Ricard Smith of Surrey, England, and Michael S. Sharp of Tulsa, OK, for pointing this out.*

GREAT LINES

"Nice legs...for a human."—Worf commenting to Data, La Forge, and Troi after taking a gander at Vash and getting caught in the act.

ALTERNATE VIEWPOINTS AND CORRECTIONS

• Shortly after Q transports the senior staff to Sherwood Forest, Worf attacks

Sir Guy of Gisbourne—the latter on horseback. In the *NextGen Guide,* on page 258, I asked why Worf doesn't just stab the horse. I received a wide variety of responses to this query. Some nitpickers pointed out the value of the horse. Others painted an attack on the animal as strategically foolish. Thoroughly confused, I called a couple of friends, Charles Gragg and Janetta Flippo of Ozark, MO, who are members of the Society for Creative Anachronisms—a group that studies and reenacts medieval warfare. According to the information they have gleaned from history books, the warhorse was indeed a very valuable commodity and preserved if at all possible. Given the rainy conditions of England, sometimes one side of the conflict would even attempt to trap the opponents' horses in mud. However, horses could become prime targets as well, and in that case the attacker would simply sweep the horse's legs with his sword. If the rider survived the fall, the battle continued on foot.

TRIVIA QUESTIONS

1. Into what animal does Q threaten to turn Vash?

2. Where did Troi's arrow impact Data?

PLOT OVERSIGHTS

• As the show begins, Troi visits a nervous Picard in his ready room. She realizes that he is still working on his speech before the Federation Archae-ology Council but chides that it is quite late and eventually bids him good night. Yet when Troi leaves, the bridge lights appears to be at full intensity, not dimmed, as demonstrated for the night shift in "Data's Day."

• Surprisingly, Data doesn't "bleek" when pierced by Troi's arrow. (See "The Naked Now.")

• And speaking of said arrow, what has happened to Data's reflexes? He dodges laser blasts in "We'll Always Have Paris," and he can't get out of the way of an arrow? (I thought he would do one of those Kung Fu things where he grabs the arrow in midflight.)

EQUIPMENT ODDITIES

• I want to know where Riker was hiding his staff. Just as the big fight commences, the first officer slings off his robe and pulls out a sword. Then, a few shots later, he is using his staff. It's not exactly like he could keep the thing under his clothes. It's as tall as he is!

CONTINUITY AND PRODUCTION PROBLEMS

• Pay attention. This is a fun one, but it will take some concentration on your part. After helping Sir Guy capture Picard, Vash writes a letter to Riker. When finished, she first folds the top third of the letter down and then the bottom third up to complete the trifold. However, Q discovers the letter, and unfolds the outermost flap. He leaves that flap toward the top, and he unfolds the rest. In other words, he holds the letter *upside down* as he looks at it! Clever Q that he is, he still has no trouble reading the note.

• In the big battle at the end of the

episode, Picard stabs Sir Guy. In the wide shot, there's no blood on Picard's sword. Then, suddenly, in a closer shot, there is!

TRIVIA ANSWERS

1. A Klabnian eel.
2. Just above his sixth intercostal support.

THE DRUMHEAD

Star Date: 44769.2

When an investigation turns up a Klingon spy for the Romulans on board the *Enterprise,* Starfleet sends retired Admiral Norah Satie to hold further hearings. Unfortunately, Satie's proceedings soon take on the air of an inquisition, enveloping even Picard in a cloud of suspicion.

TRIVIA QUESTIONS

1. From what sickness does Lieutenant J'Ddan suffer?

2. What is the Federation's Constitution's equivalent of the U.S. Constitution's Fifth Amendment?

ALTERNATE VIEWPOINTS AND CORRECTIONS

• On page 259 of the *NextGen Guide* I asked if exobiology sounded like a believable line of work for a Klingon,

given that it probably offers a *lot* of chances for glory. Sharla Smith of Minneapolis, MN, suggested that the Klingon society must have individuals who pursue the sciences in order for it to advance technologically.

PLOT OVERSIGHTS

• Admiral Satie must be a great student of history. She certainly uses enough arcane twentieth-century expressions. She tells Picard that her father loved it when she "nailed" one of her brothers in a debate with some subtle point of logic. Later she tells the captain that spies don't like the bright lights of an inquiry, that they are like roaches scurrying for the dark. (Then again, maybe some problems—such as insect infestation—are ageless!)

• After establishing Lieutenant J'Ddan's guilt as a Klingon spy and Romulan collaborator, Satie's investigation turns on Simon Tarses, a medical technician who claimed that his grandfather was a Vulcan on his Starfleet application when his grandfather was actually a Romulan. His nervousness that Satie will uncover this fact sends off a warning in the mind of her Betazoid associate. I wonder why Troi doesn't sit in on the initial questioning of Tarses. Wouldn't it be good to have two Betazoid opinions on the matter? (Okay…it really wouldn't be two, it would be one and one-half.)

• Satie's court reporter takes an interesting approach to her duties. It appears that the female enters only the responses of the interrogated and not the questions of the interrogators. Aren't both important?

• So much for the fabled open-mindedness and tolerance of the Federation. Poor old Simon Tarses is one-quarter Romulan, and the powers that be hound the guy, whereas Sela has a Starfleet officer for a mom, and the Romulan government lets her mastermind two conflicts with the Federation. (Possibly three if you count "The Mind's Eye." And, yes, I know this was the whole point of the episode—that we must be vigilant lest these attitudes rear their ugly heads. I just thought it an interesting juxtaposition.)

• Picard seems to forget the name of Satie's Betazoid associate. In a moment of tension he calls Sabin Genestra "Mr. Sabin."

EQUIPMENT ODDITIES

• In the *Classic Trek* episode "Wolf in the Fold," Kirk used some type of computerized lie detector on Scotty. Sure would be helpful to have one of those gizmos during these hearings, wouldn't it?

CONTINUITY AND PRODUCTION PROBLEMS

• I realize that Admiral Satie is supposedly retired, but she certainly acts like she's official in this episode. But if she's official, why isn't she wearing a uniform and a communicator? Or is she not official enough to warrant a uniform and that's why she had to have Admiral Thomas Henry sit in on the hearing?

• For some reason, Satie's court reporter takes the scenic route when bringing Picard a summons. She gets off the upper turbolift on the bridge, walks behind Worf, down the ramp on the *starboard* side, then strolls over to the *port* side of Picard's chair to deliver the "invitation."

TRIVIA ANSWERS

1. Ba'ltmasor syndrome.
2. The Seventh Guarantee.

HALF A LIFE

Star Dates: 44805.3—44812.6

Kaelon II scientist Dr. Timicin joins the *Enterprise* to perform a test on the revitalization of a star. Kaelon II's star nears death, and Timicin has made it his life's work to find a way to reenergize it. Unfortunately the test fails and Timicin—who will soon reach sixty—must return home to end his life voluntarily, as dictated by his race's culture.

RUMINATIONS

*T*he creators slipped in a little inside joke that J. Seth Farrow of Independence, MO, brought to my attention. As La Forge gives Timicin the readouts on the test for revitalizing a star, the label for the screen reads, "COMPOSITE SENSOR ANALYSIS 4077." David Ogden Stiers, who plays Timicin, starred in a series called M*A*S*H that featured a mobile surgical hospital numbered 4077.

ALTERNATE VIEWPOINTS AND CORRECTIONS

• In the *NextGen Guide,* on pages 260 and 261, I noted Picard's unsophisticated greeting of Timicin with a handshake. I noted that I could think of only one other instance where Picard shook hands with a visitor, and even then only after greeting the man according to his custom ("Final Mission"). David J. Ferrier of Washington, DC, remembered Picard trying to shake hands with Minister Campio in "Cost of Living." As David put it, "Of course, Campio stands there and looks at Picard as if to say, 'A person with earlobes like these doesn't shake hands with the likes of you!'"

TRIVIA QUESTIONS

1. What dish does Lwaxana prepare for Timicin and bring to Main Engineering?

2. How old is Timicin's grandson?

EQUIPMENT ODDITIES

• One has to wonder what effect Lwaxana has on the equipment when she marches into Main Engineering, sweeps several padds onto the floor, and sets up a table on an engineering workstation.

CONTINUITY AND PRODUCTION PROBLEMS

• The actress who plays Timicin's daughter in this episode, Michelle Forbes, returns as Ensign Ro in the fifth season.

TRIVIA ANSWERS

1. Mantickian paté.

2. Six.

THE HOST

Star Dates: 44821.3—44824.4

Dr. Crusher finds love with a Trill ambassador named Odan, on board the *Enterprise* to mediate a dispute between the two inhabited moons of Peliar Zel. When a shuttle accident reveals that Odan is actually a "symbiont" who lives within a humanoid host, Riker volunteers his body until a new Trill host can arrive.

ALTERNATE VIEWPOINTS AND CORRECTIONS

• On page 264 of the *NextGen Guide,* I engaged in a discussion of my evaluation of the relationship between the Trill host and symbiont. I characterized that relationship as one of parasite and host—an exploitation, if you will, of the humanoid host's opposable thumbs! Several nitpickers took exception to this description—no doubt spurred on by the new "revelations" about the Trill in *Star Trek: Deep Space Nine.* I will deal with those below. As part of her rebuttal, Jessica P. M. Lawyer of Lancaster, VA, was kind enough to supply me with definitions for the three types of symbiotic relationships: parasitism (in which the symbiont damages the host), commensalism (in which the symbiont benefits but the host does not), and mutualism (in which both benefit). On the other hand, Lee Zion of the USS

Kitty Hawk suggested that I be chastised for my incorrect characterization and be forced to go to the blackboard and write "The slugs are our friends" a hundred times.

However, may I direct your attention to the scene in which Odan reveals his nature to Beverly? Odan is injured during an attack on a shuttle. Crusher takes readings on him in sick bay and states, "It's as though there's a parasite at work." She tells Odan about this and that she wishes to do exploratory surgery. Odan takes her hand and places it on his stomach. Odan's stomach starts moving, at which point Crusher says, "Eeeeeewwwwww, gross!" (Just joking. She really says something like, "What is that?") Odan then replies— and this is important because he's describing himself—"That is me. This body is just a host. I am that *parasite*." (Emphasis mine.) Now…a parasite can be called a symbiont because parasitism is a form of symbiosis and therefore "symbiont" is a more general term. On the other hand, if someone identifies himself or herself as a parasite, that is a *specific* functional term and cannot be lightly discarded. You cannot say that just because the rest of the show refers to Odan as a symbiont, the relationship between Trill "lobsteroid" and host should be elevated to commensalism or mutualism. (I realize that the information in *DS9* attempts to do so, but I will deal with that below.) According to the evidence in this episode, *Odan is a parasite*! Case closed! (Chuckle, chuckle, chuckle.)

TRIVIA QUESTIONS

1. Who calls Picard to inform him that the shuttle is ready to take Odan to the surface?

2. At age eight, what did Crusher name her three imaginary children?

PLOT OVERSIGHTS

• Ever wonder how this Trill "joining" ever got started? It's not like this is a discovery that you just *happen* upon. A creature must be *surgically implanted* in a humanoid host! As James R. Collier of Georgetown, Ontario, asked, "Was there some medieval Trill, Vlad the Impaler, who would get rid of his enemies by slitting open their bellies and inserting a small animal?" (And one wonders how many animals Vlad went through before he happened upon the lobsteroid.)

• And another thing: Exactly where does Odan go when it wiggles down into Riker's stomach? The lobsteroid is bigger than a softball and it has a large tail! Do men really have that much extra space in their innards?

CHANGED PREMISES

• My, oh my, oh, my oh, my. The Trill certainly have *changed*! I must tell you at the outset of this nit that I am genuinely confused as to why the creators just didn't call Dax's race something different in *Star Trek: Deep Space Nine*. Granted, we can explain away the *physical* differences between the Trill in this episode and Dax on *DS9* by saying that there are different races on the Trill home planet. (Even though Dax looks surprisingly like the empathic meta-morph Kamala from "The Perfect Mate." Lots-o-dots. I bet some makeup artist has fun with those.) But there are far more fundamental problems that cannot be reconciled.

First, as stated above, Odan characterizes the relationship between host and symbiont as parasitism, and this episode supports this label. When Odan occupies Riker's body, the first officer is continually spoken of in the third person. Odan never once refers to the joining in any type of plural term. He says "I," not "we." It's as if Riker doesn't exist as long as Odan inhabits his body. And, given the strong suggestion that Riker and Crusher are intimate as Odan inhabits his body, it's pretty obvious to me that Riker doesn't have much say in the matter. (Not that there's anything wrong with Crusher. Riker simply has never expressed an interest in her, and the good doctor even characterizes his relationship to her as one of a "brother.") Yet, in DS9, the relationship between host and symbiont is one of mutualism and great honor for the host. This brings us to our next topic.

According to DS9, being selected as a host is a great honor open only to a few—only the best and brightest earn the privilege of joining. I have no wish to be unkind, but consider the Trill host at the end of this episode. Does she strike you as the "best and the brightest"? (You know, the one who looks like she's on heavy doses of Valium?)

Then there's the bit with the transporter. According to Odan, the process of beaming will harm the symbiont.

Yet Dax does it frequently in DS9.

Beyond all of this, however, is the worst inconsistency of all. This episode indicates that the Trill are somewhat unknown to Starfleet. Think about it. A medical doctor dates a Trill. As she gets to know him, she probably wants to know more about him. So she checks Starfleet's medical data base—if nothing else, to determine if Trills and humans have a histamine incompatibility with respect to mucous membranes. Obviously the data base says very little. It doesn't say anything about the Trill being a "joined" species (a nice euphemistic term if I've ever heard one). It doesn't say anything about transport damaging a Trill. This type of background information would be very important. What if Odan had been knocked unconscious during the shuttle attack? Would the Enterprise crew have killed Odan because no one thought to send along some simple instructions? Yet even though Starfleet's medical data base is obviously lacking with regard to the Trill, we find out in DS9 that there's a Trill in Starfleet! Star Trek: Deep Space Nine started halfway through the sixth season of NextGen. This episode occurs near the end of the fourth season. That means in a little over one and one-half years from now Jadzia Dax will appear in DS9 as a lieutenant. Wasn't she attending Starfleet Academy when this episode occurs? Even more amazing, DS9 establishes that Commander Sisko had a decades-long relationship with Dax's former host Curzon. All this exposure to Trills and no one entered anything about them in the medical data base?

TRIVIA ANSWERS

1. Ensign Taggart.
2. Andrew, Alexander, and Jennifer.

THE MIND'S EYE

Star Dates: 44885.5—44896.9

After his capture and brainwashing by the Romulans; La Forge returns to the *Enterprise* programmed to create an incident between the Federation and the Klingon Empire. Just in time, Data uncovers the plot and thwarts the plan.

TRIVIA QUESTIONS

1. What are the resonances of the subquantum states associated with transitional relativity in descending alphabetical order?

2. Prior to this episode, Kriosian rebels attacked Ferengi and Cardassian freighters near what celestial region?

PLOT OVERSIGHTS

• So the Klingon Empire occupies Krios, which has been at war with Valt for centuries according to "The Perfect Mate"? Isn't it awfully hard to maintain a war with one race if you are occupied by yet another race? The Klingons don't seem the type of conquerors who would allow this.

• Under Romulan influence, La Forge transports a load of Federation weapons down to the surface of Krios. The scene shows him inserting isolinear optical chips in a black box. Later, La Forge has the computer erase all records of his modifications. The subsequent investigation thrashes about trying to determine who beamed down the phasers. Why doesn't someone dust the chips for fingerprints!

EQUIPMENT ODDITIES

• Evidently, after the events of "Redemption II," three episodes from now, the Federation sets up some sort of tachyon detection grid. In "Face of the Enemy," the Romulan commander says that they cannot enter Federation space because of the sensor nets. In this episode, the Romulan warbird flies into Federation space and grabs La Forge.

• This episode features several views of the output from La Forge's VISOR that are very different from the view in "Heart of Glory"?

• During one scene, La Forge and Data test a phaser rifle in Main Engineering. Does this seem like a good idea? Doesn't the *Enterprise* have labs for this type of work?

• The footage of the three Klingon ships taking up their positions in front of the *Enterprise* comes from "Reunion."

TRIVIA ANSWERS

1. Universal, stable, phased, inverted, and asymmetrical.
2. The Ikalian asteroid belt.

IN THEORY

Star Dates: 44932.3—44935.6

As the *Enterprise* investigates an M-class planet within a dark nebula, a romance blooms between Data and Lieutenant Jenna D'Sora. A series of odd and sporadic incidents soon awakens the crew to the dangers of the nebula, and they barely escape with the ship intact. Unfortunately, D'Sora quickly discovers that she cannot sustain herself with Data's nonemotional nature and soon breaks off the relationship.

GREAT LINES

"When I have some, I'll let you know."—Picard to Data, cutting him off after the android attempts to ask Picard for advice on understanding women.

TRIVIA QUESTIONS

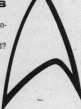

1. What comprises the concoction that Guinan asks Data to try in Ten-Forward?

2. Who is injured when the cryogenic control conduit explodes in Main Engineering?

CONTINUITY AND PRODUCTION PROBLEMS

• In the teaser, Data works to modify a photon torpedo with D'Sora. She walks over to the torpedo and tells Data that she saw a former boyfriend in a turbolift. As per a prior agreement, Data reminds D'Sora why she broke up with the guy. She stands, leaving behind a small, hand-held, box-shaped device on top of the torpedo. Data replaces the cover on the torpedo and stands as well. When the camera angle changes to a wider shot, Data's "sequencer" jumps from his left hand to his right. At the same time, the device disappears from the top of the torpedo and magically reappears in D'Sora's hands.

• Near the end of the episode, a female crew member starts walking down a hall and then screams. La Forge runs back to her position and finds her lower half "buried" in the floor. She must have spun when she died, because she was walking away from La Forge at the time of the accident but faces La Forge when he approaches.

TRIVIA ANSWERS

1. Eighty-seven percent Saurian brandy, with the rest made up of Targ milk (yum!) and Denevian mead.

2. Thorne.

REDEMPTION

Star Dates: 44995.3—44998.3

As Picard attempts to complete his duties as arbiter of succession for the Klingon High Council and install Gowron as its leader, the sisters of Duras appear with Duras's illegitimate son and mount a challenge. Eventually Picard finds in favor of Gowron's claim, but the decision drives the Klingon Empire into civil war.

TRIVIA QUESTIONS

1. Where does Kurn go to meet with the squadron commanders who are loyal to him?

2. What is the name of Kurn's ship?

CHANGED PREMISES

• After speaking with Gowron, Picard walks back onto the bridge and asks Data to begin monitoring activity along the Neutral Zone. Riker reacts with surprise, and Picard explains that the Duras family is massing support. "Backed by Romulans?" Riker asks, to which Picard replies, "I don't know. But there is too much history between the Duras and the Romulans to discount the possibility." Hold it: What would Picard know of this "history"? The business with the Khitomer mas-

sacre and the Klingon High Council covering up Duras's father's collusion with the Romulans was supposed to be a secret, wasn't it?

• In the *NextGen Guide* I mentioned that Gowron says women cannot serve on the High Council, but he offered K 'Ehleyr a seat on the council in the episode "Reunion." Several nitpickers provided additional cases where Gowron's statement seems untrue. Several women inhabit the council chambers during Worf's challenge in "Sins of the Father." In addition, *Star Trek VI: The Undiscovered Country* features a female chancellor, Azetbur.

• This episode shows that Worf has red blood (when he grasps Gowron's knife to receive back his family honor). But, but, but…didn't *Star Trek VI: The Undiscovered Country* show us that Klingons have purplish-colored blood? Or was that merely the royalty class of Klingons who have the purplish blood?

TRIVIA ANSWERS

1. The Mempa Sector.
2. The *Hegh'ta*.

TRIATHLON
TRIVIA ON SPACECRAFT

MATCH THE SPACECRAFT TO
THE DESCRIPTION TO THE EPISODE

SPACECRAFT	DESCRIPTION	EPISODE
1. *Akagi*, USS	A. Thadiun Okana's cargo carrier	a. "Descent"
2. *Archos*, USS	B. Commanded by Subcommander Taris	b. "Chain of Command, Part 1"
3. *Charybdis*, Explorer Ship	C. Lost in the Hekaras Corridor	c. "Encounter at Farpoint"
4. *Cleponji*	D. Trapped in null space	d. "Samaritan Snare"
5. *Crazy Horse*, USS	E. Where La Forge served as an ensign	e. "The *Pegasus*"
6. *Dorian*	F. Riker refused transport to its captain	f. "Ethics"
7. *Erstwhile*	G. Encountered the Children of Tama	g. "Force of Nature"
8. *Fearless*, USS	H. Commanded by Captain Conklin	h. "Unification I"
9. *Feyhman*	I. Mythical vessel on which Riker serves	i. "Hollow Pursuits"
10. *Flemming*	J. Commanded by Captain Talmadge	j. "Reunion"
11. *Gandhi*, USS	K. Encountered a wormhole with Data	k. "Starship Mine"
12. *Haakona*	L. Perished in the lower atmosphere gases	l. "Silicon Avatar"
13. *Hera*, USS	M. Part of a blockade armada	m. "Final Mission"
14. *Hood*, USS	N. Commanded by Captain Dirgo	n. "Symbiosis"
15. *Intrepid*, USS	O. Assigned to Task Force 3	o. "Second Chances"
16. *Jovis*	P. Commanded by Captain Picard	p. "Sins of the Father"
17. *Kallisko*	Q. Riker served on this vessel as an ensign	q. "Legacy"
18. *Khazara*, IRW	R. Trapped by aceton assimilators	r. "Darmok"
19. *Krayton*	S. Used by Picard, Crusher, and Worf	s. "The Most Toys"
20. *Kyushu*, USS	T. Commanded by Captain La Forge	t. "Elementary, Dear Data"

21.	*Lollipop*, USS	U.	Brought Dr. Russell to the *Enterprise*	u.	"Conspiracy"
22.	*Magellan*, USS	V.	Stolen from junkyard on Qualor II	v.	"A Matter of Honor"
23.	*Mondor*	W.	Ornaran freighter	w.	"All Good Things"
24.	*Nenebek*	X.	Barclay served on this vessel	x.	"The Enemy"
25.	*Pagh*, IKC	Y.	Thomas Riker departed for this vessel	y.	"First Contact"
26.	*Pasteur*, USS	Z.	Commanded by Captain Rixx	z.	"The Outcast"
27.	*Pegasus*, USS	AA.	Destroyed at Wolf 359	aa.	"Heart of Glory"
28.	*Pi*	BB.	Escape pod landed on Turkana IV	bb.	"Man of the People"
29.	*Potemkin*, USS	CC.	Responded to Khitomer distress calls	cc.	"Where No One Has Gone Before"
30.	*Raman*	DD.	Zibalian trader Kivas Fajo's vessel	dd.	"The Royale"
31.	*Sanction*	EE.	Brought Duras to the Rite of Succession	ee.	"Ménage à Troi"
32.	*Shiku Maru*	FF.	Klingon renegades destroyed her	ff.	"The Arsenal of Freedom"
33.	*T'Acog*, IKC	GG.	Attacked by the crystalline entity	gg.	"Redemption II"
34.	*T'Pau*	HH.	Commanded by Commander Toreth	hh.	"Interface"
35.	*Taris Murn*	II.	Crashed on Galorndon Core	ii.	"Contagion"
36.	*Thomas Paine*, USS	JJ.	Ended up in orbit around Theta VIII	jj.	"Booby Trap"
37.	*Trieste*, USS	KK.	Klingon vessel on which Riker served	kk.	"The Best of Both Worlds, Part 2"
38.	*Victory*, USS	LL.	Dr. Farek was a member of its crew	ll.	"The Outrageous Okana"
39.	*Vorn*, IKC	MM.	Commanded by Grebnedlog	mm.	"Face of the Enemy"
40.	*Zhukov*, USS	NN.	Kosinski worked on this ship as well		

SCORING
(ANSWERS)

0–3	Okay
4–9	Very good
10 and up	Most excellent

SPACECRAFT ANSWER KEY: 1. M gg **2.** BB q **3.** JJ dd **4.** R jj **5.** O a **6.** J bb **7.** A ll **8.** NN cc **9.** S b **10.** C g **11.** Y o **12.** B ii **13.** T hh **14.** F c **15.** CC p **16.** DD s **17.** GG l **18.** HH mm **19.** LL ee **20.** AA kk **21.** I ff **22.** H k ff **23.** MM d **24.** N m **25.** KK v **26.** P w **27.** Q e **28.** II x **29.** U f **30.** L hh **31.** W n **32.** G r **33.** FF aa **34.** V h **35.** D z **36.** Z u **37.** K y **38.** E t **39.** EE j **40.** X i

FIFTH
SEASON

REDEMPTION II

Star Dates: 45020.4–45025.4

Wanting to ensure that the civil war of the Klingon Empire remains an internal affair, Picard convinces Starfleet to allow him to take an armada of vessels to the Klingon/Romulan border and establish a blockade using tachyon beams to detect any cloaked vessel that might attempt to resupply the Duras. Soon Gowron and his forces emerge victorious.

TRIVIA QUESTIONS

1. According to Lieutenant Commander Christopher Hobson, members of what race do not make good engineers?

2. Where do the Klingon forces loyal to Gowron regroup after their defeat in the Mempa sector?

ALTERNATE VIEWPOINTS AND CORRECTIONS

• At the very end of the episode, Worf—having resigned from Starfleet—looks at Picard and says, "Request permission to return to duty, sir." Picard says okay, and the pair walk off happily into the sunset. On page 280 of the *NextGen Guide,* I marveled that a resignation and reinstatement could be

handled with such ease. Former army officer John Hobson of Bolingbrook, IL, suggested that Picard may have held on to Worf's resignation request for a time, knowing that the Klingon made the decision under emotional pressure. Since it was never officially processed, Picard could rescind it without any difficulty.

PLOT OVERSIGHTS

• Making his tachyon beam blockade pitch to a Starfleet admiral, Picard says, "What I propose is that we send a freet to the Romulan border." A "freet"? Now, that should strike terror into the hearts of the Romulans? ("Oh, no! A Starfleet *freet is* coming!")

• Does anyone else find it incredible that Sela—a young person in her early twenties—would command a "freet" of Romulan vessels? (And did you know that *The Star Trek: The Next Generation Companion* identifies her assistant as *General* Movar?)

• Picard seems to have a bit of trouble figuring out when the *Enterprise*-C was destroyed. He tells Guinan that it happened twenty-three years ago and then tells Sela that it happened twenty-four years ago.

CHANGED PREMISES

• I dealt with this issue under "Changed Premises" for "Yesterday's *Enterprise*," but I probably should mention it again. Picard seems to know all about the Romulan attack on Narendra III over two decades ago. Yet the dialogue in "The Neutral Zone" states that no one has heard from the Romulans in fifty-some-odd years. (See "Yesterday's *Enterprise*" for a fuller discussion.)

• After seeing Sela aboard the Romulan warbird, Picard discusses the situation with Guinan and tells her that Tasha Yar died "a year" before she came on board. "Skin of Evil" actually occurred near the end of the first season, and Guinan joined the ship at the beginning of the second season, so it seems unlikely that a year had transpired.

EQUIPMENT ODDITIES

• I wonder if Starfleet has ever considered using tachyons for communications. If I understand my physics, tachyons can never go as slow as the speed of light, and the upper range of their velocity is theoretically limitless.

• Attempting to thwart Picard's tachyon net, Sela concentrates a blast of tachyon energy at the ship commanded by Data. Romulan sensors must be quite capable. After all, Sela can tell not only that Data is on a particular ship but also that he captains it.

CONTINUITY AND PRODUCTION PROBLEMS

• Evidently Sela didn't like her latest haircut, so she ran off in the middle of a crisis and had it touched up. At the conclusion of "Redemption" her bangs come to a point in the center of her forehead. At the start of "Redemption II" they are cut straight across.

• The footage showing the *Enterprise* and the *Tian An Men* comes from "Yesterday's *Enterprise*." (In that episode, the two ships were the *Enterprise*-D and the *Enterprise*-C.)

TRIVIA ANSWERS

1. Berellians.
2. Beta Lankal.

DARMOK

Star Dates: 45047.2—45048.8

When the *Enterprise* rendezvouses with a vessel belonging to a race known as the Children of Tama in orbit around El-Adrel IV, the captain of the craft beams himself and Picard down to the surface, hoping that the challenge of defeating the beast who lives there will force the pair to learn how to communicate with each other.

TRIVIA QUESTIONS

1. Who called the Children of Tama incomprehensible?

2. What is "darmok" on Tasna V?

ALTERNATE VIEWPOINTS AND CORRECTIONS

• Many nitpickers had a great deal of trouble buying into the concept of a race that talks completely in metaphors. Mikal C. Johnson of Kirkland, WA, wondered how the Tamarians learned words like "at" and "from." Mark Carlson of Tulsa, OK, submitted that the Tamarians would have to teach their young the rudiments of language before they could understand the meaning of the wide variety of metaphors they must employ. Ian and Ruth Stuart-Hamilton of Worcester, United Kingdom, added that—if this is the case—the Tamarians should switch to "baby talk" when their "adult talk" failed. They also wondered how the Tamarian language would deal with requests such as "At what time do we meet?" or "To the nearest thousandth of [whatever], how much does this weigh?"

• At the end of this episode, Picard stands and stares out his window as the *Enterprise* travels at warp. The camera sits outside the ship, and the streaking stars reflect on the exterior surface of the pane. The stars streak toward Picard. For some reason, the picture bothered me a lot. It just didn't *look* right. So I experimented with a mirror and thought I had figured out what was wrong. On page 284 of the *NextGen Guide,* I stated that the stars should still be streaking away from Picard, because we are outside the ship looking in. I realized my error a few weeks after the *NextGen Guide* hit the bookshelves. (Brain cramp! Aaaah!) If you find a scene in Picard's ready room that features the stars streaking away from his window and hold up a mirror, you will find that the stars do in fact streak correctly. (Thanks to David Shelton of Birmingham, AL, for noticing this first.) On the other hand, Otto "Hackman" Huer in his Internet error list for *Star Trek* states that, given the camera angle, the stars should be streaking left to right on the window. Personally, I think the only way to know for sure is to build one of these *Galaxy*-class babies and take it out for spin.

PLOT OVERSIGHTS

• At one point, Riker determines to send Worf down to the surface in a shuttle to rescue Picard. He hopes that the Tamarians won't fire on the craft. Given that the *Enterprise* sits nose to nose with the Tamarian vessel, wouldn't it be prudent to back the *Enterprise* out of weapons range and see if the other ship follows? If the Tamarian vessel stays close, it might indicate that they have every intention of enforcing their captain and Picard's privacy on the planet.

• Riker is a bit rude at the end of this episode. He strolls right into the captain's ready room and then says, "I hope I'm not disturbing you." (Well...there would be *less* chance of that, Wil, if you *rang the doorbell* and waited for Picard to say, "Come.")

EQUIPMENT ODDITIES

• This episode seems to indicate that a person cannot move while in a transporter beam. As Dathon and Picard battle the beast, Riker decides to try to beam Picard through the scattering field set up by the Tamarian ship. The attempt fails but freezes Picard in place as the beast pummels Dathon. Now, if Picard could move in the transporter beam, wouldn't he be waving his arms around, trying to get O'Brien's attention, and signaling the transporter chief to leave him on the surface so he could assist his newfound friend?

• For some reason, the *Enterprise*'s phasers erupt not once but twice from the forward photon launcher.

CONTINUITY AND PRODUCTION PROBLEMS

• After the attempted rescue of Picard via shuttle fails, Riker orders

Data and Troi to find a way to communicate with the Tamarian. He makes it sound urgent. Indeed it is: Their captain is on the ground, weaponless, facing an uncertain future. Troi wears her gray unitard when Riker puts her on the case. Later we see her and Data working, and she wears her *burgundy* unitard! In other words, in the middle of this crisis she changed outfits. (Okay, okay. I have to admit that I also *think* better when I'm dressed in burgundy.)

TRIVIA ANSWERS

1. Captain Silvestri of the *Shiku Maru*.

2. A frozen dessert.

ENSIGN RO

Star Dates: 45076.3—45077.8

Under orders from Admiral Kennelly, Ensign Ro Laren joins the crew to assist Picard in locating Orta—a Bajoran terrorist accused of attacking a Federation colony. After realizing Orta's innocence, Picard discovers that the Cardassians have compromised Kennelly and are attempting to use the resources of Starfleet to locate Orta so they can destroy him.

ALTERNATE VIEWPOINTS AND CORRECTIONS

• One of the most submitted nits in the entire series occurs in this episode. While visiting a Bajoran resettlement camp, Ensign Ro kneels down, peels off her jacket, and places it around a child. I commented on page 286 of the *NextGen Guide* that the creators attempted to demonstrate Roddenberry's vision of a zipperless future during this incident. However, something else occurs as Ro disrobes that caused a fair bit of consternation among nitpickers. As James H. G. Redekop of London, Ontario, noted, it appears that Ensign Ro's communicator either magically jumps from her jacket to her sleeveless shirt underneath, or she carries two communicators. In fact, I *personally* think it's neither. Ro makes this little gesture before peeling off her jacket, and I believe that the creators had her do that to give the impression that she is moving the communicator from her jacket to her shirt. As the camera cuts to show us a front view of Ro, we see that her communicator hangs at an odd angle—as if it were put in place quickly.

TRIVIA QUESTIONS

1. With which Bajoran leader has Dr. Crusher danced?

2. Where was Ro Laren interned?

PLOT OVERSIGHTS

• When Ensign Ro firsts beams aboard, Riker makes her remove her Bajoran earring, citing some uniform code to which Starfleet officers must adhere. Obviously, Riker is simply grousing at Ro because the first officer has allowed Worf to wear his sash for more than four seasons now.

• Is there some reason why Ro wears her earring on her left ear when all the other Bajorans wear their earrings on their right ear?

• Walking through a Bajoran camp, Picard claims that he read in his fifth-grade reader how the ancient Bajoran civilization had flourished when "humans were not yet standing erect." I believe that—according to the theory of evolution—humans began standing erect about five hundred thousand years ago. One has to wonder what these Bajoran guys were doing all that time. To use a politically correct term, were they all "technologically challenged"? Why have they advanced so little in five hundred thousand years that the "lizard necks" could wander in and beat the stuffing out of them?

• Granted, Picard's plan to float an empty terrorist vessel just to see how the Cardassians will respond *is* beneficial in flushing out Kennelly's involvement in the affair, but what about Orta? He lost a perfectly good ship!

EQUIPMENT ODDITIES

• At the beginning of the episode, Kennelly comes on board, suffering from a Cardassian virus. Is there some reason why Crusher doesn't run him through the biofilters of the transporter? Or is this yet another disease that the biofilters won't filter?

• At the end of the episode, two Cardassian warships fire on a craft that they believe holds Orta. The first ship fires, and after several moments, the second ship fires. Yet, when the destructive charges reach the terrorist ship, they arrive very close together.

CONTINUITY AND PRODUCTION PROBLEMS

• Near the beginning of the episode, the *Enterprise* approaches Lya Station Alpha with survivors from the attacked Federation colony. As the *Enterprise* prepares to enter the giant space dock, the scene cuts inside to the observation lounge and a meeting between Picard and Kennelly. Surprisingly enough, although the meeting lasts for some time, the windows never show the *Enterprise* entering the space dock.

• Upon learning from La Forge that Ro doesn't deserve to wear a Starfleet uniform, Guinan wanders over to get acquainted. Ro holds a glass in her right hand. Her left arm rests between her body and the table. When the shot changes, Ro's left arm is suddenly on the table.

• After meeting with Orta and returning to the ship, Picard, Data, Troi, Worf, and Ro walk off a turbolift on the main bridge. As they walk down the ramp, they discuss the truthfulness of Orta's statements. It appears that the away team has just beamed up, gotten on a turbolift and reported back to the bridge. Yet both Picard and Troi wear outfits different from the ones they wore on during the away mission. So either the whole group went to Picard's quarters and waited for him to change and then went to Troi's quarters and waited for her to change, or Picard and Troi simply changed in the turbolift as it sped them to the bridge! (Now, *that* would be an interesting turbolift ride.)

TRIVIA ANSWERS

1. Jaz Holza.

2. At the stockade on Jaros II.

SILICON AVATAR

Star Dates: 45122.3—45129.2

D r. Kila Marr joins the *Enterprise* following an attack by the crystal entity on the colony on Melona IV. Unfortunately, Marr's need to avenge the death of her son on Omicron Theta (see "Datalore") soon leads her to use the resources of the *Enterprise* to destroy the entity—and her career in the process.

TRIVIA QUESTIONS

1. What previous attack site contained tunnels with the trace element kelbonite?

2. Who first experimented with gamma radiation scans on Omicron Theta?

PLOT OVERSIGHTS

• I let it pass in the *NextGen Guide,* but it really does strain credulity that Marr could outsmart Data and La Forge on *their own* ship and thwart their efforts to save the crystal entity.

• But for the sake of argument, let's say that Marr is such a fabulous programmer that neither Data nor La Forge can do anything to stop the graviton pulse that threatens the crystal entity. Is there some reason why Picard doesn't blast away at warp 9?

• So…why *did* the colonists on Melona IV survive? Was it because of Data's presence?

CHANGED PREMISES

• I mentioned this nit in "Datalore," but I should log it here as well. The rapid destruction of the colony on Melona IV raises a question about the events in "Datalore." In that episode, children actually had time to draw pictures of the crystal entity before they died. Given the events in this episode, this seems unlikely.

EQUIPMENT ODDITIES

• Does the crystal entity have some sort of probe it can use to extract crew members from a sealed ship? (Sort of like an anteater's tongue?) After figuring out how to track the crystal entity, the crew set out on its trail. A freighter soon contacts the *Enterprise* and reports that it is under attack from the crystal entity. When the *Enterprise* arrives, everyone is dead and the entity has fled. Yet the ship looks perfectly intact.

TRIVIA ANSWERS

1. Forlat III.
2. Dr. Clendenning.

DISASTER

Star Date: 45156.1

hen two quantum filaments
slam into the *Enterprise,* the
various members of her
crew must deal with a variety of crises. Troi takes command of
the bridge, while Picard attempts to
escape a damaged turbolift with three
children. Crusher and La Forge face
death from radiation or chemical detonation as Riker and Data make their
way to Engineering.

TRIVIA
QUESTIONS

1. The *Enterprise* completes
its mission on what planet
prior to striking the filaments?

2. To what starbase does
Picard set course at the
end of this episode?

ALTERNATE VIEWPOINTS
AND CORRECTIONS

• In the *NextGen Guide,* on page
292, I expressed my incredulity at
Troi's lack of knowledge about the
basic operation of the *Enterprise.* On
the bridge, O'Brien and Ro advise her
that the containment field for the antimatter is losing its integrity and there
is a danger of a containment breach
(which will result in the destruction of
the ship). Troi then asks for an expla-

nation of "containment breach." That's
when I became confused. John Burrows of Middlesex, England, offered
a possible explanation. He suggested that since Troi is the ship's counselor and advises the captain on many
matters, she was assigned the rank of
lieutenant commander as a specialist
rank commensurate with her duties.
As such, she would have little knowledge of any technical aspect of the
ship. However, if she is a specialist,
she shouldn't be in charge of the
bridge. That duty should have fallen
to O'Brien—assuming that Starfleet
uses some system like that in *Classic
Trek,* where McCoy was never even
considered to command the bridge.
And initially in "Encounter at Farpoint,"
Crusher stated that her interests lay
outside the command structure.

• The back cover of the *NextGen
Guide* comments that there is a control panel in a turbolift in only one
episode, "Brothers." Many, many nitpickers corresponded to remind me
that Picard's young "Number One" in
this episode operates a control panel in this episode as well. (Leslie
Tymko of London, Ontario, was the
first.) If you will look closely at the location of the control panel you will see
that it resides inside a rectangle with
slightly rounded corners. I believe the
control panel seen in this episode is
actually inside the motion indicator for
the turbolift. Apparently Picard
removed the motion indicator panel
prior to our joining this scene.

PLOT OVERSIGHTS

• After doing a preliminary damage
survey, Data tells Riker that they might

be able to reach Engineering through the "starboard service crawlway." Then they exit Ten-Forward through the *port*-side doors!

• At one point La Forge convinces Crusher to let him open the cargo bay doors and evacuate the atmosphere. By doing so he believes that all the dangerous chemicals will be sucked out into space. To quote Data in "The Naked Now," "Correction, sir: That's blown out."

• Try as I might, I cannot figure out how Picard got out of the turbolift with a broken ankle and only three small assistants.

EQUIPMENT ODDITIES

• Shortly after Picard boards the turbolift with the three children, a shot from inside the car shows us that it travels *up*. This seems like an odd direction to go, given that everyone boarded from the main bridge, the highest point on the ship. (Obviously the turbolift *didn't* read the script.)

• So the main power goes out on the ship, the computer goes down, and the *communicators* quit working? This is not a good design. In the good old days of *Classic Trek,* at least their communicators worked without benefit of the ship's power and computer.

• After discovering that the turbolifts don't work on the bridge, O'Brien observes that they are trapped. (Note: This is before the discussion about the emergency bulkheads closing.) So there's no staircase or crawl-space ladder off the bridge? Didn't Riker attempt to gain access to the bridge by climbing up a ladder in "Brothers"?

• Why is there gravity in the turbolift tubes? According to the *Tech Man-*

ual, there are gravity generators on every deck—each of them contributing to the overall natural feeling of gravity on the ship. Why not just put a gravity generator in the bottom of the turbolift car? Why put one in the bottom of the turbolift tube? If you put one at the bottom of the turbolift tube, won't the system have to fight against it every time the car goes up?

• And another thing: Where are the horizontal connecting tubes that supposedly branch off the vertical shafts? We get to see about nineteen decks' worth of this turboshaft, and I can't find a single horizontal shaft.

• The fact that sound doesn't travel in a vacuum brings up an equipment oddity. If Crusher and La Forge were trapped in the cargo bay without any air and they had to rely on their communicators to call for help, what would they do? Is there some way to send Morse code on those things? (Didn't the *Classic* communicators have an emergency transport button?)

TRIVIA ANSWERS

1. Mudor V.
2. Starbase 67.

THE GAME

Star Dates: 45208.2—45212.1

 esley visits the *Enterprise* just in time to uncover a plot to take over Starfleet by sublimating its members through the spread of a highly addictive game. Working together, Data and Wesley thwart the plans of the Ktarians—Starfleet's would-be conquerors.

GREAT LINES

"Chocolate is a serious thing." — Troi to Riker after he comments on the ritualistic nature of her consumption of the delicacy. Nominated by Noreen A. Demers of Epsom, NH.

TRIVIA QUESTIONS

1. What ship brings in five science teams at the beginning of the episode?

2. What dessert does Worf make for Wesley?

PLOT OVERSIGHTS

• Just after arriving on the *Enterprise,* Wesley walks down a hall with Data and the pair talk of their experiences at Starfleet Academy. Both recall with discomfort the "Sadie Hawkins Dance." If a twenty-fourth-century dance of this nature is equivalent to its twentieth-century counterpart, this is an event in which the "girls" must ask the "boys" to attend instead of the other way around. I find it amusing that the normally politically correct *Star Trek: The Next Generation* would submit that in the twenty-fourth century it will *still* be the normal custom for males to do the asking when it comes to dating—as signified by the implied unusual quality of the "Sadie Hawkins Dance" where the roles are reversed.

• After becoming addicted to the game, Crusher asks Data to come to sick bay. She shuts him off and severs some positronic links at the back of his head. The next scene shows Picard, La Forge, and others standing over Data's body and looking worried as Crusher explains that Data came in complaining of a malfunctioning servo and then suddenly collapsed. Wait a minute: La Forge was standing right beside Data when Crusher asked him to come to sick bay. Shouldn't the chief engineer say something like, "That's odd. That servo must have gone bad just after you called him to sick bay because he didn't mention it to me"?

• The big surprise at the conclusion of the episode comes when Data bursts onto the bridge with a palm beacon whose flashes are attenuated to release the senior officers from the control of the game. One question: Why didn't Ensign Robin Lefler tell the other infected crew members that Wesley was trying to reactivate Data? She was with Wesley when they discovered the addictive qualities of the game. She was with Wesley when they found that someone had tampered with Data. At the end of the program, she comes under the game's influence. Doesn't it make sense that she would tell the others to keep an eye on Data?

• After catching Wesley, Riker and Worf bring him to the bridge, plop him in the captain's chair, and force his eyes open. They intend to make him view the game. Yet, in the midst of this coercion, Wesley blinks! A good, full-bodied blink—a "he could shut his eyes if he wanted to" blink!

EQUIPMENT ODDITIES

• It's amazing that the game apparently affected everyone on the ship in the same manner, regardless of species. What about Worf, for example? Isn't his brain substantially different? And who could force him to play the game?

• Is there some reason why the tractor beam comes out of the forward photon launcher at the end of the episode?

CONTINUITY AND PRODUCTION PROBLEMS

• After Wesley finds her playing the game in his quarters, Crusher attempts to convince him to play it as well. She walks over and stands directly in front of her son, holding the game between them. From one angle the eyetips of the game point down. From the other, they point up.

• Is that Brent Spiner in the background in a blue uniform near the window when Wesley and Lefler play their second scene in Ten-Forward?

TRIVIA ANSWERS

1. The USS *Zhukov*.
2. Tarvokian pound cake.

UNIFICATION I

Star Dates: 45233.1—45240.6

After receiving intelligence that Ambassador Spock has gone to Romulus, Starfleet sends Picard and Data on a mission to determine his intent. At the same time, the crew of the *Enterprise* investigates the remains of a Vulcan ship stolen from the Federation junkyard on Qualor II.

TRIVIA QUESTIONS

1. Whom does Picard suggest that Worf contact on the Klingon Home World when Gowron fails to respond to the *Enterprise*'s hails?

2. What is the name of Pardek's political district?

PLOT OVERSIGHTS

• In this episode, Picard and Data ride aboard a Klingon Bird-of-Prey that flies straight up to the Romulan border and cloaks. It then proceeds to Romulus and drops into orbit around its enemy's home planet. Shouldn't the Romulans be patrolling their borders? One would think that the security-minded Romulans would keep a fleet of cloaked Romulan warbirds strategically located along their borders, constantly monitoring the line. In addition, if this cloaking device is so good that the Romulans can't even detect it, what's to stop a fleet of Romulan warbirds from taking up orbit around Earth or the Klingon Home World? Or what's to stop a fleet of Klingon Birds-of-Prey from taking up orbit around Romulus?

CHANGED PREMISES

• Wow! Starfleet Intelligence certainly has improved in the past few years. In "The Defector," Data told

Admiral Jarok that little was known of the Romulan Home World. In this episode, Starfleet long-range scanners pick out *one person* standing among a crowd on the surface of Romulus.

• While attempting to fit Data for pointed ears, Crusher asks if the android's ears are removable. Data replies no, that they are fully integrated components. Yet in "Datalore," Data picks up Lore's head, and it appears that the head lacks ears. Some sort of connecting slot lies flush against the side of the head, looking like a place where an ear would connect. And Dr. Soong—the creator of both androids—said in "Brothers" that Lore and Data were virtually identical except for "a bit of programming."

TRIVIA ANSWERS

1. K'Tal.
2. The Krocton Segment.

UNIFICATION II

Star Date: 45245.8

Locating Spock, Picard learns that the venerable Vulcan ambassador has come in response to an invitation from members of the Romulan government to discuss the reunification of Vulcan and Romulus. The true Romulan intent of the invitation soon becomes clear. The Romulans will send an invasion force to Vulcan using stolen Vulcan ships and force their own brand of reunification on the populace.

TRIVIA QUESTIONS

1. What is the name of the "fat Ferengi" who visits the bar on Qualor II?

2. What is the only vessel in range of the colony on Dulisian IV when the Romulans send out a bogus distress call?

PLOT OVERSIGHTS

• Is Spock posing as a Romulan on Romulus? Granted, he's got the ears and the eyebrows, but the forehead ridges are missing.

• Needing more information on the arms trader who died when his ship exploded, Riker goes to a bar on Qualor II. He locates the arms trader's wife—she plays keyboards at the bar—and attempts to charm the information out of her. Since Riker did her the favor of killing her husband, she acquiesces and suggests that he drop a few coins in her bowl. At this Riker replies that he doesn't carry money. Doesn't this seem like a good time to carry a few coins? Surely Starfleet has some method for providing payment to those outside Federation structures. Or is Riker merely trying to bluff his way through, knowing that if she won't budge he can always go back to the *Enterprise* and grab some gold-pressed latinum? (This brings up another question. The woman at the bar mentions coins. Apparently coins still exist. So…what's stopping some unscrupulous person from getting a replicator and mass-producing them? Do replicators have some sort of anti-counterfeiting circuitry built into them?)

• After learning that the fat Ferengi delivered the stolen Vulcan ship to a Barolian freighter near Galorndon Core, Riker sets course for the planet. On arrival, the crew finds nothing, but Troi suggests that there may be a cloaked Romulan base on the surface. This seems unlikely. "The Enemy" established that the magnetic fields of the planet wreak havoc with Romulan and human nervous systems. And in "The Defector," Data states that a cloaking device on the surface of a planet would produce visible distortion effects.

• Isn't it just a tad bit too convenient that Sela leaves Picard, Spock, and Data in her office without any guards to watch them so they can plan their escape?

• Many members of the Nitpicker's Guild remain unconvinced that Sela's plan for forcing the reunification of Vulcan and Romulus—using Vulcan ships carrying two thousand Romulans traveling at warp 1—has merit. Aside from the obvious problem of conquering an entire planet with two thousand soldiers, what good will it do for the Romulans to try to control the stoic Vulcans? How do you bend someone to your will who relies on logic alone? Control requires emotion. In addition, just how far is it from Romulus to Vulcan? The ships carrying the invasion force travel at warp 1. At warp 1 it would take at least *four years* to get from Earth to its nearest star system. And why would the Romulans use *Vulcan* ships in the first

place? Vulcan ships imply some sort of Vulcan involvement in the initiative. Don't the Romulans know that somebody is going to dial up Vulcan and say, "Pardon me for asking, but…did you send some ships to Romulus to pick up a peace delegation?" *And…*if the Klingons can actually send a cloaked ship to ferry Picard and Data to Romulus—apparently without the Romulans' knowledge—what is to stop Sela from sending a fleet of cloaked Romulan warbirds to Vulcan instead of these wimpy Vulcan ships? (I know that "Face of the Enemy" makes some mention of a Federation detection grid, but if there is a detection grid on our side of the border for cloaked Romulan ships, why don't the Romulans have a detection grid on their side of the border for cloaked Klingon ships? Answer: Because then Picard and Data couldn't get to Romulus and there wouldn't be a show!)

• When Riker decides to investigate the Vulcan ships crawling through the Neutral Zone at warp 1, the Romulans send a bogus distress call from the Federation colony on Dulisian IV. Amazingly enough, Crusher walks off the turbolift and states that they have just received it. Why is Crusher receiving medical distress calls? Isn't this Worf's job?

• In keeping with the portfolio confusion created when Crusher brings notification of a distress call to the bridge, Riker soon orders *La Forge*—at the *Engineering* station—to set course for Dulisian IV!

TRIVIA ANSWERS

1. Omag.
2. A Rutian archaeological vessel

A MATTER OF TIME

Star Dates: 45349.1—45351.9

When a small, unusual craft appears near the *Enterprise*'s flight path, the crew finds a vessel inhabited by a man named Rasmussen, who claims to be a historian from the twenty-sixth century. The crew soon discovers that Rasmussen is in fact a failed inventor from the past—come to steal devices from the *Enterprise*.

TRIVIA QUESTIONS

1. Among how many musical compositions, played simultaneously, can Data distinguish?

2. Where does Picard intend to take Rasmussen after this episode?

ALTERNATE VIEWPOINTS AND CORRECTIONS

• Several nitpickers wrote to wonder how Rasmussen could have located the *Enterprise* in the first place, given the vastness of space and time. Personally, I always thought that Rasmussen had seen some historical records from the twenty-sixth century on the USS *Enterprise* under the command of Captain Jean-Luc Picard

prior to his arrival. Otherwise, the episode made no sense to me because Rasmussen beams aboard with an amazing amount of knowledge about the crew and the ship. He could be faking some of it, but he is a fabulous con man if he's faking everything. Either the time-traveling craft contained detailed historical records, or Rasmussen first took a trip into the future, picked out a target for his attempted thievery, and then came back to meet the *Enterprise*.

• In the end, Picard refuses to allow Rasmussen to return to the twenty-second century, choosing to rip him out of his own time when the time-traveling craft returns to the twenty-second century by itself. On page 304 of the *NextGen Guide,* I questioned Picard's course of action and offered another. Let Data take Rasmussen home, kick him out, bring the machine back to the twenty-fourth century, step out, and send the machine back to the twenty-sixth century. In the company of other nitpickers, Phillip Thompson of Surrey, England, rejected this plan, believing that Rasmussen could do more harm by returning with knowledge of the future. Phillip also believed that the fact that nothing changed when Picard made the decision to keep Rasmussen shows that it was the correct decision. (I still wonder how Picard knew it was the correct decision in the first place. Did the historical records of that era show that Rasmussen disappeared without a trace? Perhaps, but in my own defense, I would offer a small addition to my plan to dispose of the scoundrel safely: Have Crusher wipe

Rasmussen's memory and then send him home!)

PLOT OVERSIGHTS

• At one point during the initial briefing in the observation lounge, Picard claims that he has inspected Rasmussen's credentials and they seem to be in order. How does one determine that a person from the future has credentials that are in order?

• At the briefing, Data escorts Rasmussen to his quarters. Once there, the android asks the historian if he still lives in the twenty-sixth century. Of course Rasmussen refuses to respond, but Data should deduce the answer, given the events during the rest of the episode. Rasmussen continually asks about Data's capabilities and is often amazed at how the android functions. He even asks Data for a set of schematics. Wouldn't Data realize that this indicates that he will not survive until the twenty-sixth century?

• At one point Rasmussen wanders down to Main Engineering to give Data and La Forge his questionnaires. As La Forge gets up from his seat to walk to the center island, Rasmussen starts questioning him about his VISOR. Then it sounds like Rasmussen says, "Ya know, I have a picture of you wearing that, Lev," but that can't be right, because the chief engineer's name is Geordi La Forge, not LeVar Burton. Or does Rasmussen say "Laf," short for "La Forge"? (It's awfully hard to tell.)

• The creators treat us to a large time jump in this episode when the *Enterprise* makes its first attempt to help the colony on Penthara IV. An asteroid has struck the planet, sending debris into the atmosphere and causing a decrease in the amount of sunlight that reaches the surface. La Forge comes up with a plan to drill holes in the planet, using the phaser to release subsurface pockets of carbon dioxide. He hopes this will create a greenhouse effect, trapping more heat near the surface, thereby keeping the planet from freezing. Within seconds after completing the drilling, La Forge reports an increase at two equatorial stations. Brad Higgins advises me that atmospheres of planets simply do not change this quickly. For instance, on Earth the hottest part of the day comes between three and four o'clock in the afternoon, even though the sun is at its highest at noon. That's called thermal lag.

CHANGED PREMISES

• At the beginning of the episode, Rasmussen meets with the senior staff in the observation lounge. Riker asks when historians began to use time travel for research. Well…Kirk and crew were engaged in historical research several decades *prior* to this episode in "Assignment: Earth."

• In Ten-Forward, Crusher responds to Rasmussen's statement that he just returned from the twenty-second century by saying that he probably saw a lot of surgical masks and gloves, because quarantine fields weren't invented yet. But Crusher used gloves during the operation to implant Odan in Riker in "The Host" and uses them again when replacing Worf's backbone in "Ethics."

EQUIPMENT ODDITIES

• In his quarters, while talking with Rasmussen, Data receives a call from La Forge on the surface of Penthara IV. The music that plays in the background instantly stops. This makes sense. It ensures that the music does not interfere with the conversation. However, after the conversation, the music stays off. Shouldn't it restart?

• After accusing Rasmussen of stealing equipment from the *Enterprise,* Picard refuses to allow the "historian" to enter his craft unless accompanied by Data. Once inside, Rasmussen pulls a phaser on the android and attempts to stun him. The phaser fails to function. Picard later explains that the computer deactivated it. Indeed, the *Tech Manual* says that the hand phasers contain both a safety interlock and a subspace transceiver array, indicating that the main computer would have the capability to perform this function. Why, then, is this capability not used on other episodes such as "The Hunted" and "Power Play"?

CONTINUITY AND PRODUCTION PROBLEMS

• In preparation for its second attempt to help the colony on Penthara IV, the *Enterprise* rotates to face the planet. Subsequent shots of the viewscreen show the planet as if the *Enterprise* still sits in a standard orbit.

TRIVIA ANSWERS

1. One hundred fifty.

2. Starbase 214.

NEW GROUND

Star Date: 45376.3

Helena Rozhenko suddenly comes to the *Enterprise* with Alexander and advises Worf that his son needs him. As the crew tests a new method of warp propulsion called the soliton wave, Worf discovers that Alexander suffers from feelings of anger and abandonment caused by the death of his mother, K'Ehleyr. In response, Worf asks Alexander if he wants to stay on board the *Enterprise.*

TRIVIA QUESTIONS

1. On what planet will a Federation colony generate a scattering field to disperse the soliton wave?

2. What would Worf rather face than his child?

ALTERNATE VIEWPOINTS AND CORRECTIONS

• During this episode, La Forge reports a power efficiency rating of 98 percent for the soliton wave. Data then states that this is 450 percent—or four and one-half times—more efficient than the *Enterprise*'s warp drive. On page 307 of the *NextGen Guide* I noted that La Forge in "Allegiance" managed to raise the efficiency of the warp drive to 95 percent. Then, I wondered how you could calculate a 450 percent increase by going from 95 percent to 98 percent. Several nitpickers made a valiant attempt to do so. Scott Charrington of County Antrim, Northern Ireland, started with the assumption that everything in the dialogue is true. Since La Forge said the wave was 98 percent efficient and Data said that was 4.5 times greater than the *Enterprise*, obviously the *Enterprise* engines only operate at about 22 percent optimum efficiency, and La Forge in "Allegiance" increased engine efficiency to 95 percent of that figure, or almost 21 percent efficiency. Sunshine of Philadelphia, PA—figuring that the crew might be using a logarithmic scale—juggled some figures to come out at a relatively close 550 percent increase in efficiency. (I must tell you, with all due respect, I remain *unconvinced*!)

PLOT OVERSIGHTS

• If Worf's last name is Rozhenko—evidenced by the fact that his adoptive parents *and* his son carry the last name of Rozhenko—I wonder why he isn't addressed as "Lieutenant Rozhenko" instead of "Lieutenant Worf." (Personal preference, maybe?)

• During this episode, the *Enterprise* transports two of only twelve remaining Corvan gilvos creatures to a protected haven on another planet. Granted, Picard has a pretty good track record in keeping the *Enterprise* from exploding, but wouldn't it be safer to transport these endangered species on a vessel that isn't a continual target for Klingons, Romulans, Cardassians, Ferengi, temporal disturbances, etc.?

• Toward the end of the episode, Riker and Worf rescue Alexander and the Corvan gilvos from a room that will receive a lethal dose of radiation when Picard fires photon torpedoes to dissipate the soliton wave. The room must be *right* on the edge of the *huge* contamination area displayed on Riker's monitor early in the episode, because Worf and Riker simply run out into the hall and everyone is fine.

EQUIPMENT ODDITIES

• In this episode, Alexander's class goes on a field trip to see a bunch of plastic models of extinct animals. Wouldn't the holodeck serve this purpose *much* better by presenting animated versions of the beasts?

• At one point Alexander runs off to join the holodeck and play with Worf's beasties. Worf walks in and commands the holodeck to "freeze program." For some reason the fog keeps moving in the background.

TRIVIA ANSWERS

1. Lemma II.
2. Ten Balduk warriors.

HERO WORSHIP

Star Date: 45397.3

The crew of the *Enterprise* locates the science vessel *Vico* ripped apart with only one survivor—a boy named Timothy. As part of the investigation, the *Enterprise* travels into a "black cluster"—a region of space with high gravitational waves. Its crew is unaware that shield energies reflecting off the waves destroyed the *Vico,* and their ship as well.

TRIVIA QUESTIONS

1. What metal can inhibit transporter function?

2. What does Timothy order while visiting Ten-Forward with Troi?

ALTERNATE VIEWPOINTS AND CORRECTIONS

• On page 310 of the *NextGen Guide* I observe that the *Vico* must have a humongous computer core. At one point in the episode, Picard—looking at a side view of the *Vico*—points to the midpoint on the saucer and identifies it as the hallway outside the core. La Forge then points at the lower portion of the star drive section and identifies it as part of the core. So the computer core starts in the saucer, travels all the way down the yoke, and ends near the bottom of the star drive? Michael Hollick of Brampton, Ontario, asked why the core couldn't be that big, noting that it is a science vessel. In reviewing the episode, I find a fact that I neglected to mention. The *Vico* does not have a single yoke in the center of the ship. It has two yokes on either side that connect the saucer to the star drive. That means the computer core starts in the saucer section, runs over to one side of the ship, makes a right-angle turn at the yoke, travels down the yoke, and ends in the star

drive. I suppose it's ▮

PLOT OVERS▮

• Data forgets La F▮ momentarily before buildi▮ ▮er of a temple for Timothy, re▮rring to the chief engineer as "Lieutenant" when, in fact, his rank is "lieutenant commander" and he should be addressed as "Commander."

• Shortly after Timothy gives a true recounting of the events on the *Vico,* a gravitational wave hits the *Enterprise.* Timothy comments that it felt just like it did when the trouble began on the *Vico.* His face shows concern. But the *Enterprise* experienced a similar shaking earlier in the episode, and moments later we see Timothy crack a smile in school. The bridge shook. Engineering shook. Did the school not shake?

EQUIPMENT ODDITIES

• Toward the end of the episode, Timothy breaks down and confesses that he believes he caused the destruction on the *Vico* when his arm bumped a computer terminal panel. Data reassures him that this is impossible because the on-board control systems on all Starfleet vessels require a user code clearance. In other words, you have to punch in a code to get access to the terminal? Do all Starfleet vessels have codes for every member in Starfleet? If not, how can away teams beam over and start operating a ship, as the crew did in "The Naked Now," "Night Terrors," "Realm of Fear," and—for that matter—in this episode? (Or is there some sort of generic code you can punch in? How often is this changed? And if terminals really take a code, why was Worf worried about the Cardassian fooling around with the computer terminal in "The Wounded"?)

CONTINUITY AND PRODUCTION PROBLEMS

• After Timothy decides to become an android to repress the pain he feels over the loss of his parent, Picard and Troi suggest that Data spend time with the boy to reinforce the new persona. Data begins by styling Timothy's hair into an android hairdo. After Data finishes, a lock of Timothy's hair still sticks out on the left side of his head. Then the shot changes and the hair is smooth.

• Worf gets just a little jumpy when the gravitational waves start rocking the ship. Just after La Forge tells the bridge that he will smooth things out in just a minute, keep your eyes on the chief of Security. A wave hits; Picard, Riker, and Worf move together. Then Worf moves, and a moment later Picard and Riker join him. (Missed it by *that* much!)

TRIVIA ANSWERS

1. Victurium alloy.
2. A Tamarian frost.

VIOLATIONS

Star Dates: 45429.3—45435.8

When the *Enterprise* transports a group of Ullians—memory archaeologists who recover the recollec-

tions of individuals to understand their race—one of them, named Jev, turns out to be a psychic rapist. After assaulting Troi and sending her into a coma, Jev incapacitates Riker and Crusher, trying to cover his crime. In time, Data and La Forge uncover his activities.

TRIVIA QUESTIONS

1. Which doctor assists Crusher during this episode in sick bay?

2. Who became trapped near the warp core during a failure of the matter/antimatter system?

PLOT OVERSIGHTS

• After Troi falls into a coma and is taken to sick bay, Riker pays her a visit. While talking to her, the first officer says that he isn't sure if she can hear him or not. Given Crusher's statement in "The Battle" that twenty-fourth-century medicine has mapped the brain, are we to believe that—in the *twenty-fourth* century—they still don't know if a person can hear you while in a coma? Can't they do some type of neural scan to determine this?

EQUIPMENT ODDITIES

• Near the end of the episode, the display above the replicator in Troi's quarters looks very odd, almost as if it comes from one of the first six *Star Trek* movies. You can see only bits and pieces of it through the scene, but it is definitely not standard issue for the *Enterprise*-D.

CONTINUITY AND PRODUCTION PROBLEMS

• During the famed conversation mentioned above, Riker starts out on Troi's left. Then a close-up shows him on Troi's right. There is time for him to move around the bed, but no sound accompanies the movement. Then Riker walks around the bed to Troi's left. It looks like the editor grabbed a piece of film from later in the scene to use as an establishing shot.

TRIVIA ANSWERS

1. Dr. Martin.
2. Ensign Keller.

THE MASTERPIECE SOCIETY

Star Date: 45470.1

The *Enterprise* helps an isolationist, genetically engineered colony on Moab IV avert disaster by working with the colonists' scientists and engineers and discovering a way to ensure that the colony's sealed environment can withstand the gravitational disruptions caused by the near passage of a stellar fragment. In the process, many colonists decide to leave.

TRIVIA QUESTIONS

1. From what type of celestial body did the stellar fragment originate?

2. How many colonists leave?

ALTERNATE VIEWPOINTS AND CORRECTIONS

• While working with Hannah Bates, the colony's chief scientist aboard the *Enterprise,* La Forge says that his eyes feel like they have lead weights attached to them. In the *NextGen Guide* on page 316, I stated that I found this an odd statement for La Forge to make. Normally a person makes this statement because he or she is struggling to keep his or her eyes open and—for whatever reason—the circumstances do not allow the individual to close them. I noted that it makes no difference if La Forge closes his eyes because he sees with his VISOR. John E. Cherman of Glendale, CA, had a different opinion. He felt that La Forge needed to keep his eyes open so he would not fall asleep—feeling that even visually impaired people begin to fall asleep when they close their eyes. My standard response to this type of statement was that sighted people go to sleep when they close their eyes because of a reduction in the amount of sensory input combined with a learned response. Since the closing of La Forge's eyes does not result in a reduction of sensory input, I *still* didn't think it made any sense for him to struggle to keep them open! My feeling was that La Forge's equivalent to closing his eyes would be to take off his VISOR (something that he does several times in the series when he goes to sleep and, in fact, does in *this* episode just shortly after making the "lead weights on my eyelids" statement).

Joy A. Frost of San Antonio, TX—an occupational therapist with training in neuroanatomy and neurophysiology—added some interesting information to this discussion. She stated that the phenomenon of sleep is quite complex, primarily regulated by certain neurotransmitters. Sleep deprivation is one of the strongest stimuli in the production of these transmitters for persons with normal brain chemistry. If you haven't had any sleep in a while, the brain figures you need some. Another strong stimulus is fatigue. Sensory stimulation or deprivation also affects sleep, but not as much as sleep deprivation and fatigue. (Remember when your mom told you just to lie in bed and stay quiet until you fell asleep? Well, she was partially right.) In other words—given a high enough level of sleep deprivation and fatigue—La Forge would start snoring no matter what he did, just like very tired sighted persons fall asleep with the TV blaring in a brightly lit room or even driving down a road in broad daylight.

But the question remains: Do individuals blind from birth experience "heavy eyelid" syndrome? In fact, they do! I spoke with Rachel Schroeder, a visually impaired Trekker who's still waiting for a VISOR just like Geordi's. (One that works, that is!) Rachel tells me that she has trouble keeping her eyes open and frequently rubs them when she's tired. On the other hand, Rachel added that she *can* close her eyes and keep going.

• The answer to the second trivia question on page 316 should be "one to one hundred thousand terra*hertz*," not "terrawatts." (Thanks to James Furlong of East Sussex, England.)

• Dorothy E. Clark of Decatur, GA, wrote to point out correctly that the piece played by the young boy in this episode is not Chopin's "Prelude in C Minor," as I stated on page 316 of the *NextGen Guide*. (Personally, I think that page was jinxed!) In fact, the musical selection is Chopin's "Prelude in *E* Minor." Sorry, I was confused. I've played both of the lovely little selections and switched their titles.

CONTINUITY AND PRODUCTION PROBLEMS

• At the very beginning of the episode, La Forge gives Picard a report from his Engineering workstation on the bridge. As he moves toward the curved, wooden railing, you can see the reflection of a boom mike in the large upright black panel that hangs on the wall between the Engineering workstation and the upper turbolift.

• The redoubtable Commander Riker almost walks into a wall on his way to meet Hannah Bates, the colony's chief scientist. Watch him as the away team and Aaron Conor approach her work area. Riker has his head down. He's striding forward in typical Riker style. Suddenly he realizes he isn't going to clear the door and makes a quick course correction!

TRIVIA ANSWERS

1. A disintegrating neutron star.
2. Twenty-three.

UPDATED
CONUNDRUM TOTE BOARD

1. Given Riker's insistance in "Encounter at Farpoint" that Picard remain on the ship for his own safety, the number of dangerous planets visited by the captain: twenty-five
2. Given Crusher's assertion in "The Battle" that humanity no longer suffers from the common cold (and presumably other viral-type illness), the number of respiratory viruses that show up in the series: two
3. Given Data's inability to use contractions, the number of times he does: at least thirty-two
4. Given Troi's ability to sense the emotional states of others, the number of times she can't sense deception in humans: two
5. Given Picard's statements in "Elementary, Dear Data" that holodeck matter cannot leave the holodeck, the number of times it does: five
6. Given the fact that the *Enterprise* can fly at warp and most shuttles fly at impulse, the number of times crew members take multiple-hour trips when the *Enterprise* could take them to their destination in seconds: five
7. Given Gene Roddenberry's assertion that zippers would be obsolete in the twenty-third century, the number of times female crew members grope for zippers: two
8. Given that the *Enterprise* is filled with Starfleet's best and brightest crew members, the number of times Wesley, who has trouble getting into the Starfleet Academy, comes up with the needed solution: seven
9. Given the kindness the crew shows toward other races in the twenty-fourth century, the number of times they resort to bashing twentieth-century humans: five
10. Given the close proximity of the turbolift near Picard's ready room, the number of times the crew uses it: very few

REFERENCES

1. Deneb IV in "Encounter at Farpoint," Ligon II in "Code of Honor," Rubicun III in "Justice," Mordan IV in "Too Short a Season," Aldea in "When the Bough Breaks," Minos in "Arsenal of Freedom," Vagra II in "Skin of Evil," Iconia in "Contagion," Delta Rana IV in "The Survivors," Mintaka III in "Who Watches the Watchers," the first Gatherer outpost in "The Vengeance Factor," Angosia III in "The Hunted," Rutia IV in "The High Ground," the Klingon Home World in "Sins of The Father," Ventax II in "Devil's Due," Malcor III in "First Contact," the Klingon colony in "The

Mind's Eye," the Klingon Home World again in "Redemption" and "Redemption II," a Bajoran refugee camp in "Ensign Ro," Moab IV in "The Masterpiece Society," Devidia II in "Time's Arrow" and "Time's Arrow II," a war-torn planet in "Man of the People," Celtris III in "Chain of Command, Part 1," Vilmor II in "The Chase," Borg world in "Descent," and Kesprit III in "Attached."

2. A virus ravages the crew in "Angel One," and Admiral Kennelly suffers from one in "Ensign Ro." (A note of explanation: Since the "common cold" does not come from one but hundreds of different viruses, successful elimination of the common cold would involve a broad-based cure for viral-type infections. At the very least, running a person through the transporter and its biofilters should eliminate the viruses, shouldn't it?)

3. This is by no means a complete list, but here's a sampling: At least four times in "Encounter at Farpoint." Three times in "The Naked Now." At least five times in "Code of Honor." At least twice in "The Last Outpost." At least twice in "Where No One Has Gone Before." "It's elementary, my dear Riker," "...he's in trouble," and "He's in the ship's circuitry" in "Lonely Among Us." At least five times in "Justice." At least four times in "The Big Goodbye" when playing Picard's sidekick, along with "I'm at a loss, sir." "I'm quite deficient...," "I've always felt...," and "I've been most anxious..." in addition to "I'm fine" in "Datalore." "Time flies when you're having fun" in "We'll Always Have Paris" in addition to "It's me!" and "There's insufficient data to make..." in "Conspiracy." "Okay, you're ugly, too," in "The Outrageous Okona." "I'm aware of your interest..." and "...it's a waste of time now" in "The Schizoid Man." "I'm taking part..." in "The Measure of a Man." "I'm puzzled..." in "Tin Man." Several times when playing the angry lover in "In Theory." "I've locked out..." in "The Quality of Life." "I've been meaning..." in "Starship Mine." "I'll break his neck" in "Descent, Part II." "We'll be returning..." in "Inheritance." (And so it goes, and so on.)

4. Rasmussen's deception eludes her in "A Matter of Time," as do Timothy's lies in "Hero Worship."

5. Wesley walks out of the holodeck and he's still wet in "Encounter at Farpoint." A snowball flies out and hits Picard in "Angel One." Lipstick remains on Picard's face during "The Big Goodbye." Data carries out a piece of paper in "Elementary, Dear Data." Picard walks out with a different uniform in "Ship in a Bottle."

6. Troi travels back to the *Enterprise* in "Skin of Evil." Picard comes from Starbase 718 in "The Neutral Zone." Picard and Wesley go to Starbase 515 in "Samaritan Snare." Picard and Wesley fly off to meet with miner in "Final Mission." La Forge travels to Risa in "The Mind's Eye."

7. Crusher in "The Naked Now" and Troi in "The Price."

8. He changes the tractor beam to a repulser beam in "The Naked Now." He points out the similarity of wave forms in "The Battle." He fixes the holodeck in "The Big Goodbye." He figures out they could use a neutrino pulse to contact La Forge in "The Enemy." He makes the crucial connection to the Elway Theorem in "The High Ground." He recognizes Riker's signal in "Ménage à Troi." He notes the game's addictive nature in "The Game."

9. "Encounter at Farpoint" claims that humans were a dangerous, savage child race when they wore World War II uniforms. In "Code of Honor," Picard states that Ligonian customs are the "same kind of pompous strutting charades that endangered our own species a few centuries ago." Riker compares us to the Ferengi in "The Last Outpost." In "Haven," Crusher says that the Tarellians had reached earth's late twentieth-century level of knowledge and then concludes, "That's all you need if you're a damn fool." And finally, Riker during "The Neutral Zone" comments on the recently thawed humans by saying, "From what I've seen of our guests, there's not much to redeem them. It makes one wonder how our species survived the twenty-first century."

10. (Sorry, I'm still not going to list them!)

CONUNDRUM

Star Date: 45494.2

After a memory-erasing beam hits the *Enterprise* and its crew, Picard and the others find the Federation at war with the Lysian Alliance. According to the crew's orders, the *Enterprise* must fly to the Lysian Central Command and destroy it—orders concocted by Commander MacDuff, a Satarran and archenemy of the Lysians who poses as a human member of the crew.

TRIVIA QUESTIONS

1. What is a standard response to the Kriskov Gambit in three-dimensional chess?

2. What book—a present from Troi—does Riker have in his quarters?

ALTERNATE VIEWPOINTS AND CORRECTIONS

• For my second trivia response in the *NextGen Guide*'s review of this episode, I stated that the *Enterprise* has ten phaser banks. I took this piece of information from Worf's dialogue when he reviews the tactical arrangements of the ship. But according to my reading of the *Tech Manual,* the *Enterprise* actually has eleven! (They are: one Saucer Module dorsal array, two Battle Section upper arrays, two Battle Section dorsal aft arrays, one Saucer Module ventral array, one Battle Section forward array, two nacelle pylon arrays, and two Battle Section ventral aft arrays. Thanks to Michael Mueller of San Jose, CA, for pointing this out.) In addition, "Arsenal of Freedom" shows a phaser array on the cobra head of the Battle Section.

PLOT OVERSIGHTS

• Won't MacDuff's memory-erasing beam work on the Lysians? Is there some reason why MacDuff and the Satarrans haven't used this awesome weapon on their foes?

• After everyone gets zapped, a new crew member instantly appears on the *Enterprise.* Sometime later we discover that he is the first officer, Commander MacDuff. This begs these questions: Why didn't MacDuff make himself captain? Or get rid of the crew and staff it with his own people?

• It's a bit amazing to me that everyone believes the *Enterprise* is on a secret wartime mission to destroy the Central Command of an enemy who has fought a "genocidal" war against the Federation but no one finds it odd that there are families on board the ship.

EQUIPMENT ODDITIES

• In the moments after the memory-erasing beam hits, Picard attempts to use the computer by talking to the ceiling. Riker replies that there's no voice interface. To this La Forge claims, "no interface, period." Presumably he's speaking of a user interface to the computer. Amazingly enough, La Forge's workstation still shows lots of buttons. He can still enter commands on those buttons. And just a few seconds later, he brings up a beautiful graphic of the *Enterprise* on his display. He then proceeds to give the status of the major sections of the ship. From my perspective, it sure looks and sounds like the computer has a user interface!

CONTINUITY AND PRODUCTION PROBLEMS

• Shortly after the memory-erasing beam hits the *Enterprise,* La Forge states that he has some intermittent energy readings. At this point, look closely at his right hand. It looks like he's tapping some buttons on the Engineering workstation—and it certainly sounds like he's hitting buttons—but the area underneath his fingers is blank!

• When Picard and MacDuff report to Worf in the ready room on their progress, the stars in the window move along at a pretty good clip given that the *Enterprise* supposedly hangs motionless in space.

• The creators took the opportunity to reuse the Edo "god" ship from "Justice" and recast it as the Lysian Central Command for this episode.

TRIVIA ANSWERS

1. The el-Mitra Exchange.
2. *Ode to Psyche* by John Keats.

POWER PLAY

Star Dates: 45571.2—45572.1

While an away team searches for faint life signs on an uninhabited moon, three noncorporeal prisoners exiled to the moon take over Troi, Data, and O'Brien. When the trio returns to the *Enterprise* they attempt to commandeer the ship, but Picard and crew outsmart them before the entire vessel can become a new sanctuary for the convicts interned below.

TRIVIA QUESTIONS

1. Who was the sector commander for the *Essex*?

2. From where did the prisoners originate?

PLOT OVERSIGHTS

• After sensing life on the moon, Troi accompanies Riker and Data as they fly down to the surface in a shuttle. Once the craft loses a thruster, Riker tells everyone to ready themselves for a crash. Troi pushes herself into her seat and forces her head against the back wall. This is a good position if you expect a rear impact, but since the craft will undoubtedly crash-land while moving forward, it probably would be better for her to put her head down and avoid the whiplash.

• The away team returns and in short order Data hits Riker, sending him backward. Riker struggles to rise, and O'Brien stuns him. Meanwhile, Troi knocks Picard unconscious in his ready room. Then the possessed trio boards a turbolift. Picard comes out of his ready room and asks for a report. Riker says that Data, O'Brien, and Troi tried to commandeer the ship. But Riker was unconscious when Troi came out of the ready room. How did he know that she was involved?

EQUIPMENT ODDITIES

• I should point out that in this episode Troi, Data, and O'Brien leave their communicators in a turbolift. The computer then reports the turbolift as their present location. Yet, in "Reunion" and "Identity Crisis," Worf and La Forge, respectively, are separated from their communicators and the computer says they are no longer on the ship.

CONTINUITY AND PRODUCTION PROBLEMS

• Would that be some of Brent Spiner's *makeup* that rubs off on the Ops panel where Data pounds his fist?

TRIVIA ANSWERS

1. Admiral Uttan Narsu.
2. The Ux-Mal System.

ETHICS

Star Date: 45587.3

When Worf sustains an injury that paralyzes him from the waist down, Dr. Toby Russell joins the *Enterprise* to assist. Knowing that Worf will commit suicide if he doesn't regain his mobility, and certain that conventional therapies will not succeed, Russell proposes a controversial procedure over Crusher's objections. Thankfully, the procedure proves successful.

TRIVIA QUESTIONS

1. What ship brings Russell to the *Enterprise*?

2. Where does the *Denver* crash-land?

PLOT OVERSIGHTS

• At the end of the episode, after Worf dies, we learn that (insert trumpet "ta-da" here) Klingons have a *backup* to their synaptic functions and he really isn't dead (insert nitpicker "groan" here). Makes one wonder how hard Klingons have to work to commit suicide.

• During the operation, the members of the surgical team have their hair neatly tucked away under their caps, but Worf's is completely exposed. Shouldn't his be up in some kind of "warrior" shower cap?

CHANGED PREMISES

• During Worf's operation, the members of the surgical team wear cool little hats and surgical gloves. Yet, in "A Matter of Time," didn't Crusher make a point to mention that surgical gloves were still used in the twenty-second century because the sterile field hadn't been invented yet?

• I hate to bring this up again but…would that be *red* blood that Worf bleeds during his operation? (One more time: Doesn't *Star Trek VI: The Undiscovered Country* lead us to believe that Klingons have purple-colored blood?)

EQUIPMENT ODDITIES

• Many of the Guild found it completely untenable that Starfleet would exhibit such wanton disregard for crew safety as evidenced by the state of the barrels in the cargo bay where Worf sustains his injury. In a vessel constantly jostled about by enemy fire and all manner of energy distortions, Starfleet has industrial shelving units filled with tall stacks of large barrels but not one *restraining strap* in sight!

TRIVIA ANSWERS

1. The *Potemkin*.
2. On a planet in the Mericor System.

THE OUTCAST

Star Dates: 45614.6—45620.4

R iker falls in love with a member of the J'naii race named Soren. Soren responds to Riker's attentions but is soon apprehended by the authorities. Because of the androgynous nature of the populace, any feelings of gender on her planet are quickly repressed. In short order, psychotectic treatments bring Soren in line with the norm.

TRIVIA QUESTIONS

1. Who was Soren's flight instructor?

2. What is the name of the missing shuttle?

PLOT OVERSIGHTS

• Two minor additional items on this episode. While we do not have an ending star date for the previous episode, "Ethics" begins with a star date of 45587.3. "The Outcast" occurs within star dates 45614.6 through 45620.4. First, Crusher tells Worf in the previous episode that it is going to take some time for his muscles to learn to respond to the new nerve signals traveling along his newly replaced spinal column. This seems reasonable, and it appears at the end of "Ethics" that Worf attempts to learn to walk again. Yet, in this episode, Worf seems fully recovered and even engages in a fight at the end. Second, La Forge sports a fairly full beard in this episode, whereas in the previous episode he was clean-shaven. Neither of these items would be odd providing the time that elapses between the episodes is adequate. Several times in the *NextGen Guide* I offered evidence that 1000 star date units translate to one year. Given that ratio, some simple math can give us a rough idea of how much time passes between these two episodes. From the start of "Ethics" to the end of "The Outcast" is 33.1 star date units. Normalizing this figure using a year of 365 days, we find that just over 12 days have elapsed from the time of Worf's accident through the decision to operate, the operation itself, to Worf's convalescence to his reinvigorated stature as a warrior. Likewise, just over 12 days have elapsed for La Forge to go from clean-shaven to a fairly nice-looking beard. (Actually, I know some guys who could pull off this latter nit!)

TRIVIA ANSWERS

1. Krite.
2. The *Taris Murn*.

CAUSE AND EFFECT

Star Date: . . .45652.1, 45652.1, 45652.1, 45652.1

After a collision with the USS *Bozeman*, the *Enterprise* becomes trapped in a temporal causality loop that repeats the events that lead up to the collision and the collision itself over and over. Experiencing an ever deepening feeling of déjà vu, the crew finally determines what is happening to them, avoids the collision, and breaks out of the loop.

TRIVIA QUESTIONS

1. What card first appears on the bottom of the deck when Data shuffles the cards during the opening credits?

2. What medication does Crusher give La Forge to combat his dizziness?

PLOT OVERSIGHTS

• Coming upon a temporal distortion, Picard attempts to back the *Enterprise* away, but soon the ship loses power. Moments later, the *Bozeman* comes flying through the distortion, and Data calculates that it is on a collision course. Picard asks for options. Riker suggests decompressing the main shuttle bay. Data suggests using the tractor beam. Picard opts for the latter, but the tractor beam doesn't deflect the *Bozeman* enough to keep it from hitting the starboard engine nacelle. Why not use both? Why not take advantage of every opportunity to save the ship? On top of that, why *doesn't* the tractor beam work? Since the *Enterprise* has lost its propulsion systems, there is nothing to anchor it to a specific point in space. There is no gravity, so when the tractor beam strikes the *Bozeman,* not only should it shove the *Bozeman* away, it should shove the *Enterprise* backward as well.

• Riker displays his "sea legs" in this episode: During each collision sequence, as the ship bounces around after impact, the first officer stands with one foot on the ground and the other propped up on Data's console. He lasts quite a while before tumbling down to the floor.

• There are some major time discrepancies between the loops. For instance, La Forge always happens to show up in sick bay at precisely when it is convenient for Crusher to leave the poker game. For instance, in the poker game that runs during the opening credits, almost one and one-half minutes elapse between the time Riker raises the bet to fifty and Crusher's nurse pages her. Yet later, when Riker realizes that Crusher will call his bluff, fewer than twenty seconds elapse from the time he raises the bet to fifty until the nurse pages. In the third complete run-through of the loop, Crusher records the voices in her quarters, takes them to Main Engineering, and then calls a special meeting of the senior staff some-

time before their normal meeting at 0700 hours. (If you recall, the *Bozeman* consistently appears during this meeting.) At the conclusion of this special meeting, Data, Crusher, and La Forge go to Main Engineering and install a device to allow Data to send a message into the next cycle of the loop. In the fourth and last complete run-through of the loop, Crusher again records the voices in her quarters and takes them to Main Engineering. Presumably she calls a special meeting of the senior staff. Yet this time the distortion appears near the end of this meeting instead of the normally scheduled one at 0700 hours. Finally, during each run-through of the loop until the last, there are only a few seconds from the time Worf engages the tractor beam until the *Bozeman* hits the *Enterprise.* Yet, during the final loop, Data has time to swing his head up dramatically to look at Riker's collar, reach a decision, and then decompress the shuttle bay.

• After discovering that they are caught in the loop, Worf suggests that they reverse course to avoid the explosion. Picard and Riker both reject this idea, stating that their reversal might be the action that got them into the loop in the first place. (Insert really obnoxious buzzer sound here.) Wrong! Since they weren't in the loop the first time through, there wouldn't be any déjà vu to alert them to any potential danger and therefore they would have no possible reason for turning around in the first place. Therefore it is reasonable to assume that they didn't turn around as part of the events that led to the creation of the loop, so turning around is probably the right thing to do!

• Captain Morgan Bateson seems a bit dazed by his experience in the causality loop. Remember that he comes from the year 2278. According to the official chronology of *Star Trek,* this is a few years after the events in *Star Trek: The Motion Picture.* But Bateson has very little reaction to seeing a very odd-looking ship that has *"Enterprise"* scrawled across its saucer. Neither does he react to seeing a Klingon on the bridge of a Starfleet vessel. And finally, he takes it all in stride when Picard introduces himself as the captain of the *Enterprise.* Given Bateson's time frame, one would expect him to say, *"Enterprise!?* What do you mean, you're the captain of the *Enterprise*? That's James Kirk's ship!" (Okay, okay. We don't know for sure that Kirk was commanding the *Enterprise* in 2278, but Bateson would know who was. The *Enterprise* is one of the most famous ships in Starfleet.)

EQUIPMENT ODDITIES

• Every time through the loop Crusher breaks a glass in her quarters. Each time this occurs it has a strong impact on the good doctor. The first two times, the glass breaks because Crusher is groping for the control panel that turns on the lights. Of course, it would be much too simple for Crusher to say simply, "Computer, lights," wouldn't it? Of course, the fall from Crusher's small nightstand to the carpeted floor also seems insufficient to break the glass.

• When Data decompresses the main shuttle bay, the exterior graphic shows it filled with shuttlecraft. If the force of the air blowing out into space is sufficient to shift the entire mass of the *Enterprise,* doesn't it seem likely that it could blow a few shuttlecraft out the door as well?

CONTINUITY AND PRODUCTION PROBLEMS

• Toward the end of each loop, Worf reports a distortion off the starboard bow. Picard then tells Ro at conn to back them off slowly. Then the *Bozeman* comes through on a collision course. The next exterior shot shows the tractor beam shoving the *Bozeman* away from a head-on collision. If the *Bozeman* came out of the distortion, and if the distortion is to the starboard side of the ship, shouldn't the *Bozeman* approach from the starboard side?

• The second time through the loop—just before the ship explodes for the third time—the creators show us a shot of the viewscreen. The camera bounces around to show us the current distress of the ship, but the stars on the viewscreen bounce even more violently. Is the universe shaking as well?

TRIVIA ANSWERS

1. The nine of diamonds. (Sorry. There wasn't much to pick from in this episode.)

2. Vertazine.

THE FIRST DUTY

Star Date: 45703.9

When an accident results in the death of one of its members, Nova Squadron—a precision flying squadron whose pilots include Wesley Crusher—refuses to answer for the irregularities of the incident. Picard soon discovers that the squadron had attempted a banned maneuver and challenges Wesley to put his duty to the truth above his loyalty to the group.

TRIVIA QUESTIONS

1. To what city did Wesley go with Josh Albert?

2. What prestigious award did Nova Squadron win?

ALTERNATE VIEWPOINTS AND CORRECTIONS

• Now that the Nitpicker's Prime Directive allows the use of authorized reference manuals from Pocket Books, Lee Everett Patterson of University, MS, answered the confusion I express on pages 332 and 333 of the *NextGen Guide*. On those pages I tried to calculate the age of Captain Picard based on Data's statement in "Encounter at Farpoint" that he grad-

uated with the class of '78. In fact, this statement is wrong, and Picard is sixty-three at the time of this episode.

PLOT OVERSIGHTS

• As Riker, Picard, and Troi speak of academy days, Riker states that during his academy days the Vulcan superintendent had memorized the records of every cadet. Riker says it was like being with your parents. Since his mother died when he was very young and his father left when he was fifteen, how does Riker know what it is like to be with his parents?

CONTINUITY AND PRODUCTION PROBLEMS

• Wesley Crusher seems to have an affinity for twentieth-century antique collectibles. I believe that's a Franklin Mint version of the original *Enterprise* in his quarters at Starfleet Academy.

TRIVIA ANSWERS

1. Calgary.

2. The Rigel Cup.

COST OF LIVING

Star Date: 45733.6

Lwaxana Troi pays a visit to the *Enterprise* and almost immediately begins to meddle in Worf and Deanna Troi's attempt to make Alexander a bit more responsible. As an aside, she also announces that she has decided to marry a dour judge named Campio. However, when Lwaxana appears naked in typical Betazoid style for the wedding, Campio's protocol master pronounces the whole thing scandalous and hustles him out of the room.

GREAT LINES

"You're just supposed to sit here?"— Worf grousing about the fact that he's covered up to his neck in mud at the end of the episode.

TRIVIA QUESTIONS

1. At the beginning of the episode, Picard and crew keep an asteroid from hitting what planet?

2. What is Campio's official designation?

ALTERNATE VIEWPOINTS AND CORRECTIONS

• On pages 335 and 336 of the *NextGen Guide* I asked, "Does it strike anyone as odd that Troi—a person who has never had children and can't even get along with her own mother—is providing parenting advice for Worf?" Several nitpickers, including Phillip Martin of Anniston, AL, wrote to remind me that Deanna Troi did have a child in "The Child." Granted, I should have said that Troi has never raised a child, but I'm just not sure that experience counts for much. Many nitpickers also wrote to say that Troi is qualified to give parenting advice because she has had so much counseling training.

PLOT OVERSIGHTS

• Why is everyone sweating at the end of the episode when the bridge crew members struggle back to their feet after Data rids the ship of the metal parasites? Life support is out. There's no oxygen. Is there heat? Isn't space cold? Shouldn't they be freezing?

EQUIPMENT ODDITIES

• As part of her meddling, Lwaxana takes Alexander to a mud bath on the holodeck. Interestingly, as the holodeck doors close, they already show the background of the setting. Normally the doors close and then fade from view.

• As part of the plot, metal parasites threaten the ship by devouring nitrium, a metal used throughout the vessel. When the ship shudders at warp, Worf reports that there is an intermittent failure of the inertial damping system. Picard immediately tells the ensign at the conn to take them out of warp. After the commercial, Riker tells Data to try a manual bypass of the inertial dampeners, and Picard states that they shouldn't fail without automatically engaging the bypass. This makes it sound like the *Enterprise* is without its inertia damping field (IDF). Just what does this marvelous, magical field do? According to the *Tech Manual,* the IDF keeps the crew from turning into "chunky salsa" when the *Enterprise* experiences rapid acceleration. Somehow it compensates for the law of inertia. (A body at rest tends to stay at rest. A body in motion tends to stay in motion.) When the *Enterprise* jumps to warp, it starts out at about 25 percent of the speed of light (full impulse) and accelerates to faster than the speed of light in mere seconds. The acceleration would crush the crew into their seats without the IDF which exerts an opposite force on the crew, thereby nullifying the effects of the acceleration. One assumes that deceleration also would be a problem without an IDF. Since the *Enterprise* appears to decelerate as rapidly as it accelerates, a drop out of warp without the inertia damping field should plaster the bridge personnel all over the main viewscreen. Thankfully for the fearless crew of the *Enterprise*—even though Picard thoughtlessly orders a drop out of warp when the IDF fails—everyone manages to survive.

• At the conclusion of the episode, Data activates the Bussard collectors but apparently never uses them.

• The *Enterprise* makes another amazing recovery. The metal parasites have degraded the integrity of the antimatter containment field to 28 percent, yet moments after they leave the ship, everything seems back to normal. (Actually it probably isn't, but the creators just don't want us to worry about it.)

CONTINUITY AND PRODUCTION PROBLEMS

• While enjoying a mud bath on the holodeck, both Lwaxana and Alexander create continuity errors. At one point Lwaxana tells Alexander he must never be afraid to take the little voices inside him with him wherever he goes. The shot changes, and Lwaxana continues, saying you never know when you might need one of them.

Between these two shots, the bite in Alexander's cup moves from facing to his left to facing to his right. In addition, Lwaxana's right arm suddenly drops lower into the mud.

TRIVIA ANSWERS

1. Tessen III.

2. The third minister to the Conference of Judges from the planet Kostolain.

THE PERFECT MATE

Star Dates: 45761.3—45766.1

While hosting a peace conference between Krios and Valt Minor, Picard discovers that the Kriosian ambassador has brought a "gift" for Alrik, the representative from Valt. She is a beautiful, empathic metamorph named Kamala. Attempting to discover if Kamala performs this service of her own will, Picard finds himself strongly attracted to the unusual woman.

RUMINATIONS

Sometimes I try to figure out if a man or a woman wrote a certain script before I pay attention to the credits. Some episodes of Trek *present very little challenge. Take Kamala, for instance. She was separated from her parents at age four. (That means she doesn't have any pesky in-laws.) She is widely read and versed in many different areas of learning. (She can* hold an interesting conversation on any topic, so you never have to worry about what to say.) She is empathic. (She can immediately sense exactly what you're feeling, so you don't have to go to all the bother of verbalizing your emotions.) She is a metamorph. (She changes herself into exactly the type of woman that her mate desires.) She is tall and beautiful and she runs around all day wearing an outfit that barely qualifies as more than lingerie! Now, I ask you: Do you think a man or a woman invented this character?

GREAT LINES

"I make it a policy not to open another man's gift."—Riker to Kamala, struggling to find some reason not to give in to her charms.

TRIVIA QUESTIONS

1. Where does the *Enterprise* stop to pick up a group of miners?

2. To what does Kamala compare the sounds produced by certain Valtese horns?

PLOT OVERSIGHTS

• Wanting to allow Kamala some freedom to tour the ship, Picard chooses Data as her chaperon. He knows that Kamala's heightened pheromone production will not affect the android. I wonder why Picard didn't choose Crusher or Troi to act as chaperone. Kamala's pheromones wouldn't affect them. Or would they? And while we are on that topic, why don't we ever see Kamala in the company of women? Whenever she is with men, she changes to their liking. In the company of women, would Kamala have a chance to be herself?

CHANGED PREMISES

• In this episode, Krios and Valt Minor are close to concluding one hundred years of war. Yet, in "The Mind's Eye," Krios is a Klingon colony struggling to win back its independence. I suppose they could be the same planet, given that the Kriosians in "The Mind's Eye" were close to throwing off the shackles of their oppressor. But does it seem likely that the Kriosians could maintain a hundred-year-old war while they themselves are dominated by the Klingons? (Or is this another case for the Galactic Court for Race Name Conflict Resolution? See "The Creator Is Always Right" on pages 350–55 of the *NextGen Guide*.)

CONTINUITY AND PRODUCTION PROBLEMS

• During the first breakfast with Crusher, Picard takes a drink of his tea. When he sets the cup back down on the table, you can see that it is half full. The camera angle changes, and on the left side of the screen, the cup appears to fill with tea. There are a few close-ups, none of which features any sound of liquid pouring, and the scene returns to the original shot. Now you can clearly see that the cup has indeed refilled itself.

TRIVIA ANSWERS

1. Harod IV.
2. The bray of a Targhee moonbeast.

IMAGINARY FRIEND

Star Date: 45852.1

An energy being enters the ship and assumes the persona of Isabella, the imaginary friend of a little girl named Clara Sutter. Isabella finds the rules aboard the ship restrictive toward children and soon pronounces that others of her kind are coming and all the crew will die. Thankfully, Picard soon convinces Isabella that the rules she despises exist solely to protect the children on the ship from harm.

TRIVIA QUESTIONS

1. What did La Forge's father study in the Modean System?

2. What two shapes does Guinan make out in the nebula while speaking with Data?

PLOT OVERSIGHTS

• At one point Clara takes Isabella to Main Engineering—an area off-limits to children for obvious reasons. Does this seem sensible? With all the computer intelligence on the ship, why would the turbolift take children there?

• Why can't Troi sense a change in Clara's emotional state when Isabella transforms from an imaginary friend to a real-life entity?

• Attempting to reduce Isabella's influence on Clara, Troi takes the little girl to a pottery class. Isabella gets mad and destroys a clay cup Alexander makes for his father, Worf. Blind to Isabella's presence, Alexander accuses Clara of the deed. As Clara tries to explain, a piece of clay flies out and hits Alexander in the head. Terrified, Clara runs to the gardens to have a cry. Later, in Ten-Forward, Troi reports on Clara's day to Guinan, stating that Clara "made some new friends and had a good time." This must be some new definition of "had a good time." (Or Troi never checked back on Clara and was merely guessing that everything went okay.)

CONTINUITY AND PRODUCTION PROBLEMS

• When Clara visits Ten-Forward, Guinan brings her a glass of papalla juice with "extra bubbles." Oddly enough, the clear drink seems to be missing its bubbles.

TRIVIA ANSWERS

1. Invertebrates.
2. A Samarian coral fish and a Mintonian sailing ship.

I BORG

Star Date: 45854.2

Picard brings an injured Borg aboard the ship, intending to infect it with an invasive computer virus that will then be carried back to the Borg collective. Then the Borg—whom La Forge names Hugh—becomes self-aware, causing Picard to abandon the plan. As Hugh returns to the collective, Picard hopes that his individuality will be the most powerful virus of all.

TRIVIA QUESTIONS

1. What area of the galaxy does the *Enterprise* chart at the beginning of this episode?

2. The away team finds the crashed Borg scout ship on a small moon orbiting which planet of the star system?

PLOT OVERSIGHTS

• When compiling his away team at the beginning of the episode, Riker calls Crusher and asks her to report to a transporter room *with* a medical away team. Then an away team of Riker, Worf, and Crusher materializes on the planet. What happened to the medical team?

• When the Borg first comes aboard, Picard explains a few things about his anatomy. This makes sense, as he was one of them. He should know these things. Yet later Crusher explains to Picard that the Borg uses energy for food. Did Picard forget this fact and remember all the others?

• Just after bringing the Borg to the lab, La Forge introduces Beverly as "Dr. Crusher." The Borg immediately asks for the definition of "doctor." Question: How does the Borg know that "doctor" needs further explanation, whereas Crusher doesn't? We know that "doctor" is an occupation, but for the Borg, it could simply be similar to a first name (like the actor Judge Reinhold).

• After the introductions, the Borg asks, "Do I have a name?" He does this apparently before his emergence into self-identity. From this point until the ready room scene with Picard, the Borg uses "we" or "us." In the ready room scene when Hugh uses the pronoun "I," Picard is stunned. Considering the rest of the episode, shouldn't the Borg say "Do *we* have a name?"?

• One final thing: If the Borg are really one massive, interconnected consciousness, as this episode indicates—after all, Hugh *did* recognize Locutus—why haven't the Borg come after the Federation again? They must know that Locutus destroyed thirty-some-odd ships at Wolf 359. They must know that Starfleet is struggling to rebuild. Why have they suddenly lost interest? Are they afraid that Picard will tell them all to go to sleep again? (At least Picard has a career to fall back on in case the Starfleet thing doesn't work out. He could be a hypnotist. "Sleep… sleep. You're getting sleepy. Listen only to the sound of my voice. You will believe everything you hear me say. You love the *Nitpicker's Guides*…." Sorry. Couldn't resist.)

CHANGED PREMISES

• The crucial moment in this episode comes when Hugh uses the pronoun "I," stating that he will not assist the Borg in assimilating the life forms on the *Enterprise*. Picard recognizes—partially because of Hugh's use of this pronoun—that the Borg has achieved self-identity. Interestingly enough, when the newly Borgerized Picard introduces himself at the end of "The Best of Both Worlds, Part 1," he says, "*I* am Locutus of Borg."

EQUIPMENT ODDITIES

• Attempting to install a food spigot in the detention cell, La Forge and Worf enter cautiously. Worf tells a guard standing right by the controls at the side of the opening to lower the force field and then raise it once he and La Forge are inside. The guard reaches up and punches a few buttons. The force field dissipates. The pair steps inside. You can hear the control panel beep, and the force field is reinstated. Oddly enough, the guard doesn't appear to operate the controls! (It is possible that the guard set it to reinstate automatically. But when La Forge and Worf exit, the guard operates the controls manually, both to lower and then to raise the field.)

• Does it seem a bit weird to have an easily accessible junction that obviously connects to the energy system of the *Enterprise inside a* detention cell?

• Do the dampening fields move around the ship? We see Hugh in his detention cell, in a laboratory, and in Picard's ready room. Yet La Forge speaks of installing the dampening field—to screen out Hugh's transmission and kill his reception of the signals that comprise the Borg's collective consciousness—only at the detention cell.

CONTINUITY AND PRODUCTION PROBLEMS

• After speaking with Hugh, Picard holds a staff meeting in which he abandons the plan to use the invasive computer virus. When Picard states that Hugh seems to be a fully realized individual, Crusher sits with her right arm on the table, clasping her hands. Her left elbow bends down into her lap. The shot changes, and her left arm instantly rests on one of the marble uprights that support the table.

TRIVIA ANSWERS

1. The Argolis Cluster.
2. The fourth planet.

THE NEXT PHASE

Star Date: 45892.4

A transporter accident while beaming back from a disabled Romulan ship turns La Forge and Ro invisible and allows them to pass through normal matter.

After several unsuccessful attempts, the pair finally alerts the crew to their presence and are "dephased" just in time to report a Romulan plot to destroy the *Enterprise*.

TRIVIA QUESTIONS

1. What is the name of the transporter chief who mans the console when La Forge and Ro disappear?

2. When did the transporter malfunction occur?

ALTERNATE VIEWPOINTS AND CORRECTIONS

• On page 344 of the *NextGen Guide*, I said that the star date for this episode was unknown. Larry Nemecek in his tome *The Star Trek: The Next Generation Companion* states that the star date 45892.4 is shown on Ro's death certificate in Crusher's office. (Thanks to Josh Thompson of Montgomery, AL, for pointing this out.)

PLOT OVERSIGHTS

• Just after the transporter accident, Picard asks Troi if she senses La Forge and Ro. She says no. Why not? Do cloaking and phasing block telepathic transmissions as well? She senses the last feelings of the harvested humans in "Time's Arrow." The life forces of those humans exist ahead in time of the away team. If she can sense that, why can't she sense La Forge and Ro?

• Riker gets really strong in this episode. Worf and a Romulan manually prep the core for ejection and then start struggling to move some debris that blocks a door. Unable to move one particular piece, Worf calls for Riker, who strides over, easily picks it up, and shoves it to one side.

• La Forge and Ro hitch a ride on a shuttle over to the Romulan ship, trying to find out what's happened to them. Once there, La Forge determines that they've been cloaked and phased. He and Ro also overhear a plan to destroy the *Enterprise.* Immediately they hurry back to catch the next shuttle home. Well, actually they *walk around* a large center control area when already at this point in the episode they have become quite used to walking straight through furniture and walls. Why not just walk through it, as the phased Romulan does mere seconds later?

• I wonder if Data's detection of the chroniton distortions was refined enough to allow him to read a message from La Forge such as "HELP!"

• At the end of the chase, Ro and the Romulan struggle in a room as a couple enjoys dinner. Data and La Forge come to the door. The male gets up and answers the door. La Forge sees Ro struggling with the Romulan and charges into the room. Data takes a quick step back to let La Forge by and then enters. Why would Data step back? He can't even see La Forge. (I do need to say that Brent Spiner covers this action very, very well. He almost makes the motion perfectly believable.)

• After charging into the room, La Forge shoves the Romulan out into space. The Romulan begins the trip facing La Forge with his back to the hull. The impact from La Forge sends the Romulan backward through the hull, and he leaves the ship still facing La Forge. The next shot of the Romulan shows him cartwheeling freely, head over heels, through space. When he is upright, he is facing *away* from the ship. That means he executed an about-face between the time he departed the ship and the following shot. But if he did an about-face, wouldn't he still be spinning as well as cartwheeling?

• Why isn't O'Brien at La Forge's funeral? Aren't they close friends?

• To create the highest possible level of chroniton distortions, Ro sets the Romulan phaser on overload. Then she and La Forge jump behind a couch for cover—a *normal* couch, that is. How will a normal couch protect them from a phased explosion?

CHANGED PREMISES

• During the wake for La Forge and Ro, Picard says that Ro would have made lieutenant commander already had it not been for the incident on Garon IV. "Ensign Ro" establishes that the aforementioned incident occurred on Garon II.

EQUIPMENT ODDITIES

• Shortly after arriving on the Romulan ship, Riker sends La Forge and Ro back to the *Enterprise* with a piece of equipment. The accident that phases and cloaks them occurs during this transport. The creators show the pair's patterns materializing halfway on the transporter pad a few times before completely disappearing. Yet the piece of equipment never materializes. What happened to it? (By the way, the creators also used a little visual clue to

hint at the transformation going on in La Forge and Ro, by momentarily showing their positions reverse on the pads. It made me wonder if this type of thing ever happens in the transporter. With all those body parts slushing around in the pattern buffer, it could be a bit embarrassing if the reconstruction subroutine made a mistake!)

• I spent a considerable amount of time talking about the communicators in the *NextGen Guide*, but this episode contains a prime example of inappropriate usage. When La Forge and Ro disappear during beam-out, Riker yells for the transporter chief and *then* slaps his communicator before continuing his message.

• When it appears that the Romulan vessel may soon self-destruct, Picard tells the ensign at conn to lay in a course away from the craft and engage at warp 1 if there is any sign that it is going to explode. Moments later, the engine core destabilizes. Worf and a Romulan eject it manually. The *Enterprise* extends its shields around the Romulan ship. The core detonates. Everyone is safe. Isn't the engine core the most volatile element on a starship? Doesn't it explode with the most force? If the shields of the *Enterprise* could protect it even after it had extended its shields around the Romulan vessel, why did Picard tell the ensign at conn to make preparations to run away? The shields protected the *Enterprise* when the *Yamato*'s engine core lost containment in "Contagion." The shields also protected the *Enterprise* when the Romulan scout ship self-destructed in "The Defector." What's different this time that Picard feels he must leave the area?

• After the phasing, La Forge and Ro's communicators quit working even though the phased Romulan we meet later has a phaser that still works.

• There must be a *bunch* of shuttles going back and forth between the Romulan ship and the *Enterprise.* After hearing about the Romulan plan to destroy the *Enterprise,* La Forge and Ro hop a shuttle back to their ship. A phased Romulan follows them, only seconds behind. Yet they obviously take different shuttles back to the *Enterprise* because La Forge and Ro don't see the Romulan until he appears on the bridge. If they all traveled back on the same shuttle, wouldn't La Forge and Ro notice him?

• This question could be raised in any number of episodes, but how does the turbolift know where to drop a person on a given deck? Traveling down to La Forge and Ro's wake in Ten-Forward, Picard and Riker board a turbolift on the bridge. Picard asks for deck 10, and the turbolift proceeds. Isn't deck 10 one of the largest decks in the saucer section? How does Picard know that the turbolift won't drop him somewhere on the back side? (Or is this a case of the Starfleet designers ensuring that the crew gets plenty of exercise?)

• To create lots of chroniton fields and to attract attention, Ro walks around Ten-Forward during the wake for her and La Forge and fires the phased Romulan phaser. Wouldn't the energy from the phaser travel through multiple decks and create chroniton distortions all over the forward end of the saucer section? Apparently not, because the crew on the bridge reports chroniton distortions only in Ten-Forward.

• Obviously Romulan phasers aren't as powerful as Starfleet phasers. In "The Hunted," when Worf finds a Starfleet phaser on overload, he gives instructions to seal off the entire deck. Yet in this episode, Ro puts a Romulan phaser on overload, but the resulting explosion doesn't even appear to fill Ten-Foward.

TRIVIA ANSWERS

1. Brossmer.
2. At 1430 hours.

THE INNER LIGHT

Star Date: 45944.1

A s the *Enterprise* crosses its path, an unusual probe sends out a beam that transmits a lifetime of experiences to Picard. In only twenty-five minutes, he lives the life of an inhabitant of Kataan. Knowing that their planet was dying, the people of Kataan crafted the probe to find and train a teacher who would speak of their existence to others.

ALTERNATE VIEWPOINTS AND CORRECTIONS

• In the *NextGen Guide,* on page 347, I went into a little tirade expressing my shock and disbelief that this episode actually expects us to believe that a little primitive farming society that's just begun to launch missiles can actually manufacture a probe that can encounter an alien brain and remotely implant a fantasy in that brain that's so flawless that Picard would remark that his life on the *Enterprise* was as real as his life on Kataan. Several nitpickers have written claiming that I have a cultural bias, that Kataan might look primitive in appearance but be extremely sophisticated in a very narrow area of expertise, such as machine-to-mind interfaces. Some have cited examples of China building massive cities in the 6th century A.D., and the ancient Aztecs constructing incredible stone walls, all without the invention of the nail. I've gone back and thought about this some more and *I still don't get it!* Advances in technology have a tendency to act like a shotgun blast. They normally don't stay confined to a niche. Take the transistor. It was invented at Bell Labs, but it didn't just stay in telephones. It spread to televisions, radios, musical instruments, recording devices, logic circuits. The invention of the transistor led to the integrated circuit (IC), raising the sophistication of the control mechanisms for the devices we use. These devices impact our society and change it. We, in turn, utilize these devices to invent new devices, and so it goes and so on. If the events of this episode are true, Kataan somehow invented an extremely sophisticated technology for the creation and delivery of a mental holodeck, and that technology *never* touched their society in *any* observable way. That's the picture they present of themselves to Picard.

Of course, the other option would be to say that the mental holodeck did actually impact their society—that Kataan society decayed to the point where the Kataans just sat around all day hooked up to their brain suckers. In the end, they were so ashamed that they didn't make any attempt to emigrate off their dying world that they constructed a primitive probe with a sanitized, unsophisticated version of their lifestyle and shipped it off to seek out some gullible alien, hoping that a pleasant memory of their world would somehow redeem their miserable existence! (I'm just joking!)

TRIVIA QUESTIONS

1. The *Enterprise* completes a magnetic wave study in what sector just prior to encountering the Kataan probe?

2. Where is the community of Ressik located on the planet of Kataan?

PLOT OVERSIGHTS

• If Kataan was destroyed a thousand years ago and no one on the planet survived to bring word of their civilization to other races, how can La Forge access the computer and determine the name of the probe's origin point?

• I am told by amateur astronomer Mike Mader that when Picard looks through his telescope on Kataan, the illumination from the porch light directly behind him would render the instrument almost useless.

• Where's Troi in this episode? She was of service during "Shades of Gray," informing Pulaski of Riker's mental state. Why isn't she up on the bridge?

• Picard sure recovers from this experience fast! The next episode starts on star date 45959.1, and our beloved captain seems well and in command. This episode begins on 45944.1. That's a difference of 15 star date units. Using our handy dandy ratio of 1,000 star date units per 365 Earth days, we find that just over 5 days have transpired. Five days to relearn what it is to be a Starfleet captain after a probe has just crammed thirty years of alien experiences into your head!

CONTINUITY AND PRODUCTION PROBLEMS

• Shortly after Riker orders Data to cut off the beam from the probe, Picard experiences a seizure. Crusher struggles to keep him alive as Data races to reinstate the beam. They succeed, and Crusher leans back with a heavy sigh. Take a good look at her hair. The episode wanders back to Picard's experiences on the planet Kataan and, shortly, returns to the bridge of the *Enterprise*. Now look at Crusher's hair. Notice the beautiful curls that have suddenly appeared at the ends of her locks. Remember that Picard is under the influence of the probe for only "twenty, twenty-five minutes." After almost losing him, did Crusher say to herself, "Well, I'm not doing much good here, I reckon I will keep that hair appointment I made with Mr. Mot this morning"?

TRIVIA ANSWERS

1. The Parvenium Sector.
2. In the northern province.

TIME'S ARROW

Star Dates: 45959.1—45965.3

The discovery of Data's head in a cave beneath San Francisco brings the *Enterprise* to Earth. A fossil in the cave leads the crew to Devidia II, where they find aliens who travel back to nineteenth-century Earth to harvest humans for their life energy. When Data is swept back to the past, Picard and an away team follow.

TRIVIA QUESTIONS

1. How do the phase-discriminating amplifiers differ between Data and Lore?

2. In front of what building does Data appear after traveling into the past?

ALTERNATE VIEWPOINTS AND CORRECTIONS

• On page 349 of the *NextGen Guide*, the answer to the first trivia question states that .45-caliber double-action cavalry pistol was invented by Colt Firearms in 1873. Though this information comes directly from the dialogue of the episode, apparently, it is wrong! Joseph Gidi of Allen Park, MI, wrote to inform me that double-action revolvers (handguns that allow the user to cock the hammer by simply pulling the trigger instead of manually drawing the hammer back, as is the case of the single-action revolver) weren't introduced by Colt until 1878, and were chambered for .38- or .41-caliber ammunition. Paul Czaplicki of Palos Verdes Estates, CA, added that the weapon pictured in the episode is, in fact, a *single*-action revolver.

PLOT OVERSIGHTS

• Obviously San Francisco in the nineteenth century was a happenin' kind of town. The people have seen it all and probably done it all. Data gets caught in the temporal anomaly caused by the Devidians and arrives in San Francisco lying in the middle of the street. He gets up, and life goes on completely unperturbed all around him. In fact, a street sweeper practically bumps into him. I guess a being with gold skin wearing his pajamas and suddenly appearing out of nowhere isn't that big a deal to these people!

• To raise some money, Data engages in a friendly round of poker with some professional gamblers. For his stake, Data sells his communicator to one of the gamblers for three dollars. The gambler gives him three coins. Data tosses one of the coins into the center of the table. In other words, he antes up with one dollar. Yet the dialogue moments earlier indicated that the ante was "four bits," or fifty cents. Surprisingly, none of the other players points out Data's error.

• When Picard decides to send a larger away team back to look for Data, Worf makes the statement that it might be their place to die in the cav-

ern under San Francisco as well. He says that their remains would have turned to dust long ago. Really? Wouldn't some bones and teeth still be around after five hundred years?

EQUIPMENT ODDITIES

• At one point, Riker and Troi board a turbolift with Data but do not state their destination. I assume that they assume he's going to the bridge, but how does the turbolift assume that they are assuming that it will assume the same thing and therefore not need a destination?

• Where does Data stash his phaser during the poker game?

• There's something a bit odd about the subspace field that La Forge creates and within which the away team moves forward in time. After he activates it, a blue beam races around the perimeter. Then each member of the away team begins stepping inside the target area. Each time they cross the boundary, the blue beam flashes…except for La Forge. When he steps across, no flash. At first I thought the blue beam races around the perimeter at regular intervals, but after watching the scene again I think the creators simply forgot to make the generator shoot its beam when La Forge crossed over.

CONTINUITY AND PRODUCTION PROBLEMS

• When discussing why the away team can't see the Devidians, La Forge says that the aliens exist slightly ahead in time. He says that even a millisecond would be enough to make them disappear. This makes sense. I can't see you if you aren't there *when*

I'm trying to look. However, when Data moves ahead in time, he gradually fades. Yes, it's a nice effect, but shouldn't he just wink out?

• Gul Dukat of *Star Trek: Deep Space Nine* apparently has a deep, dark secret in his past. As a Cardassian, Dukat probably would be appalled to learn that he has some portion of *human* blood floating around in his system. As proof, I direct your attention to one Frederick La Rouque, a professional gambler with whom Data plays poker in this episode. Does not La Rouque bear a striking resemblance to Dukat and even sound like the Cardassian Gul?

TRIVIA ANSWERS

1. Lore has a Type "L" amplifier, Data has a Type "R."

2. The No. 5 Fire House.

★
THE LOVELIES

've spent a great deal of time over the past few years picking apart *Star Trek* and *Star Trek: The Next Generation*. But for all that activity, I am happy to admit that the shows do hold together quite well. And often I come across wonderful touches that the creators add to their product to increase its realism. These are beyond the easily observable facts that the *Enterprise* has tremendous visual appeal, the computer displays are gorgeous, and the general look and feel of the show are of the highest quality. They are little extras that easily can be missed—little extras for which the creators deserve credit.

1. "The Big Goodbye." When Picard enters the holodeck for the first time, a female vocalist sings, "You came to me from out of nowhere."

2. "11001001." Riker and Picard prepare to beam to the bridge and recapture the ship. Riker tells Picard that he has set the transporter for a ten-second delay. Riker hits the button, and the console begins beeping at one-second intervals. Ten seconds later, the transporter energizes.

3. "Coming of Age." There's a beautiful series of transitions as Remmick questions members of the senior staff about Picard's conduct since taking command of the *Enterprise.*

4. "The Vengeance Factor." In one scene in Ten-Foward, the camera pans while the ship flies at warp. The image of streaking stars in the windows changes exactly as it should as the camera moves.

5. "The Best of Both Worlds." This episode has wonderful, original music to add to the tension of the events.

6. "Future Imperfect." When the creators crafted new communicators for everyone, they integrated the rank insignia into the new design.

7. "Time's Arrow, Part II." While in Mrs. Carmichael's boardinghouse, discussing the next course of action with the rest of the away team, both Crusher and Troi feel their sides as if uncomfortable with the constraints of nineteeth-century feminine fashions.

8. "Relics." Unable to access the name of an alcoholic beverage he finds behind

Guinan's bar, Data describes it to Scotty by saying, "It is green." This line pays homage to Scotty's performancè in the *Classic Trek* episode "By Any Other Name."

9. "Dark Page." At the beginning of this episode, during a reception in Ten-Foward, Worf finally resigns himself to the fact that Lwaxana will always call him "Mr. Woof."

10. Opening Credits. Watch very carefully as the *Enterprise* saucer section appears at the bottom of the screen just before the ship blasts into warp for the last time. Focus on the observation lounge windows as they become visible and you'll see an itty-bitty person walking through the room.

SIXTH SEASON

TIME'S ARROW, PART II

Star Date: 46001.3

After locating the murderous aliens and their time-traveling device, Picard and his senior officers return to the cave beneath San Francisco. Suddenly the aliens reappear. A struggle erupts, and the time-traveling device blows off Data's head and flings his body into the future. The senior officers follow. La Forge attaches the five-hundred-year-old head to Data's body and the crew destroys the aliens' departure point on Devidia II.

RUMINATIONS

*T*here's *a lovely little touch of realism that the talented Marina Sirtis and Gates McFadden add to their performances in this episode. When we first see the women discussing the next course of action with Picard and the rest of the away team in Mrs. Carmichael's boardinghouse, both of them feel their sides, as if uncomfortable with the constraints of nineteenth-century feminine fashions. Of course, the creators may have purposefully cinched up the ladies' corsets a bit tight to ensure this realism!*

TRIVIA QUESTIONS

1. What is the name of the doctor Crusher speaks with at the Sisters of Hope Infirmary?

2. Into what role did Picard suggest casting Mrs. Carmichael?

PLOT OVERSIGHTS

• I wonder what happened to the clothes that the away team wore when they went back to the nineteenth century. Isn't anyone worried about the consequences of twenty-fourth-century clothing being examined by nineteenth-century tailors? (My guess is that the cat suit fashion somewhat popular in certain circles today actually derives from a temporal corruption caused when Troi left her outfit in the nineteenth century! On the other hand, it probably would be *very easy* for Troi to hide her standard twenty-fourth-century attire somewhere within the nineteenth-century outfit she wears for the first part of this episode. As tight as her bunny suit fits, it is most likely constructed from some type of stretchy material and probably isn't much bigger than a lady's handkerchief once she takes it off.)

• From the events of the last episode, it's apparent that Picard and the away team are soon to embark on an excursion to the nineteenth century. Surprisingly enough, no one thinks to change into period clothing before departure or even to take along some legal tender.

• Would it be proper in nineteenth-century San Francisco for men and women to share the same boarding-house room?

• La Forge starts out this episode using a fair amount of caution with respect to his VISOR. Unfortunately, there are many scenes where the VISOR *should* attract considerable attention. But, of course, it doesn't. For instance, in the hospital scene that opens with Picard installing the sensor on the ceiling lamp, a doctor walks up and speaks with Crusher, then turns and walks out of the room. La Forge stands in full view wearing his VISOR, but the doctor says nothing. (And even if he took the VISOR off and put on his sunglasses, wouldn't the flashing lights at his temples attract suspicion?)

• When the away team first encounters the aliens, Data works with his time distortion detector in his hotel room. He registers a disturbance, checks a chart, checks his machine, and then rechecks his chart. It's a very human gesture, but doesn't Data remember everything? Why does he need to check this chart twice?

• Fleeing the hospital after the first encounter with the aliens, the team gratefully encounters Data driving a horse and buggy. They all hop in and on, finding space wherever they can. Oddly enough, Riker gets inside, forcing Picard to hang on to the back. Does this seem right, given Riker's normally overprotective attitude toward the captain? Shouldn't the first officer shove Picard inside and take up the more exposed position as the team flees from the San Francisco police (and possibly their bullets)?

• After Samuel Clemens returns to the twenty-fourth century with the away team, Troi volunteers to escort him to his quarters—and presumably keep track of him on the ship. The pair departs the transporter room arm in arm and, a short time later, strolls down a hall. Two points of interest. First, Troi has changed into one of her bunny suits. I suppose she made Clemens come back to her quarters, locked him in, and proceeded to change. (Would that be a smile I see on Clemens's face?) Second, Clemens says he can't get a fine, hand-wrapped cigar in the twenty-fourth century. Michael A. D. Reid tells me that true cigar aficionados would say cigars are "rolled," not "wrapped."

• When we see Data's five-hundred-year-old head in "Time's Arrow," the hair is mussed and the features soiled. Yet, in this episode, after La Forge attaches it to Data's body, it looks brand new. Did La Forge take it up to Mr. Mot for a quick trim and buff?

CHANGED PREMISES

• Guinan was probably just being evasive in "The Child" when she told Wesley that she had never met Picard before coming on board the *Enterprise*. However, this episode does establish that she met him a very long time before coming on board the *Enterprise.*

• After attaching Data's five-hundred-year-old head, La Forge reactivates the android by pressing the center of his back. That's funny. I could have sworn that "Datalore" established that Data's off switch was on his right side.

EQUIPMENT ODDITIES

• In the previous review, I discussed the fact that my nitpickers have identified the weapon that Clemens carries as a single-action .45-caliber revolver. (Single action means that you must cock the hammer manually before pulling the trigger so the gun can fire.) As such, the weapon that Clemens waves at the away team near the end of the episode isn't a threat. The hammer isn't cocked, and he stands close enough to Data for the android to wrestle it away before Clemens could bring it to lethal status. Both Clemens and Data would know this.

TRIVIA ANSWERS

1. Dr. Appollinaire.
2. Titania.

★

REALM OF FEAR

Star Dates: 46041.1—46043.6

Lieutenant Barclay must confront his fear of the transporter and his belief that he has contracted transporter psychosis after seeing wormlike objects moving through the matter stream while beaming over on an away mission to the distressed USS *Yosemite*. He later discovers that the worms are actually the missing crew of the *Yosemite*.

PLOT OVERSIGHTS

• Obviously, when Troi relieves an officer of duty, the information isn't posted throughout the ship. Some time after the counselor sends Bar-

clay to bed, the neurotic engineer shows up in the transporter and tries to give O'Brien a direct order. Yet O'Brien doesn't say, "Excuse me, sir, but I believe that you have been relieved of duty."

• In this episode, La Forge, O'Brien, and Crusher cleanse Barclay of quasi-energy microbes by putting him in the transporter and holding him at the point where matter is converted to energy. Presumably this is *after* the transporter has deconstructed him at the *quantum subatomic level.* Yet somehow Barclay remains *conscious*!?

TRIVIA QUESTIONS

1. Where did O'Brien reroute an emitter array filled with Talarian hook spiders?

2. Who taught Barclay's Transporter Theory class at Starfleet academy?

EQUIPMENT ODDITIES

• With the *Yosemite* trapped in a plasma streamer, La Forge, Barclay, and O'Brien link a transporter with the *Yosemite*'s transporter to allow an away team to beam over and investigate. Sometime later, Worf states that an explosion occurred on the *Yosemite*'s transporter pad. La Forge has the same reaction as many nit-pickers to the chief of Security's statement. The chief engineer responds, "How is that possible? The transporter is still functioning!"

• As the away team investigates the *Yosemite,* Picard has a conversation with a Starfleet admiral. The conversation ends with a picture of the admiral saying, "Very well." Then the screen switches to the United Federation of Planets icon. The admiral didn't close the connection, because her hands are folded in front of her. It is unlikely that Picard closed the connection, because he stands with one arm draped over his chair and his hands folded. Who closed this communication channel?

• The away team brings the pieces of a container back to the *Enterprise* for analysis. Later, in Engineering, the reassembled container sits on a small table between the center island and the warp core. Barclay moves into a Jefferies tube; La Forge follows and suggests that he take some time off. When La Forge walks back into Engineering, the container is in pieces on the table.

• Attempting to rest in his quarters, Barclay heads to bed. He asks the computer to play some soothing music, and immediately the lights dim. Shouldn't Barclay need to tell the computer to dim the lights as well? Or has he set up some kind of macro since he always listens to music with dimmed lighting?

• Crusher's tricorder behaves a bit oddly during the observation lounge meeting after Barclay wakes up the senior staff. In the long shot, the little lights inside the hood at the top of the tricorder move back and forth. In the close-up, they do not.

• Dr. Crusher needs to requisition maintenance to replace a lightbulb on the scanner she uses with Barclay. Look closely at the vertical stack of LEDs on the left side and you'll see that the fourth bulb from the top is burned out!

CONTINUITY AND PRODUCTION PROBLEMS

• Barclay's nervous habits seem to include fiddling with his pips. Just before beaming over to the *Yosemite,* a close-up reveals that his pips—reading from the inside out—are solid and then hollow. When Barclay beams back from the *Yosemite,* the order has somehow reversed.

• In this episode the *Enterprise* hangs in space investigating the disappearance of the crew on the *Yosemite.* Yet, in the observation lounge scene, the stars move.

• Why does Barclay start his transporter decontamination trip facing the transporter console and end it facing the back wall of the transporter chamber?

TRIVIA ANSWERS

1. The starbase on Zayra IV.
2. Dr. Olafson.

MAN OF THE PEOPLE

Star Dates: 46071.6—46075.1

When his mother dies while traveling with him on board the *Enterprise* to his latest diplomatic endeavor, Ambassador Ves Alkar asks Troi to join him in a ritual of mourning. Unknown to the counselor, the ritual actually establishes a psychic link between the pair that allows Alkar to use Troi as an emotional waste receptacle.

TRIVIA QUESTIONS

1. Who commands the transport vessel *Dorian*?

2. What is the name of Alkar's "mother"?

PLOT OVERSIGHTS

• Why does Picard choose Troi to welcome Ambassador Ves Alkar and his "mother" aboard? Given the importance of the ambassador's diplomatic mission, doesn't a formal welcoming by a higher-ranking officer—Picard or Riker, for instance—seem in order?

• I can understand why Troi doesn't immediately sense Alkar's deception when he introduces his "mother"—a woman he is merely exploiting as a repository for emotions he would rather not feel. I would imagine that the emotive side of the deception immediately flushes out of Alkar and into his humanoid septic tank. What I don't understand is why Troi didn't sense some malevolence from Alkar after his mother died. Obviously he has very little grief for the woman he has just killed. His attitudes are very much self-motivated. He is only interested in securing another toxic waste site. Why does Troi participate in this so freely?

• Follow along as I recall a sequence of events. Riker escorts seductively dressed, "garbage dump" Troi out of Ten-Forward and back to her quarters. Then she proceeds to come on to Riker. He resists. She scratches him. A bit later, we see Riker in sick bay, where Crusher heals the scratch-es. Strangely enough, he refers to seeing Troi "last night." Why did Riker wait until morning to see Crusher about the scratches? (Answer: If he had gone to Crusher immediately, she would have located Troi and taken her to sick bay. This would have deleted the scene in the transporter room where Troi stabs Picard and lead to the infamous "short show" syndrome.)

• After the thwarted attempt to bring Alkar back to the *Enterprise,* Picard and Worf beam back to the ship. Picard steps off the pad and tells the transporter chief to lock on to Alkar's signal and beam him aboard. Before the transporter chief can even try, Worf interrupts, saying that the security field on the planet is certainly back in place. It very well might be, but is there any harm in trying?

• Determined to kill Troi and thereby force Alkar to break his psychic connection with her, Crusher states that she must revive the counselor in thirty minutes. Picard gives her the go-ahead. On the surface of the planet we see Alkar have a small seizure. Evidently Troi is either dead or dying and the thirty-minute countdown has begun. Picard then pages Alkar, sounding very urgent and insisting that Alkar return to the ship immediately. The captain also threatens to beam him up whether he agrees to come or not. A short time later, Alkar and a lady friend come to sick bay. Alkar makes a few quick remarks about the tragedy of Troi's death and reminds Picard of the Federation's agreement to return him home safely. Alkar leaves. *Moments* later, Crusher announces that she must revive Troi in the next three minutes and forty seconds. Wait a minute: Did it really take Alkar more than twenty-five minutes to get from the surface to sick bay?

• Shortly after Alkar leaves, Picard tells Transporter Room 2 to lock on to the female in Alkar's quarters. Then he turns to Worf and tells the Security chief to station himself outside *her* quarters. Thankfully, Worf understands what Picard means and goes to Alkar's quarters instead.

• How does Worf know that Alkar is dead at the end of the episode without even checking a pulse?

EQUIPMENT ODDITIES

• Medical tricorders must be readily available all over the ship. After healing Riker's scratches, Crusher sets down her tricorder and takes off her coat. She asks the computer for the location of Counselor Troi. Then Crusher and Riker leave to find her. Note that the good doctor leaves her office *empty-handed*. Yet, moments later, she appears in the transporter room with a tricorder.

CONTINUITY AND PRODUCTION PROBLEMS

• Evidently Data wasn't paying attention when he mounted his pips before taking his station at Ops at the beginning of this episode. He wears the standard two solid and one hollow, but the hollow pip rests closest to his throat. Normally the hollow pip is the outermost one.

• It must have been "backward pip" day on the *Enterprise*. When Crusher comes to Engineering to discuss Alkar's dead "mother," La Forge wears his standard three pips, but he has

two hollow and one solid—instead of two solid and one hollow.

• The creators forgot to add in the dissipating blue field effect when Crusher tells Nurse Ogawa to shut off the restraint field around Troi.

TRIVIA ANSWERS

1. Captain Talmadge.
2. Sev Maylor.

RELICS

Star Date: 46125.3

On the surface of an immense sphere, the crew finds the wreckage of the USS *Jenolen,* and one survivor kept alive in a specially modified tractor beam for seventy-five years. He is Montgomery Scott, former chief engineer of the original starship *Enterprise.* When the *Enterprise*-D becomes trapped inside the sphere, La Forge and Scott combine their skills to free it.

RUMINATIONS

In this episode, the creators of NextGen paid a nice little homage to the Classic *episode "By Any Other Name." In "Relics," when Data tries to identify the contents of a bottle of whiskey for Scott, he finally uses the nondescript phrase "It is green." In "By any Other Name," after drinking through almost all the liquor in his quarters with a Kelvan, Scott finds one last bottle for them to consume. The Kelvan asks* what it is. *Scott* replies with some unsteadiness, "It is green." (Thanks to Andrew La Mance of East Ridge, TN, for noticing this.)

TRIVIA QUESTIONS

1. Scott's quarters on the *Enterprise* remind him of a hotel room on what planet?

2. Who does La Forge first suggest to accompany Scott back down to the *Jenolen*?

ALTERNATE VIEWPOINTS AND CORRECTIONS

• In the *NextGen Guide,* on page 368, I made an offhand comment about Data subbing at the bar in "Disaster." In fact, I should have said, "Conundrum." (Thanks to Nick Zielinski of Hales Corners, WI, for pointing this out.)

PLOT OVERSIGHTS

• At the beginning of the episode, the *Enterprise* drops out of warp and encounters a strong gravitational field. Picard asks why the sensors didn't detect it sooner, and Data replies that the enormous sphere is causing a great deal of gravimetric interference. In other words—stripping away the technobabble—the *Enterprise*'s sensors couldn't detect the gravitational field of the Dyson sphere because it generated too much gravity?

• Scott materializes with his arm in a sling, and we find out later that the arm has a hairline fracture. Yet, walking down the hall to sick bay, he gestures with the arm.

• From what exotic origin point did

Scott begin his trip to Norpin V? The *Jenolen* spent seventy-five years on the surface of the Dyson sphere, and no one heard its distress call. Presumably ships pay an occasional call on Norpin V—Scott's destination while riding on the *Jenolen*—even if it is a retirement colony. So why hasn't someone found the sphere before now?

• In this episode, the entire crew—with the exception of Picard—seems to display a singular lack of interest in the rich perspective that Scott could bring to their understanding of the history of the organization in which they serve. Aren't there at least some historians on board this ship who would be overjoyed at the chance to interview him? (Then again, Troi does seem *very* friendly with Scott at the end of the show. Did they spend some time together that we don't see? You know…the *only* time the creators don't show us the time that two people spend together is when it's…*that* kind of time! Blush, blush.)

• At one point, tractor beams from the Dyson sphere reach out and drag the *Enterprise* inside. Heading into the star at the sphere's center, Picard orders "Port thrusters ahead full. Starboard thrusters back full." Unfortunately, in real life, this maneuver would only succeed in spinning the *Enterprise* like a top unless the ensign at conn understood what Picard *really* wanted and adjusted the firing pattern of the thrusters as soon as the *Enterprise* turned perpendicular to its former line of travel. (Picard probably should have had all the thrusters fire to one side of the ship or the other, thereby forcing the *Enterprise* sideways and into orbit.)

• As soon as La Forge and Scott wedge the doors of the Dyson sphere open, Picard tells the ensign at conn to make a run for it, and immediately the ship takes off. Now, wait a minute: Weren't the solar flares from the star buffeting the ship as it held a close orbit just moments before? If the *Enterprise* could fly off just like that, why didn't Picard increase the distance between the ship and the star earlier? Does he just like to see how much punishment the *Enterprise* can really take? (I remind you that when his double pulled a stunt like this in "Allegiance," Riker relieved him of duty.)

EQUIPMENT ODDITIES

• Evidently—had the *Enterprise* not detected the distress call from the *Jenolen* and dropped out of warp at the beginning of the episode—the very real possibility exists that the ship could have warped right past it without the sensors detecting it. Does this seem right? What if the Dyson sphere happened to be in the path of the *Enterprise*? Would the ship smack into it?

• Why do the transporters on the *Jenolen* sound and look just like the transporters on the original *Enterprise* and not like the transporters in the movies? The ship doesn't look old enough to be a contemporary of the *Classic Enterprise*.

• Who fixed the replicators so they couldn't produce real alcohol? When Scott comes to the bar and orders scotch, he gets the synthehol version and finds it unpalatable. Yet, in "Up the Long Ladder," Worf simply ordered real alcohol from the replicators, and from the looks of Danilo Odell's face when he tasted it, the drink packed quite a punch.

• Slightly drunk and lonely for the good old days, Scott goes to the holodeck and asks to see the bridge of the *Enterprise*. The computer asks for a registry number, and Scott replies "NCC-1701." Moments later the doors of the holodeck open on the bridge of the *Enterprise* as seen in the *Classic* episodes. One question: How did the computer know to display this bridge and not the one shown in the first or second movies? That *Enterprise* also had a registry of NCC-1701. (Of course, one has to wonder why Scott didn't ask for the engine room of the old *Enterprise*. After all, he did spend a lot of time there.)

• The main computer eavesdrops on bridge conversations again. After the *Enterprise* settles into a stable orbit around the star at the center of the sphere, Riker announces that he is going to Main Engineering to get main power back on line. He gets up from his chair, and the camera cuts to Picard. In the background, the turbolift doors open well before Riker gets anywhere near them.

CONTINUITY AND PRODUCTION PROBLEMS

• Just prior to entering the holodeck, Scott's hair is neatly combed to the side, but as he steps through the door, it is suddenly mussed.

• When Scott first enters the holodeck, there are clearly two segments in the section of railing on the port side of the ship that separates the center command area from the outside workstations. Yet, when Scott stands to leave the holodeck, the lower left-hand side of the screen shows that the same railing has suddenly shrunk to one section. (Some have suggested that this is actually the end of the full-size set.)

• La Forge must be a very fastidious worker. Just consider this sequence of events. He beams down to the *Jenolen* with one satchel slung over his shoulder and carrying a tool kit in his hand. He and Scott jury-rig the transport ship and wedge open the doors of the Dyson sphere. The *Enterprise* makes a mad dash for them. La Forge tells Picard that they can't get out of the way—the *Jenolen* is literally coming apart at the seams. Picard calls for transport and then blows up the *Jenolen* with two photon torpedoes. La Forge steps off the transporter pad with the satchel slung over his shoulder and carrying a tool kit in his hand. Obviously he jumped out of his chair at some point and collected everything he brought aboard just before the *Enterprise* beamed him home.

TRIVIA ANSWERS

1. Argelius.
2. Lieutenant Bartel.

SCHISMS

Star Dates: 46154.2—46191.2

The night terrors of the crew turn out to have some basis in fact. Experiments by La Forge into the deeper regions of the sub-

space domain have attracted the attention of Solanagen-based aliens who are abducting members of the crew for a series of hideous experiments. In time, the aliens' particular interest in Riker allows the crew to locate and seal the gateway between the domains.

RUMINATIONS

Data's "Ode to Spot" in this episode really is a wonderfully constructed little ditty. I would imagine someone had a blast crafting that poem. It is a delightful touch in the episode.

TRIVIA QUESTIONS

1. The poem that Data recites prior to "Spot" is written in what meter?

2. What two crew members does the computer report as missing from the *Enterprise* in response to Picard's request?

ALTERNATE VIEWPOINTS AND CORRECTIONS

• Sandy Anderson of Taft, CA, wrote to augment my nitpicking of this episode on page 370 of the *NextGen Guide*. Under "Continuity and Production Problems" I noted that Worf locates a crew member's quarters on deck 9, section 17, while Crusher calls an emergency medical unit to deck 9, section 19. Sandy noticed that the numbers on the crew member's door read, "09-1947." The *Tech Manual* identifies the "19" as the section number. Therefore Crusher was right, Worf was wrong!

PLOT OVERSIGHTS

• When Riker comes to sick bay complaining of sleeplessness, Crusher prescribes a shot of Picard's Aunt Adele's hot toddy. Has our good doctor suddenly decided in favor of naturopathic cures? What happened to "load 'em up, shoot 'em up" Beverly?

CHANGED PREMISES

• At the beginning of this episode, La Forge identifies deck 4 as the location of Cargo Bay 4. Yet, when the computer registers an EPS explosion, the flashing indicator on the large ship schematic in Main Engineering makes it appear that Cargo Bay 4 is somewhere around deck 10. On the other hand, when the possessed Troi, Data, and O'Brien take Picard, Worf, and Keiko to Cargo Bay 4 in "Power Play," Ro reports that they disembark the turbolift on deck 18! (I suppose they could get off at deck 18 and then climb through the Jefferies tubes back to deck 10 or deck 4, but why would they?)

EQUIPMENT ODDITIES

• At one point Riker tries to show an ensign how to set a new course in a nebula. He sits down at conn, and a close-up shows the station's display. For some reason it looks very similar to the configuration for Ops—not conn—as shown in the Tech Manual. (The Tech Manual does say that the workstations can be reconfigured. Maybe the ensign is running conn and Ops from her station?)

• Cargo Bay 4 must have two major entrances, even though we see only one. A scene in the cargo bay begins with a crane shot from above. An officer later identified as Shipley works a transporterlike console. From other shots in the cargo bay we know that the main doors sit directly behind him on the opposite side of the cargo bay. Data and La Forge enter from Shipley's right—accompanied by the "big door" opening and closing sounds. Shipley directs their attention to the area between his position and the main cargo bay door. A column of light dances there. Of course, if Data and La Forge had used the entrance that the crew uses for the rest of the show, they would have seen the light before Shipley brought it to their attention. This would have created a contractual dispute, given that Shipley belongs to the Official Columns-of-Odd-Light Identification Contractors' Union (O-COOL-ICU). No doubt the infraction would have lead to endless labor disputes about who's supposed to do what on the *Enterprise*. Wisely, Data and La Forge choose to use the little-known—and never-seen—auxiliary entrance to Cargo Bay 4.

TRIVIA ANSWERS

1. Anapestic tetrameter.
2. Lieutenant Hagler and Ensign Rager.

TRUE Q

Star Dates: 46192.3—46193.8

Amanda Rogers's visit as a student intern to the *Enterprise* prompts a call from Q. Unknown to her, Amanda—though human in appearance—is actually a member of the Q Continuum. According to Q, the continuum has decided that she must join them or refrain from using her powers. Unable to do the latter, Amanda goes with Q.

RUMINATIONS

Lee Zion of the USS Kitty Hawk *nominated the moments when Q turns Crusher into an Irish setter and Amanda turns her back—all without any notice by the good doctor—as one of the all-time greatest sight gags of the series.*

TRIVIA QUESTIONS

1. Where is the current location of Amanda's adoptive parents, and what do they do?

2. What is the name of the engineer from Tagra IV?

PLOT OVERSIGHTS

• Putting Amanda to work, Crusher has the young lady test a series of tricorders and then deliver them to a shuttle bay. The doctor tells Amanda that Nurse Ogawa will help her carry the tricorders. Yet when Amanda shows up in the shuttle bay, she walks in alone.

• Every outside shot of the ship and every starfield seen through the windows seem to indicate that the *Enterprise* flies at impulse for the entire show. Isn't the crew supposed to be rushing to assist Tagra IV?

EQUIPMENT ODDITIES

• Why doesn't Amanda wear a communicator in this episode?

CONTINUITY AND PRODUCTION PROBLEMS

• This isn't really a nit. Nor is it a problem. Actually, it's quite cute. Evidently someone in the sound effects department decided to have a little fun with the lovely Dr. Beverly Crusher. At the very end of the episode— after Q and Amanda disappear —Picard looks at Crusher for a reaction. She looks down and blinks twice with a very distinctive rhythm. Listen closely to the background and you'll here button-pushing beeps in perfect sync with her blinks! (It's "Droid-Doc"!)

TRIVIA ANSWERS

1. They are marine biologists living in the Bilaren System.

2. Orn Lote.

RASCALS

Star Dates: 46235.7—46236.3

A transporter accidently turns Picard, Ro, Guinan, and Keiko into children again. Unfortunately, a band of rogue Ferengi chooses this time to attack and capture the *Enterprise,* using two Klingon ships. Capitalizing on the misperceptions of the Ferengi, Picard and the others assist Riker in regaining control of the ship.

PLOT OVERSIGHTS

• Picard and his younger self seem to have a few differences. Their accents are quite dissimilar. The adult version of Picard has a dimple in his chin; the younger does not. The adult version of Picard has blue eyes; the younger has brown.

• Riker makes a pitiful showing as the Ferengi take on the flagship of the Federation with two surplus Klingon Birds-of-Prey. Unfortunately, his strategy does follow a pattern established in many of the *Enterprise*'s engagements. (This pattern can even be seen in *Star Trek Generations*.) It goes like this. Let the enemy ships hit you about two hundred times with their phasers. Then ask Worf for a damage report. Let the enemy ships hit you another two hundred times with their phasers and photons. Ask for shield status. Let the enemy hit you another two

hundred times with phasers and photons. Fire back at the enemy *once.* Do some fancy flying around. Begin cycle again! Why doesn't Riker just lay into these old rusting Klingon ships with his full complement of weapons?

TRIVIA QUESTIONS

1. Who invited Picard to study the ruins of Suvin IV with her?

2. Guinan claims that Ro cannot resist jumping around like what beast?

EQUIPMENT ODDITIES

• At the beginning of the episode, Picard, Ro, Guinan, and Keiko are beamed from the shuttlecraft in seated positions and materialize on the transporter pad standing up.

• According to "Samaritan Snare," Picard has an artificial heart—presumably an adult-size artificial heart. So...how did it fit in the younger Picard's chest cavity without causing problems? Surely it didn't revert to a younger version of itself, did it?

• As part of Picard's plan to recapture the *Enterprise,* the children use communicators to identify the location of various Ferengi and beam them onto a transporter pad cordoned off with a force field. Where did the kids get these communicators? Picard and Guinan keep theirs, yet the children use *four* others to trap the Ferengi. In addition, one capture deserves special attention. Picard attaches a communicator to the back side of a remotely controlled car. He uses this car to distract the Ferengi so Keiko can secure some phasers in the transporter room. As the pair run for cover, we see the Ferengi returning with the car. He brings it into the transporter room and overlooks the communicator attached to the back of the vehicle. Later, Picard rams the car into the Ferengi's foot, thereby activating the communicator and providing a signal lock so the captain can beam the Ferengi onto the transporter pad. Aside from the fact that this Ferengi must be incredibly unobservant to miss the communicator in the first place, how does the communicator activate? It sits on the back side of the car. If communicators can activate with a jostle as small as this one, why don't we hear them activate when crew members hug or accidently place their hands on another's communicator during a tender moment?

CONTINUITY AND PRODUCTION PROBLEMS

• Obviously Guinan plucks her eyebrows. The younger version of herself comes "eyebrow-equipped."

• Shortly after we join a scene featuring O'Brien and a de-aged Keiko, Keiko gets her husband and herself some coffee from the replicator. She picks up a cup of creamed coffee in her left hand and a cup of black coffee in her right. As she turns, the camera cuts to O'Brien, who sits on the couch. When Keiko walks into the scene, the cups have switched sides. She now holds the black coffee in her left hand and the creamed coffee in her right.

• On the shuttle at the beginning of the episode, we see Keiko holding a tray with five spherical containers and one uncovered plant. Keiko still holds this tray when she rematerializes as a child on the transporter pad. Supposedly this same tray arrives in Crusher's area. Later, however, there are *six* spherical containers and a plant on which Crusher has accelerated the growth.

• The Ferengi apparently bought their hand-held weapons from the Romulans.

• The first few minutes of the engagement between the *Enterprise* and the Ferengi show two Klingon ships. All subsequent exterior shots show only one Klingon vessel. Is the other one cloaked to make it a more difficult target should Riker regain control of the *Enterprise*?

• At one point, Picard sends Alexander to sick bay to fetch some hypos. Keiko later uses one of these hypos to drug a Ferengi into unconsciousness. Yet, close inspection of the hypos as Alexander crawls out of the Jefferies tube and hands them to Picard should reveal that the vials at the bottom of the hyposprays are completely empty!

TRIVIA ANSWERS

1. Dr. Langford.
2. A Tarkassian razorbeast.

A FISTFUL OF DATAS

Star Dates: 46271.5—46278.3

A malfunction in Engineering caused by Data transforms an Ancient West holodeck program enjoyed by Worf, Alexander, and Troi. Suddenly every enemy in the town of Deadwood looks exactly like Data. After constructing a personal force field from some spit, baling wire, and his personal communicator, Worf faces down the head villain and shoots the gun from his hand.

TRIVIA QUESTIONS

1. Where will the *Enterprise* pick up new personnel in a few weeks?

2. Who runs Deadwood's house of pleasure?

PLOT OVERSIGHTS

• As the show begins, Crusher attempts to enlist Picard to play the role of the butler in her play and then tells him that the practices start at "one thirty." One thirty? AM? (I realize that "one thirty" might mean 1:30 PM to you and me but the *Enterprise* runs on military time, doesn't it?)

EQUIPMENT ODDITIES

• Just when it looks like Eli Hollan-der is about to shoot Worf, a rifle shot sounds and Hollander's hat flies off. Eli still holds his .45-caliber revolver. He looks over at Troi, who holds a rifle to her shoulder as she sights down the barrel. In short order, Eli drops his weapon. If I am not mistaken, Troi holds a *lever-action* rifle. To eject the spent cartridge that's in the firing chamber—a result of shooting Eli's hat from his head—and load up a live round—our dear counselor needs to cock the lever. In real life, Troi wouldn't have a live round of ammunition in the rifle, and Eli Hollander could simply shoot her with his revolver!

• Obviously Alexander and Barclay programmed the holodeck characters to call Troi "the Stranger" continually. When she first appears to shoot the hat off Eli Hollander's head, Alexander comments that he invited Counselor Troi to join them. Later, with Eli in jail just in the other room, Worf calls her "Troi," to which she replies that her name is Durango. Yet when Frank and Eli ask about "the stranger," Eli cannot offer a name.

• Alexander and Barclay must have programmed the holodeck to make Worf the hero. In the final gunfight, Frank Hollander draws his weapon, crouches down, and empties his gun at Worf by fanning the hammer—a method used to fire single-action revolvers rapidly, since the hammer must be cocked before pulling the trigger. Once Frank runs out of bullets, a henchman throws him another gun. Worf watches it arc through the air. Frank—still crouching—grabs the gun with his left hand, aims the gun at Worf, and brings his right hand up to fan the hammer. From this position, Frank Hollander can fire the weapon in about one-half second! All he has to do is hit the hammer with his right hand and pull the trigger with his left. No doubt a holodeck character with the reflexes of Data could fire the weapon in *less* than one-half second. However, at this point the scene cuts to Worf. He draws and then shoots the gun from Hollander's hand *before* Hollander can get off the shot. In addition, when the gun flies from his hand, Hollander stands upright, with his right hand *at his side!* This makes sense only if Hollander dropped his arm, stood up, and simply waited for Worf to draw and fire.

CONTINUITY AND PRODUCTION PROBLEMS

• The following nits might simply be holodeck malfunctions, but I'll note them anyway. When Frank Hollander visits his son in jail, pay close attention to Frank's left arm. As the elder Hollander turns to walk away from the jail cell, a thin portion of the arm around the elbow disappears. (It is a bit difficult to spot but definitely there.)

• Evidently the creators didn't want to pay another extra to stand in the cell and pretend to be a Data version of Eli Hollander when Frank walked back into the front room of the jail. Either that, or some extra got paid good money to look *exactly* like a bad mannequin!

• The actual shoot-out between Worf and Frank Hollander provides some interesting shadowplay. Worf and Eli Hollander walk out of the jail. In the aerial shot of the street, they stand just behind a large shadow of a tall building. Yet, when the shot changes

to a reverse angle set on the ground, the shadow directly in front of them has disappeared. Then Frank Hollander and Alexander come out. They stop in the middle of the street quite far from any shadows. When the scene returns to the aerial shot, a roof shadow now is fairly close.

TRIVIA ANSWERS

1. Starbase 118.
2. Miss Langford.

THE QUALITY OF LIFE

Star Dates: 46307.2—46317.8

To assist in the construction of a particle fountain, Dr. Farallon invents some helper droids she names exocomps. Data soon comes to the conclusion that the droids have become sentient and refuses to let the crew sacrifice them to save the lives of Picard and La Forge until the droids themselves volunteer for the mission.

TRIVIA QUESTIONS

1. What game does Crusher call for as she deals the cards at the beginning of the episode?

2. Starfleet is considering the use of the particle fountain for mining operations on what planet?

ALTERNATE VIEWPOINTS AND CORRECTIONS

• Brian Fitzgerald of Acworth, GA, wrote to point out that I incorrectly called Dr. Farallon's invention a "plasma" fountain in the *NextGen Guide*. The correct term is "particle" fountain.

PLOT OVERSIGHTS

• Near the end of the episode, Riker decides to use the exocomps like little bombs to shut down the particle fountain and rescue Picard and La Forge, both of whom are still trapped on the station. Data reacts badly to this plan and locks out the transporters, stating that he cannot allow Riker to sacrifice the lives of the exocomps just to save Picard and La Forge; to use the android's words, it is "not justified to sacrifice one life form for another." This line of reasoning from Data deserves some examination. In prior episodes we have seen that the Federation guarantees certain rights to sentient beings. Yet in all previous cases, an individual entity must not simply live, it also must be *sentient* to acquire protected rights status under Federation law. Presumably these rights preclude the violation of the autonomy of self-destruction. In other words, under Federation law, someone can't arbitrarily order me to sacrifice myself to save another (unless maybe I'm a member of Starfleet and a superior officer is doing the ordering). This is supposed to be the point that Data is making—that the exocomps deserve protected rights status under Federation law, and therefore Riker cannot destroy them to save Picard and

La Forge. *However,* nothing in this episode indicates that the exocomps are *sentient*. This episode merely focuses on whether the exocomps are *alive*. Data bases his entire argument for protection on the fact that the exocomps have proven they are alive by exhibiting a survival instinct. Well…a *cockroach* exhibits a survival instinct when I chase after it with shoe in hand. Does this mean that Data would refuse to beam three bomb-equipped cockroaches to the particle fountain to save Picard and La Forge? Cockroaches are life forms, right? (Yes, I know that the exocomps are supposed to be very intelligent, but I would submit that cockroaches ain't too shabby in the intelligence department either. After all, they have managed to survive as a species despite humans' attempts for years to eradicate them.)

• Riker makes a deal with Data. The first officer says that he will ask the exocomps to go on the mission to save Picard and La Forge. Data then states that he will release transporter control if the exocomps agree to go. Then the action moves to the transporter room, the exocomps agree to go, and the transporter chief beams them over. So…when did Data release the transporter controls?

• *Star Trek: The Next Generation* really needs a character like Spock to rock the humans back on their pompous heels every so often. At the end of the episode, Data explains his actions to Picard, and the captain—thinking he is paying Data a compliment—tells the android that it was "the most human decision" Data has ever made. At times like this I would really like to hear someone respond like Spock did in *Star Trek VI: The Undiscovered Country*. When Kirk tries to assert that everyone is human, Spock comes back, saying that he finds that statement insulting!

CHANGED PREMISES

• In sick bay, Crusher and Data discuss the definition of life. After Crusher lists qualities such as movement, consumption, and reproduction, Data replies that fire has those qualities but is not considered alive. Crusher then states that the same arguments could be applied to growing crystals but obviously "we don't consider them alive." I believe, Dr. Beverly, that you considered crystals alive in the episode "Home Soil"—and not only alive…but sentient!

• In the same discussion, Data wonders about himself stating that he cannot reproduce yet is considered alive. What about Lal? Wasn't she considered Data's child in "The Offspring"? Granted, she ceased to function, but for a time she *did* live.

EQUIPMENT ODDITIES

• After an exocomp refuses to enter a tunnel that explodes only seconds later, La Forge and Farallon take it to Main Engineering for a full analysis. Data joins them. A viewscreen shows a close-up of the exocomp's central processor slowly scrolling downward. La Forge spots something and asks Data to increase the magnification of section "gamma 4." Data complies and a few moments later a piece of the screen at the very top on the right-hand side enlarges. Oddly enough—since the graphic continually scrolls downward—the section that enlarges *was not visible* on the screen when La Forge asked Data for an enlargement! It hadn't scrolled into the picture yet. (With the screen constantly moving, I would have expected La Forge to say something like "Enlarge section gamma 4…no, wait…gamma 5…no…gamma 6…wait…7!")

CONTINUITY AND PRODUCTION PROBLEMS

• Worf's sash is missing at the beginning of this episode. (It's probably at the metal cleaners.)

• To test an exocomp's survival instinct, Data, La Forge, and Farallon stage an experiment. They send the exocomp into a long Jefferies tube and simulate a plasma conduit explosion. The Jefferies tube begins in the Jefferies tube access room on the port side of the center island in Main Engineering and runs toward the warp core. It appears to run parallel to the walls in Main Engineering, but that can't be right, because the walls widen on both sides when they reach La Forge's office. Then they widen again when they reach the warp core. And finally, there's an elevator tucked into the wall on the port side of the warp core. If the Jefferies tube runs straight, it would come right out of the wall at some point!

TRIVIA ANSWERS

1. Seven-card stud, one-eyed jacks are wild.
2. Carema III.

CHAIN OF COMMAND, PART 1

Star Dates: 46357.4—46358.2

Using an elaborate scheme, the Cardassians convince the Federation that they are constructing a horrific metagenic weapon. Starfleet assigns Picard to lead a search and destroy mission, transferring Captain Edward Jellico to the *Enterprise*. Unfortunately, the weapon proves to be a hoax, a lure that the Cardassians use to capture Picard.

TRIVIA QUESTIONS

1. What is the name of the shuttle that Picard, Crusher, and Worf use for their mission?

2. What are the names of Gul Lemec's aides?

PLOT OVERSIGHTS

• Where does the light come from that permeates the caves beneath the surface of Celtris III?

• I'm told by veteran rock climber Robert Chisnall that the away team does not carry enough rope to descend five hundred meters, that there is no need for them to descend all at once—they could have saved the amount of rope they had to carry by going one at a time—and that bouncing down the rock face may be what SWAT teams do and may look good on television, but it has nothing to do with safe or efficient rappelling technique.

EQUIPMENT ODDITIES

• Why isn't Vice Admiral Nechayev wearing a communicator when she comes aboard the *Enterprise* to tell Picard that she is giving command of the *Enterprise* to Captain Jellico?

• After inspecting a wall that he must cut through with a phaser, Worf states that a setting of level 16 "should suffice." I would hope so! According to the *Tech Manual*, level 16 is the highest possible setting and results in "explosive/disruption effect" with "heavy geologic displacement." (By the way, just after Worf vaporizes the rock face, does it seem odd that Picard can climb over the "certain to be blazing hot" rocks so quickly?)

CONTINUITY AND PRODUCTION PROBLEMS

• Looking for passage to the Cardassian world of Celtris III, Picard, Crusher, and Worf go to Torman V and visit a bar. A guy in the background to whom Picard speaks looks like he's a member of the Children of Tama. But that can't be, because they speak only in metaphor.

TRIVIA ANSWERS

1. The *Feyhman*.
2. Glin Corak and Glin Tajor.

CHAIN OF COMMAND, PART 2

Star Date: 46360.8

As a prelude to a new aggressive incursion into Federation space, Cardassian Gul Madred tortures Picard for information about Starfleet's strategies and deployment of ships. Meanwhile, Captain Jellico conducts negotiations with Cardassians before staging a preemptive strike on Cardassian positions and forcing Picard's return.

TRIVIA QUESTIONS

1. To what neutral planet does Gul Madred claim to have sent a message concerning Picard?

2. Where do the Cardassians hide their invasion force?

ALTERNATE VIEWPOINTS AND CORRECTIONS

• In the *NextGen Guide,* on pages 384 and 385, I wondered if the creators had George Orwell's *1984* in mind when they wrote this episode—citing what I felt were similarities. Alas, alack, my memory evidently failed on the details of Orwell's actual story. I mentioned that the torturers in the book required that their victims recite "2+2=5." Graham Buckingham of Thompson, Manitoba,

wrote, "Yes, I too picked up the similarities between Picard's torture and that of Winston Smith in *1984*. The similarities are even more glaring when reported properly. O'Brien, Smith's *only* inquisitor, holds up four fingers and asks Smith how many he can see. Under torture, Smith maintains there are four. Then, to stop the pain, agrees to five. Then, as the pain increases, he can't tell how many there are. Nowhere is Smith told to recite '2+2=5.' He writes in his diary that 'Freedom is the freedom to say that two plus two make four.' The Party wish him to believe that two plus two can be four, five, three or all of these at the same time, if the Party says so."

PLOT OVERSIGHTS

• After Jellico relieves Riker, Data changes into a red uniform. Yet when Data serves as first officer for Picard during the war games of "Peak Performance," he remains in gold. Why? Just what do these colors on the uniforms mean? Blue evidently denotes medical or scientific specialties, but why do Picard, Riker, and ensigns wear red, with everyone else in gold?

• During the episode, Gul Madred's daughter pays a visit, and she is decked out in full military garb. Surely she can't be in the military. Or is she just passing through that "I want to be just like my daddy" phase?

• Needing the best pilot on board, Jellico goes to the former first officer's quarters. Is Riker really a better pilot than Data? Or is Jellico looking for the best *expendable* pilot on board?

EQUIPMENT ODDITIES

• Speaking of mining the Cardassian ships, just how many trips did Riker have to make with this shuttle? Jellico ordered Worf to prepare five hundred of them, and only a few actually come along during the first trip. And how did Riker and La Forge actually deploy these mines? Open the shuttle door and kick them out?

CONTINUITY AND PRODUCTION PROBLEMS

• Near the beginning of the episode, Gul Madred has his minions implant a pain-giving device in Picard's chest. The operation leaves behind an ugly scar that sits in the center of the captain's left pectoral muscle just below his collarbone. Yet, just after Gul Madred's daughter pays a visit, you can see at least part of that area through the opening in Picard's garment, and the scar has disappeared.

• There are times in this episode when Picard supposedly stares at the four lights behind Madred, but the shadows don't seem to support this premise. For instance, after Picard says he will always see Gul Madred as a powerless little boy, the angry Cardassian cranks up the painmaker to an excruciating level. As Picard screams that Madred cannot hurt him, watch the shadows in the moments that follow. To me, they don't seem to indicate that "there are four lights."

TRIVIA ANSWERS

1. Tohvun III.
2. The McAllister Nebula.

SHIP IN A BOTTLE

Star Date: 46424.1

The Moriarty holodeck program awakens and tricks Picard, Data, and Barclay into believing that he has found a way to leave the holodeck when, in fact, he holds them hostage within. At the same time, Moriarty demands that the crew enable him to live in the real world. Discovering what Moriarty has done, Picard and Data create yet another fantasy within the fantasy, convincing Moriarty that he has succeeded in his quest.

TRIVIA QUESTIONS

1. What log should have the results of Data and Barclay's attempt to beam a chair off the holodeck?

2. Where does Riker suggest that Moriarty and the Countess Barthalomew go in their shuttle?

PLOT OVERSIGHTS

• At one point, Data deduces that he, Picard, and Barclay are still on the holodeck. A proof for this statement involves La Forge. Data sees the chief engineer working a padd with his left hand. He then throws an object at La Forge, who catches it with his left hand. From this, Data deduces that La Forge is a holodeck character with a glitch in that the real La Forge is right-handed. John Watson decided to test this theory of hand dominance and went around throwing things at people. He found that people tend to catch with the hand that is closer to the object, not with the hand that is dominant. (By the way, Debbie Sleeter of Albuquerque, NM, also wrote to say that she's left-handed but catches things quite often with her right hand.)

• After discovering that they are still on the holodeck, Picard and Data also come to the conclusion that Moriarty has set all the holodeck controls to respond only to his voice. Why doesn't Data rummage around in that fancy positronic brain of his, find an impersonation of Moriarty, and get them off the holodeck?

CHANGED PREMISES

• For all his protestations and self-proclamation as the champion of the rights of artificial life forms—as demonstrated in "The Quality of Life"—Data seems singularly unimpressed with Moriarty's desire to exist in the real world.

• Data seems to have lost his ability to tell when he's on the holodeck. In "Encounter at Farpoint" he easily found the back wall of the room.

EQUIPMENT ODDITIES

• Why is Picard concerned that Moriarty will vanish if he leaves the holodeck? Isn't Moriarty's program stored in the protected archives? In twentieth-century computer systems, when I start an application, it gets pulled from long-term storage and loaded into RAM. If something happens to the copy in RAM, I can always go back to the hard drive. Wouldn't some corollary to this exist in the twenty-fourth century? If not, why doesn't Picard simply make a backup of Moriarty, let him walk off the holodeck, and see what happens?

• At one point a holodeck-recreated La Forge says, "Holodeck matter doesn't have any cohesion unless it's inside the [holodeck] grid." That being true, it then follows that our captain had a most embarrassing moment (perhaps even in the literal sense) as he trudged off the holodeck at the end of the episode. Originally, Picard entered the holodeck wearing his gray shirt and red jacket. He leaves wearing his standard uniform. Where did he get this uniform? On the holodeck. Of what would this new uniform be composed? Holodeck matter. What happens to holodeck matter when it comes off the holodeck? It loses its cohesion. In other words, it vanishes!

• At the very end of the episode, Barclay—in his typical nervous style—worries that he may just be a program running on someone's desk and says, "Computer, end program." Of course, nothing happens. But that's the problem—*nothing* happens. The computer doesn't chirp. It doesn't say, "Please restate request." It ignores Barclay, as if to say, "That's one of the stupidest things you've ever said and I'm not even going to dignify it with an acknowledgment signal!"

TRIVIA ANSWERS

1. Transport log 759.
2. Meles II.

AQUIEL

Star Date: 46461.3

When a coalescent organism—one that consumes its victims before assuming their appearance—absorbs Lieutenant Keith Rocha just prior to his posting to Relay Station 47, the station's other officer, Aquiel Uhnari, must flee for her life, casting suspicion on her as Rocha's murderer. With La Forge's help, she proves her innocence.

TRIVIA QUESTIONS

1. Where was Uhnari posted prior to her assignment to Relay Station 47?

2. What, in full, was Counselor Troi's dialogue for this episode?

PLOT OVERSIGHTS

• Worf makes a confusing decision when escorting the Klingon Morag to the quarters where he will be held on the *Enterprise*. From the observation lounge, Worf takes Morag through the doorway that leads to the bridge! Presumably the chief of Security then marches the Klingon all the way across the bridge to the turbolift and finally to his quarters. Of course, it's possible that Worf just wanted to give the *murder suspect* a tour of the *Enterprise* and decided to start with

the bridge, since it is the most fascinating and sensitive area on the ship.

• On the first away mission, Crusher finds a glob of goo on the floor. It turns out to be part of a coalescent organism that can absorb and mimic anything it touches. When the organism assumes the shape of Crusher's hand—*without* absorbing it, by the way—Picard and Riker come down to sick bay to gawk at the sight. The goo appears to sit, uncovered and unrestrained, in the middle of the room. Shouldn't the crew be just a tad bit more careful with this stuff?

• At the conclusion of the show, we discover that the coalescent being had previously absorbed Uhnari's dog and assumed its shape. The being then attempts to attack La Forge. The chief engineer puts on an amazing display of dexterity—bobbing and weaving to avoid absorption—but never once cries out, "Security to La Forge's quarters!"

EQUIPMENT ODDITIES

• I am constantly amazed by Starfleet technology. Shortly after an away team arrives on Relay Station 47, Worf cuts out a section of the deck plate. It contains a glob of goo that Crusher wants to take back to the *Enterprise* for analysis. His phaser looks like it's aimed well beyond the glob, but somehow the targeting mechanism correctly interprets what the Security chief desires to hit and adjusts the angle of the beam accordingly.

• La Forge must really crank up the power of his phaser at the end of the episode. Previous dialogue in the episode seems to indicate that the goo on the deck plate had been hit with a phaser on level 10 for thirty or forty seconds. Yet, once La Forge gets the phaser powered up, it takes only a few seconds to vaporize the coalescent being. (I wonder what happened to the "lethal phaser discharge" alarm that the *Enterprise*-A had in *Star Trek VI: The Undiscovered Country*?)

CONTINUITY AND PRODUCTION PROBLEMS

• All the exterior shots of the relay station show it rotating. Yet all interior shots of Aquiel's quarters that feature her window show the stars standing still.

• Attempting to piece together the events on the station, La Forge tries to access Uhnari's personal logs. At one point he throws a doodad into his tool kit in frustration. To the right of the case there's a smaller cylindrical tool and a large padd. La Forge asks the computer for a diagnostic check and then orders ice coffee from the replicator. When he looks back at the console and sees a picture of Uhnari, the doodad has disappeared from the case, the cylindrical object has moved, and the padd is gone. (Spooky, huh?)

• Going over Uhnari's logs, La Forge finds a place he wants to review. He asks the computer to rewind the log, and then La Forge begins to play back the section a second time. In the recording, behind and to the left of Uhnari, a boom mike makes an appearance.

TRIVIA ANSWERS

1. Deriben V.

2. "Concerned." (Thanks to Geoffrey Cook of Hammond, IN, for pointing this out. As Geoffrey observed, "I'm sure Marina Sirtis was ashamed to pick up her paycheck. However, she did make up for it in the very next episode.")

TREK TECHNOBABBLE GENERATOR

t's fun! It's fascinating! It's fast! Now you, too, can develop that special lingo used in many *Star Trek: The Next Generation* episodes. Simply choose a number from each of the four columns and put together the resulting words. Instant technobabble! For instance, choosing "3 1 2 3" would result in "annular confinement beam." Or how about "1 2 4 3"? That's "anaphasic energy being"! Amaze your friends! Impress your relatives! Start sounding just like La Forge and Data *today*!

1. [blank]	1. [blank]	1. [blank]	1. [blank]
2. ambient	2. anaphasic	2. confinement	2. beam
3. annular	3. axionic	3. containment	3. being
4. quantum	4. biomimetic	4. energy	4. bubble
5. spatial	5. cosmic	5. flux	5. burst
6. trans-	6. duodynetic	6. impulse	6. capacitor
	7. dynamic	7. particle	7. conduit
	8. genetic	8. plasma	8. converter
	9. interphasic	9. vertion	9. core
	10. isomiatic	10. warp	10. discriminator
	11. magnascopic		11. field
	12. metagenic		12. scanner
	13. metaphasic		13. sensor
	14. nueucleonic		14. shell
	15. osmotic		15. stream
	16. plasmonic		16. string
	17. positronic		
	18. static		
	19. subharmonic		

FACE OF THE ENEMY

Star Date: 46519.1

Troi awakes on a Romulan vessel dressed and physically altered to look like a member of the Tal Shiar, Romulan Intelligence. The Romulan underground is smuggling three high-ranking members of the Romulan senate into Federation territory, where they will seek asylum, and they need her help in case they must defeat Starfleet's gravitic sensor nets at the border.

TRIVIA QUESTIONS

1. What is the name of Commander Toreth's vessel?

2. What award did Commander Toreth earn in her attack on a Klingon outpost?

PLOT OVERSIGHTS

• I wonder if the Romulans keep visual records similar to Starfleet's? If so, did Commander Toreth look up Majors Rakal's records? And, if she did, does the dissident movement have enough pull to alter the records, or does Troi just happen to look exactly like Rakal?

• This episode also features a man named DeSeve, who defected to

Romulus twenty years earlier and has decided to return to the Federation. Yet, according to "The Neutral Zone," at the time of that episode, the Romulans hadn't been heard from in fifty-three years! So—twenty years ago—after *complete silence* from the Romulans for more than thirty years, this guy decided to defect to them?

• How does Troi know her way around this massive Romulan warbird? She goes to a cargo bay without assistance. Then she goes from the cargo bay to the wardroom. Then she leaves the bridge and goes to her quarters. Maybe I can grant the last one because Subcommander N'Vek had previously escorted her from her quarters to the bridge, but it seems like the other incidents would require a guide. Then again, maybe the computer on the Romulan warbird showed her how to get around.

• Supposedly the Romulan dissident movement recruited Troi because she would know the codes for the subspace listening devices along the Federation border. Does this seem right? A *counselor* on a starship knows how to disable a defense grid?

• Most everyone in the episode identifies M'ret, the leader of the defectors, as "Merret." But DeSeve calls him "Emret."

CHANGED PREMISES

• In "Unification," a Klingon Bird-of-Prey waltzes right up to the border of Romulan space, cloaks, and flies straight to Romulus. Yet, in this episode, we discover that the Federation has subspace listening devices littered all along their border with "gravitic sensors" that evidently can somehow detect the passage of a cloaked ship. If the Romulans know the Federation has this technology, why haven't they done the same thing to their own borders? Surely they could steal a few gravitic sensors if they didn't know how to build them.

EQUIPMENT ODDITIES

• Who designed the doorways on this Romulan warbird? Each has a threshold raised several inches off the floor!

• At one point, DeSeve tells Picard that the *Enterprise* must rendezvous with a freighter. When the freighter misses its appointment, DeSeve fills in more details. He states that the freighter is an old *Antares*-class vessel with limited range. He says that it picked up its cargo a day ago and therefore could not be more than fifteen light-years distant. However, *The Star Trek Encyclopedia* says that it takes the *Enterprise* twenty-three hours—almost a day—to go five light-years at a maximum warp of 9.6. So this old freighter is almost three times as fast as the *Enterprise*?!

CONTINUITY AND PRODUCTION PROBLEMS

• For most of the episode, Troi wears the typical short, straight hairdo of a Romulan. Just after Crusher restores her face to normal, Troi suddenly has her thick, curly, generous mane back. Is she wearing a wig at the end of the episode?

TRIVIA ANSWERS

1. The Imperial Romulan Warbird *Khazara*.
2. The Sotarek Citation.

★ TAPESTRY

Star Date: unknown

Meeting Picard in the afterlife, Q senses the captain's remorse over his brash ways as a young man and sends him back in time to live those experiences again with the wisdom of maturity. Then Q returns Picard to a present that the captain finds lacks any challenge. After pleading for a second chance, Picard goes back to set things right, after which Q restores his life and returns him to the *Enterprise*.

GREAT LINES

"*I refuse to believe that the afterlife is run by you! The universe is not so badly designed.*"—Picard to Q after Q claims to be "God." Nominated by Matt Cavic of Ballwin, MO.

TRIVIA QUESTIONS

1. What is the last name of Penny, the woman whom Picard meets at the bar in the Bonestell Recreational Facility?

2. Who commanded the USS *Ajax* thirty years ago?

PLOT OVERSIGHTS

• Near the beginning of the episode, Picard claims that the incident with the

Nausicaans occurred thirty years ago. Yet this episode also states that Picard graduated with the class of '27 and then went to Starbase Earhart to await his first deep space assignment. The established chronology for *Star Trek* puts "Tapestry" in the year 2369. Thirty years prior would be 2339. So Picard waited around Starbase Earhart from 2327 to 2339 for his first deep space assignment?

• When allowing Picard to redo his redo of the fight with the Nausicaan, Q starts the events rolling at the actual fight. Evidently it isn't Q's intention to put everything back the way it was before this episode began, because a significant change occurred in Picard's timeline prior to this fight. He slept with his buddy Marta Batanides the night before.

CHANGED PREMISES

• The alien "background filler" at the Bonestell Recreational Facility contains representatives from an interesting collage of races. Of special interest, an Antican and a Selay peaceably stand a few feet from each other. "Lonely Among Us" established that these two races were archenemies and took any opportunity to kill the other.

• After Picard ensures that the Nausicaan does not stab him in the back, Q returns the former captain to the *Enterprise*. Picard still lives, but as an astrophysicist with a rank of lieutenant, junior grade. Picard describes himself in these present circumstances as a "dreary man in a tedious job." A *tedious* job? In the *twenty-fourth* century? I thought that every human had a *fabulous* existence in the twenty-fourth century—that the real challenge of the twenty-fourth century was "to improve yourself, to enrich

yourself." (Picard says this in "The Neutral Zone.") A "tedious job" doesn't sound very *enriching*, does it?

EQUIPMENT ODDITIES

• Shortly after an injured Captain Picard materializes in sick bay, Crusher begins waving her medical wand over him. In the first two shots that show this activity, the lights on the scanner are not blinking. Finally, the third time, they are.

• Back at Starbase Earhart, Picard asks the computer for the time, and the computer responds, sounding just like it does on the *Enterprise* (i.e., Majel Barrett-Roddenberry reads for the computer). That's interesting, because in the first few shows of the first season, the computer used different voices (both male and female). Those shows imply that the current voice of the computer didn't come into use until several decades *after* Picard's visit to Starbase Earhart.

• When Lieutenant Picard finds himself on the bridge of the *Enterprise*, Worf takes a padd from his hand, advises him that it should go to La Forge in Engineering, and hands it back. Yet when boarding the turbolift to go to Engineering—after meeting with Riker and Troi in Ten-Forward —Picard carries no padd.

CONTINUITY AND PRODUCTION PROBLEMS

• In the reenactment of the fight between the *young* Picard and the Nausicaans, watch the first Nausicaan as he flies backward from a blow by Picard. His wig comes loose as he falls, and when he rolls off-screen, the wig stays behind. (I believe the stunt guy is actually blond!) Of course, this raises all sorts of questions. Were the Nausicaans actually Starfleet officers surgically altered to look like the vicious aliens? And why would they pick a fight with Picard and friends? Just what did this trio of young officers know that was so dangerous to someone obviously high up in the echelons of Starfleet?

• Picard must be a compulsive pillow fluffer. Moments after Zweller leaves Picard's quarters because Picard refuses to help him rig the dom-jot table to beat the Nausicaan, Q enters with a bouquet of flowers. A reaction shot from Picard and Batanides shows Picard's pillow lying flat on the bed. Then Batanides says a few last words to Picard and leaves. The scene cuts to Q, who asks if he interrupted anything sordid. And when the shot returns to Picard for an answer, we discover that in this short time, our captain—overwhelmed with the untidiness of the bed—proceeded professionally to fluff and set the pillow at a delightful angle.

TRIVIA ANSWERS

1. Muroc.
2. Captain Narth.

BIRTHRIGHT, PART I

Star Date: 46578.4

Worf makes his way to a Romulan POW camp after hearing rumors that his father may still live. Shortly after arriving at the camp, he does indeed find Klingon prisoners from the last Klingon/Romulan war. Unfortunately, his father is not among them, and the prisoners who remain demand that Worf stay with them to hide their shame.

RUMINATIONS

*A*lma Jo Williams of Ithaca, NY, noted that the Yridian in this episode has the appearance of a nude mouse, a standard laboratory animal for immunological research. "Without a doubt," she continued, "more neat aliens could be modeled after laboratory animals, such as woodchucks, ticks, intestinal parasites.... The list is endless and disgusting!"

PLOT OVERSIGHTS

• Approaching the planet that houses the Romulan prisoner camp filled with Klingons, the Yridian tells Worf it will be necessary to "transport" him to the surface thirty kilometers from the installation to avoid the sensors. The precedent in *Star Trek* dialogue indicates that the Yridian intends to beam Worf to the surface. But the next scene shows the Yridian on the ground with Worf telling the Klingon that he won't land in the same place when he returns.

TRIVIA QUESTIONS

1. Where does the Rite of *MajQa* take place?

2. What is the name of the Yridian information dealer who brings Worf word concerning his father?

EQUIPMENT ODDITIES

• To explore the meaning of a dream, Data goes to his quarters to paint. In about six and one-half hours, the android creates twenty-three paintings. Then he walks around his quarters and shows them to La Forge—handling them with his fingers against the *freshly* painted surfaces. Yet he leaves no smudge marks, and no paint appears on his hands. Is he using some sort of advanced twenty-fourth-century rapid drying acrylics?

• So…what *was* the function of the machine that Bashir brought aboard the *Enterprise*?

CONTINUITY AND PRODUCTION PROBLEMS

• Beginning to paint in his quarters, Data lays down several strokes with his brush and then steps back to look at his work. If you listen carefully, you can still hear the brush working away on the canvas in the background even though Data stands several feet from the painting!

• When Data takes flight in his dream, he traverses a corridor and then passes his father the blacksmith

before exiting the ship. If you look down the corridor just as Data leaves the *Enterprise,* you can see a person sitting on the floor.

• Near the end of the episode, Bashir walks with Data down a series of corridors. Several shots clearly show that he wears regulation black boots. However, after thanking Data for allowing him to write up the android's experiences, Bashir's shoes suddenly turn white. Watch carefully as Bashir walks out of the picture.

TRIVIA ANSWERS

1. In the caves of No'Mat.
2. Jaglom Shrek.

BIRTHRIGHT, PART II

Star Date: 46759.2

Worf soon discovers that Tokath, the Romulan camp commander, gave up his military career so that the captured and dishonored Klingons could live out their lives in seclusion. Unfortunately, Worf's very presence evokes a desire in the prisoners' children to know of true Klingon ways. Rather than execute Worf and the children, Tokath allows them to leave.

TRIVIA QUESTIONS

1. What jeweled amulet is given to a Klingon female when she becomes old enough to take a mate?

2. What does Tokath insert in Worf's neck as a tracking device?

PLOT OVERSIGHTS

• The great dishonor comes for the Klingons in the camp when they allow themselves to be captured alive during the Romulan attack on Khitomer. Yet, when Worf makes his first escape attempt, he allows himself to be taken alive as well. Does this mean that Worf has been dishonored again?

TRIVIA ANSWERS

1. A *jinaq*.
2. A boridium pellet.

STARSHIP MINE

Star Date: 46682.4

Terrorists attempt to abscond with a dangerous warp core waste product called trilithium during a baryon particle sweep, a standard maintenance procedure. Accidently, Picard gets trapped on board and must stop the terrorists from succeeding.

ALTERNATE VIEWPOINTS AND CORRECTIONS

• In my plot summary on page 399 of the *NextGen Guide,* I indicated that the head terrorist beamed off the *Enterprise* to a scout ship, the scout ship blew up, and Picard called for help. Michelle Sutherland of London, Ontario, correctly advised that, in fact, the terrorist beams off, Picard calls for help, the baryon particle sweep ceases, and then the scout ship blows up.

TRIVIA QUESTIONS

1. Where was Captain Edwell born?

2. Who did a poetry reading for the *Magellan's* crew talent show?

PLOT OVERSIGHTS

• Just after knocking the first terrorist unconscious, Picard tries to get off the *Enterprise.* Presumably he wants to alert his crew to the incursion against the ship. Once main power shuts down, he never makes the attempt again. Why not? Couldn't he use an emergency transporter in one of the shuttles? What about the fabled lifeboats or the captain's yacht? (Both are mentioned in the *Technical Manual.*)

• The first time a terrorist captures Picard, she takes him to Main Engineering. For some reason the head terrorist forgets to frisk the captain and leaves him in possession of a laser welder, a communications device, and a door opener.

• It's really very fortunate that the head female terrorist has a soft spot in her heart for Picard. Moments before rendezvousing with the terrorist who holds Picard, the head terrorist kills one of the remaining members of her team. Obviously she has no scruples concerning murder. Yet she allows Picard to live even though he poses a constant threat to the mission.

• Not a nit, just an observation. At the very end of the episode, Picard comments that he only wished that he could have used the saddle on a horse. Worf replies, "Of course." The crew finds this interaction delightful. Was this dialogue intended as a homage to *Mr. Ed*?

EQUIPMENT ODDITIES

• The long-stemmed Arkarian glasses used during Hutchinson's reception appear to present a bit of a challenge. The liquid goes all the way down the stem to the base of the glass. I would imagine that if you tilt the glass up too quickly, the liquid would splash you in the face!

• Many nitpickers found it hard to believe that the captain of the *Enterprise* could not halt the autoshutdown of the *Enterprise* and beam off the ship.

• The computer shuts off main power while Picard stands on the transporter pad, but there is still enough illumination to see the captain in a closed room with all the main lights turned off. (Of course, it wouldn't be much of a scene if we couldn't see Picard stroll off the pad with a look of chagrin on his face. Wink, wink.)

• How come Hutchinson gets shot and dies and La Forge gets shot and lives?

• After capturing Picard, the terrorists seat him on the floor in Main Engineering. He just happens to be near some kind of interface, an interface very low to the ground. He puts a laser welding tool in the interface. The tool just happens to fit, and firing the tool just happens to cause something akin to a coolant leak that just happens to close the big confinement door.

CONTINUITY AND PRODUCTION PROBLEMS

• Arkaria Base bears a striking resemblance to the Darwin Genetic Research Station of "Unnatural Selection."

• Near the end of the episode, Picard walks into Ten-Foward and steps over a blue line on the floor. A female terrorist follows, but when she steps on the blue line, it suddenly has several black bumps. (The bumps are probably the explosives that the creators were loath to attach to the tape when Patrick Stewart walked across it, lest they were to go off accidentally and injure the actor.)

TRIVIA ANSWERS

1. Gaspar VII.
2. Captain Conklin.

★ LESSONS

Star Dates: 46693.1—46697.2

Falling in love with Lieutenant Neela Daren, Picard learns again the demands of a romantic relationship between the captain of a starship and a member of his (or her) crew. When a difficult away mission convinces Picard that he must never allow Daren to experience such danger again, she resigns her post and leaves the ship.

RUMINATIONS

Stephanie Ibach of Peace River, Alberta, wrote to compliment the creators on using a real musician for Daren's hand double during the close-ups of Daren's piano performances. This allows viewers to see the correct notes being played on the instrument—something that Stephanie finds pleasing, since she has perfect pitch and can immediately tell when performers press the wrong key!

TRIVIA QUESTIONS

1. Which archaeologist does Picard ask Data to contact at the beginning of the episode?

2. What is the name of the nurse Crusher gained during the *Enterprise*'s recent visit to Starbase 218?

ALTERNATE VIEWPOINTS AND CORRECTIONS

• In the *NextGen Guide,* on page 402, I referred to Daren playing the piano for a Mozart trio. In fact, the piece was a Chopin trio. (Thanks to Margaret A. Basta of Oak Park, MI, for pointing this out.)

PLOT OVERSIGHTS

• After Daren's performance of Chopin's Trio in G Minor with two other musicians, Picard compliments her on the substitution of an F minor chord in place of a D diminished. If the trio played the piece in the traditional classical style, Picard's statement is a bit ridiculous. Performers of classical music usually do not have the option to improvise new harmonies in an established, centuries-old piece. (It is true that pianists have a great deal of latitude in Mozart cadenzas. However, that's Mozart, not Chopin.) I suppose we could say that performance techniques of the twenty-fourth century allow this sort of thing.

EQUIPMENT ODDITIES

• Throughout the show, Daren carries around a roll-up keyboard that has a gorgeous acoustical piano tone. It apparently also has some sort of pop-up legs. She unrolls it flat against the floor in a Jefferies tube intersection, and the next time we see the keyboard, it has sprouted supports.

• After enjoying a kiss, Picard and Daren ride a turbolift together. A crew member enters the turbolift, the doors close, and the car continues on its way without the crew member giving the turbolift any directions. Is she simply *hoping* that the turbolift will drop her somewhere near her desired destination?

• Watch the doors in Daren's lab the second time Picard comes down. A crew member enters, and the doors close behind him…almost. There's a gap of several inches when the doors stop moving.

• In this episode, Daren heads the Stellar Cartography department. Stellar Cartography…Stellar Cartography...why does that sound familiar? Oh, I know. That's the gigantic, monstrously sophisticated room that Picard and Data use in *Star Trek Generations* to determine Dr. Soren's objectives. Stellar Cartography must have had an upgrade, because when Picard visits it in this episode, it's nothing spectacular.

• The transporter consoles in the transporter rooms must be movable. Near the end of the episode, Crusher calls the bridge, and the shot shows the console facing a wall with people coming off the transporter pads beyond it. Normally the transporter console faces the transporter pads.

• In her final talk with Picard, Daren tells the captain that her team used phasers to create a protective pocket in the firestorm. Yet, when the away team beams down, no one carries a Type II phaser (the kind that goes in the hip holster). Perhaps the away team carried Type I phasers in those tiny hip pockets, but Daren's uniform fits quite snugly and I certainly didn't spot any out-of-place bulges.

CONTINUITY AND PRODUCTION PROBLEMS

• As Daren's away team prepares to beam down, Riker tells the transporter chief to maintain a lock on their signals. He then addresses the transporter chief as "Ensign." However, the shot of the transporter chief standing behind Picard clearly shows that she wears two pips on her collar—identifying her as a lieutenant.

TRIVIA ANSWERS

1. Dr. Mowray on Landris II.
2. Beck.

★ THE CHASE

Star Dates: 46731.5–46735.2

When one of Picard's former professors discovers that human DNA contains part of a coded message, the crew goes on a chase to collect the other pieces—cooperating even with the Klingons and Cardassians. The message turns out to be a greeting from a long-dead race who claim they seeded most of the existing humanoid worlds.

TRIVIA QUESTIONS

1. What is the night blessing of the Yash-El?

2. How does Galen expect to get from DS4 to Caere?

ALTERNATE VIEWPOINTS AND CORRECTIONS

• On page 407 of the *NextGen Guide,* I stated that the stars in Picard's quarters move from right to left. In fact, the stars move from left to right. (Thanks to W. D. Timmones of Mesa, AZ, for mentioning this.)

• On page 406 of the *NextGen Guide,* I used Data's statements in "Q Who" to establish a maximum warp speed for the *Enterprise.* I claimed that Data told Picard it would take the

Enterprise over two and one-half years to travel 7,000 light-years. As Rod Tyrell of Victoria, Australia, pointed out, this isn't what Data says. Q throws them 7,000 light-years, and Data says it will take over two and one-half years to reach the nearest starbase. (Presumably the starbase lies between the *Enterprise* and its original position. Otherwise Riker would just ask how long to get back to their original position. In reality, then, it would actually take the *Enterprise* *longer* to traverse 7,000 light-years and, in this case, strengthening the point I was attempting to make!)

PLOT OVERSIGHTS

• I do have to admit that Galen is one impressive archaeologist. If I understand the dialogue correctly, Galen made a short side trip to the planet Kurl and managed to unearth an extremely rare artifact before gallivanting off to continue his research and present it as a gift to Picard.

• This gift brings up another subject: Just what is the Federation's policy toward the cultural heritage of nonaligned worlds? Shouldn't there be some corollary to the Prime Directive that states that members of the Federation will not plunder the archaeological resources of a planet for their amusement? Apparently Galen isn't restrained by any such command. If this artifact is as rare as Picard claims, shouldn't it be in a museum? (By the way, after the destruction of the *Enterprise* in *Star Trek: Generations,* Picard picks up the top of this artifact and then casually discards it. I guess that's one rare artifact that museumgoers

will simply have to live without!)

• After Picard refuses to join his expedition, Galen leaves the *Enterprise* in a huff. Some time later, a distress call comes in from Galen. Data locates the professor's shuttle. The *Enterprise* drops out of warp, and Worf fires the phaser. All this happens within seconds. How in the world did the *Enterprise* get to the location of Galen's shuttle *so* quickly?

• There's an odd little bit of dialogue as the crew searches for more pieces to the DNA puzzle. Congregating in Main Engineering, Picard, Crusher, Data, and La Forge discuss the protein fragments and the way they fit together. La Forge says that they have tried all the DNA material in the Federation data base but haven't found any other matches. Then Picard asks Data if there are any personnel aboard from non-Federation worlds, and Data responds in the affirmative. The crew then tests these persons' DNA. So...these nonaligned persons are on the *Enterprise,* and Crusher doesn't have a sample of their DNA? Is there some Federation medical ethics law that says you can't get a sample of a race's DNA until they join the club? Or is the Federation simply uninterested in people on board the *Enterprise* whose races haven't been logged into the data base?

• This episode would have us believe that a humanoid race approximately 4.5 *billion* years ago seeded various planets in our galaxy with DNA that was smart enough to create humanoid races 4.5 *billion* years later. Not only that, but this selfsame DNA also somehow managed to get many of the races to very similar levels of technology simultaneously. Just coincidence? I wonder. After all, even a .00001 percent difference (450 years) would result in a great disparity and discourage the various races from working together as the supposed progenitors desired.

EQUIPMENT ODDITIES

• At the end of the episode, the DNA program modifies a tricorder to project a recording made 4.5 billion years ago. Oddly enough, the projection has a shadow!

TRIVIA ANSWERS

1. "Dream not of today."
2. By Al-Leyan transport.

FRAME OF MIND

Star Date: 46778.1

While on a covert mission to Tilonus IV, Riker is captured and interrogated using a neurosomatic technique of memory extraction. His mind creates a defense mechanism based on recent events and patches together a hodgepodge of memories from recent weeks on the *Enterprise,* including a performance of *Frame of Mind—* a play set in a brutal mental institution.

PLOT OVERSIGHTS

• This next comment applies to almost all of the nits listed below. For the most part, this episode occurs within Riker's

mind. As I said in the *NextGen Guide,* this fact makes it a bit difficult to nitpick! All the nits could simply be fallacies of Riker's ruminations. Yet there are a few things that struck nitpickers odd when they watched the show. For instance, La Forge brings an injured man to sick bay at one point. Were all the emergency medical teams on their coffee break?

TRIVIA QUESTIONS

1. Whom does Dr. Syrus claim to have contacted on Starbase 29?

2. Whom does Jaya claim to be?

EQUIPMENT ODDITIES

• The phaser Riker holds during the conclusion of the episode has no power level readout as described in the *Tech Manual* and shown at the end of "The Vengeance Factor."

• What happened to the subcutaneous transponder technology that Starfleet had in the *Classic* episode "Patterns of Force"? In that episode, McCoy injects Kirk and Spock with transponders that would allow the *Enterprise* to beam them back to the ship even if they lacked their communicators. Doesn't this seem like a good thing to have on dangerous away missions? On the other hand, Riker's communicator sat nearby during his interrogation. Doesn't it have a locator signal?

CONTINUITY AND PRODUCTION PROBLEMS

• When Picard speaks with Riker in

his ready room, the stars creep by slowly in the window. But when Riker exits onto the bridge, the stars on the viewscreen stand perfectly still.

TRIVIA ANSWERS

1. Admiral Budrow.
2. Commander Bloom of the *Yorktown*.

SUSPICIONS

Star Dates: 46830.1—46831.2

Crusher organizes a special scientific conference to give a Ferengi scientist named Reyga a chance to prove his metaphasic shielding—a technology that should allow a shuttle to enter a star's corona. Unfortunately, a scientist named Jo'Bril sabotages the first test and fakes his death—hoping to steal Reyga's invention. Only Crusher's intervention keeps Jo'Bril from succeeding.

TRIVIA QUESTIONS

1. Where did Crusher first meet Reyga?

2. What is the name of Dr. T'Pan's husband?

PLOT OVERSIGHTS

• I guess it's a good thing Jo'Brill knew Dr. Crusher wouldn't do an invasive autopsy on him. Or was this just a lucky guess?

• Okay, so this Jo'Bril guy is in the morgue, right? And Crusher—also in the morgue—decides to take the shuttle out and prove the metaphasic shielding works, right? She takes the shuttle out, proves the shield works, and Jo'Bril pops up behind her after extricating himself from a storage bin on the shuttle. First, how does Jo'Bril get out of the morgue? The last time we see him, he's on a slab. From previous scenes, we know that Nurse Ogawa is probably going to shut the enclosure when she leaves. This means that Jo'Bril must be strong enough to shove the thing open from the inside. Next, after extricating himself from the storage unit in the morgue, Jo'Bril wandered around naked until he found his clothing. Then he used the Jefferies tubes to get to the shuttle bay so that no one would see him. And finally, Jo'Bril hid in the shuttle. Amazingly enough, he accomplished this before Crusher—who apparently goes directly from the morgue to the shuttle bay—arrives to pilot the *Justman*.

• By a process of elimination, the creators lead us to believe that Jo'Bril murdered Reyga, but the dialogue never states this. But if he didn't, who did?

TRIVIA ANSWERS

1. At the Altine Conference.
2. Dr. Christopher.

RIGHTFUL HEIR

Star Date: 46852.2

Seeking to renew his faith at Boreth, Worf witnesses the return of Kahless—the greatest of all warriors. In time, Worf discovers that this Kahless is actually a clone of the greatest Klingon warrior, but he convinces Gowron that even this Kahless can be a spiritual guide for the Empire in the honorary role of emperor.

TRIVIA QUESTIONS

1. Who serves at Tactical at the beginning of the episode?

2. Where does Crusher get the sample of Kahless's blood for the DNA comparison she runs on the cloned Kahless?

ALTERNATE VIEWPOINTS AND CORRECTIONS

• On page 413 I pointed out that, in this episode, Data states that Starfleet officers activated him, but in "Datalore," the android says that a sensing device activated him when the officers approached. I reminded my readers that Data is an android and usually speaks fairly specifically. Robert Breneman of Muskogee, OK, made the case that Data's statements are *technically* correct, given that we say a burglar sets off an alarm when in fact the burglar activates a sensor that then sets off the alarm.

PLOT OVERSIGHTS

• At one point, Kahless relates a vision that Worf had as a child. Yet the end of the episode indicates that Kahless is merely a clone and all his memories were constructed by the clerics of Boreth. So how did Kahless know about Worf's childhood vision? Did Worf tell the clerics about it?

CHANGED PREMISES

• Kahless has changed a bit since the days of *Classic Trek*. The *Classic* episode "The Savage Curtain" features a reincarnated Kahless as well. It portrays him as an infamously evil person, someone who looks very humanoid in appearance and can even do voice impersonations. This episode shows Kahless as an honorable warrior (probably because the Klingons are our buddies now). And, in this episode, Kahless sports the turtleshell head. (He probably had it in "The Savage Curtain" but you just couldn't see it because he had his hair combed forward to cover it.) As to the voice impersonations, the cloned Kahless of "Rightful Heir" never exhibits *this* capability, but he probably has it, and that's a good deal. If the emperor deal doesn't work out, there's always the entertainment palaces of the Pleiades Cluster.

• The term "emperor" for Klingons must be synonymous with "Empire." In

"Sins of the Father," Worf's nanny tells Picard that Worf's father, Mogh, was "loyal to the emperor." But in this episode, Gowron states that there hasn't been an emperor in three centuries.

EQUIPMENT ODDITIES

• In the first scene with the holodeck, the doors hiss open and shut like the ones in Ten-Forward instead of like cargo bay doors, as they should.

CONTINUITY AND PRODUCTION PROBLEMS

• At the beginning of the episode, when Riker reports to the bridge for duty, his pips run at a fairly severe angle. However, moments later, standing before Worf's quarters, the pips sit on his collar in a more normal configuration. Obviously Riker slapped them on as he hurried to report to the bridge on time for the start of his duty shift. Then he adjusted them in the turbolift on the way to Worf's quarters.

• Just after appearing, Kahless tells the loyal seekers at Boreth the story of the bat'leth. As he ends it, he holds his bat'leth with the upper portion leaning against his right shoulder. The shot changes as a high cleric kneels, and suddenly the bat'leth rests on Kahless's left shoulder. (I'm sure it looked better in the shot.)

• Is the Klingon symbol reversible? On the arms of Kahless's chair on the holodeck, it's upside down.

TRIVIA ANSWERS

1. Ensign Torigan.
2. From the Knife of Kirom.

SECOND CHANCES

Star Dates: 46915.2—46920.1

Attempting to recover data (*information,* not the android) left behind during a rescue mission led by Riker eight years ago, an away team beams down to Nervala IV, only to find *Lieutenant* William Riker—a duplicate created by a transporter anomaly those many years ago.

TRIVIA QUESTIONS

1. What is the name of the song that Troi requests in Ten-Forward at the beginning of this episode?

2. What drink does Troi order from her replicator just before finding the first note in Lieutenant Riker's "love hunt"?

ALTERNATE VIEWPOINTS AND CORRECTIONS

• On page 415 of the *NextGen Guide* I mentioned that Lieutenant Riker's doorbell doesn't ring when Troi first comes to visit. John Digianno of East Elmhurst, NY, wrote to say that the doorbell sounds on his tape. On the other hand, Marcie Terril of Zanesville, OH, corresponded that the first time she saw the episode the doorbell didn't ring, but the second time it did. (I think someone's fixing a few nits here and there!)

PLOT OVERSIGHTS

• At one point, Lieutenant Riker sends Troi on a "love hunt"—leaving little notes and presents around the ship for her to find. A clue leads her to the dilithium chamber. She finds another note hanging on the chamber, with a piece of chocolate attached. So no one in Engineering noticed a note hanging from this sensitive piece of equipment? Lest you think that Lieutenant Riker secured permission to leave the note dangling from the core, La Forge wanders up as Troi departs and casts a confused look at the situation.

• Shouldn't Lieutenant Riker get the same promotion as Commander Riker did for his actions on the previous rescue mission to Nervala IV? And what about back pay and accrued vacation time? Carl Fields tells me that Vietnam POWs received promotions to account for the time they were interred.

• So, good old Lieutenant Riker has been isolated from people for eight years—out of touch with any technological advances—and Starfleet ships him off on another assignment just over a week after he is discovered. Wouldn't this be a good time for him to undergo some adjustment time—maybe even counseling—at a starbase?

EQUIPMENT ODDITIES

• I mentioned this possibility in the *NextGen Guide*'s review of "Lonely Among Us," but a further examination might be helpful. This episode proves that you can create a duplicate of someone using a transporter beam.

(And don't say that this was just a special circumstance and could never be repeated. Most scientific discoveries happen by chance, and then everyone scrambles around until they get it to happen again.) "Relics" proved that you can keep a person intact in a pattern buffer for seventy-five years. So why doesn't the *Enterprise* have a failsafe for dangerous away missions? Take the away team and scan them twice. Then shunt one of the patterns into a setup like the one Scott created on the *Jenolen*. If the away team returns healthy, let the second pattern degrade. Otherwise, reconstitute the second pattern and let the individuals continue to enjoy the good life on board the flagship of the Federation.

• When the away team is waiting for Lieutenant Riker to join them in the transporter room, the transporter console looks completely blank but the transporter chief still manages to get a reading from it. (Maybe the only part that's illuminated is the part we can't see.)

CONTINUITY AND PRODUCTION PROBLEMS

• The star field remains stationary in the wide shots of an observation lounge meeting and then starts moving in the close-ups.

• For the most part, the creators do a very believable job in this episode convincing us that there really are two William T. Rikers. Unfortunately, during the second away mission, when Commander Riker spins Lieutenant Riker around for disobeying an order, the red-sleeved arm that holds Lieutenant Riker's shoulder *obviously* doesn't belong to Commander Riker!

TRIVIA ANSWERS

1. "Night Bird." (I probably will remember this trivia question for the rest of my life! Max Grodenchik, the actor who plays Quark's brother Rom on *Star Trek: Deep Space 9* as well as several other Ferengi roles in *NextGen*, stumped me with it.)

2. Valerian root tea.

TIMESCAPE

Star Dates: 46944.2—46945.3

Coming back from a conference, Picard, Data, La Forge, and Troi find the *Enterprise* and a Romulan warbird frozen in time. Eventually they discover the cause of this unusual occurence, save a group of alien embryos incubating in the warbird's core, and avert disaster for the *Enterprise*.

TRIVIA QUESTIONS

1. Who asked Troi to assist him in his empirical research on interspecies mating rituals?

2. On what topic did Dr. Vassbinder speak?

ALTERNATE VIEWPOINTS AND CORRECTIONS

• On page 417 of the *NextGen Guide* I incorrectly listed the star dates for this episode as "46944.2-48945.3." It should be "46944.2-46945.3." (Thanks to Oso Murillo-Shaw of Dundas, Ontario, for catching this.)

PLOT OVERSIGHTS

• Does it seem a bit odd that the captain, the second officer, the chief engineer, and the ship's counselor would all be gone from a starship at the *same* time?

• During the first part of the episode, Picard, Data, La Forge, and Troi experience temporal distortions while flying in a runabout toward a rendezvous with the *Enterprise*. First the men freeze. Then Troi freezes. Then the starboard nacelle runs out of fuel and Picard's nails grow. In other words, small portions of the runabout experience temporal distortions as the runabout moves through space. Every time the four talk about these distortions, they speak of them as spherical. The graphics support this premise. Also, at one point Picard asks La Forge to back them away from a distortion, implying that the distortion itself is somewhat stationary. But if the distortions are spherical and stationary, the entire first part of this episode makes no sense. For anyone to freeze on board the runabout for any length of time, the ship would need to be enveloped completely by a distortion and then travel through it— since the distortion is *not traveling with* the runabout and the distortion is spherical. But if the distortion completely envelops the runabout, why are some of its inhabitants affected while others are not? Possibly the distortions could be like long tubes. The runabout just happens to be traveling along them. But in that case Troi should have been frozen along with Picard at the beginning, since she sat aligned with the captain and the direction of travel for the runabout. The only way these distortions make any sense is if they *stick* to the runabout as it travels forward. In that case the distortions could be small enough to envelop only part of the runabout. But if the distortions stick to the runabout, how can La Forge back away from one?

• While on the runabout, Picard reaches for a bowl of fruit. According to the dialogue, his hand intersects a temporal anomaly that races fifty times normal. This causes his fingernails to grow. But wait: The rest of his body is outside this acceleration. How can his system provide blood and nutrients to his hand when his hand is aging—and using those nutrients and oxygen—at fifty times its normal speed? Wouldn't it have the same characteristic as if someone put a tourniquet around his wrist? Do your fingernails grow once you cut off the blood supply to a hand?

• And speaking of this accelerated time frame, in the *NextGen Guide* I ran the calculations and asked if Picard could really grow fingernails that long in just twenty-five minutes (the amount of time Picard keeps his hand in the distortion multiplied by 50). I didn't mention the bowl of fruit. It decays to a dreadful-looking pile of guck in just a few minutes. Let's say it took an hour to get to that state. That would be fifty hours—or four days—of normal time. I've let fruit sit on a kitchen counter for four days and it's still edible. It doesn't turn into *that* type of mess for…weeks!

• After Data determines that a spherical temporal distortion envelops the starboard nacelle and the bowl of fruit, Picard asks La Forge to move them away from it. La Forge begins to do so when the runabout hits another temporal distortion to the rear of the ship. The next shot shows Picard and Troi getting up from the table that holds the bowl of fruit. Troi is sitting on the side of the table supposedly *enveloped* by the temporal distortion! I don't know about you, but *I* wouldn't sit there!

• The frozen-time scenario of the episode causes an unavoidable plot oversight when it comes to the runabout crew's away team missions to the *Enterprise*. (An "unavoidable plot oversight" is called a "UPO" in nitpicking lingo. A UPO is a nit that can't be fixed without killing the entire episode.) If time has slowed to a virtual standstill, so has the flow of electrons in power cables and the photons that the lights emit and the gravitons that the gravity generators spew forth faithfully. In short, Picard, Data, and Troi shouldn't be able to see anything; they would be floating around and probably would freeze to death very quickly.

• During the first away mission, Data discovers that time has not stopped, only slowed. He does this by detecting movement in the blast working its way outward from a warp core breach. Wouldn't the power transfer beam or the weapons fired from the Romulan have just as much motion in them? Data looked straight at them when the runabout first approached and still pronounced everything frozen.

• As Data scans the alien embryos in the Romulan engine core, the emanations from his tricorder cause time to go forward and then reverse. Moments later, La Forge notices that a new Romulan has appeared in the engine room. Wouldn't Data notice this first? Doesn't he remember everything to which he's exposed? In addition, Troi tells Picard that she *thinks* she heard someone saying *something* about the power transfer beam. True, there were many voices, but didn't Data record the sequence and can't he decipher each voice—just as he deciphered the multitude of voices Crusher recorded with her tricorder during "Cause and Effect"?

• In her first visit to sick bay, Troi walks past two Security guards, apparently rushing into Crusher's area with phasers drawn. They must have been going someplace else because, once time resumes, they never enter sick bay.

EQUIPMENT ODDITIES

• Shortly after an away team from the runabout makes its first foray onto the *Enterprise,* Data states that the terminals are not functioning. Yet, moments later, Picard seems to get information from the Tactical station, pressing buttons to bring up additional information. The same thing happens later, when La Forge looks over the displays in the Romulan engine room.

• During the first away mission to the *Enterprise,* Troi visits sick bay. As she walks down the hall, all the indicator lights are on, showing the status of red alert. Someone must have reprogrammed them, because during "Time Squared" we see that the indicator lights in the hallways flash in sequence.

• Having failed to prevent the initiation of the fated power transfer beam, Data

attempts to stop it, but a crew member tells him they can't turn it off. Can't turn it *off*? The *Enterprise* turned off the power transfer beam in "The Next Phase"; why can't they do it this time?

• As part of the final away mission, Troi positions herself in sick bay to prevent Crusher's death. When time starts moving forward, a camera shot of a Romulan shows the tracer light behind him flashing to indicate red alert. Yet the close-up of Troi shows the lights stuck on.

• At the end of the episode, when time returns to normal, the Romulan warbird fires on the *Enterprise.* Riker asks for a damage report, and someone reports that shields are "down to 27 percent." Hold it! *Shields* are down to 27 percent? So the shields were up all this time? And Picard's team has beamed on and off the *Enterprise* with abandon?

• To break the power transfer beam, Picard flies the unmanned runabout into its path between the *Enterprise* and the Romulan warbird. A less expensive probe wouldn't do?

CONTINUITY AND PRODUCTION PROBLEMS

• At one point, near the beginning of the episode, an exterior shot shows the runabout jumping to warp. But the following interior shot looking out the forward windows shows the craft traveling at impulse.

• During the trip in the runabout, Picard reaches for a bowl of decayed fruit. According to the dialogue, his right hand intersects a temporal anomaly in which time travels fifty times faster than normal. Seconds later, Picard displays his hand for the camera, and his nails show incredible growth. Oddly enough, if you watch very carefully as Picard enters the aft area of the runabout—*before reaching toward the bowl of fruit*—you will notice that he keeps his right hand cupped. Then he sits at a computer terminal and begins to operate it with his right hand. Look closely and you'll see that his right hand already has long nails. I remind you that this is *before* he reaches into the bowl of fruit.

• Interestingly enough, Picard's nails suddenly return to normal just a few moments later. Probably Troi gave him a quick manicure. (It never hurts to have a second trade in life!)

• The initial dialogue about their ship from the four in the runabout doesn't match the graphics of the *Enterprise* and the Romulan warbird. Troi comments that there is damage to the port engine nacelle, but all the shots from the Romulan warbird hit the leading edge of the saucer. Also, Picard states that an energy beam comes from the deflector dish, when multiple shots show it coming from the port side of the yoke, in the vicinity of decks 15 to 20.

• An away team of Picard, Data, and Troi beams over to the *Enterprise* bridge encased in subspace time bubbles. As they materialize, a woman sits at the Ops position. Then the camera angle changes and comes back to the trio before following them in a slow pan. From the position of the camera, it certainly seems as if the woman at Ops should still be visible, but she isn't.

• Moments later, Picard finds Riker on the floor, with a Romulan reaching toward him. Watch the Romulan's

hand just before it goes out of the picture. It twitches, though it's supposed to be frozen.

• Then Picard goes to the transporter room. He walks across the room to a female Security officer who is pointing her phaser at three Romulans on the transporter pad. Both she and the Romulan in front of her have movement spasms.

• After the second away mission returns to the *Enterprise,* Picard and the others take a closer look at Data's tricorder readings. At this point you can just barely see the stars through the runabout's windows. Oddly enough, the stars are moving. Isn't this a bad idea, given that the runabout sits on the edge of a time anomaly that freezes everything that drifts into it?

TRIVIA ANSWERS

1. Dr. Mizan.
2. The ionizing effect of warp nacelles.

✦
DESCENT

Star Dates: 46982.1—46984.6

Responding to a distress call from Ohniaka III, the crew of the *Enterprise* finds a new breed of Borg, independent and very aggressive. They also learn that these new Borg are led by none other than Lore, and somehow the errant android has convinced Data to join his cause to destroy the Federation.

TRIVIA QUESTIONS

1. What are the three ships assigned by Admiral Nechayev to Task Force 3?

2. From what colony does the *Enterprise* receive a false distress call?

PLOT OVERSIGHTS

• I wonder if Starfleet is ever going to do anything with the transwarp conduit technology discovered in this episode. La Forge said it was twenty times faster than the *Enterprise*'s current maximum speed.

• Looking for Data on the surface of a planet, Picard, La Forge, and Troi team up together. Three *senior* officers on the *same* search team in *dangerous* territory. Right.

• At the end of the episode, Picard, La Forge, Troi, and a soon-to-be-toast Security guard enter a building. There's a huge Borg icon on the floor and one on the wall. Doesn't Picard recognize this symbol? After all, it's used on the toy action figure of the Borg!

• What happened to those cool commando unit uniforms that Picard, Crusher, and Worf wore in "Chain of Command, Part 1"? Why are these Starfleet officers running around on the surface of a planet, searching for a friend among deadly enemies, while wearing brightly colored outfits?

CHANGED PREMISES

• After the away team to Ohniaka III returns, the senior staff meet in the observation lounge. They discuss the differences in the Borg. After hearing that one Borg called another by name, Troi interjects that the only Borg with a name was Hugh (see "I Borg"), and the crew of the *Enterprise* gave it to him. It is inconceivable that Troi forgot the other Borg who had a name—namely "Locutus." After all, she helped counsel Picard back to mental health following the events of "The Best of Both Worlds, Part 1" and "The Best of Both Worlds, Part 2."

• Data's memory doesn't fare any better in this episode. After becoming angry during the away mission to Ohniaka III and after killing a Borg, Data tells La Forge that he believes he has experienced his first emotion. Evidently Data forgot about the laughter Q gave him at the end of "Déjà Q."

• Also, when counseling Data over his anger, Counselor "Explore your dark side and have fun with it" Deanna Troi tells him that emotions aren't negative or positive. They certainly seemed to be negative and positive in "Shades of Gray." During that episode, Pulaski evoked negative emotions in Riker by making him recall a series of bad experiences on the *Enterprise,* thereby boring some microbes to death. (I'm sorry. That was catty. I simply do not like flashback shows.)

EQUIPMENT ODDITIES

• Attempting to re-create his anger, Data goes to the holodeck. He runs several tests, eventually asking the computer to increase his opponent's strength until it endangers the android's life. When the computer balks at the request, Data asks La Forge to help him override the holodeck's safety routine. He then states that such an action requires two senior officers. Obviously someone reprogrammed the holodeck after the events in "Elementary, Dear Data"—when La Forge put the entire ship in danger by creating a too-powerful Moriarty with one misspoken word.

• In "Déjà Q," Picard controlled the force field to the brig with a voice command. In "I Borg," a Security guard standing beside the cell controlled the force field by tapping on a panel to the left of the cell entrance. In this episode, the guard sitting at the desk on the other side of the room controls the force field. Does the Force Field Controllers' Installation Team have too little work to keep them busy (and therefore keep changing this)?

• The *El-Baz* is back! Avid readers of the *NextGen Guide* will recall that the last time we saw a shuttle named *El-Baz* it was a sleek, rounded-edged, multiple-passenger unit. (See "The Nth Degree" on page 256 of the *NextGen Guide*.) In this episode, the name gets busted back down to the subcompact two-seater model.

• After entering the Borg building, La Forge states that his tricorder isn't even registering any emissions from the light fixtures. Picard says there must be a dampening field in place. So…this dampening field keeps any type of sensor from even registering light? Why is La Forge's VISOR exempt from its effects? Shouldn't La Forge be blind?

CONTINUITY AND PRODUCTION PROBLEMS

• The matte painting used for the buildings on Ohniaka III is the same as the one—with slight modifications—used for Arkaria Base in "Starship Mine" and the Darwin Genetics Research Station in "Unnatural Selection."

• I usually don't say much about stunt doubles. The creators normally do a good job of masking the double's face in some way. However, in this episode—during the hand-to-hand battle between Data and the Borg at the beginning of the episode—it's pretty obvious where the stunt double takes over.

TRIVIA ANSWERS

1. The *Enterprise*, the *Crazy Horse*, and the *Agamemnon*.

2. New Berlin.

TRIATHLON
TRIVIA ON STARBASES

MATCH THE STARBASE TO
THE DESCRIPTION TO THE EPISODE

CHARACTER	DESCRIPTION	EPISODE
1. Starbase 12	A. Kahlest went there to recuperate	a. "Frame of Mind"
2. Starbase 14	B. Quinteros commanded	b. "Reunion"
3. Starbase 23	C. La Forge sent Logan and saucer there	c. "Homeward"
4. Starbase 24	D. Dr. Dalen Quaice worked there	d. "Tin Man"
5. Starbase 29	E. Received distress call from *Lalo*	e. "Redemption II"
6. Starbase 47	F. Picard dropped Rasmussen there	f. "Realm of Fear"
7. Starbase 67	G. Destination of *Stargazer*	g. "Q Who"
8. Starbase 73	H. Admiral Haden stationed there	h. "Parallels"
9. Starbase 74	I. Data was put on trial there	i. "The Arsenal of Freedom"
10. Starbase 83	J. Nearest starbase after Q snapped	j. "The Defector"
11. Starbase 84	K. Nearest to the Devron System	k. "Phantasms"
12. Starbase 87	L. Admiral Chekote commands	l. "Lessons"
13. Starbase 103	M. Admiral Nechayev boards here	m. "Sins of the Father"
14. Starbase 117	N. Picard sent Par Lenor and Qol there	n. "Unnatural Selection"
15. Starbase 123	O. The Argus Array took its picture	o. "11001001"
16. Starbase 133	P. After damage by Gomtuu, then there	p. "Code of Honor"
17. Starbase 152	Q. Thoroughly tested the *Enterprise*	q. "Power Play"
18. Starbase 153	R. After the quantum filaments, then there	r. "Journey's End"
19. Starbase 157	S. O'Brien faced hook spiders there	s. "A Matter of Time"
20. Starbase 173	T. Dr. Leah Brahms boarded there	t. "The Battle"
21. Starbase 185	U. Commanded by Admiral Budrow	u. "Thine Own Self"
22. Starbase 212	V. After Caldos Colony, then there	v. "Disaster"

23.	Starbase 214	W.	After first contact with Borg, then there	w.	"All Good Things"
24.	Starbase 218	X.	Picard got a new heart there	x.	"The Perfect Mate"
25.	Starbase 227	Y.	*Enterprise* received new warp core there	y.	"The Measure of a Man"
26.	Starbase 231	Z.	Intended destination after Borel II died	z.	"The Icarus Factor"
27.	Starbase 234	AA.	Worf sent Alexander there	aa.	"Aquiel"
28.	Starbase 310	BB.	Admiral Uttan Narsu commanded	bb.	"The Emissary"
29.	Starbase 313	CC.	Hanson returned there after Borg came	cc.	"Sub Rosa"
30.	Starbase 324	DD.	Troi went home from there	dd.	"The Best of Both Worlds", Part I
31.	Starbase 336	EE.	Picard waited there for assignment	ee.	"Samaritan Snare"
32.	Starbase 514	FF.	Nurse Beck came on board there	ff.	"Hide and Q"
33.	Starbase 515	GG.	*Vico* assigned from there	gg.	"Hero Worship"
34.	Starbase 621	HH.	Picard leaves here with armada	hh.	"Remember Me"
35.	Starbase Earhart	II.	Sent message on Anchilles fever	ii.	"Galaxy's Child"
36.	Starbase G-6	JJ.	Detected transmission from *T'Ong*	jj.	"Gambit, Part I"
37.	Starbase Lya III	KK.	Launched K'Ehleyr in probe		
38.	Starbase Montgomery	LL.	Site of Troi's academy reunion		
39.	Xendi Starbase 9	MM.	Helped to search for Unari		
40.	Zayra IV Starbase	NN.	Sensed warbirds heading for Gomtuu		

SCORING

(BASED ON NUMBER OF CORRECT ANSWERS)

0-3	Normal
4-6	Good
7 and up	Outstanding.

(This is easily the toughest triathlon I've ever created—
unless, of course, you use *The Star Trek Encyclopedia*!)

CHARACTERS ANSWER KEY: 1. BB q **2.** II p **3.** K w **4.** A m **5.** U a **6.** O h **7.** R v **8.** AA b **9.** B o **10.** W g **11.** Y k **12.** Z c **13.** C i **14.** N x **15.** NN d **16.** D hh **17.** P d **18.** KK bb **19.** E n **20.** I y **21.** J g **22.** MM aa **23.** F s **24.** FF l **25.** L jj **26.** LL u **27.** HH e **28.** M r **29.** T ii **30.** CC dd **31.** JJ bb **32.** GG gg **33.** X ee **34.** V cc **35.** EE ee **36.** DD ff **37.** H j **38.** Q z **39.** G t **40.** S f

INDEX

Lemma II, 314
"Lessons," 96, 223, 377–379, 392
Lewis, Lieutenant, 171
Leyrons, 165
"Liasions," 7–8, 197, 223, 224
Liator, 223
Ligon II, 109, 319
Ligonians, 109–110, 321
Liko, 176, 205–207
Lin, Ensign, 282
Little John, 153
Locarno, Cadet, 45
Lockman, 202
Locutus, 176, 246, 253, 334, 335, 390
Lombard, Brian, 82, 163
"Lonely Among Us," 113–115, 129, 176, 237, 274, 320, 373, 385
Lonka Cluster, 234
Lore, 3–5, 28, 29, 91, 125–127, 231, 240, 256, 257, 274, 309, 389
Loren, Minister, 23
Lorenze Cluster, 143
Lornak clan, 216
"Loss, The," 93, 267–269
Lote, Orn, 357
"Loud as a Whisper," 164–165, 223
Louvois, Captain Phillipa, 172, 173
"Lower Decks," 44–45, 78
Lunar V, 220
Lursa, 81, 86, 91
Lutan, 109–110
Lya III, 218
Lyaaran, 7
Lya Station Alpha, 303
Lysian Alliance, 322, 323
[IN]:MacDougal, 109
MacDuff, Commander, 322, 323
Macet, Gul, 271, 272
MacPherson nebula, 66
Maddox, Commander Bruce, 171–173, 269, 275
Madeline, 224
Mader, Mike, 339

Madred, Gul, 61, 77, 365, 366
Maid Marion, 153, 285
Makto, 112
Malcor, Karen P., 278
Malcor III, 277, 278, 319
Malcorians, 128
Malencon, Arthur, 138
Malmstrom, Carl, 163
Mandl, 138, 139
Manheim, Dr. Paul, 146
Manheim, Jenice, 146–148, 223
"Manhunt," 7–8, 140, 176, 188–191, 197, 224
"Man of the People," 77, 296, 320, 350–352
Maques, 19, 21
Maquis, 69–71
Marcus, Dr. Carol, 88
Marejaretus VI, 191
Mariposa, 177
Mariposans, 187–188
"Mark of Gideon, The," 22
Marouk, 216, 217
Marr, Dr. Kila, 304
Mars, 32, 209
Martin, Dr., 317
Martin, Phillip, 330
Martin, Wells P., 225
Masaka, 49–51, 78, 274, 275
"Masks," 49–51, 78, 176, 274, 275
"Masterpiece Society, The," 96, 168, 174, 223, 317–318, 320
"Matter of Honor, A," 26, 96, 128, 170–171, 197, 254, 296
"Matter of Perspective, A," 128, 225–226, 278
"Matter of Time, A," 311–313, 320, 325, 392
Maxwell, Captain Ben, 271, 272
Maylor, Sev, 352
McAllister Nebula, 366
McClain, Jennifer, 82
McCoy, 101, 103, 106, 114, 305, 381

McKenzie, Ard'rian, 223
McMillen, Corinne C., 57
McNary, 125
McNeil, Ann, 161
"Measure of a Man, The," 96, 107, 127, 171–173, 215, 275, 320, 393
Meles II, 367
Melian, 137
Melona IV, 304
Mempa Sector, 294, 299
"Ménage à Troi," 137, 176, 197, 243–244, 296, 321
Mendak, Admiral, 270
Mendenhall, Stephen, 261
Mendez, 284
Mendon, Ensign, 170, 171
Menegay, Paul, 36
Menthars, 208
Merculite rockets, 142
Mericor System, 325
Metal parasites, 330, 331
Meyers, Annie, 274
Miller, Mrs., 122
Miller, Wyatt, 120–122
Milligan, Merak, 159
"Mind's Eye, The," 288, 292, 319–320, 332
Minos, 142, 319
Mintaka III, 204, 207, 319
Mintakans, 153, 204–207, 232
Minuet, 133, 134, 224, 265
Mirasta, 278
Mirek, Debbie, 282
Mitchell, Gary, 118–119
Mizan, Dr., 223, 389
Moab IV, 317, 320
Modean System, 333
Mogh, 232, 384
Mondor, 186, 296
Moore, David T., 86
Morag, 368
Mordan, 254
Mordan IV, 135, 136, 319
Mordock, 243
Morgana Quadrant, 161
Moriarty, Professor, 128, 161, 162, 224, 366, 367, 391

ATTENTION
ALL NITPICKING TREKKERS!

JOIN THE NITPICKER'S GUILD TODAY!

J ust send in a mistake that you've found in an incarnation of Star Trek—the original series, the movies, *Next Generation, Deep Space Nine* or *Voyager*—or even a mistake that you've found in any of the *Nitpicker's Guides*. Simply mailing that entry will make you an official member of the Nitpicker's Guild! (Please understand. I get *a lot* of mail and I try to read every letter, but it is very difficult to send out personal responses.)

Send your mistake to:
Phil Farrand, Chief Nitpicker
The Nitpicker's Guild
P.O. Box 6248
Springfield, MO 65801-6248

Note: All submissions become the property of Phil Farrand and will not be returned. Submissions may or may not be acknowledged. By submitting material, you grant permission for use of your submission and name in any future publication by the author. Should a given mistake be published in one of the mediums of the Nitpicker's Guild, an effort will be made to credit the first person sending in that mistake. However, Phil Farrand makes no guarantee that such credit will be given.